Tramping in New Zealand

Jim DuFresne

Tramping in New Zealand
2nd edition

Published by
Lonely Planet Publications
Head Office: PO Box 617, Hawthorn, Victoria 3122, Australia
US Office: PO Box 2001A, Berkeley, CA 94702, USA

Printed by
Colorcraft, Hong Kong

Photographs by
Jim DuFresne (JD)
Ingvar Kenne (IK)
Front Cover Photograph: Trampers on the Routeburn Track (IK)
Back Cover Photograph: Dart Glacier (JD)

Line illustrations
from *New Zealand: Its Physical Geography, Geology and Natural History* by Ferdinand von Hochstetter
(a German Publication, 1863)

First Published
November 1982

This Edition
May 1989

Although the author and publisher have tried to make the information as
accurate as possible, they accept no responsibility for any loss, injury or
inconvenience sustained by any person using this book.

National Library of Australia Cataloguing in Publication Data

Du Fresne, Jim
  Tramping in New Zealand.

  2nd ed.
  Includes index.
  ISBN 0 86442 076 5.

  1. New Zealand – Description and travel – 1981 – Guide-books. I. Title.

919.31'0437
© Copyright Jim DuFresne, 1989

Jim DuFresne

A former sports and outdoors editor for the *Juneau Empire* Jim was the first Alaskan sportswriter to win a national award from Associated Press. He is presently a freelance writer, specialising in outdoor and travel writing. His other publications include wilderness guides to Isle Royale, Voyageurs and Glacier Bay National Parks and he is also the author of Lonely Planet's *Alaska – a travel survival kit*.

From the Author

There are now 12 national parks in New Zealand. There is a new track and new huts where old ones use to be. There is even a new governmental department overseeing it all (introducing new fees and new policies).

Much has changed as far as tramping in this country is concerned but one thing has remained constant – the people of New Zealand. From the walkers and hut wardens you meet out on the track to the ranger back at the visitor centre and the driver on the Magic Bus, this is a nation of warm-hearted people who love their rugged land and are enthusiastic about sharing it. Tramping in this part of the world is a wonderful experience for as much as the people you'll meet as the scenery you'll gaze upon.

I am indebted to everybody in the Department of Conservation whom I worked with, from rangers and trail crews to information officers, district conservators and chief rangers. Special thanks to Bruce Young of the Northern Region, Rex Mossman of Hauraki Gulf Maritime Park, Don Woodwock at Great Barrier Island and Sue and Ian Case of the North Egmont Visitor Centre in Egmont National Park. In the South Island I received much assistance from Bill Hislop, chief ranger of Mt Aspiring National Park, Joy Paterson of Fiordland National Park and Ron Tindall at Stewart Island.

A summer tramping in New Zealand could not have been possible without the help of Diane Anderson and J B Moir of Air New Zealand, Edward Beckett, Prue Norling and Jan Brooks of Mount Cook Lines, David Wells of New Zealand Rail and Road Services and Ann Rowley of Southern Air. Assisting me with my travel arrangements was Colin Taylor of the New Zealand Travel and Publicity Office in Los Angeles while Mary Ann Fisher of the NZTP office in Auckland provided me with a desk, typewriter, paper etc, when I was organising the book and wrapping up the research.

Information came from a variety of sources including those who provide crucial services to trampers. People like Glynn Kemp of Glenorchy Holiday Camp, Darryl Wilson of Abel Tasman National Park Enterprises, Dick William of Matukit Services, the fine guides at Alpine Guides in Mt Cook and Tim McGeorge of Magic Bus.

The best information and most memorable moments came of course from trampers themselves. To my backpacking partner Carl Vogelsang who came to New Zealand only to tramp and eat ice cream.

To Barb Pietsch and her spirit of determination, Bruno Corletto at Mt Cook, Brent Matheson in Arthur's Pass and Michael Crampton in Kaimanawa State Forest Park.

Supporting me and my passion to improve this book was my wife Peg, and Amy Jeschawitz back in Clarkston, Michigan, Ray Richards in Auckland and the dedicated staff at Lonely Planet in Australia. But most of all this book is for those of us, Kiwi or not, who live for peaks, ridges and other high places. To Donna who went to New Zealand and discovered a passion for the alpine and the Swedish girl who cried when she reached the top.

If you don't climb the mountain, you can never look down in the valley.

Lonely Planet Credits

Production Editor	James Lyon
Maps	Margaret Jung
	Valerie Tellini
Cover design, design & title page illustrations	Margaret Jung
Typesetting	Tricia Giles

Copy Editor: Andrew Kelly. Thanks also to Katie Cody and Lyn McGaurr for proofreading and Jon Murray for indexing.

A Warning & a Request

Things change – prices go up, schedules change, good places go bad and bad places go bankrupt – nothing stays the same. So if you find things better or worse, recently opened or long since closed, please write and tell us and help make the next edition better! All information is greatly appreciated and the best letters will receive a free copy of the next edition, or any other Lonely Planet book of your choice.

Extracts from the best letters are also included in the *Lonely Planet Update*. The *Update* helps us make useful information available to you as soon as possible – it's like reading an up-to-date noticeboard or postcards from a friend. Each edition contains hundreds of useful tips and advice from the best possible source of information – other travellers. The *Lonely Planet Update* is published quarterly in paperback and is available from bookshops and by subscription. Turn to the back pages of this book for more details.

Contents

INTRODUCTION   7

FACTS ABOUT THE COUNTRY History – Geography – Climate – Natural History   9

FACTS FOR THE TRAMPER Visas – Customs – Money – General Information – Health –   15
Hazards – Accommodation – Tramping Information – Maps – Food – Clothing –
Equipment – Fishing – When To Go

GETTING THERE   38

GETTING AROUND Air – Bus – Train – Boat – Driving – Hitching – Local Transport   41

NORTH ISLAND

THE FAR NORTH
Te Paki Coastal Park Ninety Mile Beach-Cape Reinga Walkway   48
Great Barrier Island State Forest Recreation Area Great Barrier Island Trek   52
Coromandel State Forest Park Coromandel State Forest Park Walk   59

SOUTH OF AUCKLAND
Urewera National Park The Lake Track – Whakatane River Track – Other Tracks   64
Whirinaki State Forest Park The Whirinaki Track   76
Tongariro National Park Round Mt Ngauruhoe Track – Other Tracks   80
Kaimanawa State Forest Park Te Iringa-Oamaru Circuit – Other Tracks   88
Mt Egmont National Park Mt Egmont Round-The-Mountain Track – The Pouakai Track   93
Whanganui National Park Matemateaonga Walkway – Other Tracks   104
Tararua State Forest Park Mt Holdsworth Circuit – Totara Flats Track – Other Tracks   109

SOUTH ISLAND

NELSON REGION
Abel Tasman Coastal Park Abel Tasman Coastal Track – Other Tracks   120
North-West Nelson State Forest Park Heaphy Track – Wangapeka Track – Leslie-Karamea   127
Track – Other Tracks
Mt Richmond State Forest Park Pelorus River Track – Other Tracks   140
Nelson Lakes National Park Travers-Sabine Circuit – D'Urville Valley Track   144
Lewis Park National Reserve & Others St James Walkway   155

WEST COAST & SOUTHERN ALPS
Paparoa National Park Inland Pack Track – Other Tracks   161
Arthur's Pass National Park Goat Pass – Waimakariri-Harman Pass Route – Harper Pass –   167
Other Tracks
Craigieburn State Forest Park Cass-Lagoon Saddle Track   184
Mt Cook & Westlands National Parks The Copland Pass – Mueller Hut – Other Tracks   187

THE FAR SOUTH
Mt Aspiring National Park Routeburn Track – Greenstone Track – Caples Track –   198
Rees-Dart Track – Cascade Saddle Route – Wilkin-Young Valleys Circuit – Other Tracks
Fiordland National Park Milford Track – Hollyford Track – Kepler Track – Dusky Track –   220
Other Tracks
Stewart Island Link Track – Northern Circuit   243

INDEX Map Index   255

Introduction

A tramping holiday is the best way to explore the NZ bush and the only way to see much of the country's unique flora and fauna. This guide is an aid for the Kiwi who wants to progress from day hikes to overnight outings of two or more days, while the overseas traveller will find it invaluable in choosing the tracks they want to walk and fitting in as many as possible during the time they have available.

Forty tracks are featured and each track description has an accompanying map. All these tracks are walks of several or more days and all but two have huts along them.

The track descriptions encompass tramps from Cape Reinga in the far north of the North Island to a tramp on the south side of Stewart Island. Tracks in all 12 national parks and seven out of 20 forest parks are included, and most of the interesting geological features of New Zealand are found in one track or another.

The tracks present a good cross-section of the country's tramping opportunities, from easy beach walking in the Abel Tasman National Park to the technical and highly challenging alpine crossing of the Copland Pass in the Southern Alps. There are the very popular walks of the Milford and Routeburn Tracks in Fiordland National Park and the often overlooked areas such as the Wilkin Valley in Mt Aspiring National Park and the Whirinaki Track in Whirinaki State Forest Park.

At the end of every section there are brief descriptions of additional tracks in the same park. Together the tracks mentioned in this book represent a good range of difficulty, lengths and landscapes, providing you with the best possible selection of New Zealand's natural wonders and scenery.

MAP LEGEND

▬▬▬	Road
▬ ▬ ▬	Walking Track – well defined
• • • • • •	Route – not well defined
+++++	Railway Line
➤—	River, Stream
▲	Mountain, Peak
⚐	Campsite
—750—	Contour line, height (m)
⧛	Mountain Pass/Saddle
⊣⊢	Bridge
⌂	Hut/Shelter
∧	Bivvy/Natural Shelter
✝	Church
⣿	Glacier
◎	Spring

Facts about the Country

HISTORY
Maori History

The original inhabitants of New Zealand were known until fairly recently as Morioris. Recent evidence now indicates that the Maoris arrived in Aotearoa – or the 'land of the long white cloud', as they called New Zealand – in a series of migrations and that the Morioris were the first wave of Maori migration rather than being a separate and distinct race. It was these early settlers who hunted the huge flightless bird, the moa, both for food and its feathers until it became extinct. Today, the name Moriori refers to the original settlers of the Chatham Islands where the last full-blooded Moriori died in 1933.

Since the Maoris had no written language, their history and culture is recalled through story-telling and songs, which means it's probable that the saga of Kupe, Hawaiki and the 'great migration' has been embellished over the centuries. While it would be unwise to take the legend absolutely literally, there's obviously a good deal of truth in it. One of the heroes of the story, Kupe, a particularly brilliant Polynesian navigator, is said to have set sail from Hawaiki in the 10th century for the 'great southern land, uninhabited and covered with mists' – and managed to return to tell the tale.

Centuries later, when things weren't going so well in Hawaiki – over-population, shortage of food and all those other familiar problems – the decision was made to follow Kupe's instructions and head south. Despite the similar names, Hawaiki is not Hawaii; experts believe it was more likely to have been an island near Tahiti. The similar spelling and pronunciation however, suggests that another party of emigrants from Hawaiki settled in Hawaii, naming it after their home island.

According to legend, 10 great canoes sailed to New Zealand in the 14th century, though historians now feel the great arrival may actually have been much

earlier. The names of the canoes are all remembered, and their landing points, crews and histories also recalled. Today, Maoris still trace their lineage back to those passengers in one or other of the canoes of the great migration. Of course the 'moa hunters' were there, and some other Maoris from an earlier small migration, but the new immigrants from the great fleet soon established themselves in their adopted home.

Maori culture developed without hindrance from other cultures for hundreds of years but being warriors the people engaged in numerous tribal battles. While they did not develop a written language the Maoris created a complex art form involving beautifully carved war canoes and meeting houses and intricate tattoos on both men and women. They also produced exquisite greenstone (jade) ornaments and war clubs.

European Exploration & Settlement

In 1642 the Dutch explorer Abel Tasman, who had just sailed around Australia from Batavia (modern day Jakarta, Indonesia), dropped by. He decided not to stay long after several of his crew were killed and cooked. His visit, however, meant that Europeans now knew of New Zealand's existence and in those days of colonialism it also meant that they would eventually want it. The Dutch, after their first uncomfortable look, were none too keen on the place and it was left alone until Captain Cook sailed by in 1769, claimed the whole place for Britain, sailed right round both islands mapping as he went, and split for Australia.

When the British started their antipodean colonising they opted for the even more lightly populated Australia so the first European immigrants to New Zealand were temporary visitors – sealers (who soon reduced the seal population to nothing) and then whalers (who did the same with whales). They were hardly the cream of European society and they introduced diseases and prostitution. By

1830 the Maori population was falling dramatically.

The arrival of Samuel Marsden, the first missionary, in 1841 righted the balance a little and by the middle of the 19th century the raging impact of *Pakeha*'s (white man's) diseases and his modern armoury had been curbed. But the unfortunate Maoris now found themselves spiritually assaulted and much of their tradition and culture destroyed. Despite the missionary influence their numbers continued to decline.

During this time settlers were arriving in New Zealand and beginning to demand British protection from the Maoris and from other less savoury settlers. The threat of a French colonising effort stirred the Crown to despatch James Busby in 1833 to be the British Resident. The fact that this was a very low-key effort is illustrated by poor Busby even having to pay his own fare from Australia; and once he'd set up shop his efforts to protect the settlers and keep law and order were somewhat limited by the fact that he had no forces, no arms and no authority. He was soon dubbed 'the man-of-war without guns'.

Clashes with the Maoris

In 1840 the British sent Captain William Hobson to replace Busby. Hobson was instructed to persuade the Maori chiefs to relinquish their sovereignty to the British Crown. In part this decision was made in the expectation that if the government didn't get in there and organise things every Tom, Dick and Harry settler would be buying land off the Maoris for two axes and a box of candles and chaos would soon result.

With a truly British display of pomp and circumstance, Hobson met with the Maori chiefs in front of Busby's residence at Waitangi at the Bay of Islands. It is now known as the Treaty House and the anniversary of 6 February 1840 is considered the birthday of modern New Zealand. Forty-five chiefs signed the treaty (or rather Hobson signed for them) and eventually 500 chiefs from around the country agreed to British rule.

This orderly state of affairs didn't last long. When settlers wanted to buy land and the Maoris didn't want to sell, conflict inevitably resulted. The admirable idea that the government should act as a go-between in all Maori-Pakeha deals to ensure fairness on both sides fell apart when the government was too tight-fisted to pay the price. The first visible revolt came when Hone Heke, the first chief to sign the Waitangi Treaty, chopped down the flagpole at Kororareka (now known as Russell), across the bay. Despite new poles and more and more guards Heke or his followers managed to chop the pole down four times, and after the last occasion it was covered with iron to foil axe-wielding Maoris! As well as destroying the pole on the last occasion, Heke burnt down the town of Kororareka for good measure, an action which has since been acclaimed as a sign of his good taste because it was a pestilent place.

In the skirmishes that followed, the British governor put a £100 reward on Heke's head, to which Heke brilliantly responded by offering a matching £100 for the governor's head. This was only one in a long series of skirmishes, battles, conflicts, disputes and arguments which escalated between 1860 and 1865 into a more-or-less full-fledged war. The result was inconclusive, but the Maoris were effectively worn down by sheer weight of numbers and equipment.

Modern New Zealand

Things calmed down and New Zealand became an efficient agricultural country. Sheep farming, that backbone of modern New Zealand, took hold when refrigerated ships made it possible to sell New Zealand meat in Europe. Towards the end of the last century New Zealand went through a phase of sweeping social change that took it to the forefront of the world. Women were given the vote in 1893, 25 years before

women in Britain or America and more like 75 years ahead of those in Switzerland. The range of far-sighted social reforms and pioneering legislation included old-age pensions, minimum wage structures, the establishment of arbitration courts and the introduction of child health services. The latter included the foundation in 1907 of the Plunket Society, an organisation of nurses who care for expectant mothers and young babies.

Meanwhile the Maoris floundered. New Zealand grew through immigration (a very selective immigration), but by 1900 the Maori population had dropped to an estimated 42,000 and was falling fast. The Maoris were given the vote in 1867, but the continuing struggle to hold on to their culture and their ancestral lands sapped their spirit and energy for some time. In the last few decades there has been a turn-around and the Maori population has started to increase at a faster rate than that of the Pakeha. Today they number about 280,000.

New Zealanders are proud of their record of racial harmony; there has never been any racial separation and inter-marriage is common. (In *Return to Paradise* James Michener tells of the outraged New Zealand reaction when WW II GIs stationed in New Zealand tried to treat Maoris like they treated American blacks.) Despite this the Maoris are a disadvantaged race sharing a less than proportional part of the nation's wealth and leadership. It's a problem New Zealanders are wrestling with but without great success as yet.

New Zealand Today

Today New Zealand is still predominantly an agricultural country but the '70s and '80s have been hard. The closure of much of its traditional European market for agricultural products, combined with the oil crisis price hikes of many of its mineral and manufactured imports, has done no good at all to the country's economic situation. Unlike Australia, New Zealand has little mineral wealth to supplement its agricultural efficiency. Furthermore the inefficiencies of small-scale manufacturing that afflict Australia are magnified by New Zealand's even tinier population. It's still an affluent, organised, tidy country but things simply aren't as rosy as they once were.

New Zealand follows a party system, the two main political groups being the National (conservative) and Labour parties. Among the others is the Social Credit Party. The party that wins a majority of seats in an election automatically becomes the government and its leader, the Prime Minister. In July 1984 the Nationals, in office for three terms under the leadership of Sir Robert Muldoon, were bundled out unceremoniously by the landslide victory of the Labour Party led by David Lange. In August 1987 Lange won a second election –a mandate to continue his sweeping changes to the New Zealand economic system.

Internationally New Zealand has become by far the most interesting and important country in the South Pacific region. It has taken a strong stand on nuclear issues, refusing entry to nuclear-equipped US warships and condemning French nuclear testing in the Pacific. This brave policy has caused more than a few problems for the Kiwis. The US dumped them from the ANZUS treaty agreements and the French even went so far as to send government-sponsored terrorists to sink the anti-nuclear Greenpeace ship the *Rainbow Warrior* in Auckland's harbour.

GEOGRAPHY

New Zealand stretches 1600 km from north to south and consists of three large islands and a number of smaller islands scattered around the two main ones. The two major land masses are the 115,000 square km North Island and the 151,000 square km South Island. Stewart Island, which covers an area of 1700 square km, lies directly south of the South Island. The

country is 10,400 km south-west of the US, 1700 km south of Fiji and 2250 km east of Australia. Its western coastline faces the Tasman Sea, the part of the Pacific Ocean which separates New Zealand and Australia.

New Zealand's territorial jurisdiction also extends to the islands of Chatham, Kermadec, Tokelau, Auckland, Antipodes, Snares, Solander and Bounty (most of them uninhabited) and the Ross Dependency in Antarctica.

CLIMATE

The usual weather pattern in New Zealand is a cycle of a high pressure system (anticyclones or ridges) followed by a low pressure system (troughs or depressions), travelling from west to east. The anticyclones normally pass the northern portions of the country at intervals of three to seven days, bringing fine weather with light or moderate winds. In between them are depressions of rain, strong winds and cooler temperatures. One early warning sign of approaching bad weather is an increase in wind speed and the appearance of high cloud sheets. These sheets, which look as if they are stacked on top of each other, are known as 'hog's back' and are the outriders of northwest storms. As the depression moves on the wind changes direction, often quite suddenly, and a change in weather results.

The wind is the key to reading the weather out in the bush. As a general rule, northwesterlies bring wet weather and storms while southerlies are a sign of a cool frontal change, often followed by clearer conditions. Northeasterlies are also a sign of good weather approaching and southwesterlies are cool, rain-laden winds.

Most important, however, is to keep in mind that weather in New Zealand changes quickly and is highly unpredictable beyond a day or two. Long-range forecasts are virtually impossible and mountains, because most ranges run roughly north to south, make their own weather. It is not uncommon to have rain on the windward or western side of a range, fine weather on the lee side and miserable conditions of heavy wind and rain along the ridges on top.

Almost all DOC offices and national park headquarters and visitor centres receive the latest weather forecasts at around 9 am and another report in the evening. It is a wise practice to stop in at such an office before any tramp to check the weather and leave your intentions. If heavy storms move in once you are out on the track, the best practice is to stay put in the hut and take a day off, especially if you are in an alpine area. Be patient and don't worry about missing a bus or train at the end of the walk. Pressing deadlines and time limitations are one of the main causes of mishaps in the bush. An excellent brochure to pick up is *Weather Wisdom In New Zealand Mountains*, published by the NZ Mountain Safety Council and available at most park centres.

NATURAL HISTORY

For all its grandeur, natural beauty, numerous tracks and excellent huts, the only thing New Zealand tramping seems to lack is wildlife. On most tracks an encounter with anything other than a handful of birds is rare.

Originally, before the days of Maoris, New Zealand had only one land mammal, a bat that came in two species, but there was a thriving bird population including the famous moa, an ostrich-like bird that grew to a height of four metres. Today just the reverse is true. Beginning with the Maoris, who hunted the moas to extinction, and continuing with the Europeans, humans introduced mammals and drove birds to extinction. Rats, dogs, cats, deer, goats, possums, hares, wild pigs and ferrets were introduced into the forests. Some didn't fare so well; others went on a breeding spree because of a lack of natural predators. Today in many national and forest parks deer, goats and possums are

Moa and Kiwis

so abundant that they are causing serious problems with native plants.

The native birdlife, meanwhile, suffered greatly. Rats, wild cats and ferrets attacked flightless birds or ate the young and eggs until many of the native species either became extinct or extremely rare. Those that survived the ordeal and which are often spotted by trampers are the kea or mountain parrot, found in the alpine areas of the South Island, and the weka or wood hen. The kea is known as a comical bird who displays little fear of trampers to the point stealing watches, spoons, cups or any other shiny items left unattended. Weka is a flightless bird of brown feathers seen in many lowland areas of the South Island. Other birds seen along the track include fantails that flutter around you and wood pigeons, large and distinctively colourful birds.

The national bird, the kiwi, is also around but rather difficult to spot in the wild since it is nocturnal – sleeping during the day, feeding at night – and shy by nature. But if you are willing to lose a few winks, it may be seen occasionally during night walks. Your best bet is to look in thick bush after midnight and around areas which have been overturned, since the kiwi hunts the ground for insects with its long beak. Stewart Island may be the best place to spot a kiwi as the birds outnumber humans on the remote island and are not as nocturnal as their cousins to the north. Most trampers, however, spare themselves that midnight search and just visit one of a number of nocturnal houses in zoos around the country.

Surprisingly not extinct is the tuatara, the sole survivor of a group of ancient reptiles somewhat akin to the dinosaurs. Sometimes mistakenly referred to as a lizard it is now found only on a few offshore islands and is absolutely protected. New Zealand has no snakes and only one spider that is dangerous to humans, the rare katipo which is a close relation of the North American black widow or the Australian redback.

Unlike the fauna, the flora of New Zealand is diverse and very interesting. Native forests fall into three types. Podocarp-mixed broadleaf forests contain rimu, miro, silver pine and matai trees and, like rainforests, they have a thick understorey of ferns and mosses with orchids, more ferns and other shrubs hanging from the branches of the trees. Kauri forests of the upper portions of the North Island are similar to the podocarp forests in character except that the towering kauri, which dwarfs all other trees, is the dominant species. Beech forests are found in the drier regions and are made up of several beech species. The trees of these forests are of uniform height and form a dense canopy. The floor of the forest is open and dry, easy for trampers to walk through, unlike the jungle-like kauri and podocarp forests.

Three species of trees that fascinate most trampers are mamuku or the black fern tree, which grows to heights of 15 metres; the nikau, which is New Zealand's only native member of the palm family and is found along the warmer coastal areas of the country; and the ti or cabbage tree, which can grow to 20 metres in height and is recognised by its distinctive grouping of narrow leaves.

Native Forest

Facts for the Tramper

VISAS

Everyone needs a passport to enter New Zealand. Until recently, Aussies technically didn't need their little blue book to enter if they were coming direct from Australia, although they did need it to get home again! However, since November 1987, Australians have also had to present their passports to immigration officers on entry. All passports must be valid for three months beyond the intended departure date.

Australians do not need visas and can stay indefinitely. British passport holders (who have UK residence rights) do not need visas and can stay up to six months. With certain exceptions, you do not need a visa for stays of up to three months if you're from a country of Western Europe or from Canada, Iceland, Japan, Singapore or the USA. If you're from another country or you wish to stay for longer than those periods then you must have a visa. Check with New Zealand consular offices for more visa information.

As with almost anywhere in the world, entry requirements are likely to change so check the situation shortly before you depart. There's nothing worse than arriving at the airport when you leave home and finding you must have a visa, when you thought you didn't need one! All visitors must have onward or return ticketing and sufficient funds to maintain themselves without working for the duration of their stay.

CUSTOMS

The usual sort of x cigarettes, y bottles of liquor regulations apply. Like their counterparts in Australia the customs people in New Zealand are very fussy about drugs. They are also fussy about animal products and the possibility of animal disease, which is not surprising as they've got 60 million sheep. Before you bring tramping gear into the country, it should be thoroughly cleaned and there should be no traces of dirt or you will be delayed while it gets fumigated at the airport.

There's a $2 departure tax at the airport.

MONEY

Unless otherwise noted all dollar prices quoted in this book are New Zealand dollars.

New Zealand currency is dollars and cents – there are one, two, five, 10, 20 and 100 dollar notes and one, two, five, 10, 20 and 50 cent coins very similar to Australia's. You can bring in as much of any currency as you like and unused foreign currency or traveller's cheques that you brought in with you may be exported without limitations. Unused NZ currency can be changed to foreign currency before you leave.

Banks are open Monday to Friday from 9.30 am to 4 pm. All the usual brands of traveller's cheques are accepted and they can be changed at banks or large city hotels. Australian Bankcards are widely accepted throughout New Zealand; as are Visa, Mastercard, American Express and Diners Club.

If you're intending a long stay it may be worth opening a Post Office Savings Bank account. You can withdraw money from this at any post office in New Zealand – very handy for trampers – and the Post Office Savings Bank is open for longer hours than the other banks. Apart from saving on traveller's cheques you also get a free safe deposit envelope when you open the account. You can put airline tickets or other valuables in this envelope and deposit it with the bank while you tramp around New Zealand. They'll even forward it on to the city you depart from if you don't leave from the same place as you arrive.

Inflation & GST

Inflation is hot and heavy in New Zealand. One recent cause for the rapid price hikes was the introduction in late '86 of GST – Goods & Services Tax. It's a European-style VAT (value added tax) which added 10% on to the price of just about everything. Most prices in New Zealand are quoted inclusive of GST but when you're paying for something beware of any small print announcing that the price is GST exclusive; you'll be hit for the extra 10% on top of the stated cost. GST has been such a wonderful money spinner for the government that there are strong rumours that it will be increased, possibly to 15%.

GENERAL INFORMATION

Post

Post offices are generally open weekdays from 8.30 am to 5 pm; and to 8 pm on Fridays. You can have mail addressed to you care of 'Poste Restante, CPO' in whatever town you require. CPO stands for Chief Post Office. Telephone facilities are also available at post offices.

Telephone

From private phones local calls are free, from phone boxes they cost 20c. Although new electronic phones are now being introduced, pay phones have generally lagged far behind inflation. Most of them are the old fashioned button A and button B type. When the call is answered you press the button on the front and your money is swallowed up. If there's no answer press the button on the side and your money is returned. They have coin slots for 1c, 2c (both blanked off) and 10c. So even the cheapest local call requires two coins!

Conceivably you could make a three-minute call to Australia from a pay phone – as long as you had 55 10c coins ready to feed into the phone! Actually if you want to make an international telephone call what you do is make your call through a post office – you go in, pay a deposit, they connect you and afterwards you collect the change or pay the excess. You can even do this for after-hours phone calls – pay now and when you want to make the call the operator should have a record of your deposit on hand.

For emergencies in the major centres dial 111 and say whether you want the police, fire or ambulance authorities.

Electricity

Electricity is 230 volts AC, 50 cycle.

Time

Being close to the international date line, New Zealand is one of the first places in the world to sta of the first places in the world to start a new day. New Zealand is 12 hours ahead of Greenwich Mean Time and two hours ahead of Australian Eastern Standard Time. In summer New Zealand observes Daylight Saving Time, which means that the clocks are advanced one hour on the last Sunday in October and turned back on the first Sunday of the following March. Usually when it's 12 noon in New Zealand it's 10 am in Sydney or Melbourne, 2 am in London, 5 pm the

previous day in San Francisco or Los Angeles.

Business Hours

Office hours are generally 9 am to 5 pm Monday to Friday. Shops are usually open weekdays from 9 am to 5.30 pm, and to 9 pm on Fridays. In most places shops are also open on Saturday mornings. Additionally there are now many convenience stores open much longer hours. This is a considerable improvement on just a few years ago when doors clanged shut at 5 pm Friday and absolutely everything was closed up like Fort Knox until 9 am on Monday.

HEALTH

There are no vaccination requirements. New Zealand is a healthy, disease-free country. Medical attention is high quality and reasonably priced but you should have medical insurance. If you suffer personal injury by accident in New Zealand you are entitled to compensation as a right – irrespective of fault – and may no longer sue in the courts for damages. This covers such things as medical expenses and payments for permanent incapacity, but note that it covers only accidents, not illnesses. If you simply get ill and require medical attention you'll have to pay for it.

HAZARDS

Insects

If the kiwi ever became extinct, the sandfly could replace it as the national symbol – the little bugger is found almost everywhere. Only high alpine areas are free from its torment (or we should say her torment for, like the mosquito, it's the female sandfly who is intent on biting you), Fortunately, the sandfly has a couple of characteristics that enable trampers to survive. As long as you are moving, the insect doesn't land on you, making walking pleasant even in the most infested areas. If they do land on you they're easy to kill as quickness and

alertness are not two of the sandfly's strong points. Best of all, the insect usually disappears at night, allowing you a well-deserved sleep after swatting them all day.

You encounter sandflies mostly before or after rain or on cloudy days. Mosquitoes don't seem to be the problem they are in North America or Australia. Occasionally you may venture into an area – Martins Bay at the end of the Hollyford Track is a classic example – that has both. Now you have a problem. The sandflies work on you during the day and the mosquitoes take over at night. *Take insect repellent* – Dimp is a popular brand in New Zealand – regardless of when you are tramping. Trampers planning to use a tent should also double check their netting for any holes.

Safety Precautions

The most important thing on any tramping adventure is to return safely and the best way to guarantee that is to leave a note of your intentions somewhere, preferably with park officials where you will be hiking. Most visitor centres have intention boards and boxes and only a minute or two is required to fill out a card with your trip details and expected date of return. The park holds on to the card and if for some reason you don't return to sign-out they organise a search.

The system works well if trampers do two things: sign every hut log book as they pass through and, most importantly, take the time to sign out at the end. By registering at each hut, you enable search parties to eliminate a lot of territory if they do have to look for you. But if you forget to sign out, park rangers can only conclude you're lost or hurt on the track and must follow up with an expensive search and rescue effort. Even if you're not returning to the park headquarters, just stop at the next visitor centre or DOC office you pass on your travels and they will inform the proper officials of your departure from the track.

At many rivers and major streams you'll find either swingbridges, wires or even cableways to insure a safe crossing. Smaller streams are normally a quick wade through to reach the track on the other side but any crossing must be carefully considered. Take the me to choose a good spot to ford and remember that a strong current that reaches higher than your knees is often too hard to cross without the mutual support of several people with a pole between them.

During and immediately after heavy rains is a particular dangerous time to ford. It doesn't take long, sometimes less than an hour of hard rain, to turn a mountain creek into an impassable thunder of whitewater. If such is the case, either search for a bridge or wire nearby or camp and wait rather than attempt a crossing. Remember that streams and rivers rise quickly but by the same token return to their normal levels almost as fast. Often by waiting a day or even until late afternoon the water will lower enough to ford safely.

Safe tramping also means knowing your capabilities and expectations and then planning the right trip. Most trampers feel comfortable with walking five to six hours a day, plus an assortment of rest stops and a 30-minute lunch break. That allows them to leave at 9 am and be at the next hut by 3 or 4 pm. If you take more breaks for whatever reasons then plan accordingly and tackle shorter daily sections.

Avoid the common mistake of over-estimating your abilities or endurance. There might be enough daylight for 10 hours of walking but most trampers are too tired towards the end to enjoy any of it. And if your only experience in the bush is day-walks, then don't attempt strenuous eon't attempt strenuous expeditions such as the Copland Pass or a tramp over Cascade Saddle. It's better to select a shorter track than to try and squeeze a five-day tramp into four days.

ACCOMMODATION

New Zealand has a wide range of places to stay but to all of it there is one catch: the Kiwis are great travellers. So during the holiday season you may well find a long queue at popular places. This applies particularly to youth hostels and almost any other cheap accommodation in major holiday areas. The answer is to book ahead if you are going to be arriving in popular places during holiday periods.

Hostels

Hostels offer cheap accommodation in locations all over New Zealand. At a hostel you basically rent a bed, usually for around $10 to $12 a night. Some hostels have male and female bunkrooms for 10 or more people. Others have smaller bunkrooms or even double or single rooms. You usually have to provide your own bedding, although sometimes this can be rented. There's usually a communal kitchen, probably a dining area and a lounge area.

Hostels have always been popular in New Zealand but the recent growth in demand has been phenomenal, which has, of course, created the need for more hostels – both YHA and private.

Apart from being just about the most economical form of accommodation, particularly if you're travelling solo, hostels are also a great place for meeting people, making friends and finding people to go tramping with. They're also wonderful information sources – almost every hostel has a noticeboard smothered in notes, pieces of advice and warnings and the hostel managers are also often great sources of local information, including information on tracks and tramping. Hostels, both private and YHA, often negotiate special discounts and deals for their hostellers with local businesses and tour operators.

YHA Hostels YHA hostels are only open to members of the Youth Hostel Association. You can either join the YHA in your home country (don't forget to bring your membership card) or in New Zealand either at the Auckland or Christchurch office, at any YHA hostel or at Westpac banks. There's a joining fee of $10 and annual membership is then $27.50. You must have sheets or, much better, a sheet sleeping bag when you stay at YHA hostels. A regular sleeping bag is not good enough – it has to go in a sheet sleeping bag or a regular sheet must be used to separate your bag from the mattress. Blankets and sheets or sheet sleeping bags are available for hire at some hostels but you're better off having your own. The YHA handbook shows the approved dimensions if you want to make one from a couple of sheets or you can buy ready made new ones at the YHA shops in Auckland or Christchurch for $14 or from the YHA in your home country.

It is wise to book ahead, particularly during school holidays and at popular hostels . You can do this either directly with the hostel in question, through the New Zealand offices. Alternatively, one hostel can make a reservation for you at another hostel. Reservations have to be paid for in advance; again, the handbook has full details on what to do.

Christchurch National Office
    28 Worcester St (PO Box 436) (tel 799-970)
Auckland Office
    Australis House, 36 Customs St East (PO Box 1687) (tel 794-224)
Wellington Office
    40 Tinakori Rd (tel 736-271)

Private Hostels Although there is no formal association between the private hostels they do produce a useful *Budget Accommodation in New Zealand* leaflet which covers a number of private hostels around the country. As with YHA hostels, nightly costs are typically around $10 to $12.

Many of the private hostels operate just like regular YHA hostels, with bunkrooms, kitchen and lounge facilities and so on. Some of them are operated by ex-YHA managers so they're fully aware of all the plus and minus points about YHA hostel operations.

YMCA & YWCA Hostels There are YMCA and YWCA hostels in several larger towns which offer straightforward, no frills accommodation and are generally reasonably priced. A few of them are single-sex only but most of them take men and women. Although the emphasis is on 'permanent' accommodation – providing a place to stay for young people coming to work in the 'big city' – they are increasingly going after the 'transient trade'.

Accommodation in these hostels is often almost all in single rooms. They've got one extra plus point – they are often less crowded during the holiday seasons, when every other place is likely to be short of space.

Guest Houses & Bed & Breakfasts

There's a wide variation in types and standards in this category. Some guest houses are spartan, cheap, ultra basic accommodation in some cases defined as 'private' (unlicensed) hotels. Others are comfortable, relaxed but low key places, patronised by people who don't enjoy the impersonal atmosphere of many motels. Others are very fancy indeed and try to give their guests a feeling for life with a New Zealand family.

Although breakfast is definitely on the agenda at the real bed & breakfast places it may or may not feature at other places in this category. Where it does it's likely to be a pretty substantial meal – fruit, eggs, bacon, toast, coffee or tea are all likely to make an appearance. Many guest houses seem to really pride themselves on the size, quality and 'traditional value' of their breakfasts. If you like to start the day heartily it's worth considering this when comparing prices.

Also guest houses can be particularly

good value if you're travelling on your own. Most motels, hotels, cabins and so on are priced on a 'per room' basis whereas guest houses usually charge 'per person'. Typically bed & breakfast singles cost $25 to $40 but in some of the more spartan breakfastless guest houses the price can drop to $20 or less while a double in some of the country's best bed & breakfasts can cost $100 or more. Except at the most expensive bed & breakfasts and guest houses, rooms generally do not have attached bathrooms.

Hotels

As in Australia, a hotel essentially has to be licensed to serve alcohol. So at one end of the scale the hotel category can include traditional older-style hotels where the emphasis is mainly on the bar and the rooms are pretty much a sideline. At the other end it includes all the brand new five star hotels in the big cities, hotels which are pretty much like their relations elsewhere in the world in facilities and in their high prices. In between, many places that are essentially motels can call themselves hotels because they have a bar and liquor licence. At the cheapest old-sward $20 while at the most luxurious new establishments a room could be $200 or more.

Scattered around New Zealand are a number of THC (Tourist Hotel Corporation) hotels. The THC is a government-run organisation whose intention is to operate hotels in tourist areas where it would be difficult for privately run hotels to charge reasonable rates and make a profit. Actually some of the THC places are so expensive it would be difficult to make a loss!

Motels

Motels are pretty much like motels anywhere else in the world although New Zealand motels are notably well equipped. They always have tea and coffee making equipment and supplies, usually there's a fridge, very often there's a toaster and electric frypan if you just feel like whipping yourself up scrambled eggs. Even a real kitchen is not at all unusual, complete with utensils, plates and cutlery.

A motel room typically costs around $55 to $65. Sometimes you can find them cheaper, even down towards $40, and there are lots of more luxurious new motels where $70 to $100 is the usual range. There's usually only a small difference in price, if any, between a single or double motel room.

TRAMPING INFORMATION
Information Centres

When you arrive in New Zealand you should spend an afternoon gathering the latest information on parks, walks and transportation and buying any gear that was left behind at the last minute.

Auckland The best information centre for trampers is on the first floor of the DOC Northern Regional Office (tel 379-279), Liverpool House on the corner of Liverpool St and Karangahape Rd. The centre, open from Monday to Friday from 9 am to 4.30 pm, sells brochures, maps and books for most tracks and parks in the North Island and the popular ones in the South Island.

Also check out the Outdoor Recreation Information Centre (tel 775-380) on the second floor of the Auckland Aquatic Centre, next to the Union Fish Co Restaurant on 22 Quay St and open from 9 am to 4 pm weekdays. ORIC provides information and sells books and maps on all types of outdoor activities from hang gliding to climbing but the majority of the material is about tramping. There are three of these centres in New Zealand.

All maps, including topographicals, can be obtained from the Infomap Centre on the 11th floor of the State Insurance Building, downtown on the corner of Wakefield and Rutland St. The centre (tel 771-899) is open weekdays 8 am to 4 pm. Just up Rutland across from the Auckland

Public Library (another good source of New Zealand information) there is also the Government Book Store for a smaller selection of national park maps and handbooks.

Travellers arriving without the basic tramping needs (sleeping bag, pack and stove) might first check the bulletin boards at the Auckland City Youth Hostel on Churton St in Parnell as often someone is unloading their gear before departing the country. Some used equipment and decent prices on new gear can also be obtained at Douglas Surplus Store (tel 796-704) at 66 Hobson St. The YHA headquarters (tel 794-224) at 36 East Customs St sells a limited amount of packs and tramping gear and offers a 10% discount to YHA members while the best selection of equipment (and the most expensive) is found at Alp Sports (tel 394-615) on the corner of Queen and Rutland Sts.

Christchurch Tramping information can be obtained in Christchurch at the DOC regional office (tel 799-758) which in 1988 moved to a new location on Hereford St in the city centre. It is open weekdays 9 am to 4.30 pm. The Outdoor Recreation Information Centre (tel 799-395) is located across from the YHA National Office in the Arts Centre at 28 Worcester St and is open 9 am to 4 pm Monday to Friday and Saturday 10 am to 1 pm during the summer. The ORIC sells books, brochures and maps, the YHA Office (tel 799-970), open weekdays 9 am to 5 pm sells a limited amount of equipment with members receiving a 10% discount.

Other places to check out for tramping equipment are Wilsons Army & Navy Stores (tel 65-374) with two locations at 469 Colombo St and 112 Manchester St and Alp Sports (tel 67-148) at 235 High St. Maps and national park handbooks can also be purchased at the Infomap Centre (tel 799-793) in the State Insurance Building on Worchester St.

Around the Country Trampers can obtain information, brochures and, usually, maps and books on tracks around the country from the following Department of Conservation regional and district offices.

Northern Region
> Northern Region Office, Liverpool House, Cnr Liverpool St & Kanangahape Rd, Auckland (tel (09) 379-279)
> Kaikohe District Office, Marino Place, Harrison Building, Kaikohe (tel (0887) 80-109)
> Whangarei District Office, Jounneaux Building, Bank St, Wh (tel (0887) 80-109)
> Whangarei District Office, Jounneaux Building, Bank St, Whangarei (tel (089) 480-299)
> Hauraki District Office, 60 Cook St, Auckland (tel (09) 371-140)
> Great Barrier District Office, Port Fitzroy, (tel Port Fitzroy 4K)

Waikato Region
> Waikato Regional Office, Level 1, White Stewart House, 18 London St, Hamilton (tel (071) 383-363)
> Hamilton District Office, Ground Floor, White Stewart House, 18 London St, Hamilton (tel (071) 383-379)
> Maniapoto District Office, 78 Taupiri St, Te Kuiti (tel (0813) 87-297)
> Tongariro District Office, Turangi Place, Turnagi (tel (0746) 8607)
> Coromandel District Office, 404 Queen St, Thames (tel (0843) 89-732)
> Taupo District Office, Ruapehu St, Taupo, (tel (074) 85-450)

Wanganui Region
> Wanganui Regional Office, Conservation House, Cnr Victoria Ave & Dublin St, Wanganui (tel (064) 52-402)
> Raukawa District Office, 4th Floor, Challenge House, 85 The Terrace, Wellington (tel (04) 725-821)
> Hawkes Bay District, NZI Building, Tennyson St, Napier (tel (070) 350-415)
> Rangitikei District Office, 2nd Floor, Govt Life Bldg, Cnr Queen & Rangitikei Sts, Palmerston North, (tel (063) 89-004)
> Waiarapa District Office, Government Bldg, Chapel St, Masterton, (tel (059) 82-061)
> Taranaki District Office, Atkinson Bldg, Devon St West, New Plymouth (tel (067) 80-433)

CONSERVATION

Eastern Region

Eastern Regional Office, 1st Floor, Housing Corp. Bldg, Amohau St, Rotorua (tel (073) 479-179)

Urewera District Office, Mill Ave, Minginui (tel Murupara 65-601)

Raukumara District Office, 359 Gladstone Rd (above post office), Gisborne (tel (079) 78-531)

Nelson/Marlborough Region

Nelson/Marlborough Regional Office, Munro State Bldg, 186 Bridge St, Nelson (tel (054) 69-335)

Golden Bay District Office, 1 Commercial St, Takaka (tel (0524) 58-026)

Waimea District Office, Cnr Edward & High, Motueka (tel (0524) 89-117)

Picton District Office, Picton Harbour Board Bldg, Auckland St, Picton (tel (057) 37-582)

Blenheim District Office, 68 Seymour St, Blenheim (tel (057) 88-099)

West Coast Region

West Coast Regional Office, Cnr Sewell & Gibson Quay, Hokitika (tel (0288) 58-301)

Inangahua District Office, Crampton Rd, Reefton, (tel (02728) 390/391)

Buller District Office, Palmerston St, Westport (tel (0289) 7742/7743)

Canterbury Region

Canterbury Regional Office, Hereford St, Christchurch (tel (03) 799-758)

Twizel District Office, Twizel, (tel (05620) 802)

Rangitata District Office, 39 Church St, Timaru (tel (056) 48-320)

Southern Region

Southern Regional Office, John Wickcliffe House, Princes St, Dunedin (tel (024) 770-677)

Otago District Office, Royal Insurance Bldg, 23 Dowling St, Dunedin (tel (024) 778-267)

Lake District Office, Cnr Ballarat & Stanley Sts, Queenstown, (tel (0294) 27-933)

Takitimu District Office, Fiordland NP Visitor Centre, Te Anau Terrace, Te Anau (tel (0229) 7921)

Murihiku District Office, State Insurance Bldg, Don St, Invercargill (tel (021) 44-589)

Rakiura District Office, Halfmoon Bay, Stewart Island, (tel (021) 391-130)

Parks & Park Authorities

The biggest change in New Zealand tramping the past 10 years occurred in April 1987 when the newly created Department of Conservation replaced the Lands and Survey Department and the New Zealand Forest Service as well as assuming functions from several other government agencies.

It was an unprecedented reorganisation of the country's crown lands and natural resources, touching every national park, state forest, maritime park and scenic reserve. In short, practically all of New Zealand's tracks now fall under the jurisdiction of the Department of Conservation, or as one ranger from Arthur's Pass National Park put it, 'we all work for DOC now'.

Not only are national parks, wilderness and ecological areas under the management of DOC but so are the care and welfare of the country's wildlife and fauna and the promotion and development of recreational policies. Described as a 'voice for conservation' in one brochure, DOC is responsible for conserving New Zealand's natural resources and has a staff of 1900 dispersed around eight regions and 34 districts to carry out that task.

The full impact of the reorganisation may not be felt for years but already changes have rippled down to those who are eager to tramp in New Zealand's bush. Trampers now search out a DOC office, whether it is a regional or district centre, when seeking information. Once having found one, many trampers then painfully discover another policy the new department has instituted.

It's called 'user pays' and it means if you want a brochure on the Hollyford Track or a *Birds of Mt Aspiring National Park* pamphlet it's going to cost you 20 cents or 30 cents. User pays is being applied to most visitor services, from the summer nature programmes presented in national parks to the country's hut system. Whereas in the early 1980s trampers were only charged for using huts along the Routeburn and Milford tracks, now all national parks charge hut users a fee. Eventually even huts in forest parks and other obscure preserves will be charging some kind of fee in an effort to recover their construction and maintenance costs.

National Parks In 1887, Te Heuheu Tukino IV, paramount chief of the Maori tribe, the Tuwharetoa, was worried about the future of his people's sacred ancestral mountains, the North Island's Central Plateau. Rival Maori tribes were eyeing the peaks as were European settlers who saw the tussock lands around the volcanoes as potential grazing country. With remarkable foresight, the native chief offered the land to the New Zealand government as a gift to all the people with one stipulation: it had to be kept tapu (sacred) and protected. The area became Tongariro National Park, New Zealand's first park and the start of the world's fourth national park system following those of the US, Australia and Canada.

With the recent creation of Whanganui National Park in 1986 and Paparoa National Park in 1987, there are now 12 within the country, four in the North Island and eight in the South Island. They are the crowning jewels of New Zealand's natural treasures, each preserving a distinct area of the country, ranging from volcanoes, glaciers and the Southern Alps to coastal beaches, native forests and the longest navigable river. They are under the jurisdiction of DOC but each park is administered by a chief ranger from its headquarters, usually located within the town or city that serves as the major access point.

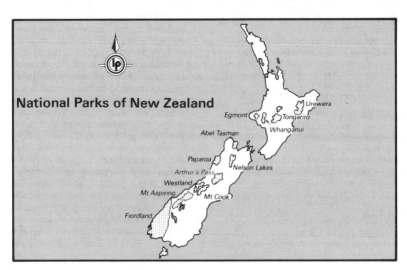

Park headquarters and visitor centres are good places to visit before tramping off into the bush or mountains. They can provide trampers with the latest weather report as well as track and hut conditions. They sell maps, brochures and park handbooks that explain the natural and historical significance of the area. Most of them have visitor centres that contain a series of interesting displays along with a small theatre where a video presentation on the park is shown on request. These are also the best places to leave your intentions and pay hut fees.

North Island

Urewera The park headquarters and visitor centre are at Aniwaniwa on the eastern arm of Lake Waikaremoana. The address for inquiries is: The Chief Ranger, Urewera National Park, Private Bag 213, Wairoa (tel Tuai 803)

Tongariro The headquarters and visitor centre are at Whakapapa Village and the address for inquiries is: The Chief Ranger, Tongariro National Park, Mt Ruapehu (tel Ruapehu 729)

Egmont The headquarters is in New Plymouth but the visitor centre is at North Egmont within the park. The address for inquiries is: The Chief Ranger, Egmont National Park, PO Box 43, New Plymouth (tel 80-829)

Whanganui The headquarters is at the DOC office in Wanganui while a visitor centre and river museum are at Pipiriki. The address for inquiries is: The Chief Ranger, Whanganui National Park, C/-DOC, Private Bag, Wanganui (tel Wanganui 52-402)

South Island

Abel Tasman The headquarters is on Commercial St in Takaka and the address for inquiries is: The Chief Ranger, C/-DOC, PO Box 53, Takaka (tel Takaka 58-026)

Nelson Lakes The headquarters and visitor centre are in the small village of St Arnaud. The address for inquiries is: The Chief Ranger, Nelson Lakes National Park, St. Arnaud (tel St Arnaud 806)

Arthur's Pass The headquarters and visitor centre are in the alpine village of Arthur's Pass. The address for inquiries is: The Chief Ranger, Arthur's Pass National Park, PO Box 8, Arthur's Pass (tel Arthur's Pass 500)

Paparoa For information there is the DOC office in Punakaiki while a visitor centre is a km south at the Pancake Rocks. The address for inquiries is: The Punakaiki Conservation Officer, DOC, Private Bag, Greymouth (tel Barrytown 893)

Westland The headquarters and a visitor centre are at Franz Josef while there is another visitor centre at Fox Glacier. The address for inquiries is: The Chief Ranger, Westland National Park, PO Box 14, Franz Josef (tel Franz Josef 727)

Mt Cook The headquarters and visitor centre are in the village of Mount Cook, and there are plans to build a mountaineering museum there as well. The address for inquiries is: The Chief Ranger, PO Box 5, Mount Cook (tel Mount Cook 819)

Mt Aspiring The headquarters and a visitor centre is located in Wanaka. The address for inquiries is: The Chief Ranger, Mt Aspiring National Park, PO Box 93, Wanaka (tel Wanaka 7660)

Fiordland The headquarters and an impressive visitor centre are in Te Anau on the southern shore of Lake Te Anau. The address for inquiries is: The Chief Ranger, Fiordland National Park, PO Box 29, Te Anau (tel Te Anau 7521)

State Forest Parks There is more bush and wilderness preserved in New Zealand's state forest park system, with 13 parks in the North Island and seven in the South Island. Forest parks fall under the jurisdiction of DOC and are managed under a different philosophy from that of the national parks. While the theme of national parks is to preserve 'an area in its natural state', state forest parks follow a multiple-use concept. In a national park, everything is secondary to preservation, tramping included. But state forest parks are managed to sustain a balance of land uses which might include timber production, live deer harvesting to provide stock for farms, possum hunting for the fur industry and, of course, recreational activities.

State Forest Parks of New Zealand

The main recreational activity in most of them is tramping and there are huts and a variety of tracks in all the state forest parks. The Heaphy, one of the country's best known walks, lies in North-West Nelson State Forest Park. Ten other tracks described in this guide also lie in state forest parks, ranging from the easy two-day Whirinaki Track near Urewera National Park to the challenging alpine treks found in the Tararuas north of Wellington.

State Forests & Scenic Reserves Other types of preserved lands in New Zealand include state forests, of which two – Great Barrier Island in the Hauraki Gulf and Stewart Island south of Invercargill – contain a network of tracks and huts. Trampers will also find walking opportunities in many of the scenic reserves, most notably in the Lewis Pass area, which contains a portion of the St James

Walkway. For up-to-date information on forest parks, state forests and scenic reserves, contact the nearest DOC regional or district office.

STATE FOREST PARKS

Walkways

The idea of a national walkway – a path from one end of New Zealand to the other, captured the enthusiasm of Kiwis in the 1970s and by 1975 the country's legislators passed the Walkways Act which set up the framework for this immense project. Under the direction of the New Zealand Walkways Commission, the ultimate goal is a network of inter-connecting tracks to provide a path from Cape Reinga at the north end of the country to Bluff at the south end. In the beginning, the main emphasis was to provide access for short family walks into the countryside from major urban areas. But now there are walkways all around the country that vary in difficulty and terrain.

The Commission has since set up a system of track classifications that rate all walkways. The easiest rating is a *walk*, which is 'well formed and suitable for the average family', while a *track* is a 'well-defined walking track suitable for people of good average physical fitness', and the most difficult is a *route*, which is 'a lightly marked track for use only by well-equipped and experienced trampers'.

Several of the walkways lend themselves to tramps of several days' duration including the three described in this book – the St James Walkway in the South Island and the Matemateaonga and Ninety Mile-Cape Reinga Walkways in the North Island. For more information on New Zealand Walkways write to: The Secretary, New Zealand Walkway Commission, C/-Department of Conservation, Private Bag, Wellington.

Walking Standards

Each track is rated according to difficulty in the subsection called The Track. *Easy* tracks are those that are well maintained and frequently used, with planking over most wet areas, swingbridges over major streams and directional signs. These tracks can be attempted by trampers with just day-hiking experience.

Those rated as *medium* are tracks that are well cut and which are usually well marked with small metal tags but are more strenuous than easy tracks with numerous stream crossings. They require a greater degree of physical stamina and better map-reading skills . *Difficult* tracks are often not tracks at all but routes that are marked only by rock cairns and snow poles in alpine areas or maybe not marked at all, such as a route along a river valley. These trips should be attempted only by experienced trampers with the right equipment and a good knowledge of New Zealand's bush and frequently changing weather patterns.

Keep in mind that no matter what the track is rated, even if it is easy, it will most likely involve some climbing and descending of ridges or passes. It's almost impossible to find a completely flat walk in New Zealand, it's just the nature of the country.

Approximate walking times are also provided, most often from one hut to the next. It is important to remember these are only *average* tramping times based on the average tramper covering a km of well-marked and somewhat level track in 20-25 minutes. Your hiking time will most likely be different. What one person thinks is a backbreaking trudge, the next will judge as a pleasant stroll. Determine your own endurance and speed and then adjust the times in this book accordingly.

The times do not include major rest periods, lunchbreaks or afternoon teas. They are also based on good weather conditions. Swollen streams or muddy tracks will slow you down.

The distances given within the text are approximate figures only. This is especially true of routes where there is no exact track, for example up a river bed or over an alpine ridge. On these routes the path followed and the distances covered will differ from one party to the next.

Huts & Camping

Camping Even when you're not actually tramping or in a national park, New

Zealand is a great place to camp. All you need is a tent and sleeping bag – there are a lot of sites, particularly in touristy places, and they are very well equipped. Many of them have kitchens and dining areas where the cooker, hot plates and often kettles and toasters are provided; all you need to bring is the utensils, plates, bowls, etc and the food. There are also laundry facilities and often TV rooms too.

How you are charged varies fairly widely. Sometimes there's a site charge and then an additional cost per person. Sometimes it's just a straight site charge. But most of the time it's a straight per person charge and that's typically around $5 to $8 per adult, and half price for children. Most sites charge a dollar or two more per person if you want a powered site for a caravan or campervan as opposed to a tent site without power.

At most sites the kitchen and showers are free but at a very few sites there are coin-in-the-slot operated hot plates and/or hot showers. At most sites laundry facilities are coin operated.

Sites in the Parks There are Department of Conservation camping sites in reserves and national, maritime and farm parks. Most of these camping grounds have minimal facilities – fresh water, toilets, fireplaces and not much else – but they also have minimal charges, often $5 or less.

Cabins & Tourist Flats Many of the campsites near the start and end of tracks will also have cabins which are simply equipped rooms where you have to provide your own sleeping gear (a sleeping bag is fine) and towels. Cabins can be very cheap, often less than $20 for two which makes them even cheaper than hostels. They generally charge per two adults, plus so much for each additional person, but some charge per cabin and some per person. Usually you can rent sheets and blankets if you come unequipped.

On-site caravans (trailer homes in US parlance) are another campsite possibility. Many campsites have regular motel rooms or an associated motel complex and hostel-style bunkrooms are another possibility.

Huts Most tracks in New Zealand are blessed with huts. Although occasionally taken for granted by Kiwis, overseas travellers often marvel at the New Zealand hut system. Huts come in all shapes and sizes, from modern 40-bunk structures like those on the Kepler Track with separate kitchens, gas rings and flush toilets to single-room hunter's shacks that provide little more than a fireplace, table and canvas mattresses.

They are usually placed about a day's walk from each other along a track and used on a first-come, first-one-to-get-a-bunk basis. While some fill-up quickly during the summer – most notably the huts on the Routeburn, Abel Tasman and Heaphy Tracks – trampers are very accommodating to each other. Nobody is ever turned away at night even though it might mean doubling up in bunks or sleeping on the floor.

The huts not only prevent areas from being 'camped-out' but allow trampers to carry lighter packs as they do not need to carry tents, sleeping pads or, sometimes, even stoves. They provide the best protection from rain, strong winds and a

Typical walking track hut

freak summer snowfall in the mountains, guarantee a tramper dry clothing in the morning and just make life a little more pleasant in the bush.

New Zealand's excellent hut system dates back to the turn of the century when a number of them – most notably the Milford Track huts – were built for tourist purposes. As a result of the upsurge of tramping and climbing clubs in the 1920s, private groups began building huts in their favourite tramping areas. The formation of the national parks boards after WW II lead to the construction of even more huts as a way to encourage public use of the land. In the 1960s and '70s, the NZ Forest Service did the same in its State Forest Parks and New Zealand's hut system was in place along every major track or route, from one end of the country to the other.

Today all huts are administered by either DOC or a local tramping club. The system is wide spread and ranges from large dormitory huts like those on the Kepler that provide gas rings, a separate kitchen and flush toilets to a two-man bivvy that is little more than a couple of mattresses and a chair. Most huts, however, provide mattresses, a method of cooking (open fireplace, wood stove or gas rings), a common room with lines or racks for drying wet gear, table, benches and a pit toilet outside. They are usually placed four to five hours apart on the track and many huts in popular areas have a limitation on the number of nights you can stay. Although it is a good practice to obtain permission to use club huts, backcountry shelters are usually left unlocked in case of emergency.

It is wise to check with park authorities about the conditions of huts before embarking on a track. Huts a short walking distance from a road are often crowded or heavily vandalised.

With the formation of DOC and the institution of its user pays policy, hut fees have increased significantly in the last few years, especially when you consider most

of them were free in the early 1980s. This has angered many trampers but the fact remains that huts are still cheap accommodation. The most expensive ones – $11 a night – are those on popular Fiordland tracks such as Routeburn, Milford and Kepler. Most hut fees are lower, ranging from $3 to $7 – half the cost of a night in a youth hostel.

In some huts, there is a warden during the summer season to collect fees, but in most of them an 'honesty system' is used and trampers either drop their money in a box or pay it at the park headquarters afterwards. Unfortunately most trampers, Kiwis and overseas travellers alike, avoid paying anything at all if they can get away with it. In Mt Aspiring National Park, rangers estimate only 20% of all trampers pay when an honesty box is installed in a hut.

Minimum Impact Code

It has long been a tradition in New Zealand to dig rubbish pits next to huts but in recent years there has been a concentrated effort to do away with them. There is now a campaign to encourage trampers to carry out the rubbish they create, with signs in most huts urging trampers and hunters to 'pack it in and pack it out'. Still the number of empty cans and fuel canisters and the volume of other garbage left in many huts is disturbing.

The Nature Conservation Council provides this Minimum Impact Code and they're good points to remember:
1 Keep tramping parties small;
2 Plan your trip to minimise rubbish;
3 Pack out what you pack in;
4 Keep to the tracks where they exist;
5 Minimise campsite construction and avoid camping near huts;
6 Do not use soap or detergents in streams and lakes;
7 Burn or bury all toilet waste;
8 Avoid fires by using portable stoves and conserve wood when using fires;
9 Protect native wildlife and plants.

Tramper admiring the view

The Tracks

Ninety Mile Beach-Cape Reinga Walkway (easy) Part of the New Zealand Walkway system, this tramp can be a 50-km, three-day walk from Spirits Bay to the northern end of Ninety Mile Beach or up to a 133-km walk if the long beach is followed down to its southern end at Ahipara. The best part is the scenic Cape Reinga area with its sweeping coastlines and the semi-tropical beaches of Te Werahi Beach and Tapotupotu Bay. Plenty of camping but no huts.

Great Barrier Island Trek (moderate) The heart of the largest offshore island in Hauraki Gulf is a regenerating kauri forest of 80 square km with a 100-km network of tracks and two huts. You can easily spend two to four days on the island to take in the native forest, the interesting remains of kauri dams, the hot springs and the opportunities for camping, swimming and saltwater fishing.

Coromandel State Forest Park Walk (easy to medium) A three-day tramp up and around the Kauaeranga Valley, the most popular area of the forest park because of the large number of logging and gold-mining relics that can be viewed. Although there is some uphill walking, the track is well cut and easy to follow in most places.

Lake Track (easy to medium) One of the most popular tramps in the North Island, this track circles most of the shore of Lake Waikaremoana, the largest lake in Urewera National Park. Highlights of the three to four-day, 40-km walk are the spectacular views from the Panekiri Range, fine beaches encountered and excellent trout fishing in the lake.

Whakatane River Track (medium) A four to five-day circular route that begins from Ruatahuna in Urewera National Park and includes an all-weather track along the Whakatane River and two days following the banks of the Waikare River, which involves numerous fords. Not nearly as popular as Lake Waikaremoana, both rivers offer excellent trout fishing.

Whirinaki Track (easy) This all-weather track runs 27 km from Minginui to an access road off SH5 (State Highway 5) and makes for an easy two-day tramp along the scenic Whirinaki River. Trampers with more time, however, can combine this with other more challenging tracks to make a circular route of five to six days in the Whirinaki State Forest Park, located just west of Urewera National Park.

Round Mt Ngauruhoe Track (medium) This is a four-day walk which circles the perfect cone of Mt Ngauruhoe in Tongariro National Park, New Zealand's first national park. The tracks are well cut and sections of the route are well marked with snow poles. A popular walk that includes such highlights as Ketetahi Hot Springs and active volcanic areas.

Te Iringa-Oamaru Circuit (medium) A five to six-day tramp through the forests of Kaimanawa State Forest Park east of Tongariro National Park. Although there

WALK STANDARDS & SEASONS

Island	Track	Rating	Days
N	Ninety Mile Beach – Cape Reinga Walkway	Easy	3
N	Great Barrier Island Trek	Medium	2-4
N	Coromandel State Forest Park Walk	Easy to Medium	3
N	Lake Track	Easy to Medium	3-4
N	Whakatane River Track	Medium	4-5
N	Whirinaki Track	Easy	2
N	Round Mt Ngauruhoe Track	Medium	4
N	Te Iringa – Oamaru Circuit	Medium	5-6
N	Mt Egmont Round-the-Mountain Track	Medium	4
N	Pouakai Track	Medium	2-3
N	Matemateaonga Walkway	Medium	4
N	Mt Holdsworth Circuit	Medium to Difficult	2-3
N	Totara Flats Track	Medium	3
S	Abel Tasman Coastal Track	Easy	3-4
S	Heaphy Track	Easy to Medium	4-5
S	Wangapeka Track	Medium	5
S	Leslie – Karamea Track	Medium to Difficult	5-7
S	Pelorus River Track	Medium	3-4
S	Travers – Sabine Circuit	Medium to Difficult	6
S	D'Urville Valley Track	Medium to Difficult	5
S	St James Walkway	Easy to Medium	5
S	Inland Pack Track	Medium	2-3
S	Goat Pass	Medium to Difficult	2
S	Waimakariri – Harman Pass Route	Difficult	4-5
S	Harper Pass	Medium	4-5
S	Cass – Lagoon Saddles Track	Medium	2-3
S	Copland Pass	Extremely Challenging	4
S	Mueller Hut	Difficult	2
S	Routeburn Track	Medium	3
S	Greenstone Track	Easy	2
S	Caples Track	Medium	2
S	Rees – Dart Track	Medium	4-5
S	Cascade Saddle Route	Difficult	4-5
S	Wilkin – Young Valleys Circuit	Difficult	3
S	Milford Track	Easy	4
S	Hollyford Track	Medium	4-5
S	Kepler Track	Difficult	4
S	Dusky Track	Difficult	4-7
St	Link Track	Medium	3
St	Northern Circuit	Difficult	10

N North Island

S South Island

St Stewart Island

Season: E Excellent

F Fair

P Poor

NA Do Not Attempt

Transport	Summer	Autumn	Winter	Spring	Features
Bus	E	E	E	E	Beach, rugged coast
Boat, Plane	E	E	P	E	Kauri dams, hot pools
Bus	E	E	P	E	Kauri dams, forest
Boat, Bus	E	E	P	E	Lakeshore, fishing
Bus, Taxi	E	E	P	E	River, trout fishing
Bus, Taxi	E	E	P	E	River, caves, gorge
Bus	E	F	NA	F	Hot pools, volcanoes
Private	E	F	P	P	River valleys, fishing
Bus, Taxi	E	F	NA	F	Volcano peaks
Private, Taxi	E	F	NA	F	Alpine views
Boat, Taxi	E	E	F	E	Wilderness isolation
Private	E	P	NA	P	Alpine scenery, peaks
Private	E	F	P	F	Rivers, grassy flats
Boat, Bus	E	E	F	E	Coastal beaches
Taxi, Plane	E	E	P	E	Forest, beach
Taxi	E	F	P	F	Rivers, passes
Private	E	F	P	F	Gold mining history
Bus, Private	E	F	P	F	Rivers
Bus, Boat	E	F	NA	F	Alpine passes, peaks
Bus, Boat	E	F	NA	F	Alpine pass, peaks
Bus	E	F	P	F	Rivers, alpine views
Bus	E	F	P	F	Granite cliffs, caves
Bus	E	F	NA	F	Alpine pass
Bus	E	P	NA	P	Alpine pass, peaks
Bus, Train	E	F	NA	F	Rivers, alpine scenery
Bus, Train	E	F	NA	F	Alpine passes
Bus, Plane	E	NA	NA	NA	Peaks, glaciers
Bus, Plane	E	NA	NA	NA	Peaks, glacier
Bus	E	F	NA	F	Alpine scenery
Bus	E	F	P	F	Rivers, fishing
Bus	E	F	P	P	Rivers, fishing
Bus, Taxi	E	P	NA	F	Alpine pass, rivers
Taxi	E	NA	NA	NA	Peaks, glacier
Bus, Boat	E	P	NA	P	Pass, rivers
Bus, Boat	E	F	NA	F	Waterfalls, pass
Plane, Boat	E	F	P	F	Rugged coast, wildlife
Private	E	P	NA	P	Alpine scenery, peaks
Boat, Plane	E	P	NA	P	Lakes, fiords
Boat, Plane	E	F	P	F	Rugged coast
Boat, Plane	E	P	P	P	Rugged coast, wildlife

are a number of ridges and passes to climb, much of the walk is along rivers that are favourite spots for trout fishermen.

Mt Egmont Round-the-Mountain Track (medium) A popular 55-km track around the cone of Mt Egmont in Egmont National Park that takes four days, though many trampers tackle only a portion of it. Although there are excellent views of the volcano and opportunities to climb it, much of the track is in heavy bush and dense beech forest.

Pouakai Track (medium) A shorter alternative loop to the Egmont Round-the-Mountain Track that requires only two to three days' hiking time but still provides excellent views of the national park from lofty perches above the bushline.

Matemateaonga Walkway (medium) The four-day track is located in an isolated section of Whanganui National Park, which was created in 1986 and lies north of Wanganui. The 42-km track is part of the New Zealand Walkway system and provides trampers with one of the few true wilderness experiences in North Island. One end of the track can only be reached by boat up the Wanganui River.

Mt Holdsworth Circuit (medium to difficult) The two to three-day alpine walk is located in Tararua State Forest Park, a favourite area for Wellington tramping clubs. The circuit includes nights at two scenic huts above the bushline and a day following alpine ridges.

Totara Flats Track (medium) Also located in the rugged Tararua Range is a walk through Totara Flats but this trip is considerably easier with no open alpine crossings. The 38-km, three-day trip follows river valleys much of the way and conveniently ends near a youth hostel.

Abel Tasman Coastal Track (easy) This three to four-day trip that follows the shoreline of the South Island's Abel Tasman National Park is one of the best coastal tracks in New Zealand but unfortunately also one of the most popular walks. There are plenty of trampers and boaters in this area but the beaches, beautiful bays and tidal areas are unmatched anywhere else in the country.

Heaphy Track (easy to medium) Another popular and well-known walk, the Heaphy Track is a 76-km tramp in North-West Nelson State Forest Park. The scenery ranges from hilly beech forest to a stroll down a Tasman Sea beach lined with palm trees.

Wangapeka Track (medium) Lying in the same state forest as the Heaphy but not nearly as popular, this 65-km, five-day walk is a pleasant alternative. A more challenging trip overall, the track begins at Rolling River and ends 25 km south of Karamea on the West Coast and is often walked after the Heaphy to return to Nelson.

Leslie-Karamea Track (medium to difficult) Even more remote and unknown, this trip traverses the Leslie and upper Karamea River valleys in the heart of North-West Nelson State Forest Park. Access to the route is via Wangapeka Track in the south or the Tablelands to the north and all together the tramp requires five to seven days to cover the 85 km. The area contains many historical sites from the gold-mining days and good opportunities for trout fishing.

Pelorus River Track (medium) A popular three to four-day tramp in Mt Richmond Forest Park with one end just 27 km south of Nelson. The river is famous for its large trout though the track doesn't always lend itself to easy access to Pelorus's deep green pools where the fish are found.

Travers-Sabine Circuit (medium to difficult) Grassy river flats, beech forests and two alpine saddles make up the features of this circular walk through Nelson Lakes National Park in the South Island. The six-day tramp includes excellent alpine scenery and two huts above the bushline but is not nearly as busy in the summer as tracks in the Abel Tasman and North-West Nelson areas.

D'Urville Valley Track (medium to difficult)

An even more remote tramp, the D'Urville and Sabine Valleys can be combined for a five-day circular walk beginning at the south end of Lake Rotoroa in the Nelson Lakes are. (Two more days need to be added if you walk in from Rotoroa or St Arnaud rather than take a water-taxi.) The trip includes the alpine crossing of Moss Pass and a night at scenic Blue Lake Hut.

St James Walkway (easy to medium) The St James is the first walkway to be established in sub-alpine terrain and at 66 km the longest track constructed by the Walkway Commission. The five-day trip passes through Lewis Pass Scenic Reserve, beginning and ending at SH7 where there is good public bus transportation available.

Inland Pack Track (medium) This historic track, carved out by gold-miners who wanted to avoid the rugged West Coast, is located in Paparoas National Park, New Zealand's newest park. The walk features an unusual landscape of steep limestone gorges, caves and towering bluffs. There are no huts but trampers can get away without a tent on the 21-km track by staying at the Ballroom, one of the largest rock bivvies or shelters in New Zealand.

Goat Pass (medium to difficult) A popular overnight trip of 25 km over the alpine pass of Goat Pass in Arthur's Pass National Park. Much of the tramp is along rivers and is easy to follow while the highlight is a night spent at the alpine hut on Goat Pass.

Waimakariri-Harman Pass Route (difficult) A much more challenging route in Arthur's Pass, this four to five-day tramp includes ascending two alpine passes and following the upper reaches of the Taipo River, renowned for its trout fishing. Good transportation is available at both ends of the trip on SH73.

Harper Pass (medium) The four to five-day tramp begins in Lake Sumner State Forest Park, crosses the historic Harper Pass and ends up in Arthur's Pass National Park in the South Island. The pass is low and much of the route is through beech forest and along wide river flats.

Cass-Lagoon Saddles Track (medium) Located in Craigieburn Forest Park just south of Arthur's Pass, the two to three-day walk is along a well-marked track and considerably easier than most of the trips in the national park north of it. The tramp is highlighted by the spectacular views from two alpine passes and a night at impressive Hamilton Hut.

Copland Pass (extremely challenging) A highly technical trip from Mt Cook National Park to Westland National Park over the Southern Alps through the famous Copland Pass. This trip requires good physical endurance, experience in alpine travel and special equipment – crampons, ice axe and ropes – to undertake the entire route. Those without them should consider hiking the portion on the west side up to Welcome Flats Hut, well known for its hot springs.

Mueller Hut (difficult) This is the only track in which you have to return the way you came. It is included because the climb to Mueller Hut allows trampers to overnight in the Southern Alps at Mt Cook National Park without undertaking the extremely challenging Copland Pass.

Routeburn Track (medium) This is New Zealand's renowned alpine crossing that lies in both Mt Aspiring and Fiordland National Park. The three-day walk includes rainforest, sub-alpine scrub and spectacular views from ridges, peaks and saddles. Unfortunately its immense popularity has lead to heavy usage and its 40-bunk huts are often crowded at night with 60, 70 or even more trampers.

Greenstone Track (easy) The two-day walk is an easy tramp along the Greenstone River that is noted among anglers for its trout fishing. The tramp, which passes through grassy river flats and beech forest, is often combined with the Routeburn to form a circular trip back to Queenstown.

Caples Track (medium) A little more

difficult than the Greenstone, this two-day track is another way to return from the Routeburn to the car park on Lake Wakatipu where there is public transportation to Queenstown. Or for those who want to skip the mass of humanity on the Routeburn, the Caples and Greenstone can be combined for a pleasant and less crowded four-day loop.

Rees-Dart Track (medium) A classic four to five-day round-trip from Glenorchy, this track provides a pleasant variety of scenery including forests and grassy river flats along with mountain vistas and the Rees Saddle. Most of the trip lies in Mt Aspiring National Park but does not experience the heavy usage of the Routeburn Track.

Cascade Saddle Route (difficult) A steep and difficult climb, this alpine crossing can be one of the most scenic in the country in good weather. Superb views of Mt Aspiring and the Dart Glacier are enjoyed before the routes converge at the middle of the Dart-Rees Track.

Wilkin-Young Valleys Circuit (difficult) The three-day trip, part of it in the Mt Aspiring National Park, involves bush tracks, grassed valleys and the 1460-metre Gillespie Pass. The alpine scenery on the walk is exceptional while the entire area does not suffer from the heavy overuse that the Routeburn and other tracks of the Glenorchy region do.

Milford Track (easy) Undoubtedly the best known track in New Zealand, it is so popular that reservations are needed to enjoy the four-day walk. It runs from Lake Te Anau to the Milford Sound in Fiordland National Park and includes a wide variety of rainforest, alpine meadows and spectacular waterfalls. Special transportation needs to be arranged, however, and the total cost of walking the track, even for independent walkers, is not cheap.

Hollyford Track (medium) This is a tramp through thick rain forest, past Lake McKerrow and out to isolated Martins Bay on the west coast. The track lies in Fiordland National Park and features excellent trout and coastal fishing, good mountain scenery and interesting seal and penguin colonies.

Kepler Track (difficult) One of the newest tracks in New Zealand, the Kepler was finished in 1988 as an effort to reduce the number of trampers using the Routeburn and Milford. The four-day loop begins and ends near Te Anau and includes a longer alpine crossing, and thus is more difficult than its two famous counterparts to the north.

Dusky Track (difficult) At the other end of Fiordland National Park is this track which offers the isolation and wilderness experience the Milford or Routeburn cannot. It is a rugged but exceptionally scenic track and special transportation arrangements have to be made as the tramp begins and ends on remote lake or coastal shores.

Link Track (medium) Off by itself, Stewart Island is a tramper's delight with a wide system of tracks, including its newest one, the Link Track. The route was built in 1986 to connect the beginning and end of the northern circuit to form a shorter three-day tramp on the island.

Northern Circuit (difficult) This is the classic 10-day tramp around the northern portion of Stewart Island. The famous mud and bogs of the island make it difficult but for those trampers with the time and energy the isolated beaches and native birdlife make it worth getting your boots dirty.

MAPS

There is no substitute for a good map, not even a guidebook to the tracks. There are two types of maps trampers commonly use: the topographical quads or the recreational maps to national parks and certain state forest parks and tracks. Topographicals are the best and can be purchased either as NZMS 1, the original series with a scale of 1:63,360 (1 inch to 1 mile) or the new NZMS Infomap 260 series, the metric equivalent with a scale

Department of
Survey and Land Information

nfo**map**S

SOLD HERE

of 1:50,000 (1 cm to 500 metres). Any other topographical with a larger scale (such as 1:250,000) is of little use to trampers as there is not enough detail.

Recreational maps have a scale of 1:100,000 and while they provide less detail they are still suitable for most well-marked tracks. Many of them also contain tracks notes, walking times and the park's natural history on the back and are usually the maps posted in huts. The biggest advantage of recreational maps, however, is the price. A recreational map costs $5.50 and covers all the tracks in a certain park. Topographicals cost almost $8 a quad and two or three sheets may be needed to cover the entire trip.

Most maps are produced by the government's Department of Survey and Land Information and are sold at Infomap centres throughout out the country as well as at DOC offices and park visitor centres. District Infomap offices are located in Auckland, Hamilton, New Plymouth, Gisborne, Napier, Wellington, Blenheim, Nelson, Hokitika, Christchurch, Dunedin and Invercargill. If you are unsure about your map-reading skills, pick up a *Information For Map Users* pamphlet at any Infomap Centre. Although mostly devoted to how the map was created, it will help you understand what all the lines are you're staring at.

FOOD

Outfitting a trip with food is easy in New Zealand. You can find almost everything you need at small dairies (local grocers) in villages and towns or at supermarkets in the cities. Most tracks require less than a week to complete and you can get by with inexpensive items like muesli, dried soups, one-pot dinners of rice or noodles and a loaf of bread. New Zealand food markets usually carry an excellent selection of dried vegetables and fruits while their cheese, always white in colour, is tasty and inexpensive, making it a good item to put on lunchtime bread.

If you plan longer tramps of a week or more you might want to lighten your load with special freeze-dried food. In New Zealand, the most popular brand available is Alliance and while the quality is only fair the price is usually steep; $4 to $7 for a packet that makes a single serving. Freeze-dried dinners are one item overseas travellers might consider bringing with them.

CLOTHING

General Clothing Carry a change of warm clothing along with a heavy jersey, jacket or sweater to keep out cold winds, rain or possibly even snow. You should also use wool socks and carry a stocking cap and mittens. Both walking shorts and long trousers will be needed. In this country of 70 million sheep, wool is considered ideal for both its ability to keep you warm while wet and its price. The new synthetic pile fibres or spun artificial or bunting also work well though these materials are usually much more costly than wool. Avoid cotton at all costs, especially jeans and cotton socks. Cotton absorbs and retains water and thus will not hold in your body heat when wet. And, once wet, cotton seems to take forever to dry out over the wood burning stove in a hut.

Footwear More and more trampers are turning away from the traditional, and very heavy, all-leather hiking boot and choosing instead the new ultra-light boots. On most tracks, the nylon boots are excellent, providing adequate comfort and support to the feet and ankles. But where there isn't a track, when you're crossing an alpine pass or bouldering along a river, the extra support of stiff leather boots will be appreciated by the end of the day. Trampers should also take a pair of tennis shoes as a change of footwear for use in the huts at night.

Raingear Foul weather gear is a must. Pack a waterproof parka and try to avoid ponchos as they become flapping messes in heavy winds. Waterproof overtrousers are also a handy piece of gear, especially in alpine areas. Many New Zealand trampers, however, wear a parka and knit hat while leaving their shorts and bare legs unprotected. They know that a properly protected head and upper body will keep the rest of the body warm in bad weather as long as they keep up a steady pace. It is also a good idea to wrap your sleeping bag in plastic (a garbage bag is best) even if you do use a pack cover. Even a partially wet bag makes for a long night.

EQUIPMENT

Mishaps in the bush begin with people being unprepared or with people underestimating the difficulty of a track or the changeability of New Zealand's erratic weather. Tramping in this mountainous country, regardless of which track you choose to walk, should not be taken lightly. If you arrive without the proper gear, then either rent it or look into joining a guided trip where the outfitter supplies the necessary equipment.

Overseas travellers should plan on bringing all their own gear, or at least major items such as boots, packs, sleeping bags and stoves. There are excellent outdoor shops in most large towns and cities but the cost can shock, though this depends on the prices you are used to at home and the prevailing exchange rates.

Major Items
Backpack The popular choice is an internal frame pack even though on most tracks a rigid frame pack would be far more comfortable. Either one will be adequate. Overseas travellers who arrive with packs that convert into luggage should keep in mind those are fine for an easy track like the Abel Tasman but will be a painful way to carry gear on many of the more challenging tracks. If you plan to do a considerable amount of tramping bring a good backpack, not a piece of luggage, and a pack cover to keep everything dry inside.

Stove A good, lightweight backpacker's stove is not a necessity on most tracks but it makes life a lot more pleasant. With a stove you can cook dinner or make a pot of tea when you want to without having to worry about finding wood or stoking up a fire. On popular tracks, competition for a spot on the hut stove can be fierce and in some alpine areas wood for burning is almost impossible to find. Overseas trampers who use white gas in their stoves need to ask for white spirits, which can be purchased for $3 a litre at most petrol stations and hardware stores.

Tent It's a toss-up whether you need a tent. On a few of the more popular tracks, most notably the Abel Tasman, it allows you to get away from the overflowing huts, but on most tracks it will be a bulky item to carry that will rarely be used as you will usually stay in huts.

General Equipment
Torch Most trampers carry a small torch with them but candles are also a handy thing to pack along as they make for a pleasant evening in a hut.

Cooking Equipment Some walkers forget to bring a small pot and other cookware or think there will be something in the hut. This is not usually the case and they end up having to borrow pans for their entire tramp.

Gaiters Many people wear gaiters but they are not a necessity.

Sleeping Bag & Mat You will need a sleeping bag, of course, but a sleeping pad is not necessary as there are mattresses in the vast majority of huts.

Fishing Rod Take a rod if you want to make the most of New Zealand's excellent trout fishing.

Rainbow Trout

FISHING

The one animal that was introduced and seems to have made a hit with everybody is the trout. Before the Europeans arrived, there were only a few species of freshwater fish and eel. The English being English quickly imported the brown trout, via Tasmania, in 1867 and in 1883 imported and stocked the rivers with the California rainbow trout. The superb water of the lakes and rivers soon led to a thriving species that easily exceeded its ancestors in size. Today New Zealand is world renowned for its fly fishing.

Those interested in combining fishing with tramping should plan to bring either a lightweight spinning outfit or fly fishing gear. You'll also need to look into seasons and limits and purchase a fishing licence, which is sold as one-day, a week or a season-long permit. Freshwater game fish are protected and under the control of 24 Acclimatisation Societies throughout the country who stock rivers, issue licences and patrol their region. A licence purchased from one society is good all over the country with the exception of the Rotorua and Taupo districts where special permits are needed.

Overseas anglers find it best to bring a selection of their favourite spinners and spoons or flies (wet flies and nymphs being the most widely used) as well as to purchase a few local varieties once they arrive. Any good bookshop will also carry a number of trout guides to rivers for the more serious angler.

WHEN TO GO

Most national parks and state forests experience their largest influx of trampers during the Christmas school holidays, from roughly the third week of December to the end of January. This is when New Zealanders have extended vacation time, the kids are off from school and overseas travellers begin showing up in force because the weather is at its best. On some tracks there is another big influx of walkers during the April Easter holiday, the unofficial end of the summer tramping season. Most tracks, including the 40 in this book, can be undertaken any time from mid-November to early April although snow may be encountered in the alpine areas in November or March. June, July and August is the New Zealand winter and tramping at this time requires special skills and equipment to combat the cold temperatures, snow and strong winds.

For overseas travellers, the best time to explore the country's wilderness may be February and March. This is the driest time of the year, the kids are in school, mums and dads are back at work and on most tracks you can usually count on getting a bunk in the next hut. If you do plan on tramping around Christmas choose a track that lies off the beaten path or be resigned to enduring crowded huts as a price of enjoying a popular walk.

Getting There

AIR

For overseas travellers planning a tramping holiday, the first decision may not be which tracks to walk but where to enter the country: Auckland in the North Island or Christchurch in South Island. There are actually three airports that handle international flights: Auckland, Wellington and Christchurch. Most international flights go through Auckland; certainly if you're flying from the US you're going to arrive in Auckland. Wellington airport has limited runway capacity and international flights are all to and from Australia. Flights to and from Christchurch also usually connect with Australia although there are some connections with other countries.

Overseas travellers who are planning a tramping holiday, however, should seriously consider arriving at Christchurch if possible. The city serves as the gateway to the South Island where eight of the 12 national parks are located and where, unquestionably, the most varied and best tramping can be found. The renowned tracks of the Routeburn, Milford, Heaphy and Able Tasman are located in the South Island along with many others including five described in this book that are only two hours from Christchurch.

There are some special ticket types and definitions which may be of interest to trampers going to New Zealand.

Circle Pacific Fares

Circle Pacific tickets let you circle the Pacific using a combination of airlines. You can start and finish the circle at any point and it goes from the US West Coast, via various islands in the Pacific to New Zealand, on to Australia, to Asia and back to the West Coast. Circle Pacific tickets usually cost about US$200 more than a regulare fare.

Circle Pacific tickets usually have some sort of advance purchase requirement and there will probably be restrictions on changing your route once you've bought the ticket. Typically you're allowed four stopovers but additional stopovers can be included at extra cost. You will probably have to complete the circuit within a certain period of time.

Round-the-World Fares

Round-the-World or RTW fares can be a very useful way of visiting New Zealand in combination with other destinations. They work particularly well from Europe – having come half-way round the world to New Zealand in one direction you might just as well continue the same way!

Round-the-world tickets usually apply to the combined routes of two airlines. As with Circle Pacific tickets, you can join the loop at various places throughout the world. A ticket from London costs around £990. You could use an RTW ticket to make stops in Australia, New Zealand, the USA and Europe.

Apart from the official airline RTW tickets there are also RTW combinations put together by travel agents. Out of London, for example, they might put together a combination such as a cheap flight to Asia, hooking up with the popular and heavily discounted UTA trans-Pacific route and then another cheap fare back to London from the US.

Bucket Shops

Particularly in Europe special deals on air fares are often found through travel agents known as 'bucket shops'. A bucket shop is an agent specialising in discounted tickets. These tickets are usually quite legitimate.

The more obscure the airline or the more inconvenient the route the bigger the discount is likely to be. Although it's really only in Europe that ticket discounters are known as bucket shops, similar operations can also be found in the US, Australia, Hong Kong and many other places. To find a ticket discounter simply scan the travel ads in the travel pages of newspapers.

From Australia

The number of air routes between Australia and New Zealand has increased dramatically in the past few years. New Zealand cities with flights to or from Australia are Auckland, Christchurch and Wellington. Australian cities with flights to or from New Zealand are Adelaide, Brisbane, Hobart, Melbourne, Perth, Sydney and Townsville. Prices alter according to the season. Examples of cheap return fares are: Sydney to Auckland – A\$365 to A\$470; Sydney to Christchurch or Wellington – A\$452 to A\$598; Melbourne to Christchurch, Auckland or Wellington – A\$525 to A\$690. Fares from Brisbane or Hobart are a similar price, while those from Adelaide to Auckland are slightly more expensive.

It's much cheaper to take an advance purchase fare which can get you to New Zealand and back for little more than a regular one-way fare. With these fares you must book and pay for your ticket a specified period in advance, and once the tickets are issued amendment and/or cancellation charges apply should you wish to change your reservation or fail to fly. Insurance is available to protect against the advance purchase cancellation fees. You must stay in New Zealand for at least six days but no more than 120.

The fare depends on the time of the year you fly out as well as where you fly to and from. The year is divided up into peak (mid-December to mid-January), off-peak (June and July) and shoulder (the period in between). It pays to plan your flight dates carefully: if you were planning to visit New Zealand in the summer, leaving just a few days earlier in December or later in January could save you money.

From the USA

A typical advance purchase return fare from the US west coast to New Zealand is between US\$895 and US\$1295, depending on the season. The Sunday travel sections of papers like the *New York Times*, the *Los Angeles Times* or the *San Francisco Examiner* always have plenty of ads for cheap airline tickets and there are always good deals on flights across the Pacific. Council Travel and STA, the two student travel specialists, both have good fares on offer.

From Europe

There has always been cut-throat competition between London's many 'bucket shops', and with the weaker pound London is once again the European centre for cheap fares. There are plenty of bucket shops in London and although there are always some untrustworthy operators most of them are fine. You'll find advertisements from agents and examples of their fares in give-away papers like *Australasian Express* or *LAM*. The weekly 'what's on' magazine *Time Out* has plenty of travel ads and they also give some useful advice on precautions to take when dealing with bucket shops. The magazine *Business Traveller* is another good source of information and advice on discount fares. Two good low-fare specialists are Trailfinders at 46 Earls Court Rd, London W8, and STA Travel at 74 Old Brompton Rd, London W7.

Return tickets from London to Auckland can be found in London bucket shops for around £800 to £1000. Some stopovers are permitted on this sort of ticket. Since New Zealand is about as far from Europe as you can get it's not that much more to fly right on round the world rather than backtracking.

From Asia

There are now far more flights to New Zealand from Asia than there were only a few years ago. Although standard return economy fares from Tokyo to Auckland can be as much as Y462,600, cheaper fares should be relatively easy to find. From Kuala Lumpur, Malaysia, a standard economy one-way ticket can be up to M$2240, but Malaysia is a very popular place for fare discounting so shop around.

From Singapore standard economy one-way fares are as much as S$2165. Hong Kong is another popular fare discounting centre so you should have no trouble finding something for considerably less than the standard economy one-way fare of HK$8110.

Getting Around

The beauty of New Zealand for trampers lies not only in the scenery but also in the ease with which you can get from track to track. This is a compact country where it takes only hours, not days, to travel from one national park to the next. In New Zealand you can often hop from one track to the next and still have enough time left in the day to hike into the first hut, thus skipping the cost of overnight accomodation in a town or city.

The country has an excellent system of buses, trains, planes and ferries that are clean, reasonably priced (in comparison with everything else) and very dependable. And once you are at the main access point for many popular tracks, a growing number of small companies will deliver you to the start of the track and collect you at the end.

AIR

Although New Zealand is a compact country and ground transport is generally quite good there are still places where flying can make a lot of sense, particularly if you've already done the same journey by land. Travellers have quoted examples of trips between the North and South Islands where a long bus-trip is followed by the inter-island ferry and another bus trip, taking a couple of days altogether. By air the same trip could be done in an hour or two and actually cost less. There are also great views to be enjoyed, particularly if your flight takes you over the mountains or volcanoes.

Air New Zealand offers the greatest number of domestic services – some 200 flights a day to 24 towns and cities – with very competitive prices due to increased competition, most notably from Ansett New Zealand. The other major operator is Mt Cook Airlines.

For visitors from overseas Air New Zealand has a special Visit New Zealand Fare which can only be purchased prior to arrival and in conjunction with your international flight. The ticket allows either four flights for NZ$320 or six flights for NZ$440. Mt Cook has a Kiwi Air Pass which gives you 30 days unlimited travel on Mt Cook Airline services for NZ$599. Again it must be bought before you arrive in New Zealand.

Local Air Services

Apart from the three major operators there are also a host of local and feeder airlines. Services that may interest trampers include Southern Air's hop between Invercargill and Stewart Island or there's Sea Bee Air's amphibious services from Auckland to Waiheke or the Bay of Island's. Flights between the two islands are also a popular alternative to the ferry services, you can hop across from Wellington to Picton for little more than the ferry fare.

SOUTHERN AIR LTD

BUS

There is an extensive bus network that supplements and extends the rail services. The main operator is New Zealand Railways Road Services who are known by all sorts of abbreviations such as 'Road Services', 'the Railways' bus', 'Railways', 'NZR' – but more often NZRSS. With a few exceptions there is an NZRRS bus to almost any town of reasonable size in New Zealand and they often operate to and from railway stations where they share facilities. New Zealand passenger railway services contract year by year so it's a good job they have an alternative use for the railway stations!

The two other major bus operators are Newmans and Mt Cook/H&H. Although these companies have much less extensive route networks than NZRRS they also have interests in numerous other areas of tourism including local tours. Newmans operate services through both islands from Whangarei in Northland right down to Dunedin towards the bottom of the South Island. Mt Cook Landline have recently taken over H&H Travel Lines and their combined networks extend from Auckland all the way to Invercargill.

In addition there are a host of local operators including companies like Clarks Northliner which operate between Auckland and the Bay of Islands; Mainline Coachways which operate from Auckland to the Bay of Plenty, Rotorua and Taupo; or Delta Coachlines who connect Picton, Nelson and the West Coast on the South Island.

Services on the main routes usually run at least once a day, except on Sundays when some services don't operate at all. Where there is another service operating on the same route as NZRRS, the NZRRS buses will usually operate more often. Although bus travel is relatively easy and well organised it can be expensive and time consuming. Bus fares, like everything else in New Zealand, have jumped considerably in recent years and these days it pays to consider the alternatives carefully. Sometimes buying a car can actually work out cheaper than travelling by bus. Bus trips can also be slow. This problem seems particularly prevalent on

the once-a-day NZRRS services where the bus also operates as a means of local communication by picking up and dropping off mail at every little town along the way. Frequent stops at small cafes for cups of tea also slow things down, so it can take a long time to get anywhere. Although fares do vary from company to company they are generally fairly close and seem to play leapfrog with one another.

Trampers planning on walking a number of shorter tracks in a limited amount of time should look into purchasing a travel pass as the most economical way of travelling, short of hitchhiking, and undoubtedly the most convenient. Travel passes not only provide transportation from one area of the country to the next but also are a hassle-free way of getting a ride at the end of a track to the next town or park. Many treks described in this book either end on a bus route or within walking distance of one.

NZRRS offer a New Zealand Travelpass, as well as some off peak or advance purchase discount fares. Travelpasses give you unlimited travel on any NZR bus, rail or inter-island ferry service. The passes cost approximately NZ$300 for eight days, NZ$400 for 15 days or NZ$500 for 22 days and any of these passes can be extended for a further six days.

As with any unlimited travel pass of this type you have to do lots of travelling to make it pay off - they're best for people whose time is limited and want to see a lot in a short time. If you do feel a Travelpass is for you be prepared to do a lot of pre-planning to work out an itinerary you can stick to. Also it's often necessary to book ahead on the buses to be sure of a seat. The pass can be used on certain Mt Cook and Newmans services but it cannot be used on NZRRS tours in Rotorua. It can be used on the day tours to Waitomo from Rotorua or the day tours to Milford Sound in the South Island. There are some restrictions on Travelpasses during the mid-December to end of January peak summer season when the passes are only available to overseas visitors.

Kiwi Coach Passes are another travelpass possibility. These allow travel on Mt Cook Landline, NZRRS and Newmans bus services but must be purchased before you arrive in New Zealand. Newmans offer a 10/30 Pass exclusively to YHA members – it allows unlimited travel on Newmans services on any 10 days out of 30.

Off Peak Saver fares are available on NZRRS services and give a 25% discount on trips over 100 km so long as you travel at off peak times and get your tickets a week in advance. They don't apply during the summer peak period or during school holidays.

TRAIN

Railways in New Zealand are operated by a government body, New Zealand Railways (NZR for short). Their main aim appears to be to close down as many branch lines as possible and to dissuade people from using trains. For example the suburban train services in Auckland operate to a timetable which is a closely guarded secret.

New Zealand has a reasonable rail network but like the Australian equivalent it's no great shakes for speed. Fortunately the much shorter distances make rail travel feasible and the trains are quite comfortable. The main routes are Auckland to Wellington, Wellington to Napier, Picton to Christchurch, Christchurch to Invercargill, and Christchurch to Greymouth. On a map you'll notice quite a number of other branch railways, but don't be deceived – most of them no longer have any passenger trains.

The Travel Pass, described in the section on buses, also provides unlimited use of the country's railway services. The Off Peak Saver fares can also be used on New Zealand trains.

BOAT

Between Wellington and Picton there are at least four inter-island ferry services

daily in each direction, sometimes more at peak seasons. Fares vary with the seasons. The ferries are the *Aratika* and the newer *Arahura*. They handle passengers and vehicles and the crossing takes about three hours. It can get pretty rough so if you're prone to seasickness come prepared. Watch out for dolphins during the crossing.

If you arrive in Picton late at night and haven't got some sort of accommodation arranged, you can be in for an uncomfortable and cold night as they push everybody off the ferry and close the terminal building.

The Wellington Ferry Terminal is about 20 minutes' walk from Wellington Railway Station, or there's a connecting bus service to the ferry. In Picton the terminal is right in town.

DRIVING

Driving yourself around New Zealand is no problem – the roads are generally good and very well signposted. Traffic is light, distances short.

Kiwis drive on the left, as in the UK, Australia, Japan and most of South-East Asia, and there's a 'give way to the right' rule, similar to that in Australia. This is interpreted in a rather strange fashion when you want to turn left and an oncoming vehicle is turning right into the same street. Since the oncoming vehicle is then on your right you have to give way to them. Ask a New Zealander to explain it to you before setting off! This rule is interpreted the same way in some states of Australia, notably Victoria.

To drive in New Zealand you need an international driving permit or an ordinary licence from a major country. Speed limits on the open road are generally 100 kph, while in built up areas the limit is usually 50 kph although in some smaller towns you may see a sign announcing LSZ. This means Limited Speed Zone and the rule is that although there is no stated limit (except for the overall 100 kph limit) if anything happens you better have a good excuse for going as fast as you were!

Car Rental

The major operators – Avis, Budget and Hertz – have extensive fleets of cars in New Zealand and offices in almost every town of any size. Typical costs for unlimited distance rental of a small car (Toyota Corolla, Mitsubishi Mirage) are around NZ$80 per day with a minimum rental of three days. Medium-size cars (Toyota Corona, Ford Telstar) are typically around NZ$100 to NZ$110 per day with unlimited km. In addition there's a daily insurance charge which varies from around NZ$8 to NZ$12 a day, depending on the company. All sorts of special deals are available including long weekends, extended hire periods and special discounts if you use certain credit cards.

Apart from the three major international operators there are also a number of other large operators like Thrifty, Dollar and Southern Cross. Plus there are numerous purely local rental operators, found only in certain cities. Their rates often undercut the major operators but there may be more restrictions on use and one-way rentals may not always be possible. Always compare all the costs – one operator's daily charge may be NZ$5 less than another's but their daily insurance might be NZ$5 more. Be careful when comparing daily rates plus a km distance charge with a straight unlimited km charge.

Sometimes you may find special one-way rentals available when the company ends up with too many cars banked up at one place and too few at another. Operators always want cars to be shifted from Wellington to Auckland and from Christchurch to Picton – most renters travel in the opposite directions. Avis, for example, will give you a NZ$20 discount if you collect and drop in that direction. Usually you must be at least 21 years old in order to rent a car in New Zealand and

sometimes there will be an insurance excess if you're under 25.

Campervan Rental

Renting campervans (also known as mobile homes, motor homes or, in US parlance, RVs) has become an enormously popular way of getting around New Zealand. In some popular but out-of-the-way areas of the South Island almost every other vehicle seems to be a campervan.

There are numerous companies renting campervans and their costs vary with the type of vehicle and the time of year. Unlike rental cars, which are used for business as well as pleasure, campervans are strictly a pleasure business so demand, and hence costs, depend heavily on the tourist seasons.

Campervans are typically Japanese light commercial vehicles modified locally and equipped with beds, a dining area, cooking facilities, a fridge, a sink with a foot operated water system and storage space. Usually the table in the dining area folds down and the seatback cushions rearrange to make a couple of beds at night (one or two more are accommodated in a compartment above the driving cabin). They usually come well-equipped – there'll be towels, bedding, cooking utensils, plates, bowls, knives and forks and so on.

Maui Campas are one of the larger campervan operators and their choice of vehicles and rentals costs are fairly typical. As with the other operators their costs vary with the season. Costs drop to their lowest level in the mid-May to mid-October winter season, climbing in spring (mid-October to mid-December) or the autumn (mid-January to mid-May). The summer plus school holiday plus Christmas period from mid-December to mid-January is the worst time of the year when costs can be two to three times the winter rate.

Starting at the bottom the typical costs for a Maui Hi-Top, going by the seasons, are NZ$60, NZ$80 or NZ$120. This vehicle is a Toyota Hi-ace with a raised roof area. It's really only large enough for two, although you might squeeze a third, small person in. A Maui Mini-Campa is a Mitsubishi L300 which costs NZ$70, NZ$100 or NZ$140. This one is billed as a two plus two but the plus two should be very small children, as you'll be cramped with two larger children and four adults would find it impossible. Both these smaller vehicles are powered by petrol engines.

The Maui Campa, a diesel-powered Mitsubishi FB100, costs NZ$80, NZ$110 or NZ$170. This one is fine for a couple with two children or even for four adults. Finally there's the Maui Travel Deluxe which not only can accommodate six people but also has a shower, a chemical toilet, a water heater and a gas oven. The vehicle is a Mitsubishi FE100 and costs NZ$90, NZ$140 or NZ$200.

Other campervan operators include Newmans, Endeavour, Blue Sky, Adventure Vans, Mt Cook Line and Horizon. There's some variance in vehicle types and costs but each operator has colour brochures which explain all about their campervans and what they have to offer. Although they're good fun and a pleasant way of seeing New Zealand, measured strictly on a cost basis they're not the cheapest way of getting around with a rental vehicle. You could rent a car and spend the night in campsite cabins – even in motels at the high season when campervans are expensive – at comparable or lower costs.

Buying a Car

If you're planning a longer stay and/or if there is a group of you, buying a car and then selling it again at the end of your travels can be one of the cheapest ways of seeing New Zealand. You're not tied to the often inconvenient and expensive bus schedules nor do you find yourself waiting by the roadside with your thumb out looking for a ride.

You can find cars in the Saturday newspaper classified ads just like anywhere else in the world and you'll often see ads at youth hostels from other travellers keen to sell their cars and move on. I even saw two travellers standing in the arrivals lounge at Auckland airport holding a sign saying 'buy our car'! Make sure any car you buy has a WOF or Warrant of Fitness and that the registration lasts for a reasonable period. You have to have the WOF certificate proving that the car is roadworthy in order to register it.

HITCHING

Overall, New Zealand is a great place for hitchhiking and although almost anybody who does a fair amount of hitching will get stuck somewhere uncomfortable for an uncomfortably long period of time most trampers rate it highly. It's safe, the roads are not crowded but there are just enough cars to make things fairly easy and the New Zealanders are well disposed towards hitchhikers.

Generally hitching on the main routes in the North Island is good. In the South Island hitching down the east coast from Picton through Christchurch to Invercargill is mostly good. Elsewhere in the South Island there are hundreds of km of main roads with very little traffic. Expect long waits – even days – in some places. It's a good idea to have the Mt Cook, Newmans and NZRRS timetables with you so you can flag a bus down if you're tired of hitching. Make sure you show the driver the colour of your money. Quite a few drivers have been stopped by hitchhikers who have then decided they can't afford the fare so some busdrivers are wary about stopping unless they know you're prepared to pay.

It's easier hitching alone if you are male but, unfortunately, even though New Zealand is a safe country for hitching, a woman on her own may experience some tricky – if not dangerous – situations. Better to travel with someone else if possible. Many hostels have local hints for hitching (such as what bus to get out of town, where to hitch from) on their noticeboards.

LOCAL TRANSPORT
Bus
There are bus services in most larger cities but with a few honourable exceptions they are mainly weekday operations. On weekends and particularly on Sundays buses can be very difficult to find.

Train
The only city with a good suburban train service is Wellington with regular trains up the main corridors to the north. It's the only electrified railway in New Zealand.

Auckland has the crumbling remains of a suburban passenger service which, despite considerable pressure for it to be rejuvenated and improved, the government is promising to axe.

Taxis
Although there are plenty of taxis in the major towns they rarely 'cruise'. If you want a taxi you usually either have to phone for one or go to a taxi rank.

Bicycles
Bicycles can be rented by the hour or day in most major cities and in some smaller locales.

NORTH ISLAND

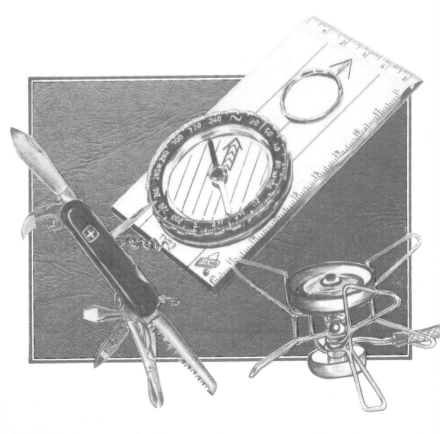

The Far North

Many overseas travellers who arrive in Auckland think they have to head south to go tramping in New Zealand. This is not so. There is Cape Reinga, the rugged point where the Tasman Sea meets the Pacific Ocean, which is the heart of the country's most northern trek, a shoreline walk from Ninety Mile Beach to Spirits Bay. Also there is Great Barrier Island within the Hauraki Gulf, where there is a 100-km network of tracks along with hot springs, native forest and even mountains; and, northeast of the metropolis is the Coromandel Peninsula, site of the Coromandel State Forest Park and its popular tramping area of Kauaeranga Valley. These three areas comprise the far north tramping region of New Zealand.

You'll encounter fascinating artifacts here, left over from the days logging and mining, or even be confronted with some steep climbs that rival those anywhere else in the North Island. About the only thing lacking is huts. There are none along the Ninety Mile Beach - Cape Reinga Walkway and only two each on Great Barrier Island and in the Kauaeranga Valley. A tent is a handy piece of gear to carry along.

Te Paki Coastal Park

The Ninety Mile Beach - Cape Reinga walk described in this section lies entirely in the Te Paki Coastal Park. The 170-square km preserve is an active sheep and cattle station, administered by DOC under the farm-park concept, where both profitable farming and recreational activities take place. The tracks are managed by the New Zealand Walkway Commission and cover a coastal area where there are sand dunes, stretches of hard beach, and rugged hills and farmland to hike through.

HISTORY

Like most regions of New Zealand, the Maoris were already well established in the far north by the time the Europeans arrived and Cape Reinga had long been regarded in Maori legend as the departure point of spirits. In 1642, Dutch explorer Abel Tasman swept by and named Cape Maria van Diemen, a point southwest of Cape Reinga. Then in 1769 on his first visit to New Zealand Captain James Cook sailed through the region, eventually rounding North Cape where he ran into a hurricane.

Ironically the French explorer Jean Francois de Surville was in the area at the same time, looking for a safe harbour in which to weather the same violent storm. Many historians believe the two probably crossed paths somewhere off Cape Reinga though in the poor weather neither one knew of the other's existence.

Europeans were attracted to the far north because it contained a number of valued resources, including whales in Hauraki Gulf, timber on Great Barrier Island and gold on the Coromandel Peninsula. The amazing kauri provided not only timber but also gum, a resin that oozed from the cracks of its bark and hardened on contact with air. The Maoris quickly recognised its value and burnt it as fuel, even carrying it as a torch. They also used it in their art of tattooing. The Europeans, when they arrived, found it ideal in the production of hard varnishes.

Gum - much of it from areas around Ninety Mile Beach and Coromandel - was New Zealand's leading export by 1890, outstripping even gold. Gum diggers would settle in fields long after the trees were gone and search for fossilised gum by digging potholes. By 1920, when only poor-quality gum was being dug, New Zealand still exported 5700 tons.

The area is now under the control of DOC and is administered as a farm-park.

CLIMATE

There is good tramping in the far north but it means packing the suntan lotion. One of the nicest features of the region is the long spells of dry weather during summer with temperatures that are warm enough at times to be considered almost tropical.

NATURAL HISTORY

To naturalists the area is known as the home of a very rare land snail. The species, *Placostylus ambagiosus*, is found only in the pockets of broadleaf forests still remaining in the North Cape region. There are also impressive stands of native bush such as giant kauri and pohutukawa trees. The wildlife most trampers encounter, however, are coastal birds such as oystercatchers, terns, gulls and the occasional white-face herons.

NINETY MILE BEACH –
CAPE REINGA WALKWAY

Once described as a 'desert coast', Ninety Mile Beach is almost concrete hard below the high-tide line and bordered much of the way by sand dunes six km wide and rising in some places to 143 metres. The walkway officially follows the beach south 83 km to Ahipara and trampers will find the 32-km portion from Hukatere to Bluff (a famous spot for surf fishing) ruler straight. Walking the entire beach requires at least three days, or you can enter it at Waipapakauri, 69 km south of Te Paki Stream; at Huatere, 51 km from the stream; or at Bluff, 19 km from the stream. The walk described here is a three-day walk from Te Paki Stream at the north end of the Ninety Mile Beach to Kapowairua at the east end of Spirits Bay.

Access

You can enter the walkway at a number of points by vehicle or you can walk the entire 83 km from the town of Ahipara at the southern end of the walkway, which would make it a seven to 10-day journey to Spirits Bay. Keep in mind, however, that cars and tour buses will be encountered daily on Ninety Mile Beach until you pass Te Paki Stream.

The main departure point for the tramp is Kaitaia – a town with a population of 5000 near the northern end of SH1 – but it also can be arranged from Paihia on the Bay of Islands or Kerikeri just to the north. All three have youth hostels and are serviced daily by NZRRS buses from Auckland. There is no regular bus transport beyond Kaitaia, but there are a number of companies which run tours up to Cape Reinga and trampers can usually arrange to be dropped off and picked up by them.

Most of these tours begin in Paihia, include stops at Kerikeri and Kaitaia, then swing onto Ninety Mile Beach, leaving it at Te Paki Stream for Cape Reinga. Once at the cape they turn around and head south through the middle of the long peninsula. Ask first, but what most companies will do for the price of a tour is to drop you off somewhere along Ninety Mile Beach (Te Paki Stream is the most common spot) and then pick you up three or four days later at Waitiki Landing, site of a tearoom, store and gasoline station. The only hassle is getting from Kapowairua, near the campground at the east end of Spirits Bay, to the Waitiki Landing, a road trip of about 16 km. Without a vehicle, hitching or walking is about the only way.

Offering Cape Reinga trips out of Paihia is King's Alternative Tours (tel (0885) 28-171) which departs at 8 am and costs $44. Both Fullers Tours (tel (0885) 27-421) and Mt Cook Line (tel (0885) 27-811) charge comparable prices and run their tours out of Paihia but have ticket offices and make pick-ups in Kaitaia as well. Mt Cook departs Paihia daily at 7.44 am, Kerikeri at 8.20 am and Kaitaia at 9.45 am. Fullers leaves Paihia at 7.30 am, Kerikeri at 8 am and Kaitaia at 9 am where the fare for the round trip is only $35. Also out of Kaitaia is Far North Magic Tours (tel Kaitaia 1028) on 27 South Rd which departs the town at 8.45 am and costs $32.

Equipment

This trip requires a tent and good sun protection, including sun block lotion, a wide-brim hat, a long-sleeve shirt and trousers of light material (not wool). You should also have a litre waterbottle per person and be aware of where water is going to be available.

Information & Maps

Most of the walk from Te Paki Stream to just west of Spirits Bay is covered by the quad M02 of the Infomap 260 Series, although to cover the entire route you would also need to purchase N02.

For additional information, either contact the DOC regional office (tel (09) 379-279) in Auckland on the corner of Liverpool St and Kauaeranga Rd or the Kaikohe district office (tel (0887) 80-109) on Marino Place in the Harrison Building in Kaikohe.

The Track

The trip can be walked in either direction but for those who are depending on the tour buses for transportation it is easier to begin at Ninety Mile Beach and then return to the bus at Waitiki Landing. The trip described is a 50-km tramp from Te Paki Stream at the north end of Ninety Mile Beach to the east side of Spirits Bay, an 18-hour walk that most people cover in three days, camping at Te Werahi Beach and the campgrounds at Tapotupotu Bay and Spirits Bay. For those with time, the trip can be extended by hiking a portion of Ninety Mile Beach, which is really only 103 km long. The tramp is rated easy.

Stage 1: Te Paki Stream to Te Werahi Beach

Walking Time: 4½ hours via Herangi Hill; five hours via Cape Maria van Diemen

Accommodation: There are no huts or developed campgrounds

Te Paki Stream marks the southern border of the coastal park of the same name but is more famous for being a 'quicksand stream'. Tour buses depart from Ninety Mile Beach at this point but trampers continue north along the Tasman Sea coast. Within an hour you cross Waitapu Stream and the marked track moves inland to ascend Scott's Point. The trail over the point is an old vehicle track that is well marked but should still be carefully followed. It takes about 1½ hours to cross the point and descend onto Twilight Beach.

Again trampers will find themselves hiking along the Tasman Sea but this time on a sandy shoreline that is usually empty of tourists. Plan on an hour to reach the north end of the beach (if the sun and sand don't delay you for an afternoon) where there is a small stream and a signposted route to the Cape Reinga road that would take 1½ hours to walk. The walkway continues towards Cape Maria van Diemen, site of a lighthouse that was built after the one on nearby Motuopao Island was closed down in 1941. After moving inland, the track comes to a signposted junction where a high level trail climbs 156 metres over Herangi Hill and then descends to Te Werahi Stream at the south end of the beach of the same name. The other track follows the cape to the lighthouse, past excellent views of the coastline, before swinging east and joining the main tramp. At the south end of Te Werahi Beach where the walkway descends from a ridge to Te Werahi Stream there is another signposted route back to the road (1 hour). It's an hour's walk along the main track over Herangi Hill and a 1½ to two hour tramp via Cape Maria van Diemen.

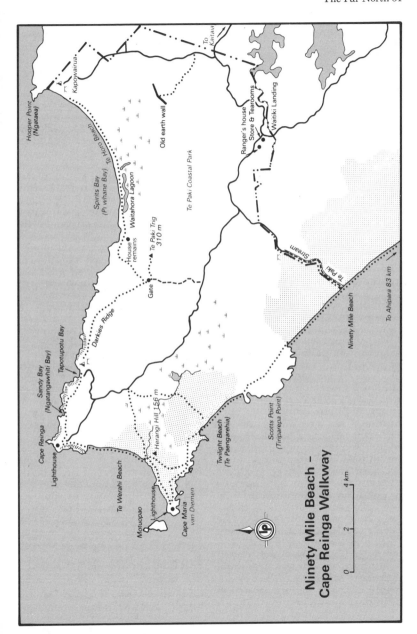

Ninety Mile Beach –
Cape Reinga Walkway

Stage 2: Te Werahi Beach to Tapotupotu Bay

Walking Time: 3½ to four hours

Accommodations: DOC campground

It takes 45 minutes to an hour to walk along the sweeping beach from Te Werahi Stream to the north end where the track begins to climb sharply. The ascent ends above Tarawamaomao Point where the track continues along cliff tops and you are rewarded on clear days with spectacular views of sandy beaches, Cape Maria van Diemen and Motuopao Island. Within an hour of the ascent from Te Werahi beach the walkway emerges at Cape Reinga a short way from the lighthouse.

The cape with its lighthouse is a scenic spot, a picture that often appears on travel brochures, and a good place to witness that often violent meeting between the Pacific Ocean and the Tasman Sea. In the Maori language, Reinga means the 'place of leaping' and according to legend it was from here that deceased spirits departed for their Polynesia homeland.

The walkway resumes in the car park near the radio masts where it follows a ridge of scrub before descending steeply to Sandy Bay, a very pleasant spot with a nice beach, freshwater stream and grassy flats beneath pohutukawa trees. On the other side of the small bay, the track begins an equally steep climb up a coastal ridge, turns inland for a spell, then returns to the cliff tops from which it descends sharply towards Tapotupotu Bay, a two-hour walk from Cape Reinga.

From the ridges above, Tapotupotu – a horseshoe bay of white sand and light green seas enclosed by forested cliffs – looks like a movie set for *Mutiny on the Bounty*. It's one of the most scenic beaches in the far north. There is a freshwater stream here, and a DOC campground, which, thanks to the gravel road which enables access from the Cape Reinga Rd, offers showers, toilets and fireplaces.

Stage 3: Tapotupotu Bay to Kapowairua (Spirits Bay)

Walking Time: eight to nine hours

Accommodation: DOC campground

To reach Spirits Bay, begin by crossing the stream in Tapotupotu Bay (easiest near the beach at low tide) and follow the track as it ascends sharply along the coastal ridge for the first hour. Eventually the walkway will head inland along Darkies Ridge and join the Pandora Track to reach a gate at the end of a partially metalled road. At the gate there is a sidetrack that continues up to Te Paki Trig, 310 metres above sea level, where you will encounter the remains of a wartime radar station and enjoy a spectacular panorama of the coastline.

From the gate a rough vehicle track heads south to the main road. Heading north of the gate is Pandora Track, which soon swings to the northeast and leads down to Pandora Beach where there are some remains of a house and gardens. If you hit the beach at low tide, you can reach Spirits Bay by the seaward route around the rocks to its western end. Otherwise follow the route above the rocks.

Once on the bay either follow Te Horo Beach or trek through the sand dunes to the eastern end to Kapowairua, where you will find the Spirits Bay campground near a small lagoon. This is a DOC facility with fresh water, toilets and showers. Waitahora Lagoon, much larger in size, will also be passed on the way and makes for a nice swimming hole. Plan on 3½ hours to walk from Tapotupotu Bay to the Te Paki Trig and five hours from the Trig to the next campground where Spirits Bay Rd leads south towards Waitiki Landing.

Great Barrier Island State Forest Recreation Area

Great Barrier Island, situated 88 km north of Auckland, features many long, white, sandy beaches on the east side and sheltered inlets with deep water on the west side.

In the middle, however, is a rugged area of steep ridges rising to Mt Hobson. At 621 metres, this is the highest point on the island.

Under the management of DOC as a state forest recreation area, the 80 square km preserve of rugged bush includes a network of tracks that are combined with a few old logging roads and tramways (where the rails have long since rotted out) to provide numerous tramping opportunities. Along with natural hot springs and towering kauri trees, one of the most interesting features of the recreation area is the remaining kauri dams from the logging era and the laid-back, 'get away from it all' feeling the island provokes.

HISTORY

Captain Cook sighted and named Great Barrier Island (it seemed to bar the entrance to the Hauraki Gulf) in 1769. Like the rest of the Far North region it was the rich resources that later led Europeans to settle on Great Barrier. The first settlement was a whaling station in Whangaparapara Harbour but it was the kauri tree and its natural by-product, gum, that was the most sought after and longest lasting resource.

As early as 1794 the British Navy began extracting the exceptionally tall and straight trees from the shores of Great Barrier to be used as ship spars. By the 1880s kauri logging was in full swing. In 1888, the Kauri Timber Company took over operations on the island and began intensive exploitation that eventually removed all trees except for those in approximately half a square km around the summit of Mt Hobson. To process the wood the company built a huge sawmill on the island in 1910, the largest in the Southern Hemisphere at the time, at the 'free port' of Whangaparapara. The tax-free arrangement was a profitable one and timber not only from Great Barrier but

also from Coromandel and the Bay of Islands was milled there and then shipped directly to Australia and Europe. The New Zealand government eventually did away with Whangaparapara's special status in 1920 and the mill closed shortly after.

The key to retrieving the timber from the rugged areas of Great Barrier was the kauri dams. These massive wooden structures were built across the upper portions of streams to trap water. For three months trees were cut and positioned in the creek bed either above or below the dam catchment. When the water was high enough a loose-plank gate in the middle of the dam was tripped and the sudden flood swept the timber through the steep and difficult terrain to navigable rivers below. Several dams were built on the island, including one on the Kaiarara Stream where enough of it remains today to envisage how it worked.

By the 1930s logging had devastated the land. Timber drives with kauri dams had been especially destructive, quickly eroding valleys and stream beds and leaving a broad silt flat at river mouths. In 1955 the New Zealand Forest Service began a programme to rehabilitate the forest and in 1973 it was declared a state forest recreation reserve.

CLIMATE

Summers on Great Barrier Island are hot and dry, sometimes as much as 3° or 4° C warmer than in Auckland, and it's not unusual for the temperature to top 28° or 30° C. The average rainfall at Port Fitzroy in the northern half of the island is 1852 mm while the southern end is even drier. Tramping takes place year round but the wet winters can quickly turn the tracks into a sea of mud.

NATURAL HISTORY

Great Barrier Island is made up predominately of volcanic rock and the heart of the island is a regenerating kauri forest of 80 square km.

GREAT BARRIER ISLAND TREK

There are three communities on Great Barrier that serve as the main arrival and departure points for the island. Claris is on the east side close to the long, white beaches that are popular for swimming, surfing and sailing while Tryphena, site of a youth hostel, is located in the southwest corner of the island. For trampers, however, Port Fitzroy is usually the best arrival point. Not only is it the most scenic harbour, with a rugged coastline and fiord-like bays, but even if you arrive late in the afternoon you can still hike to the first hut, passing the forest headquarters along the way. At Port Fitzroy there are lodges, a store that sells limited supplies, and an information hut where transportation can be arranged

Peak season for tramping is mid-December to mid-January, yet because of the cost of getting to Great Barrier the island's tracks and huts, though busy, will not be overrun like those in Coromandel State Forest Park or Tongariro National Park. Visitors begin thinning out after January and many believe the best time of the year to explore this island is March to May as the temperatures are still warm but the rainy season has yet to set in.

Access

There are are a number of ways, both by air and sea, to reach the island from Auckland. The quickest is to fly. It is usually a 20 or 30-minute flight that gives a great perspective of the island's rugged terrain. Sea Bee Air (tel (09) 774-405) runs an amphibious aeroplane that takes off on Mechanics Bay in Auckland and lands at Tryphena. If there is sufficient demand it will also land at Port Fitzroy and Whangaparapara. During the summer the company has four or five flights daily and an adult round-trip fare is $143. Great Barrier Airlines (tel (09) 275-9120) flies out of the domestic terminal of the Auckland Airport with three flights daily and additional ones during peak season to the airstrip at Claris. The daily 8.30 am

and 3 pm flights also land at Okiwi, another airstrip on the island, from where the airline company provides a free shuttle bus to Port Fitzroy.

To arrive at Great Barrier by water check the MV *Tasman* (tel (09) 734-036) which departs Tuesday and Friday at 10 am on a six-hour trip from Auckland's Kings Wharf to Tryphena. It returns on Wednesday and Sunday and the one-way adult fare is $55. Although the ship does not sell tickets to Port Fitzroy for passengers, it often is hauling cargo to the community and the practice has been to give trampers a lift to the island. In 1988, Fullers Captain Cook Cruises (tel (09) 399-901) began catamaran services from the downtown Auckland harbour to Tryphena on Wednesday, Friday and Sunday in December and January. The speedy boat is called *Supercat* and needs only 2½ hours to reach the island. The one-way adult fare is $59 and a connecting bus at Tryphena will take you to Port Fitzroy for $5. After 31 January the service runs only Friday and Sunday.

For transportation out of Tryphena contact Safari Tours (tel 22H) and out of Claris phone Claris Motors (tel 17S) concerning taxi service or rental cars.

The other possibility is to combine a tramp with a trip on the historical schooner, *Te Aroha*, which offers overnight trips in the Hauraki Gulf, leaving you at Port Fitzroy. Passage per person is $79 and bookings are best made at the NZ Adventure Centre (tel (09) 399-192) with Victoria Park Market.

Places to Stay

There are lodges in all three communities as well as the *Tryphena Youth Hostel* (tel Tryphena 20). Port Fitzroy also has a public campground near the DOC district office. For a complete list stop at the New Zealand Tourist and Publicity office on Queen St in Auckland or write to: The Secretary, Great Barrier Island Tourist Association, Port Fitzroy.

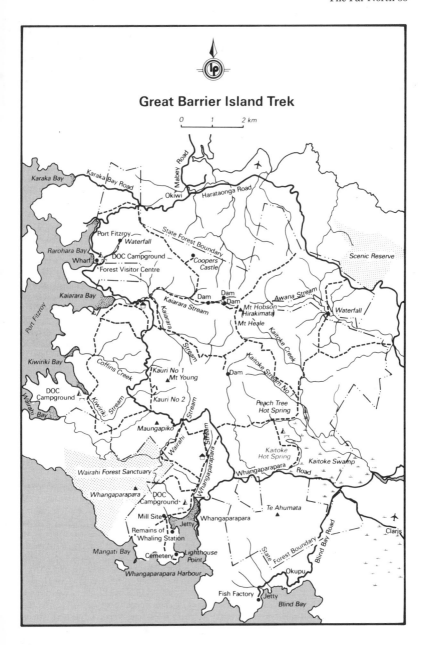

Great Barrier Island Trek

0   1   2 km

Karaka Bay

Karaka Bay Road

Mabey Road

Okiwi

Harataonga Road

Port Fitzroy

Waterfall

Rarohara Bay

Wharf

DOC Campground

Forest Visitor Centre

State Forest Boundary

Coopers Castle

Scenic Reserve

Kaiarara Bay

Dam

Dam

Dam

Kaiarara Stream

Awana Stream

Mt Hobson (Hirakimata)

Waterfall

Port Fitzroy

Mt Heale

Kaitoke Creek

Kiwiriki Bay

Coffins Creek

Kauri No 1

Mt Young

Kaiarara Stream

Dam

DOC Campground

Wairahi Bay

Kiwiriki Stream

Kauri No 2

Kaitoke Stream No 7

Peach Tree Hot Spring

Maungapiko

Wairahi Stream

Whangaparapara Stream

Kaitoke Hot Spring

Kaitoke Swamp

Wairahi Forest Sanctuary

Whangaparapara Road

Whangaparapara

DOC Campground

Te Ahumata

Mill Site

Jetty

Remains of Whaling Station

Claris

Mangati Bay

Cemetery

Lighthouse Point

State Forest Boundary

Blind Bay Road

Whangaparapara Harbour

Okupu

Fish Factory

Jetty

Blind Bay

Equipment

Don't forget sun protection but bring a bathing suit as well – and, of course, wet weather gear. Most important for an enjoyable trek is not to arrive with poor footwear or attempt to cover too much in one day. This island is rugged and some of the climbs along interior ridges are knee benders.

Information & Maps

There is a $5 hut or campsite fee which is payable at the DOC district office (tel Port Fitzroy 4K) just outside Port Fitzroy on the road to the hut. Information and maps can be obtained from the office. The quad SO8 of Infomap 260 series covers most of the tracks but the Great Barrier and Little Barrier Islands recreation map, NZMS 239, (also 1 cm: 500 metres) is just as good and cheaper.

The Track

The described trek is a four-day loop from Port Fitzroy, including travel to and from the island and two nights in DOC huts. The trip can easily be adjusted to start from Tryphena or Claris, although some transportation or hitching would be involved; with a tent it can be extended considerably. Camping is allowed around both huts, throughout the state forest and at a number of official campgrounds including the popular ones located right on Medlands and Whangapoua beaches on the east side.

Stage 1: Port Fitzroy to Kaiarara Hut

Walking Time: 1½ hours
Accommodation: Campground at DOC office; Kaiarara Hut (24 bunks)
Follow the Fitzroy-Harataonga Rd past the wharf and in the signposted direction of the 'Mt Hobson Track'. For the next 1.2 km the road climbs a high coastline bluff with views of Rarohara Bay and the sailboats that often fill the natural harbour. The DOC district office and campground, a pleasant grassy area with

water and toilets, is 20 minutes from the wharf.

Past the DOC office, the road resumes climbing, crosses the head between Rarohara Bay and Kaiarara Bay and then swings southeast and follows the coastal ridge above Kaiarara Bay. A locked gate across the road is the official border of the state forest area and prevents all but DOC vehicles from travelling further. The road drops quickly, passes Blairs Landing, a popular spot for boaters, and finally reaches Kaiarara Stream, a good hour's walk from the campground. After fording the stream (easy in normal conditions) you arrive at an information sign and map of the state forest recreational area. To the west the road fords the stream two more times, passing good swimming pools along the way, and then arrives at the hut.

Even if you are not contemplating the entire circuit over Mt Hobson, you should still consider a side trip up to the first Kauri Dam on the north fork of the Kaiarara Stream. It's a 1½ to two-hour walk (steadily uphill) to the massive structure but well worth it as the dam is one of biggest and best preserved in the country.

Stage 2: Kaiarara Hut to Whangaparapara Hut via Kiwiriki Track

Walking Time: five to six hours
Accommodation: DOC campground at Kiwiriki Bay; Whangaparapara Hut (24 bunks)
Return to the information sign and map. Follow the Kiwiriki Track where the first one km is a level walk then a slight climb to the spur track to Bush's Beach. The recreation area is a pleasant spot on Kaiarara Bay with barbecues, a little bit of sandy beach and grassy areas for camping. The main track departs from the spur track and quickly reaches a second junction. Line W Track heads east (left) to the Forest Service Rd across the Kaiarara Plateau (half an hour's walk)

while the main track (right) makes a steady descent to Coffin's Creek.

The creek is reached in one to 1½ hours from the hut and marks the point where trampers will begin to do some serious climbing on their way to Whangaparapara. The track begins a steep ascent, climbing 160 metres in a km before topping out on the crest of the ridge that separates Coffin's Creek from Kiwiriki Bay. The climb is steady but the views are good. Once on top the track reverses and sharply descends to the bay. Near the bottom is a spur track to the water. The track heads south (left) and quickly arrives at a DOC campground.

The campground, an hour's walk from Coffin's Creek, is a grassy area on the edge of the forest with a toilet and a table. It's not really near the bay, however, and is a haven for insects at times. The track follows the nearby creek for a while and then begins another steep climb, rising 100 metres in less than a km. Once near the top of the ridge, the views back on Kiwiriki Bay are excellent. The track follows the crest, working up and over two knobs and then ascending slightly at the end to emerge at the Forest Service Rd, 1½ hours from the campground.

The track is signposted from the road as is the short spur track which climbs steeply to Maungapiko Lookout, a 200-metre knob which offers good views to the south. Follow the road, which is badly eroded in places, as it descends two km to Wairahi Stream. A couple of hundred metres before the creek the Pack Track is signposted and does not begin after the stream as shown on many maps. The track provides a short cut to the Whangaparapara Hut as it drops steeply to Wairahi Stream and then climbs up and over another ridge to emerge at the tramline track. The hut is just down the old tramline or a 45-minute walk along the Pack Track from the Forest Service Rd.

Stage 2A: Whangaparapara Harbour

From the hut the track continues towards the bay, crossing bridges over a stream several times and passing the junction to the Mt Whangaparapara track (a 2½ hour round trip) just before arriving at a cow pasture. Step over the fence and cross the swingbridge to head to the village of Whangaparapara and you'll quickly spot the DOC ranger office to the left up on a small hill. Not only can information and brochures be obtained here, but the staff will also radio a taxi for those who want a lift to Claris or Tryphena. The road continues towards the harbour, passing Great Barrier Lodge where there is a small store.

If you continue past the swingbridge back in the cow pasture, a track is quickly picked up that leads to the west side of the harbour. It's about a km to the DOC campground (cooking shelter, toilets) and then another 15 to 20-minute walk over two ridges to reach the site of the Kauri Timber Company sawmill, the largest one in the Southern Hemisphere in 1910. Today all that remains is the concrete foundation and some pilings.

From the mill site the track continues, climbs two ridges (the first being quite steep) and descends into Mangati Bay, a 1½-hour walk from the swingbridge. For those who want to avoid staying at the sometimes crowded hut or the campground on the harbour, Mangati Bay is a scenic and pleasant alternative. Guarding the entrance of the secluded bay is rugged Whangara Island, giving the spot calm water ideal for swimming, snorkelling and shore fishing. You can camp on the beach but fires are not allowed.

Stage 3: Whangaparapara Hut to Kaiarara Hut via Mt Hobson

Walking Time: seven to nine hours
Accommodation: Kaiarara Hut (24 bunks)
This trek passes two hot springs before ascending Mt Hobson. Trampers should think twice, however, about soaking in the springs then climbing the island's highest point. The springs are best enjoyed as a

side trip from Whangaparapara Hut without having to endure a long tramp with a backpack afterwards.

From the hut follow the tramline track as it climbs steeply for about a km to the Forest Service Rd. Head north (left) on the road for a short way to the signposted track, which was also part of the logger's tramway to the sawmill. The wide track drops steeply through the rugged terrain to an unnamed stream, ascends on the other side and then descends again to Kaitoke Stream No 2. It follows the creek, gradually dropping towards the east side of the island until it arrives at a major junction where occasionally someone sets up camp.

The spot is signposted and points the way south to Kaitoke Hot Springs. The track immediately crosses Kaitoke Creek No 2 and then steadily marches uphill for a km to an open spot with an excellent view of Kaitoke Swamp, the surrounding ridges and even the crashing surf of Kaitoke Beach on the east side of the island. Here the track swings west and drops sharply to the thermal stream below. The first damned-up pool is rather muddy and uninviting but hike up the stream and you will encounter others, half hidden in a canopy of trees and much more delightful. From the springs, a track continues south to Whangaparapara Rd (45 mins).

Back at the junction, trampers heading for Mt Hobson continue east along the track as it follows Kaitoke Creek No 2, swings north around a corner of extensive swamp and in 45 minutes reaches Peach Tree Hot Springs. This area was an old Kauri Timber Company campsite and the thermal pool was dug out by loggers. It is smaller and hotter, but many think it a more pleasant setting than Kaitoke Hot Springs.

The track departs the hot spring area and crosses Kaitoke Stream No 1 to a signposted junction. The track to the right leads to the Fitzroy Harataonga Rd (1½ hours). Trampers with their eye on Mt

Hobson follow the track to the left as it begins a steep climb of 200 metres, levels out as it crosses a branch of upper Kaitoke Creek and then climbs again for another 240 metres before sidling around Mt Heal. Halfway up the second ascent, 1½ hours from Peach Tree Hot Springs, you pass a junction with an old bridle track that heads west along Central Ridge to the Forest Service Rd a km south of Kaiarara Hut. It's a two to three hour walk to the hut.

The final leg from the side to Mt Heal to Mt Hobson (known to the Maoris as Hirakimata) is a steep ascent of 180 metres until you reach a junction near its peak of 621 metres. The walk from Peach Tree Hot Springs to the summit is 2½ to 3½ hours but from the top you're rewarded with excellent views of both sides of Great Barrier as well as the outer islands in the Hauraki Gulf.

From the top of the island, it's a quick descent, often with the aid of black cables embedded in the rock, as the track drops to the north branch of the Kaiarara Stream. In 30 to 40 minutes you pass the spur track to the upper two dams. The upper of the two has almost totally deteriorated while the lower is in poor shape. But in another 30 to 40 minutes the track drops to the spur track to the lower dam and this one is impressive.

After following the black cables down the solid rock sidetrack you reach a massive wooden structure whose huge kauri logs still hold it in place across the gorge. The dams were built in 1926 and loggers then proceeded to cut trees and skid them below the lower dam. When sufficient water was stored, the upper dams were tripped, sending a blast of river and logs rushing towards the lower one which at the right moment was tripped as well. The result was a force of water that sent the timber all the way to Kaiarara Bay where it was gathered into huge booms and floated to sawmills in Auckland. The most unbelievable aspect of the dams is that after all the work to build them, they were used for only three years.

From the spur, more black cables are encountered, as the descent towards the hut is steep. The track levels out at a stream where a signpost declares that the hut is only '30 minutes' away (very debatable) and then climbs up and over a 200-metre knob. The stream is crossed again and another ridge is climbed over before the track becomes a very pleasant stroll, gradually dropping through the valley and crossing the north branch of Kaiarara Stream four times before emerging at an old bridle track. The hut is a short walk away at this point.

Those tramping from Mt Hobson to Kaiarara hut should plan on two to 2½ hours depending on how much time is spent at the dams. Heading in the other direction, it's an uphill climb and closer to a three to four-hour hike to reach the island's high point.

Coromandel State Forest Park

Coromandel State Forest Park, situated northeast of Thames, is a number of blocks along the peninsula that total 740 square km of rugged, forested hills. The highest point in the park is Mt Moehau, 891 metres, which is located near the northern tip of the peninsula, while Table Mountain at 836 metres is the high point within Kauaeranga Valley.

HISTORY

The Maoris were already well-established in the far north when in 1769 Captain Cook sailed into a rugged little inlet on the eastern shore of the Coromandel Peninsula. He raised the British flag over New Zealand for the first time and, after the planet appeared that night, labelled the spot Mercury Bay.

Like elsewhere in the far north it was

the rich resources of the Coromandel Peninsula that led Europeans to settle there. With the discovery of gold, bustling mining towns sprang up on the peninsula – most notably the town of Thames, which boomed during the 1866 gold rush. But the most lasting resource of the region was the kauri tree and its natural by-product, gum.

Legend has it that the Royal Navy at the Battle of Trafalgar had masts of Coromandel kauri, giving the fleet an advantage over its Spanish and French opponents. The peninsula was named by the captain of the English ship, the HMS *Coromandel*, which sailed into the area in 1820 collecting kauri for spars.

Full-scale kauri logging began in the mid-1800s and by the 1880s there were lumbermen within the Kauaeranga Valley. It was the gold rush at Thames that gave impetus to the logging efforts in the Kauaeranga Valley as there was a sudden need for building materials in the boom towns. The first trees cut were near the sea or from country where bullock teams could easily haul the logs out. But, as on Great Barrier Island, the key to retrieving the timber from the rugged areas of the valley was the kauri dam. The system was used even though a number of logs would be destroyed along the steep, narrow watercourses. It is estimated that of the 92 million feet of kauri cut in the Kauaeranga Valley, only 77 million feet reached the booms in the Thames River. Still, more than 50 dams were built throughout the valley, including 16 above the gorge on the Kauaeranga River. On a small stream near the Coromandel park headquarters there is a working replica, one-third the size of the original Tarawaere dam, and demonstrations are given on a regular basis to show what a water drive was like.

As around Ninety Mile Beach, it was not only the timber but also the gum of the kauri that was exploited, and by the 1930s much of the peninsula had been devastated by the combined effects of logging and digging for fossilised gum. As on Great Barrier Island, valleys and stream beds were badly eroded by kauri-dam timber drives.

To rehabilitate the landscape the Coromandel Peninsula was declared a state forest in 1938 and a program to re-establish the native bush began. In 1971 the status of the Coromandel area was upgraded to that of a state forest park.

CLIMATE

Although not as warm as Great Barrier Island or Cape Reinga, the climate of the state forest park is still mild and is similar to Auckland's with long dry periods in the summer and an average temperature of around 23°C. Winters are moist, but frosts are rare. The area averages 1255 mm of rain per year in the valleys and 2500 mm in the ranges.

NATURAL HISTORY

Before it was logged, the peninsula had a variety of rich forest flora unmatched by any other area of comparable size in the country. Now much of the park is regenerating native bush, including kauri and rata, the latter of which is noted for its brilliant orange-red flowers. The Kauaeranga Valley and surrounding ridges are covered with podocarps and hardwoods, a few scattered pockets of kauri and areas of bracken, fern and scrub. The predominant species is rimu and tawa while there are also miro, matai and kahikatea. The wildlife consists of the usual native birds of New Zealand (tuis, bellbirds, wood pigeons and fantails) and the introduced mammals (pigs, possums, goats, cats and ferrets).

The state forest park is known as a haven for rock collectors, rather than for its flora or fauna. In or near most streams are various kinds of jaspers, petrified wood, rhodonite and agate, which makes the place an excellent source for rare rocks and gemstones. Interested rock collectors need to pick up a permit from the park headquarters in the Kauaeranga Valley

and can only use a geological hammer to assist in removing surface material.

COROMANDEL STATE FOREST PARK WALK

As the state forest park is only a two-hour drive from Auckland, it can be busy in early summer and on weekends when school and scout groups frequent the area. If at all possible, go somewhere else during the Christmas holidays – which run from late December to mid-January – or plan your walk for the middle of the week to avoid crowded huts.

A logging boom took place in the Coromandel Range during the late nineteenth century when the stands of massive kauri were extracted. Today, like Great Barrier Island, dams, pack horse trails and tramway clearings are silent and deteriorating reminders of yesterday's feast.

Access

The departure point for trips into the Kauaeranga Valley is Thames, the first town most people pass through when touring the Coromandel Peninsula. There is a DOC district office (tel (0843) 89-732) located at 404 Queen St and any supplies you need can be purchased along Pollen St, one of the longest main streets in New Zealand. NZRRS buses travel between Thames and Auckland several times a day but there is no other public transport along Kauaeranga Valley Rd, only expensive taxis. The road begins at the southern edge of town and it's 14 km to the park headquarters and another 10 km to its end where the track begins. Hitching is usually good, however, as there is a steady flow of traffic from both day users and park employees who make it a practice to give trampers a lift to the tracks.

Information & Maps

The park headquarters and information centre (Tel. (0843) 86-381) is open daily from 7.30 am to 4 pm during the summer and on weekdays the rest of the year. Inside there are two rooms of exhibits and displays on park history from Maori settlement to the days of logging, mining and gum digging, as well as exhibits on the fauna of the area and rock collecting on the peninsula. The centre also sells maps and brochures and is the place to leave your intentions and pay the hut fees of $4 a night.

The park sells *Recreation in the Kauaeranga Valley*, a four-colour map that contains very little detail for trampers. The alternatives are quad T11 of the Infomap 260 series and the

Coromandel State Forest Park recreation map, NZMS 274/1.

The Track
The described three-day tramp is a popular walk in the Kauaeranga Valley with nights spent at two huts. It is rated easy to medium because, though the track is well cut, marked and posted with directional signs, it does involve a certain amount of climbing as does just about every walk in New Zealand. It includes passing over Mt Rowe (794 metres) where good views of the valley are enjoyed, but returns to the park road before Table

Mountain. Those tempted to hike up to the highest point in the valley should keep in mind that the route across Table Mountain is quite swampy with almost no view from the top as it is overgrown.

The track begins at the end of Kauaeranga Valley Rd and can be walked in either direction. The trek is described here by ascending Mt Rowe the first day and spending the night at Moss Creek Hut. A slightly easier climb, however, is to hike to Pinnacles Hut for the first night.

Stage 1: Road End to Moss Creek Hut

Walking Time: 4½ to five hours via Mt Rowe

Accommodation: Moss Creek Hut (24 bunks)

The tramp begins at the end of Kauaeranga Valley Rd, about 10 km past the park headquarters, where there is a large stone cairn directional sign. Follow the track towards Table Mountain and Moss Creek and it immediately crosses the Kauaeranga River by way of a wirewalk. It then follows a boardwalk for 15 to 20 minutes along the river and through an impressive forest of rata, tree ferns and nikau palms. Just before crossing Webb Creek, the track passes the signposted junction to Billy Goat Track and Hydro Camp, which is one way of reaching Pinnacles Hut.

Trampers heading to Mt Rowe cross Webb Creek and continue up the Kauaeranga Valley until the track crosses the river a second time, a 1½-hour walk from the road end. The track continues along the river's true right side for a short time and then arrives at the junction to Mt Rowe by way of Table Mountain Plateau. The track begins an immediate ascent to the plateau and steeply climbs 500 metres before reaching it. Plan on two to 2½ hours to reach the top where there is a junction with one track heading west (left) to Table Mountain. The other track heads northeast (right) along a ridge and descends slightly to a saddle before climbing to the summit of Mt Rowe, which at 794 metres offers scenic views of

the valley. The track descends from the summit and heads for the short spur track to Moss Creek Hut, reached in an hour from the junction on Table Mountain. Nearby there are the deteriorating remains of two kauri dams, including Moss Creek Dam, 50 metres before the hut.

A shorter and easier climb is to bypass the track to Table Mountain Plateau and continue along the true right side of the Kauaeranga River. Quickly the track will swing northeast and ascend directly towards the hut. From the road's end this route is a three to four-hour walk to the hut as compared to a 4½ to five hour trek over Mt Rowe.

Stage 2: Moss Creek Hut to Pinnacles Hut

Walking Time: 3½ to four hours

Accommodation: Pinnacles Hut (20 bunks)

The track continues to head east through bush and an occasional scrubby clearing, passing a kauri log dam, or what remains of it. Within 1½ to two hours it arrives at a junction with a pack-horse track to Rangihau Rd and eventually to Coroglen. The southern fork leads off towards the Pinnacles, running alongside a power transmission line at times and eventually arriving at the Kauaeranga River which it crosses.

When the river is low it's possible to hike down to the Kauaeranga Gorge by departing from the track and first passing the Main Dam, 10 to 15 minutes downstream. This was the largest dam ever constructed in the valley, built in 1921, but all that remains today is the floor and a few supporting beams. There are good swimming pools near the dam while the more adventurous can continue along the river to enter the gorge. Travel in the gorge should never be attempted when the river is swollen and even during normal water levels will involve walking through waist-deep pools.

The track continues south by dropping slightly through scrub until it reaches a signposted junction 45 minutes from the river crossing. The fork to the west (right) along with the transmission lines heads to the Webb Creek-Billy Goat Loop and a return to the road end. The other leads east (left) towards the Pinnacles but in 10 minutes comes to the short spur track to Pinnacles Hut. The hut is in a scenic location as its verandah overlooks the headwater gullies of Kauaeranga River. In a stream directly below is one of the better preserved kauri dams, the Dancing Camp Dam, which was built in 1924 and was the second largest one in the valley.

From the junction to the hut, the site of a gum-diggers' camp, built at the turn of the century and known as Dancing Camp, the main track swings to the south and in 20 minutes reaches the Pinnacle Peaks (759 metres). The route to the Pinnacles can be steep in places but the track is cut and well signposted and the views at the end are among the best in the valley.

Stage 3: Pinnacles Hut to Kauaeranga Valley Rd

Walking Time: three hours via Webb Creek; four hours via Billy Goat Track

The pack-horse track continues west from Pinnacles Hut, passing close to the Tauranikau Dam (just main structural timber remains) towards Webb Creek. There are good views along this stretch of the Pinnacles of steep-faced ridges and deep chasms as most of the vegetation is low scrub due to bushmen's fires in the 1920s. Eventually the track skirts the side of Tauranikau Peak and descends to Hydro Camp, an hour's walk from the hut.

Hydro Camp is a clearing that workmen built in the 1970s when erecting the power lines from Thames to Whitianga. It is also the site of a major junction for those heading back to the valley road. The track that heads west (right-hand fork) follows Webb Creek to its confluence with the Kauaeranga River, descending sharply most of the way and crossing the creek several times. Just before reaching the river, the track passes over a deeply worn pack-horse staircase that was cut by gum-diggers on their way to Coroglen, so-called Gumtown. Once at the river you backtrack along the track you started out on to reach the road end, a 1½ to two-hour walk from Hydro Camp.

The other fork is Billy Goat Track, a longer walk that most trampers think is far more interesting. The track heads south and immediately crosses Webb Creek where 200 metres upstream it's possible to see the remains of Webb Creek Dam. Most of the walk is downhill and in 1½ hours the track reaches the junction with the Long Trestle spur track, a short walk to view the collapsed girders. The main track swings north and follows the route of the Billy Goat Tramline down past the falls and remains of Short Trestle. It ends with a steep descent to the Kauaeranga River, crossing Atuatumore Stream and merging into the track you started out on at the wirewalk across the river. From Hydro Camp, this a three-hour walk back to the road's end.

Urewera National Park

The difference is in the trees. Urewera National Park shares the country's common traits of rugged terrain, beautiful lakes and crystal-clear trout streams. But it is the trees and the magnificent forests they make up that have set this wilderness apart and captured the imagination of those passing through.

The main access road through Urewera is SH38 which connects Rotorua to Wairoa on the east coast. The metal road curves and winds its way through the park's mountainous interior and then around the eastern shore of Lake Waikaremoana, the 'sea of rippling waters', which is bordered to the south by the towering Panekiri Bluff.

Geologists believe the 55-square km lake was formed 2200 years ago when an earthquake caused a huge landslide to dam the Waikaretaheke River. Today Waikaremoana is by far the most popular section of the national park, especially with boaters, and is the centrepiece for Urewera's most scenic and frequently used tramp, best known as the Lake Track. The four to five-day walk rings the shoreline, beginning and ending near SH38.

The northern portion of the park above SH38 is much more remote and characterised by the long valleys of the Whakatane, Waimana and Rangitaiki Rivers, all of which flow into the Bay of Plenty. Bordering Urewera to the west is Whirinaki State Forest Park, a 609 square km preserve surrounding the Whirinaki River.

HISTORY

Maori legend has it that human settlement in Urewera began when Hine-Pokohu-Rangi, the Mist Maiden, married Te Maunga, a mountain, producing 'the Children of Mist', the fierce Tuhoe tribe. Genealogical evidence points to the arrival of the Tuhoe in 1350 AD when the epic Maori migration landed on the North Island. One canoe, the Mataaua, arrived at the mouth of the Whakatane River and its occupants quickly moved up into the hinterlands.

The myth might be the better explanation, for the Tuhoe became a mountain tribe that endured hardships and isolation unknown to other Maoris in New Zealand. They could not cultivate food like most tribes because of the area's harsh climate, nor were they close enough to the sea to gather mussels or paua. The region lacked the flax bush that the Maoris used to produce clothing elsewhere and the rivers were poorly stocked with fish. The tribe evolved into fierce warriors, hardened by a difficult life, who resisted European invasion and influence long after other sections of the country were settled and tamed.

Originally the Tuhoe settled the rugged interior of Urewera but not Lake Waikaremoana. That was home for another east coast tribe, Ngati Ruapani, who believed the lake was formed when one of their ancestors, Maahu, became enraged when his daughter refused his request to fetch some water from a sacred well. The father grabbed the girl and held her in a spring until she drowned. But only her body died; her spirit was turned into a *taniwha* (water monster) that desperately tried to escape. First she thrust north and formed the Whanganui Arm before the Huiarau Range stopped her. Then she formed the Whanganui-O-Parua Arm, before attempting to escape from the lake's mouth near Onepoto. But time ran out when dawn arrived, for the sunlight, being fatal to all taniwhas, turned her into

Trampers (JD)

stone. The Ngati Ruapani identified her as a rock near the outlet of the lake.

Tribal wars soon became a fact of life in Urewera with a bitter feud forming between the Tuhoe and Ngati Ruapani. Invasions were common but reached a peak in 1823 when Ngati Ruapani warriors murdered two Tuhoe chiefs at Hopuruahine and desecrated the bodies. The Tuhoe warriors, lean and hard from living in the inhospitable interior, sought revenge and defeated the rival tribe in a battle at the Whanganui Arm that marked the beginning of an extended war. By 1830, however, the Tuhoe had completely dominated their opponent and taken over the lake.

Urewera was kept free from any outside influence by the Tuhoe who closely guarded their isolation, clinging to a natural suspicion of Europeans. Missionaries became the first whites to explore the area when Reverend William Williams travelled through the region in November 1840 and came across Lake Waikaremoana. But the Tuhoe continued to resist any intrusion by the Europeans and eventually joined several other tribes in the 1860s in warring against government troops.

They had just suffered a severe defeat when in 1868 Tuhoe destiny took a strange turn. That year Te Kooti, the notorious Maori leader, escaped from a Chatham Island prison and sought refuge in Urewera. Te Kooti and the tribe formed a pact that led to a running battle with government troops for more than three years. The soldiers used a scorched earth policy in an effort to eliminate the Tuhoe food supplies and flush them from the woods.

Te Kooti used his unique military manoeuvres to score victories over troops and stage successful raids on towns, including Rotorua. But the Tuhoe with their limited resources were no match for the government. Te Kooti only narrowly escaped several times, helped once by a premature gunshot that tipped him off. By 1871 disease and starvation had overtaken the tribe and eroded its morale. The Tuhoe finally ended their involvement in the Land War by agreeing to swear allegiance to the Crown. Te Kooti, however, never would.

The rebel leader escaped once more to King Country where he lived under the protection of the Maori chief Tawhiao. He was pardoned in 1883 and in 1891, two years before his death, the government granted him land near Whakatane.

The Tuhoe continued to distrust pakeha and in the early 1900s turned to another self-acclaimed prophet, Rua Kenana, who founded the isolated farming settlement of Maungapohatu. The tribe met with open hostility the government surveyors and construction workers who were trying to build a road through Urewera. The massive undertaking continued only after the Tuhoe could be convinced that such a road would bring trade and agricultural benefits to them. Still troops were needed to protect government workers as late as 1895 and the road was not completed until 1930.

The dark and mystic interior of Urewera was finally opened up, if only a little bit. Immediately after the completion of SH38 there was pressure to mill or farm the land but development was stalled by the government as the disadvantages of clearing the trees were already apparent. The idea of reserving the forest as a watershed was first promoted in 1925 and after WW II support grew rapidly to turn the area into a national park. In early 1954 the Tuhoe approved the name Urewera National Park at a meeting in Ruatahuna and the new park was officially gazetted later that year.

CLIMATE

Because of the mountainous nature of the area, trampers can expect a considerably higher rainfall than in either the Rotorua or Gisborne regions, which are to the west and east of it. The yearly rainfall of 2500 mm is carried in on northwest and southerly winds and in winter it can turn to snow in the higher altitudes. Fog and early morning mist are common characteristics of the area in the lower valleys but usually burn off by midday. During the summer trampers can generally expect regular spells of fine, dry weather with temperatures ranging up to 21° C or even higher during February, the warmest month.

NATURAL HISTORY

Urewera, the third largest national park in New Zealand at 2120 square km is the largest untouched native forest in the North Island. Part of the mountainous spine that stretches from the East Cape to Wellington, it is a rugged land which rises up to 1400 metres. Yet there is almost a complete absence of open peaks and ridges. The forests of Urewera form a thick blanket, covering even the mountains.

A diverse selection of trees is encountered in the forests of the park, ranging from the tall and lush podocarp and tawa forest in the river valleys to the stunted, moss-covered beech in the higher ranges. The major change in forest composition occurs at 800 metres when the bush of rimu, northern rata and tawa is replaced by beech and rimu. Above 900 metres, only beech species are usually found.

Throughout Urewera, the rivers and lakes contain some of New Zealand's finest waters for rainbow trout, while on the Lake Track it is especially productive to fly fish around the shoreline for cruising brown trout. Fishing with both fly and spinning gear is allowed in most areas but all anglers must have a licence for the Rotorua Fishing District.

THE LAKE TRACK

Built in 1962 as a volunteer project by boys from 14 secondary schools , today the Lake Track around Lake Waikaremoana is one of the most popular walks in the North Island. Highlights include spectacular views from Panekiri Bluff, numerous beaches and swimming holes and excellent trout fishing. All this makes

for a popular and sometimes crowded walk during the period from mid-December to the end of January and on the Easter weekend. During this time the park prohibits trampers from staying in any one hut for more than two consecutive nights and it's not a bad idea to carry a tent if you have access to one.

Access

Both ends of the track are within easy walking distance of SH38. The northern end is near Hopuruahine Landing, 15 km northwest of the park headquarters while the southern end is nine km to the south at Onepoto, and little more than a parking lot and a day shelter.

There is good public transport to this track. NZRRS provides a bus service along SH38 and on Tuesday and Thursday the coach travels from Murupara to Wairoa, stopping at Hopuruahine Landing (site of the northern end of the trail) at 12.45 pm. It then passes the park headquarters at 1.30 pm, reaches Onepoto at 1.55 pm and completes its route by arriving at Wairoa at 3.10 pm. On Wednesday and Friday it travels in the opposite direction, leaving Wairoa at 8.40 am, passing Onepoto at 9.50 am, Hopuruahine at 10.55 am and finally arriving at Murupara at 1.30 pm where connections can be made to continue onto Rotorua that day. If taking the bus out of the park, it's a good practice to show up at least 15 to 20 minutes early as the schedule is not always rigidly adhered to.

There is also a launch service across the lake that is especially handy for trampers wanting to return to their car from the other side. Waikaremoana Launch Service runs daily service except on Tuesday and Thursday from December 30 through January. The boat leaves Hopuruahine at 12.30 am for Onepoto and the fare is $16 for adults and $8 for children. There is no pick-up at Onepoto unless special arrangements are made. To schedule special trips contact the launchmaster

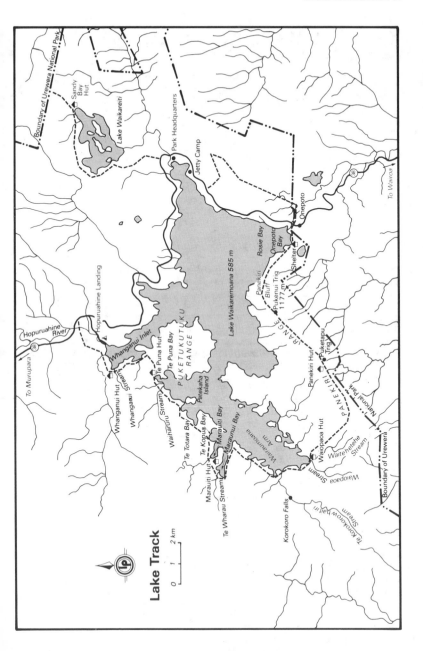

Lake Track

0   1   2 km

To Murupara

Hopuruahine River

Boundary of Urewera National Park

Sandy Bay Hut

Lake Waikareiti

Park Headquarters

Jetty Camp

To Wairoa

Onepoto

Rosie Bay

Onepoto Bay

Shelter

Panekiri Bluff

Pukenui Trig 1177 m

Lake Waikaremoana 585 m

Hopuruahine Landing

Whanganui Inlet

Te Puna Bay

Te Puna Hut

Whanganui Hut

Whanganui Stream

PUKETUKUTUKU RANGE

Patekaha Island

Waiharuru Stream

Te Totara Bay

Te Kopua Bay

Marauiti Bay

Marauiti Hut

Maraunui Bay

Te Wharau Stream

Marauiti Stream

Waiaraumana

Wairaumoana Arm

Korokoro Falls

Te Korokoro o Haumi Stream

Waiopaoa Stream

Waiopaoa Hut

Waitehehe Stream

PANEKIRI RANGE

Panekiri Hut

Puketapu Trig

National Park

Boundary of Urewera

(tel Tuai 826) at the Waikaremoana Motor Camp in January (or telephone Tuai 871 the rest of the summer).

Places to Stay

There are a number of park campgrounds throughout Urewera but the only other accommodation around the lake is at *Waikaremoana Motor Camp* (tel Tuai 826). The camp offers a variety of cabins, chalets and motel rooms with the cheapest being angler's cabins that sleep four to five people and cost $24 a night. There are also tent sites for $5 a night which includes the use of a communal kitchen and hot showers. The campground is located 1½ km south of the park headquarters.

Information & Maps

The park headquarters and visitor centre (tel Tuai 803), located on the shores of the lake at Aniwaniwa, is a good place to stop as there are a number of display rooms covering Maori tradition and legend and the natural history of the park. The centre also sells books, brochures and maps for the entire park and is open during the summer daily from 8 am until noon and from 1 to 5 pm.

Hut fees are $2.20 per night and are payable at the park headquarters; or you can post them to Urewera National Park, Private Bag 213, Wairoa.

If travelling from Rotorua, you can also stop at the Murupara visitor centre (tel 65-641), two km east of town on SH38. The centre is open from 8 am to 5 pm daily in the summer and at the same times on weekdays throughout the rest of the year. It sells maps – including topographical quads – books and brochures on the area and helps trampers choose the right walk.

The best and cheapest map to use is the Lake Waikaremoana Recreational Map (NZMS 239) that sells for $5.50 and has a scale of 1:40,000 (1 cm to 400 metres). Otherwise you would have to purchase quads 96 and 105 of NZMS 1 series to cover the walk.

The Track

The Lake Track is 43 km long and rated easy, with the only difficult section being the climb up and over Panekiri Ridge. There are five 18-bunk huts spaced along the route but most walkers need only three to four days to complete the trip. It can be hiked in either direction although by starting out from Onepoto (as described here), trampers put behind them all the steep climbing in the first few hours. For those walking in the opposite direction, an extra hour is needed from Waiopaoa Hut to Panekiri and less time from Panekiri to the end of the trail at Onepoto.

Stage 1: Onepoto to Panekiri Hut

Walking Time: five hours
Accommodation: Panekiri Hut (18 bunks)
The beginning of the track is signposted half a km from SH38 next to the day shelter. Before embarking on the walk, make sure you fill your water bottle, as there is no water available along this first leg of the journey.

There is little time to warm up at this end, as the track immediately begins a steep climb up the sandstone cliffs of Panekiri Bluff. Plan on 2½ to three hours to ascend 532 metres over four km to Pukenui Trig, one of the highest points of the trip at 1177 metres. Once at the trig you begin the second half of the day's walk by following the track along an undulating ridge of many knobs and knolls from which you get some spectacular views of Lake Waikaremoana some 600 metres below.

You continue along the ridge through mixed beech forest for almost four km until you suddenly break out at a sheer rock bluff which seems to bar the way. Closer inspection reveals a staircase and wire up the bluff where the bush has been cleared.

Panekiri Hut is another 100 metres beyond at Puketapu Trig. At an elevation of 1180 metres and only 10 metres from the edge of the bluff, this hut offers the best panoramas in the park, which include most of the lake, Huiarau Range and at times even the east coast town of Wairoa. A rainwater tank is the sole source of water at the hut while the wood stove is for heat only. A fuel stove is a necessity for any meal that needs to be cooked.

Stage 2: Panekiri Hut to Waiopaoa Hut
Walking Time: three to four hours
Accommodation: Waiopaoa Hut (18 bunks)

The track continues southwest to follow the main ridge for three km along a not-so-level course that gradually descends around bluffs and rock gullies until the track takes a sharp swing to the north. It's a one to two-hour walk to the noticeable right-angle turn, and along the way, if the weather is cooperating, are more panoramas of the lake and surrounding forest. At this point the gradual descent becomes a steep one as the track heads off the ridge towards the Wairaumoana Arm of the lake and at one point drops 250 metres in about a km.

On the way down there is an interesting change in the vegetation as the forest moves from the beech of the high country to tawa and podocarp with a thick understorey of ferns. The grade becomes more gentle as you approach the lake and eventually you arrive at the Waiopaoa Hut, which is situated near the shoreline. The hut has a wood stove and is a five-minute stroll from a sandy bay where there are good places for fishing and swimming.

Stage 3: Waiopaoa Hut to Marauiti Hut
Walking Time: four to five hours to Marauiti Bay; six to seven hours to Te Puna
Accommodation: Marauiti Hut (18 bunks); Te Puna Hut (18 bunks)

Start this day early as there are many places to linger and while the afternoon away. The track turns inland from

Waiopaoa Hut to cross Waitehetehe Stream and then follows the lakeshore across grassy flats and terraces of manuka scrub. You'll encounter a number of unbridged streams in the first hour that should be easy to ford at normal water levels. If the lake is high, however, you might have to hike up the creeks to cross them.

The signposted junction to Korokoro Falls is 2½ km from the hut, an hour's walk for most trampers, and makes for a scenic diversion. It's 30 minutes one way to the falls, which drop 20 metres over a sheer rock face, one of the most impressive displays of cascading water in the park. The main track continues around the lake by climbing 50 metres above the shore and sidling along a number of small sheltered bays that can only be reached by bushwhacking.

The track rounds Te Kotoreotaunoa Point and then drops into Maraunui Bay, three km from the junction to Korokoro Falls. It is a 30 to 40-minute walk along the south shore of the bay to Te Wharau Stream at the head of Maraunui Bay (a popular fishing spot) and along the way a Maori reserve and its private huts are passed. From here the track climbs over a low saddle and in a km dips into Marauiti Bay and passes the 200-metre side track to the hut on the lakeshore.

Continuing around the lake, the track swings northeast and in 30 minutes from Marauiti Hut arrives at Te Kopua Bay with its white, sandy beaches. This is one of the most isolated bays on the lake and abounds with campsites for those carrying a tent. The bay with its protected waters is also a favourite of trout fishermen. The track departs the bay and climbs away from the lake to cross Te Kopua headland before returning to the lakeshore. Halfway to Te Puna Hut, the track passes Patekaha Island, no longer a true island, and the shoreline that follows is dotted with a number of small sandy beaches. It's three km from the island to Te Puna Hut and trampers often reduce that at the end by cutting straight across the mud and grassy flats in front of the hut.

Stage 4: Te Puna Hut to Hopuruahine Landing

Walking Time: four to five hours

The track leaves the back of the hut and climbs over a saddle to meet the lakeshore again at Tapuaenui Bay in the Whanganui Arm, an hour's walk from Te Puna. It then follows the shoreline, with a short diversion up Tapuaenui Stream, for another hour until it reaches Whanganui Hut, situated on a grassy flat between two streams, a short way from a nice beach on the lake.

The last leg of the trip begins with a scenic walk around the lakeshore and through a short section of bush to the Huiarau Stream bridge. Once across the bridge the track continues up through the grassy flats on the northwest side of the Hopuruahine River to a point opposite the access road. A signposted spot on the river shows where to ford. It's usually an easy crossing, but if the river is swollen use the escape route which lies up the true right (west) side of the river to the concrete road bridge at SH38, an additional 30-minute walk.

Camping is allowed along the access road and there are usually a few tents and trailers among the grassy sites as Hopuruahine River and its mouth on the lake is a popular fishing spot. It's a km walk up the gravel access road to reach SH38 and the bus spot.

WHAKATANE RIVER TRACK

The Whakatane River walk is a four to five-day trip from the end of an access road off the SH38 to another near Ruatoki. The track forms a loop which eliminates the problem of finding a way of returning to your car or stored gear. The traditional route, a historic one for the Maoris, is along the river and often through it, with almost no climbing. The national park service has built an all-weather track that sidles the Whakatane

and allows trampers to avoid any dangerous fords. There is some climbing along the walking track as it works up bluffs and steep faces to avoid sharp bends in the river, but the tramp is not a difficult one. The track is well cut and formed with bridges crossing major streams.

There are six huts along the track. They are considerably smaller than those on the Lake Track. But the walk is not nearly as popular and obtaining a mattress in these huts is often easier. Carrying a stove makes cooking a lot simpler and you should also carry some extra food in case a swollen Waikare River holds you up for a day.

Access

Ruatahuna is the departure point for this trip and can be reached by a NZRRS bus from Murupara (with a connecting bus from Rotorua) on Monday, Tuesday and Thursday. On Tuesday and Thursday, the bus departs Ruatahuna at 12.10 pm and travels to and through the park and eventually to Wairoa. On Wednesday and Friday it comes from Wairoa and departs Ruatahuna for Rotorua after a lunch break. The one-way fare from Rotorua to Ruatahuna is $18.50

The bus stop is at Ruatahuna Store and Tea Room (tel 65-393), the heart of the small village. Food, gas and other supplies can be obtained here as well as transport to the track. From the store and the SH38 it's an 11-km trip up the access road to its end where the track begins. You can walk it in two hours or arrange for a lift with store-owner Dennis Smith. He charges $25-$30 per vehicle load to drop trampers off at the track. He will also store your car at his place, if you are nervous about leaving it at the end of the road. Hitching along the road is tough as there is very little traffic.

The trout fishing is renowned along the Whakatane Track, especially on the Waikare River, but bring all your tackle and flies as there is nowhere to purchase them in Ruatahuna.

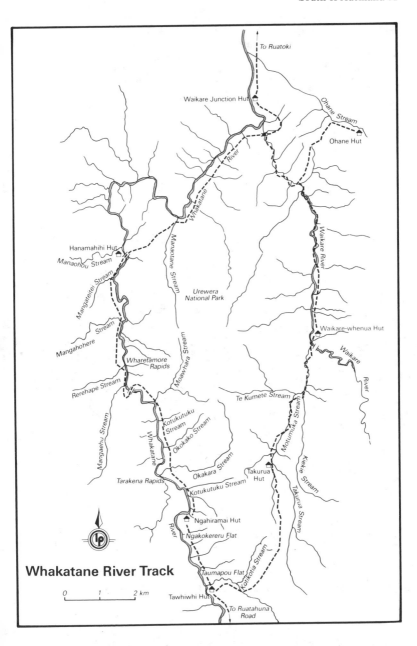

Whakatane River Track

Information & Maps

There is a ranger station in Ruatahuna, about 100 metres east of the store, where you can leave your intentions and pay the hut fees ($2.20 a night) as well as receive the latest track and river conditions. The office is open weekdays from 8 am to 4.30 pm.

Quad 86 of NZMS 1 series covers the loop trip while Quad 77 would also have to be purchased if hiking the traditional route through to Ruatoki. Many trampers, however, content themselves with the Urewera National Park recreational map, NZMS 170.

The Track

The route can be hiked in either direction but if the Whakatane River is followed first, you can avoid a night at Waikarewhenua Hut, a less than desirable place to stay. The section from the road end to Waikare Junction is rated medium and the following description applies only to the all-weather track, or 'walking track' as it is called on signposts along the way. If the water levels are normal and you don't mind getting your boots wet, you can follow the river route and save a bit of time. But the walking track is not that much longer and the views from above the river are worth the extra climbing. The stretch along the Waikare River back to Tawhiwhi Hut on the Whakatane River is a route rated medium to difficult.

The trip described here, however, heads along the river only to Waikare Junction Hut, two days short of the northern end, and then turns south and follows the Waikare River before crossing a ridge and returning to the Whakatane. Two days of this trip are along rivers and streams where there is no formed track, giving the tramp an overall rating of medium to difficult.

Stage 1: Road End to Tawhiwhi Hut

Walking Time: five hours from SH38; three hours from end of road

Accommodation: Tawhiwhi Hut (19 bunks)

The access road off SH38 is marked with a large display of the Whakatane Track system and it ends at a farm gate with a small 'track' sign on it. The track swings west (to the left) and quickly emerges high above the Whakatane River. It sidles the valley for three km until you come to a split in the track with a 'Walking Track' sign pointing the way to the all-weather route. The other track leads down to the river route along the Whakatane near Paripari Flats.

In another 20 minutes, the track descends quickly and crosses Te Mania Flats and then Mahakirua Stream. From here it continues to follow the valley for the next four km above the river but occasionally drops close to the Whakatane where it is joined by the river route. Keep an eye out for white metal tags when confronted with a choice of tracks. Ohaua is encountered next and will be recognised by the old Maori tribal house on the true left side of the river. You will see the meeting hall from the track but to view it up close requires fording the river three to four km before reaching Tawhiwhi Hut.

At Manangaatiuhi Stream you pass the junction with a track to Waiawa Hut (4½ hours) while the main track crosses the stream by way of a wirewalk. From the stream Tawhiwhi Hut is just 30 minutes away in the middle of Taumapou Flats and is a good place to spend the first night.

Stage 2: Tawhiwhi Hut to Hanamahihi Hut

Walking Time: One hour to Ngahiramai; 3½ to four hours to Hanamahihi

Accommodation: Ngahiramai Hut (nine bunks); Hanamahihi Hut (10 bunks)

Once across Taumapou Flats and Mangatawhero Stream, the track re-enters forest and in 10 to 15 minutes you actually enter Urewera National Park for the first time although there is no signposted border. Up to this point, the track has been crossing private Maori land, where there are restrictions on camping and hunting. The track remains level and in 45 minutes to an hour breaks out in a small clearing where Ngahiramai Hut is located.

From the one-room hut (nine bunks) the track continues to follow the true right bank of the river; often there are good views of the Whakatane below. The Tarakena Rapids are passed 30 minutes beyond Ngahiramai Hut and right before the track descends into Ohaerena Flats. Beyond the flats the track crosses two major streams, the second being Moawhara Stream, and from there climbs up to a swingbridge across the Whakatane River.

For the first time the track follows the true left side of the river (west bank) and immediately drops down to the river, once to cross Mangaehu Stream and a second time to cross Rerehape Stream. It then climbs up a terrace and emerges at Hanamahihi Flats, re-entering Maori land. It's six km from the swingbridge to the Hanamahihi Hut with the last two km an up-and-down walk in bush before you emerge at a small grassy flat. The one-room hut has 10 bunks and a wood-burning stove with a verandah that overlooks a scenic bend in the Whakatane River and a swingbridge to the other side.

Stage 3: Hanamahihi Hut to Waikare Junction Hut

Walking Time: three hours
Accommodation: Waikare Junction Hut (10 bunks)

To continue along the all-weather track, cross the swingbridge in front of the hut and follow the track as it begins a steep climb towards a saddle. The ascent is a knee bender for 1.2 km then levels off briefly on top before beginning a descent on the other side that's just as rapid. In an hour or so from the hut you should return to the Whakatane River.

Once on the river the track follows the true right (south) side for 4½ km until it reaches the bridge over the Waikare River.

Waikare Junction Hut

Since the valley is steep in many places, the track has quite a bit of climbing to it. In other places it cuts through grassy terraces where it might be difficult at times to see the actual track although the route is well marked with white metal tags.

If the weather is good and water levels normal, a more pleasant and easy route is to drop to the Whakatane once you have crossed the saddle. By following and fording the river at appropriate places you will avoid the bluffs and still arrive at the junction of the Whakatane and Waikare River where a sign points the way back up the shore to the swingbridge.

Near the bridge there is a sign explaining that the Waikare Junction Hut has been shifted and is now 25 minutes away on the all-weather track. The 25 minutes is a little misleading. In fact, it may be the most misleading track sign in all of New Zealand. Once over the swingbridge you begin a very steep climb as the track ascends around the bluff at the confluence of the two rivers. This is a knee-bending, two-rest climb and most people need 40 minutes to an hour to reach the hut. The only consolation is an immense view of the upper Whakatane Valley once the top is reached.

From the top the track drops quickly and then crosses a terrace (do not drop back down to the river) through a stand of bush to a clearing with the hut. The bluff makes it nearly impossible to follow the river bed to the hut while the Whakatane after the confluence is a very hard river to ford in normal conditions.

Waikare Junction Hut is worth the climb, however. It sits on a grassy terrace and from its verandah (which even has built-in benches) you can enjoy a superb panorama of the upper portion of the river, made even more spectacular by a sunset on a clear night.

Stage 4: Waikare Junction Hut to Takurua Hut

Walking Time: three to 3½ hours to Waikare-whenua; 4½ to 5½ hours to Takurua.

Accommodation: Waikare-whenua Hut (nine bunks); Takurua Hut (10 bunks)

To reach Ruatoki, the small town just north of the national park, trampers would continue down the Whakatane River along the all-weather track. The track is well cut and bridged and from the Junction Hut it is a three-hour walk to Ohora (18 bunks) and then another three hours to the road's end.

But to turn this trip into a complete loop, you return to the swingbridge at the confluence but don't cross it. Instead descend to the Waikare River and begin hiking upstream. For 4½ km (about the first 1½ hours) there is no track. Instead you follow the river bed, crossing when necessary. This part of the Waikare runs through a gorge and most likely you will have to ford it often. Needless to say, when the river is swollen the route will be impossible to follow.

An hour up the river there is a signpost on the true right (east) side, marking the start of the track to Ohane Hut (1½ hours), and in another km the river valley opens up and it's possible to locate a track along the true left side of the Waikare. This track continues for quite a distance, even marked occasionally by metal tags, until it is necessary to begin fording the river.

The Waikare-whenua Hut is reached 1½ hours or five km past the Ohane

junction but is not visible from the river, and the track to it, on the true right (east) side of the Waikare, is easy to miss. When you round a bend and see a swingbridge across the river, backtrack 50 metres and look for a track that leads up the true right side of the river to a grassy terrace that the hut is on.

This hut is one of the less desirable ones to stay at. It's a one-room shelter with nine bunks, open fireplace and mice that scurry around at night. The only reason to call it a day here is to enjoy the excellent trout fishing in the Waikare River.

At this point the route swings up the Motumuka Stream which empties into the Waikare on its true left (west) side 50 metres downstream from the swingbridge, which can be used during flooded conditions. There is a small sign marking the stream's mouth but no continuous track up the stream for the first three km, only short paths here and there. The walk involves constantly fording the stream – too often to even think of trying to keep your boots dry – but it's not unpleasant on a warm day. Kiekie Stream is passed in three km flowing into the true right side but is easy to miss. Usually it is Te Kumete a few hundred metres upstream on the opposite bank that trampers first notice.

Another km upstream an obvious track appears and climbs steeply to avoid a very narrow gorge in the stream. The gorge can be seen only by departing from the track for a short way. Further upstream the track departs again to avoid a thundering waterfall.

For the final two km to Takurua Hut, a well-worn track (even marked in a few places) appears mostly on the true right (east) bank though occasionally it swings to the other side. Eventually the track leaves the stream and quickly climbs a grassy terrace where the hut is – a much more pleasant place to spend a night than Waikare-whenua.

Stage 5: Takurua Hut to SH38

Walking Time: To Tawhiwhi Hut 1½ to two hours; access road 4½ to five hours; SH 38 six to seven hours.

Accommodation: Tawhiwhi Hut (19 bunks)

A cut and well-marked track begins behind the hut and immediately climbs the ridge. The climb is steep for the next two km until you are hiking along the crest of the Te Wharau Ridge. The track follows the ridge for about a km until it reaches Te Wharau where it begins a very steep descent. The long walk down levels out at Mangatawhero Stream in 2½ km and then works its way west towards the Whakatane River, emerging from the bush above Taumapou Flats where Tawhiwhi Hut is located. It is a 1½ to two-hour walk from Takurua Hut to Tawhiwhi but heading in the other direction the hike would be considerably harder and walking time should be increased to 2½ to three hours.

From Tawhiwhi Hut, backtrack along the all-weather track you started out on to the end of the access road. Plan on 2½ to three hours to reach the start of the road and another 1½ to two hours to hike the access road. Don't plan on hitching it, however.

OTHER TRACKS

Lake Waikareiti Track

The track begins along SH38, 100 metres west of the Urewera National Park visitor centre, and is an easy 3½ km to the secluded lake where there is a day shelter. The track continues along the western side of Lake Waikareiti and in three hours reaches Sandy Bay Hut (18 bunks) at the other end. This is a pleasant overnight trip that is rated easy. It can be shortened by renting one of the rowboats that the park maintains at the day shelter and rowing to Sandy Bay. The boats are rented at the park headquarters and the fee is $8 overnight.

Waihua-Mangamako Stream Route

In the northwest section of Urewera National Park is a network of ridge and stream routes with small huts. From Murupara, the area is reached by following the road to Te Teko just east of town and watching out for a national park sign 300 metres past the Waihua Stream Bridge. A road here takes you to the bush edge and the start of the track.

It's 4½ hours to Waihua Hut from the bridge, or three hours if you drive up to the edge of the bush. The next day you follow Te Onepu Stream, often in it, to Casino Bivouac (three bunks) and then drop down to Mangahoanga Stream to Mangamako hut (six bunks). It's a three-hour walk from Waihua Hut to Mangamako Hut and then 3½ hours back out to the Murupara-Te Teko Rd.

Whakataka Trig

This is a track rated difficult that should be considered by experienced trampers only. The route is posted along the SH38 at Taupeupe Saddle east of Ruatahuna. It is a 4½-hour walk via a slatted and undulating ridge track to the trig where there is superb panorama of the national park, including Lake Waikaremoana, as well as a small hut nearby. From the hut you can continue the second day along a steep, rugged route for four hours to Hopuruahine Landing at the northern end of the Lake Track.

Manuoha Trig

This is a tramp up to the highest point in the park at 1403 metres where there are excellent views and a small hut (three bunks). The track begins one km from the northern end of the Lake Track at Hopuruahine and climbs along a ridge for six km to the summit, a good six to eight-hour walk. Experienced parties can continue on the Pukepuke route to Lake Waikareiti, descending for five to seven hours before reaching the hut at Sandy Bay. The third day would be an easy hike out along the Lake Waikareiti Track to

SH38. This trip is rated difficult and the Pukepuke route should be considered waterless.

Whirinaki State Forest Park

Whirinaki is the newest addition to the country's State Forest Park system. As it is adjacent the Urewera National Park it shares a very similar climate and natural history.

HISTORY

Intense logging of the native bush in this area began in the 1930s. In 1946 the industry shifted from Te Whaiti right on SH38 to Minginui deeper in the Whirinaki River valley where a workers' village and three sawmills were built. In the 1970s, however, the land became a battlefield when conservation groups challenged government policy concerning the management of the forests. One result of the bitter conflict was an effort to preserve the remaining native bush. The state forest park was formed in 1984 and today no logging or development takes place in two-thirds of the preserve.

THE WHIRINAKI TRACK

The Whirinaki Track is a surprisingly easy tramp, ideal for families, novice hikers or overseas travellers who want to ease into backcountry tramping. While it lacks dramatic natural features like towering Panekiri Bluff or sweeping views of Lake Waikaremoana, it is still an interesting walk with such highlights as Te Whaiti-nui-a-toi Canyon, thundering Whirinaki River waterfall and the caves near the southern end of the track. The trout fishing is also very good in the lower reaches of the Whirinaki River up to the waterfall and more challenging above.

Access

To reach Minginui, head east on SH38 for the Te Whaiti junction, site of a former sawmill town that is 18 km from Murupara. Turn south for eight km until the road ends at the park headquarters. Hitching isn't that bad and if you get into Minginui late there's always Ohu Forest Camp. On Mondays, NZRRS runs a bus from Murupara to Ruatahuna and back that stops at the Minginui Store at 10.50 am. For a $15.50 fare you can hop on this bus and then a connecting one in Murupara for Rotorua.

The northern end of the track is seven km from the park headquarters at the end of River Rd, which begins across from Ohu Camp. The southern end is at the end of Plateau Rd which can be reached either by forest roads from Minginui or from NH5 (Napier-Taupo Rd), 2½ km south of Iwatahi. From NH5, turn north onto Low Level Rd for 27 km to its intersection with Arterial Rd. A sign for Whirinaki SFP South and Matea Lodge directs you to turn right. Once the lodge is reached, continue for another seven km and then turn right at the signposted intersection and follow the signs for 'Whirinaki Track'.

It's a 1½ to two-hour walk along River Rd unless you hitch a ride – possible at times because the most popular day walk, the waterfall loop, begins at the car park at the end. Park officials discourage trampers from leaving their cars here because of the possibility of them being vandalised while the owners are out on the track. Whirinaki Forest Holidays (tel Murupara 65-235) runs guided trips into the area but also offers a car care and drop-off service. A drop-off and pick-up at the two ends of the track would be $66 per car load or $33 if they use your vehicle.

Places to Stay & Eat

Minginui, the support centre for the sawmill and forest park, has one store, as well as Minginui Lodge ($50 a night for two people) and a community centre that may have the cheapest beer in New Zealand. The forest park also runs the Ohu Forest Camp, a 15-minute walk from the park headquarters past the sawmill and across the Whirinaki River to the start of River Rd. The hunters' camp consists of six small cabins (four to six bunks each) and an outdoor cooking pavilion. Locals have vandalised the cabins a bit but they still provide dry shelter at a convenient location near the track. Best of all they're free.

Information & Maps

The park headquarters, located in the sawmill village of Minginui, features a few displays on the area's logging history as well as selling maps of the area and providing the latest information on track and hut conditions. The office (tel Murupara 65-601) is open daily during the summer from 8 am to 4.30 pm.

Topographical maps that cover the park are quads N95 and N104 of NZMS 1 series. There is no recreational map of the park but they do sell a Whirinaki Hunting Map, minus contour lines but more than adequate for the Whirinaki Track, for $2.50.

The Track

The 26-km track, rated easy, is a wide, well-cut path with no difficult fords and so level that it even includes a tunnel through a hill. The two-day tramp includes a night at Central Whirinaki Hut, a large roomy facility near the river, but can also be extended into a four-day loop, six-day loop or even longer. The other tracks in the state forest park also have huts along them but are more difficult than the Whirinaki Track.

The following description covers the Whirinaki Track from its northern end to its southern end, a two-day walk. But also provided at the end are additional notes and times for those who want to undertake a longer loop to return to Minginui.

Stage 1: River Rd Car Park to Central Whirinaki Hut

Walking Time: three hours to Vern's Camp; five hours to Central Whirinaki Hut

Accommodation: Central Whirinaki Hut (17 bunks)

The start of the track is signposted at the car park by a map of the forest park with walking times. The entire route to the hut is surprisingly level, considering how steep the banks and bluffs are along the river. The track immediately passes the return track of the waterfall loop then in the next km comes to a bridge over an impressive rock gorge in the river known as Te Whaiti-nui-a-toi Canyon. From here it follows the true right bank of the Whirinaki River for the rest of the day.

Thirty minutes from the car park, the track passes the junction with the track to Moerangi Hut (4½ hours) and in another 30 minutes it crosses Upper Mangamate Stream and comes to its second posted junction. This one is the route up the side stream to Mangamate Hut (2½ hours). From here its a short distance to the side track to the Whirinaki River waterfall. It's only a five-minute walk and well worth it as the cascading water is an impressive sight that can be viewed from all angles as the track curves 180 degrees around it to head back to the car park. It's a great lunch spot if it's that time of day.

The main track remains in view of the river, often sidling the steep bluffs above it, and three km from the junction with the waterfall track it reaches Vern's Camp. The signposted grassy spot is about eight km from the car park and at one time was the site of a day shelter. The shelter is no longer there but the area is still an excellent campsite. In another three km the track makes one of the few descents of the day, passes a noticeable campsite along the river and then comes to the signposted Kakanui Stream.

Once over the stream, the track remains just above the river for most of the

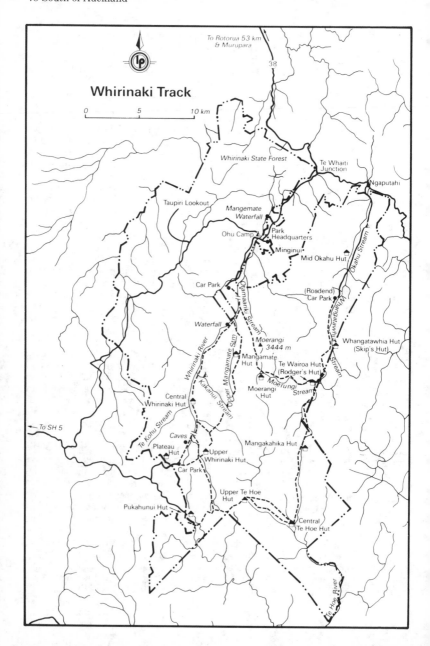

Whirinaki Track

next two hours, passing deep pools all along the way that will intrigue any angler. Anglers should keep in mind, however, that the largest trout will be found in the first hour of the walk below the waterfall. There is very little climbing at this point. Fifteen to 20 minutes before the hut, the track passes through a short and rather unusual tunnel. Central Whirinaki Hut is in a small grassy clearing near the river, 16 km from the car park.

Stage 2: Central Whirinaki Hut to Plateau Road

Walking Time: 2½ hours

A directional sign, though a little dated, is next to the hut and points the way to the track heading south. The walk resumes along the bluffs above the river and in 30 minutes arrives at Taumutu Stream and a junction with a track to Upper Whirinaki Hut (1½ hours). From the stream it's a long but gradual ascent before the track descends back to river. An hour from the hut you reach a swingbridge across the Whirinaki River.

Swingbridge on Whirinaki Track

This is a major junction of four tracks and it is well signposted along the east side of the bridge. To reach the end of the Plateau Rd or to see the caves you cross the swingbridge while trampers who are headed for Upper Whirinaki Hut or Upper Te Hoe Hut will continue along the east bank of the river. To reach the caves you turn south (left) once over the bridge on the true left side and follow the track for about 70 metres.

When the main track begins to ascend, look for a partially obscured track that continues along the river and it will quickly lead to the main cave. The huge cavern is interesting and at night it is possible to see glow-worms. It's an hour's walk from Central Whirinaki Hut. The track is wide and is an easy night-time excursion if you take a torch.

The main track climbs the ridge along the river and then heads southwest to the car park at the end of Plateau Rd.

Loop Tramps

For trampers who want to return to Minginui there are two possible loops, including a three-day trek. From the caves you would continue along the Whirinaki River for another hour while fording it perhaps a dozen times. A track, signposted on the true right side of the river, leads to Upper Whirinaki Hut (nine bunks), 20 minutes from the main track or two to 2½ hours from the caves. The hut is located in a grassy flat and a track departs from the northwest corner and follows Tatumutu Stream to its confluence with Kakaiti Stream. Here a directional sign points the way to the route to Mangamate Hut, a secondary track in the park that is marked with metal tags but not cut and bridged.

From Upper Whirinaki Hut it is 3.3 km or an hour's walk to the confluence of the two streams and then another three hours over a low saddle to Mangamate Hut (nine bunks). The next day it is a three-hour tramp out to the car park, the final hour backtracking along the northern end of Whirinaki Track.

An even longer trek would involve passing the junction to Upper Whirinaki Hut and hiking to Upper Te Hoe Hut (nine bunks), a more challenging tramp along the Pukahunui Ridge Track that takes six hours from Central Whirinaki Hut. The next day would be a five-hour walk along the ridge track to Central Te Hoe hut (17 bunks) followed by another five-hour walk on the fourth day to Te Wairoa Hut (six bunks), a rustic but charming hut built in the 1950s.

The trip ends with an easy three-hour walk to Moerangi Hut (eight bunks) from Te Wairoa Hut and then a 5½-hour return to the car park with the final 20 minutes on the Whirinaki Track. This trip is much more demanding than the Whirinaki Track and trampers should plan on five to six days to cover the loop.

Tongariro National Park

Tongariro National Park

The heart of the North Island, and the heart of New Zealand's national park system, is Tongariro. The park is a sacred ancestral homeland for the Maoris and to most trampers a walk through moonscape beauty. But more than anything else, in a country noted for its contrasts, Tongariro and the surrounding volcanic plateau offer the most

The park's trademark is volcanoes and three of them – Ruapehu, Ngauruhoe and Tongariro – form the 'top of the roof' for the North Island. The central region ranges from the stands of giant red beech and rimu in Kaimanawa State Forest Park to tussock grasslands; from alpine gravelfields and glaciers to the only desert in New Zealand. In the summer, trampers are scrambling up volcanic peaks, in the winter they are skiing down. This recreational playground can be the touristy village of Whakapapa, site of one

of the most impressive hotels in the country, or a secluded hut in the state forest where there is always an open bunk.

The variety of scenery and recreational activities is mind-boggling and this is the reason Tongariro is the most popular national park in New Zealand with more than 800,000 visitors a year. The vast majority are skiers but still the summer season draws 250,000 people who arrive to tramp, to climb to Crater Lake or just to spend their holiday around park headquarters at Whakapapa.

The area is the southern end of a volcanic chain that extends northwest through the heart of the North Island past Taupo and Rotorua and finally reaches White Island. The volcanic nature of the region is also responsible for Tongariro's hot springs, boiling mud pools, fumaroles and the maze of craters scattered throughout the park. But it is clearly the three volcanoes that attract most of the attention. At 2796 metres Ruapehu is the tallest mountain in the North Island and its snowfields the only legitimate ski area north of Wellington. Next to Ruapehu is Ngauruhoe, a nearly perfect symmetrical cone of 2291 metres and the most continually active volcano on the mainland. Mt Tongariro at 1968 metres is the smallest and northernmost of the three.

Since its establishment in 1887 the park's 750 square km have been well developed for recreational use. There is everything from the famous Chateau Hotel and a golf course to the various ski fields and a large number of tracks and daywalks around the three peaks. Although even on the longer treks you cannot get away from the more commercial activities within the park, most trampers consider that a small price to pay for their view of the park's outstanding natural features.

Along with a great variety of flora, the area offers good views of thermal activity, hot springs to soak in, peaks to climb and tracks that wind around the park above the bushline for extraordinary views. Most of the tracks lie in tussock grassland or through areas left void of vegetation by eruptions, making Tongariro the best alpine tramping in the North Island.

HISTORY

To the Maoris, the three volcanoes of Tongariro – Mt Ruapeho, Mt Tongariro and Mt Ngauruhoe – were tapu and they sought to prevent anybody from climbing them. They believed Ngatoroirangi, high priest of the Tuwharetoa tribe of Lake Taupo, arrived in the Bay of Plenty in the Arawa canoe and travelled south to claim the volcanic plateau for his people. He climbed Mt Ngauruhoe to view the land but upon reaching the top suddenly found himself in the middle of a raging snow storm. It was something the high priest had never experienced before and he cried out to priestess sisters in the north to send him warmth. The gods responded by sending fire from underneath that burst out throughout the North Island, including in the craters of Mt Ngauruhoe and Mt Tongariro, thus saving Ngatoroirangi. The high priest slew a female slave named Auruhoe and then climbed to the newly formed crater and tossed the body in, laying claim to the surrounding land for his people.

The volcanoes, especially Mt Tongariro, have been sacred to the Maoris ever since. They often travelled to Ketetahi Hot Springs to bathe but were forbidden to go any further. Europeans were also discouraged from the area. John Bidwell, a botanist and explorer, became the first European to scale Mt Ngauruhoe in 1839. While staring into the crater, Bidwell felt the volcano rumble and watched steam drift out. This frightened the explorer and even more Te Heuheu Tukino II, the

Tongariro, Ngauruhoe and Ruapehu

Maori chief who had tried to dissuade the explorer from continuing.

For the next 12 years the local tribe was successful in keeping all away from its sacred grounds. But in 1851, Mt Ruapehu fell to a climber's passion when Sir George Grey ascended one of the volcano's peaks and then hid from his Maori guides to avoid their discontent. In 1879, George Beetham became the first to scale Mt Ruapehu and see Crater Lake. During the 1880s the Maoris could no longer hold back the steady flow of geologists, explorers and botanists who were intrigued by the area. Nor could the Tuwharetoa clan keep other Maori tribes from claiming the land. After the Land Wars, where Tuwharetoa chief Te Heuheu Tukino IV Horonuku aided the rebel Te Kooti, the tribes loyal to the Crown wanted the area redistributed. In 1886, at a schoolhouse in Taupo, the Native Land Court met to determine the ownership of land around Taupo.

Horonuku showed great concern and pleaded passionately to the court to leave the area intact. At one point he turned to the rival chiefs who were longing for the land and asked 'Where is your fire? your ahi ak? You cannot show me for it does not exist. Now I shall show you mine. Look yonder. Behold my fire, my mountain Tongariro!' The forcefulness of his speech prevented the Maoris from dividing up the sacred land but Horonuku was equally worried about pakehas who were eyeing the area's tussock grassland for grazing.

The chief saw only one solution that would ensure the land's everlasting preservation. Before the Native Land Court on 23 September 1887, Horonuku presented the area to the Crown for the purpose of a national park, the first in New Zealand and only the fourth in the World. The move restored Horonuku's prestige in the eyes of the Maoris and a century later, during the country's National Parks Centennial celebration in 1987-88, the chief was remembered as a rare individual. He possessed an incredible

National Parks Centennial
1987-88

vision for a man of his time and knew that Tongariro's value lay in its priceless beauty and heritage and not as another sheep paddock.

An act of parliament created New Zealand's first national park in 1894 but its development was slow. Inaccessibility kept most New Zealanders from visiting the area, even though the Desert Rd from Wairoru to Tokaanu was completed in the first year. The first commercial adventure in the area was Allen Brothers Summer Camp where 25 shillings a day would get you a guide, a horse, meals and a bed at the wilderness resort near Desert Rd.

The main trunk railroad reached the region in 1908. By then there were huts at Waihohonu in the east with a track leading to them and to the Ketetahi Hot Springs. The railroad bought a large number of tourists to the west side and by 1918 a track and hut were built at

Mangatepopo for skiers on Mt Ngauruhoe. A road was also built to the Chateau in 1920 and within three years the Ruapehu Ski Club was formed and had a hut at the 1768-metre level on the Whakapapa slopes. The road to Top-Of-The-Bruce soon followed.

The park mushroomed in the 1950s and 1960s as roads were sealed, tracks cut and more huts built. By the early 1970s the annual number of visitors to Tongariro reached 400,000 and today it tops 800,000; often during the winter the national park will draw 10,000 skiers a day. It is only a matter of time before the sacred land of the Maoris averages a million visitors a year, the overwhelming majority pakehas.

CLIMATE

As most of Tongariro is mountainous, it has its own unpredictable weather patterns. The western slopes of all three volcanoes experience sudden periods of bad weather with heavy rain or perhaps snow on the peaks even as late as the start of summer. The winds, most often out of the west, can reach gale force on the ridges while at Whakapapa Village rain falls on an average of 191 days a year. Annual precipitation is 2743 mm.

It is usually drier on the eastern side of the mountains, and in the rain shadow of Mt Ruapehu is the Rangipo Desert, a barren landscape of patches of dark reddish sand and ash with small clumps of tussock. This unique area is the result of two million years of volcanic eruptions, especially the Taupo eruption 2000 years ago, which coated the land with thick deposits of pumice, destroying all vegetation.

NATURAL HISTORY

Geologically speaking, the Tongariro volcanoes are relatively young. Mt Ruapehu and Mt Tongariro were formed only two million years ago and were then shaped by glacial action, most strongly in the last ice age, and by further eruptions.

Glaciers at one time extended down Mt Ruapehu to below 1300 metres and have left polished rock far below their present snouts.

Mt Ngauruhoe is even younger as its formation began only 2500 years ago, in an old crater of Mt Tongariro, when eruptions started to build its cone to its present height of almost 700 metres higher than the old volcano. Today it is the most active volcano in New Zealand and it tosses out steam and dark clouds of ash every few years. All three, however, have a long history of fiery eruptions.

One eruption of Mt Ruapehu began in March 1945 and continued for almost a year, spreading lava over Crater Lake and sending huge dark clouds of ash as far away as Wellington. Mt Ruapehu was felt rumbling again in 1969 and 1973 but by far the worst disaster it caused was not the result of an eruption. On Christmas Eve, 1953, an ice wall that held back a section of Crater Lake collapsed. An enormous mud and water flow swept down the mountainside and took everything in its path including a railway bridge. Moments later a crowded Christmas Eve train plunged into the gorge and sent 151 people to their deaths in one of the country's worst accidents.

A year later Mt Ngauruhoe staged a major eruption that lasted 11 months and disgorged six million cubic metres of lava. In 1975, a brief, one-day burst sent ash 14,000 metres into the sky.

ROUND MT NGAURUHOE TRACK

Technically the Round-the-Mountain Track is the four to five-day walk around Mt Ruapehu. Many trampers, however, think of this trek as including Mt Ngauruhoe as well, making it a six to seven-day journey. The Round-the-Mountain trip described here circumnavigates only Mt Ngauruhoe and was selected for a number of reasons. The route can easily be walked in four days from either Whakapapa or the car park to Ketetahi Springs, two places connected to

Turangi by public transport. None of the days are excessively long and the walk covers the most popular and interesting thermal areas of the park. And, although it involves some climbing, it follows a well-marked track through Tongariro's most interesting areas.

Access

The circular route can be entered from four different points with the most popular places to begin being Whakapapa Village, site of the national park visitor centre, or the car park to Ketetahi Hot Spring off SH 47A. The route can also be reached from access tracks to Mangatepopo Hut and New Waihohonu Hut. There is good public transport to either place but since more trampers arrive at the park headquarters the description in this section will begin there. The advantage of beginning at Ketetahi, however, is that you will be able to enjoy a soak in the hot spring, the highlight of most treks here, on two nights instead of one.

There are a number of NZRRS buses daily from Auckland, Taupo and Napier to Turangi. From here you can reach Ketetahi car park, the Mangatepopo car park off SH 47, or Whakapapa Village through Alpine Scenic Tours (tel Turangi 8392 all hours). The tour operators run vans to these spots on a demand basis but throughout most of the summer they make an average of three trips a day. Call them up the night before to arrange drop-off or pick-up service. From Turangi to Whakapapa Village one way is $14 per person, to Ketetahi car park $8 and a lift from National Park, the nearest train station in the area, to the park headquarters is $6 (minimum two persons).

Places to Stay & Eat

Between the two information centres on Ohuanga Rd in Turangi is the *Tongariro Outdoor Centre* (tel Turangi 7492), a good place to stay where backpacker accommodation is only $13 a night.

Within Whakapapa Village there is a

pub, *Skotel Motel*, and the famous, beautiful, but a bit expensive, *Chateau Tongariro Hotel*. If you are planning to stay overnight at the village, head to the *Whakapapa Motor Camp* (tel Ruapehu 897), just past the park visitor centre, which has 47 caravan sites with power, eight tent sites and six cabins of either four or six bunks, as well as a communal kitchen and showers. Cabins are $24 a night for two people but if they're not full you can usually arrange a bunk in a shared one for $10 a night. The motor camp also has a small store with limited supplies but it is far better to bring in all your own food.

Information & Maps

Turangi, located northeast of the park, serves as an excellent place to organise the tramp. There is a relatively new information centre, open daily from 9 am to 5 pm, just off SH1 and across from it is a shopping plaza where you can pick up supplies and fishing gear. Down Ohuanga Rd at the corner of Atirau Rd is the DOC district office (tel Turangi 8520) where information, books, maps or daily weather reports can be obtained on either the national park or the Kaimanawa area.

The visitor centre and park headquarters at Whakapapa Village (tel Ruapehu 729) is open daily from 8 am to 5 pm and has a number of displays as well as a fine slide and sound presentation that explores the myths and natural history of the park. The centre is also a source of track information, maps, books, weather reports and is the place to pay for huts ($6 a night) or leave your intentions.

Tongariro is covered by four quads (T19, T20, S20 and S19) of Infomap 260 series (1 cm to 500 metres). There is also a recreation map, NZMS 273/4, that covers the entire national park including all the tracks and huts and is adequate for this trip.

The Track

The hike around Mt Ngauruhoe is a four

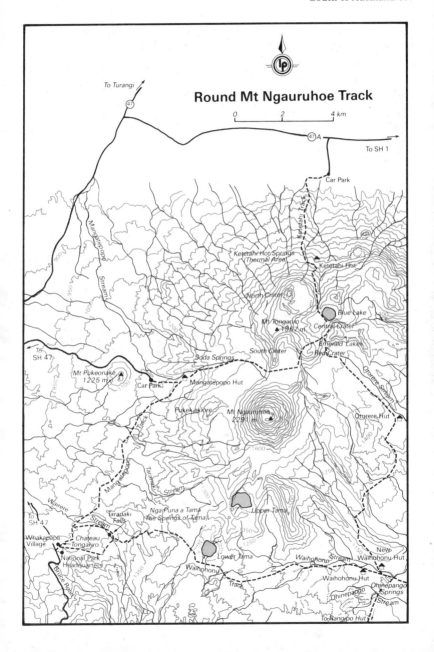

Round Mt Ngauruhoe Track

To Turangi

To SH 1

0   2   4 km

Car Park

Ketetahi Track

Ketetahi Hot Springs
(Thermal Area)

Ketetahi Hut

North Crater

Blue Lake

Mt Tongariro
1967 m

Central Crater

South Crater

Emerald Lakes
Red Crater

Soda Springs

To SH 47

Mt Pukeonake
1225 m

Car Park

Mangatepopo Hut

Oturere Stream

Pukekaikiore

Mt Ngauruhoe
2291 m

Oturere Hut

Mangatepopo

Taranaki Stream

Wairere

To SH 47

Taranaki
Falls

Nga Puna a Tama
(The Springs of Tama)

Upper Tama

Whakapapa
Village

Chateau
Tongariro

National Park
Headquarters

Lower Tama

Waihohonu

New
Waihohonu Hut

Bruce Road

Waihohonu
Track

Waihohonu Hut

Ohinepango
Springs

Ohinepango
Stream

To Rangipo Hut

to five-day trip that can be walked in either direction and is rated medium. The track is easy to follow and well marked but does involve a number of solid climbs along the way. If beginning from Ketetahi car park instead of Whakapapa Village, plan on a 2½ to three-hour hike up to the hut and a 1½ to two-hour hike down to the car park.

Stage 1: Whakapapa Village to Mangatepopo Hut

Walking Time: 2½ to three hours
Accommodation: Mangatepopo Hut (24 bunks)
From the park visitor centre, head up the road behind the Chateau Tongariro Hotel and follow it to the signposted Mangatepopo Track. The track begins as a well-maintained track that wanders through tussock grass and a few stands of beech for 1½ km. At Wairere Stream it passes a signposted junction with a track to Taranaki Falls and eventually Upper Tama Lake.

Mangatepopo Track, the left-hand fork, heads north and at this point its condition deteriorates somewhat. It crosses tussock and dozens of small streams, which have gutted the track in places and make for sloppy conditions when it rains.

Nevertheless, the track is still well marked and easy to hike and within three km of the start there are impressive views of the cones of the volcanoes with Mt Ngauruhoe and Pukekaikiore to the northeast and Pukeonake straight ahead. After a few more stream crossings, the track makes a wide swing to the east and you quickly climb a ridge to spot Mangatepopo Hut two km off in the distance.

The hut is a pleasant spot with good views of the climb to South Crater, the destination for many trampers the next day. There is also a track that heads west from the hut and in 30 minutes reaches the end of the Mangatepopo Rd, which connects to SH 47. If you decide to walk

out here, don't expect a lot of traffic on the metal access road.

Stage 2: Mangatepopo Hut to Ketetahi Hut

Walking Time: four to five hours
Accommodation: Ketetahi Hut (24 bunks)
This section of the trip is over one of the most spectacular tracks in New Zealand. It's not unusual in foul weather for trampers to walk from one hut to the next in three hours but if the weather is clear, plan on spending the whole day on the track rather than rushing off for a soak in Ketetahi Hot Springs.

The day begins with an easy trek up Mangatepopo Valley along the stream of the same name. Within an hour you pass the spur track to Soda Springs (a 30-minute round trip), which can be smelled long before they can be seen. The main track continues up the valley and quickly begins a well-marked climb to the saddle between Mt Ngauruhoe and Mt Tongariro. The ascent among the lava rocks is steep but well marked with poles and in 45 minutes to an hour you reach the top and pass the signposted route to the summit of Mt Ngauruhoe (a three to four-hour round trip). You follow the poles as they continue past the junction and cross South Crater, an eerie place when the clouds are hanging low and which, according to one writer, looks like a 'huge walled amphitheatre' when the weather is clear. The walk through the crater is flat with the slopes of Mt Ngauruhoe to the right and the summit ridge to the left.

Once across the crater the track, now more of a marked route, resumes climbing the ridge and at the top Oturere Crater is seen down a steep slope. The poles marking the track swing north (left) here and follow the narrow crest of the ridge that separates the two craters, sidling around some huge rocks. Eventually the track reaches the signposted junction to the route up Mt Tongariro (a 1½ to two-hour round trip) while to the right is steaming Red Crater, whose name comes from the dull red colour of its sides. The side of the crater is the highest point reached on the track at 1820 metres and the views from here are fantastic and on a clear day might even include Mt Egmont to the west.

The track begins its descent along the side of Red Crater, passes Emerald Lakes and then makes an even steeper drop along scoria-covered slopes into Central Crater to the signposted junction to Oturere Hut (two hours). To reach Ketetahi Hut continue across the crater and climb its north ridge to Blue Lake, another remarkable sight along the way. After skirting the lake, the track descends along the northern slopes below North Crater, reaching the hut two hours from the junction to Oturere Hut.

Ketetahi Hut has a spectacular view from its front door that includes Lake Rotoaira and Lake Taupo. The renowned hot springs are another 20 to 30 minutes along the track to the car park and are signposted on the north side of the thermal stream, though the smell and greyish water are usually noticed first. A track begins up the true left side of the stream and it's about 100 metres to the first dammed-up pools. Keep in mind that the higher upstream you go, the hotter the water gets until some pools are actually boiling. Also remember that 30 minutes in a pool usually leaves most trampers with only enough energy to climb back up to the hut.

Stage 3: Ketetahi Hut to New Waihohonu Hut

Walking Time: seven to 7½ hours
Accommodation: Oturere Hut (23 bunks); New Waihohonu Hut (22 bunks)
Return up the track towards North Crater as it ascends 200 metres to the top in a series of switchbacks. Plan on two to 2½ hours to reach the junction to Oturere Hut or even longer if the sights along the way again make you pause and ponder their unusual features. Follow the signposted track to the south (left) as it skirts the

main Emerald Lake before working its way to the old lava flow that descends into Oturere Valley.

It's an hour from the junction to the valley floor where the track follows Oturere Stream and passes clumps of tussock grass and piles of rocks and st nes in a moonscape terrain. The walk is somewhat level in the valley until you begin a gentle descent to the hut. The Oturere Hut has 23 bunks, a wood-burning stove and a view of a small waterfall in the stream.

The track departs the hut and swings southwest through open country as it skirts the eastern flanks of Mt Ngauruhoe. It descends straight towards Mt Ruapehu, working its way across numerous streams until it reaches the bridge over Waihohonu Stream, 1½ to two hours from Oturere Hut. From the bridge the walk becomes a gentle climb through stands of beech trees, descending only at the end just before it reaches New Waihohonu Hut.

The hut sits in a clearing above the stream with a nice view of Mt Ruapehu from the front door. Those heading back to Whakapapa Village might consider a short side trip along the main track south to Ohinepango Springs, an interesting bubbling pool that is a 20-minute walk from the hut.

Stage 4: New Waihohonu Hut to Whakapapa Village

Walking Time: 5½ to six hours
The day begins with the track descending from the hut and crossing a bridge over the upper branch of the Waihohonu Stream where on the other side is a signposted junction. The Round-the-Mountain Track continues south along the slopes of Mt Ruapehu while the Waihohonu Track departs east (left) towards Desert Rd (1½ hours). The track to Whakapapa Village heads west (right) and in a km passes the corrugated-iron Waihohonu Hut, the oldest building in the park with an unusual display of log signs left by tramping parties. Next to the hut is

another signposted side track to Ohinepango Springs.

The main track follows the upper branch of the Waihohonu Stream, dropping and climbing out of several streams that have eroded through the thin covering of tussock grass. The walking is tiresome at times but beautiful if the weather is clear with Mt Ngauruhoe's perfect cone on one side and Mt Ruapehu's snow-covered summit to the south. Eventually the track rises gently to the Tama Saddle between the two volcanoes and then arrives at a junction to Tama Lakes in another 1½ km. The lower lake is a short trip up the side track but it's a 45-minute walk to the upper lake along an exposed ridge.

The main track continues west (left), working down and out of another half-dozen streams until it descends to Taranaki Falls, three km from the junction with the Tama Lakes track. At the falls the Wairere Stream spills over a 20-metre rock face into a boulder-ringed pool. In the final stretch of the walk, the track passes an alternative route back to the park headquarters before making a steady descent to the Whakapapa Village, through tussock grass at first and then bush. It's a 30 to 45-minute walk from the falls to the village.

OTHER TRACKS
The Tongariro Traverse
The five-day walk crosses Tongariro National Park, from its southern border near Ohakune, across the western slopes of Mt Ruapehu and Mt Ngauruhoe, to the car park on SH 47A. The trip includes the scenic section of craters and lakes between Mt Ngauruhoe and Mt Tongariro and a night at Ketetahi Hot Springs. Public transport is available from the car park at SH 47A through Alpine Scenic Tours but getting to the top of Ohakune Mountain Rd can be tough at times in the summer. Best bet for hitching is to start early in the morning when it's often possible to pick

up a ride with ski field workers. There is a good youth hostel in Ohakune.

Kaimanawa State Forest Park

East of Tongariro National Park is Kaimanawa State Forest Park, a reserve of 765 square km that is dominated by the Kaimanawa Range and the beech forest that covers much of the land. The park contains the upper catchments of four major rivers – the Mohaka, Rangitikei, Ngaruroro and Tongariro.

To trampers, what the Tongariro National Park is, Kaimanawa isn't: one is well known, well used and is easily accessible, the other is little known, little used and is difficult to get to by public transport; in Tongariro, tracks are benched and well marked, often with poles marking the route every 40 metres; in Kaimanawa, it is always challenging to determine what is the walking track and what is just another hunter's trail.

HISTORY
Situated just to the east of Tongariro, Kaimanawa State Forest Park has a completely different history. Geologically the area is very old and the ranges are composed of sedimentary rock known as greywacke that has been dated to 200 million years. There is little evidence of widespread use of Kaimanawa by the Maoris but Europeans had arrived in the area by the 1880s, looking for gold and burning off the forest for sheep farms.

Beginning in the late 1930s and continuing for almost 40 years, splitting was the activity that dominated the northern sections of the park. Splitting was a method of producing fence posts, battens and other products from trees without the use of a sawmill. Clements Rd is actually an old splitting road and by the late 1940s there were a number of splitters living in small one-man huts built on sleds along it.

Splitting began to decrease by the late 1950s and in 1965 the Forest Amendment Act was passed to set aside sections of state forest as parks to give them more protection. By 1971 eight areas, including Kaimanawa, were turned into state forest parks, first administered by the former New Zealand Forest Service and today by DOC.

CLIMATE
Although the area receives an average of 3500 mm of precipitation a year, the summers are generally good with long dry spells and mild temperatures from December to April. In the southern, mountainous sections of the park, the weather can be unpredictable with heavy rain, sleet or even snow developing quickly in high altitudes during early or late summer.

NATURAL HISTORY
The park is renowned for its trout fishing. It is also home of the famed sika (Japanese) deer as well as red deer, and hunters make up the largest share of park users, flocking to the area during the roar (mating season) in late March and April.

Kaimanawa can be divided into two general regions. The central and southern portions of the park are steeply mountainous with forested valleys, extensive scrublands and alpine grasslands. In contrast, the area to the north and east, which is the setting for the Te Iringa Circuit, is less rugged and almost entirely forested, providing for easier tramping. The five to six-day walk climbs a number of ridges and low saddles but other sections of the park are much more rugged. The trip also touches the banks of four rivers famous for rainbow trout, making this one of the best tramps in the North Island for a wilderness fishing adventure.

TE IRINGA-OAMARU CIRCUIT
This is a four to five-day walk in a secluded corner of the North Island's popular volcanic plateau region. There are no hot springs in this area, no steaming craters, no days above the bush level and no Whakapapa Village. If trampers arrive outside the popular hunting time of mid-March to April, they'll find secluded tracks, uncrowded huts and great trout fishing along empty stretches of river.

The forest is interesting, there are some great views from the ridges, but more than anything else this is an angler's adventure. Of the five days spent walking, anglers will pass productive rivers on three of them. If you're serious about catching some trout, plan an extra day at both Oamaru Hut and, especially, Boyd Lodge. Stop at a sport shop in Taupo for advice on flies or spinners and make sure you have purchased a Taupo fishing licence for this portion of the park.

Access
Taupo is often the last town for trampers entering this area. There are plenty of stores, sport shops and outfitters for any supplies or equipment you might need and there is cheap backpackers' accommodation at Rainbow Lodge.

Getting out to this track is a challenge. If you have your own vehicle, you have it made, otherwise getting to and from the track is a two-part journey. The first is to head along SH5 (Taupo-Napier Rd) 27 km east of Taupo and turn right onto Taharua Rd. Hitching is pretty good or you can make arrangements with the NZRRS bus driver or his counterpart at Mt Cook Lines (the two depots are next door to each other) to be let off at the corner on their run to Napier.

Once on Taharua Rd you head south for 11 km and then turn onto Clements Rd for another three km to Te Iringa Campground. (Clements is an interesting forest road that continues on for another 15 km into the park.) This portion is hard to hitch as the only traffic on it is from a handful of sheep station families. They are really good about picking up trampers – it's just that it may be some time before you see one rumbling down the road going in your direction. Sometimes it's possible to contact the DOC office in Taupo and catch a ride out with a work crew. Of course there is always one sure way of reaching the starting point – on foot – in which case plan on a four-hour walk and spending the first night at Te Iringa hut.

Places to Stay

In Taupo there is cheap backpackers' accommodation at *Rainbow Lodge* (tel (074) 85-754), at 99 Titiraupenga St, where you can get a bunkroom bed for $12.50 a night.

Information & Maps

Information or maps on the state forest park can be obtained from the DOC district office (tel (074) 85-450) on Tamamutu St in Taupo, a block away from the NZRRS bus depot, and open from 8 am to 4.30 pm Monday to Friday.

The most practical map for this trip is the *Guide to Kaimanawa State Forest Park* (NZMS 274/11) that covers the entire park in a scale of 1:100,000 but has surprisingly good detail and contour lines on it. There are five huts in the park and trampers pass four of them on this trip. As of 1988, there still weren't any hut fees – something that is likely change in the future.

The Track

The following trip is a five-day loop that begins and ends at Clements Rd. There is some climbing along this track (there is almost everywhere in New Zealand!) but this trip is rated medium to difficult because the track is not cut, benched and marked every 40 metres with a pole like much of Tongariro. There will be times in Kaimanawa when you'll have to retrace your steps to locate the main track or stop

and search for that reassuring white metal tag on a tree that tells you everything is okay.

You can cut off two days by hiking to Oamaru Hut and following the poled route from the Mohaka River out to the end of Taharua Rd. Walking time is six to eight hours across the sheep and cattle paddocks and trampers need to stay on the pole route and not cut over to the private road that parallels it part of the way.

Stage 1: Clements Rd to Te Iringa Hut

Walking Time: one to two hours
Accommodation: Te Iringa Hut (six bunks)
The trip begins at the Te Iringa car park and campground, 16 km from SH5. The area is signposted on Clements Rd and the track begins before you reach the grassy area for tents. In the first km the track gently rises and then descends across a stream at which point the track begins a steady climb for 2½ km to a saddle. The climb is not hard as the track is well graded.

Once over the saddle, the track sidles the ridge for a short way where it's possible to see the roof of Te Iringa Hut just before the track descends to it. Te Iringa Hut has six bunks and an open fireplace, and though it is not new, it still provides good shelter.

Stage 2: Te Iringa Hut to Oamaru Hut

Walking Time: four to five hours
Accommodation: Oamaru Hut (12 bunks)
The track departs from the back of the hut and makes a short climb up Te Iringa, reaching a high point of 1241 metres when it passes a signposted hunter's access route. There are good views of the park's rugged interior from here and for a short distance along the track as it descends the ridge. You continue the descent for three km until reaching a branch of Tikitiki Stream where along the banks there is a popular camping area. The track crosses the branch and then follows the main

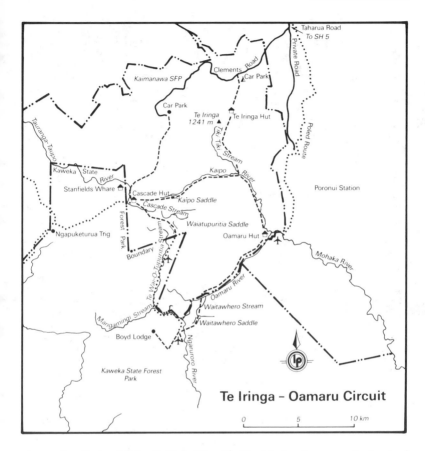

Te Iringa – Oamaru Circuit

0   5   10 km

stream along the true left (east) side for 1½ km until it empties into the Kaipo River.

A swingbridge crosses the river and the track resumes on the true right (west) bank. Most of the time it follows the edge of the forest and often climbs up ridges where it can be easy to lose. It's a two-hour walk along the river, passing some tempting pools at its lower end, until the track emerges onto the grassy flats along Oamaru River. The hut sits up on a terrace with an excellent view of the flats below and the surrounding hills. This one,

like Boyd Lodge, is very much a hunters' hut even with gun racks in the bunk rooms.

Anglers who spend an extra day here can pursue trout in a number of places, including the pools in the lower end of Kaipo River or hike up either Oamaru or down the Mohaka as all three rivers hold fish.

Stage 3: Oamaru Hut to Boyd Lodge
Walking Time: four to six hours
Accommodation: Boyd Lodge (16 bunks)
This stretch is a scenic forest walk that

provides good views and access to the Oamaru River. Trout fishermen will delight in the way the track follows much of the river bank, allowing them to search one pool after another for fish. The walk begins at the hut where steps take you quickly down to the flats and a well-beaten path begins to cross it in a southwest direction. It's a three km walk to the top of the flats and in places the grass is so tall the track is easy to lose momentarily. Just keep heading up the river and use a noticeable white bluff on the opposite side of the valley to gain a sense of direction. Once across from the landmark, it's easy to spot a 'Boyd Lodge' signpost pointing the way into the beech forest.

A well-cut track resumes here and climbs over several ridges to Ruatea Stream (Jap Creek), reached 3.4 km from the hut. Occasionally a tramper will mistake the wide stream for the Oamaru River and continue up along a hunters' track until it ends in a km or so. The main track crosses the creek and is clearly marked with white metal tags on both sides. A level walk resumes along the river for the next six km, climbing only to avoid an occasional steep bank.

At the confluence of the Oamaru and Waitawhero Stream, the track crosses the river and follows the stream up to the Waitawhero Saddle, a climb of a good hour or more. After crossing the stream several times, the track makes a final ascent to the saddle where trampers are greeted with a view of Ngaruroro River and valley. It's possible to even see the airstrip and wind sock near Boyd Lodge.

The saddle is signposted where the track swings north for a short distance and begins its descent. It drops through beech forest at first and then onto a ridge of open tussock grassland before reaching the valley floor. The Ngaruroro River should be crossed north of the airstrip to avoid swampy ground. Then you climb up the terrace on the other side to locate an old pack track. The old trail leads to the

airstrip where the final climb of the day, via steps, takes you to the hut 100 metres above it.

Boyd Lodge is generally regarded as the nicest facility in the park. It's a large roomy hut and from its verandah you can view the river below and the mountains in Kaweka State Forest Park to the east.

Ngaruroro is renowned for its excellent trout fishing and has become a favourite recently with whitewater rafters.

Stage 4: Boyd Lodge to Cascade Hut

Walking Time: five to 6½ hours
Accommodation: Cascade Hut (six bunks)

Descend to the airstrip and follow the old pack track to the Ngaruroro River. Follow the true right (west) side of the river north into the upper valley, an area of river terraces, lower hill slopes and flats of tussock grass and heath-like vegetation. The track is not cut but the route is clear as the Ngaruroro gradually curves west around Tapuiomaruahine Peak towards its headwaters and the Mangamingi Stream. Fords should not be difficult at normal water levels as you cross Mangamingi near its confluence with Te Wai-O-Tupuritia Stream.

The route continues north through the tussock valley of Te Wai-O-Tupuritia Stream and you ford the stream when necessary until the head of the valley is reached. A signpost points the way into the trees where a track ascends to Waiatupuritia Saddle. After the saddle the track climbs steeply until the high point of the catchment ridge is reached at almost 1250 metres.

A sharp descent follows until the track levels out at Cascade Stream where it follows the true left bank of it. The track skirts a narrow gorge and a series of waterfalls before reaching Cascade Hut on a terrace above the stream's confluence with the Tauranga-Taupo River. Halfway down to the hut, the track passes a signposted junction with the track to Kaipo Saddle.

Stage 5: Cascade Hut to Clements Rd
Walking Time: four to six hours via Hinemaiaia Track

Cascade Hut lies near a signposted junction that offers trampers three ways to depart the forest park. Heading off to the west is the Ngapuketurua Track that crosses the summit of the same name and terminates at the end of Kiko Rd (six to eight hours).

For those with a car at Te Iringa campground, it's possible to return to it by first heading east. Return to the signposted junction to Kaipo Saddle and cross Cascade Stream. You then climb to Kaipo Saddle at 945 metres. At the saddle the track follows the Kaipo River, fording it often in the beginning, to the confluence with Tikitiki Stream where it joins the track you started out on. It's a four to six-hour walk to the confluence and another four to five hours over Te Iringa to the car park and campground on Clements Rd.

The shortest route out is the Hinemaiaia Track which goes northwards from the hut and crosses the open flats of the Tauranga-Taupo River. Along the way, on the opposite shore to Cascade Hut, you pass a picturesque old shelter with a pumice chimney. This is Stanfields Whare, and it's open to the public. After a 30-minute walk, the track ascends from the valley along a spur to the ridge top of 1250 metres. It then drops steeply through the beech forest to the confluence of two streams, following the true left (west) bank of one of them and passes several scenic waterfalls on its way to the Hinemaiaia River.

The Hinemaiaia River is crossed below the confluence of its main tributaries and from here it's a short distance through beech forest to the car park at the end of Clements Rd. The track at this end is well cut and signposted at the car park. But for those without transport, the trip isn't over as it is 18 km to Taharua Rd and another 11 km to SH5.

OTHER TRACKS
Waipakihi Valley Route
This is an overnight trip in the west side of Kaimanawa State Forest Park that includes hiking along the Waipakihi River the second day with numerous easy crossings. The first day is spent hiking over Umukarikari, 1592 metres, and ending at Waipakihi Hut (12 bunks). The trip is almost a complete loop with both ends signposted off Kaimanawa Rd, 15 km south of Turangi on SH1. Alpine Scenic Tours (tel 8392) can provide pick-up and drop-off to the track from Turangi.

Mt Egmont National Park

First Mt Egmont tantalised the Maoris, who made it a god. Then, in 1770, Captain James Cook, on the deck of the *Endeavour*, was fascinated by the mountain. Today thousands make the pilgrimage to the summit of this lonely volcano that accents the Taranaki region of the North Island.

The near perfect symmetry of its cone makes Mt Egmont a twin to Japan's Mt Fuji and one of the most beautiful mountains in New Zealand. The easy accessibility of its tracks and the magnificent views of patchwork dairy farms, the stormy Tasman Sea and the rugged Tongariro peaks make it a favourite with trampers. The volcano that the Maoris call Taranaki is generally regarded as the most climbed summit in the country.

Mt Egmont's present shape comes from a series of eruptions that occurred 16,000 years ago and gave the cone its smooth lines and eye-pleasing beauty. The only flaw in the symmetry of the mountain is Fanthams Peak on the south slope. Snow-capped on a clear winter day, Egmont is surely one of the country's most stunning sights.

The entire mountain along with

Kaitake and Pouakai Ranges, a line of volcano activity, lies in Egmont National Park. The park includes 335 square km of native forest and bush, more than 300 km of tracks and routes and 16 huts and shelters scattered throughout the area. There are three main access roads into the park – Egmont, Pembroke and Manaia Roads – and motorists can drive up to the 900-metre level, almost to the bushline, along each one. There are accommodation and restaurants near the end of Manaia and Pembroke Roads and there is a large bunkhouse at North Egmont on the Egmont Road.

The easy accessibility allows inexperienced trampers to scale the 2516-metre summit – not a technical climb from Dawson Falls or the Stratford Plateau – during good weather in the summer. The roads and the availability of accommodation also encourage families, school groups and novice trampers to tackle a number of day hikes and overnight tramps. All this means that the park is busy with both experienced trampers and day hikers from the Christmas holidays to early February. In the winter, Mt Egmont is the second major ski area in the North Island.

The Round-the-Mountain track is the traditional four to five-day tramp around Mt Egmont and much of it is below the bushline. To many, a more pleasant and shorter alternative in Egmont National Park is the Pouakai Track. This trip is a two-day semi-loop that includes the northern slopes of Egmont as well as trekking across the rolling tops of the Pouakai Range from which you get excellent views of the volcano.

The heavy rain of Mt Egmont is responsible for the numerous streams that flow down the volcano's slopes like the spokes of a wheel. The streams have carved numerous gorges and valleys and in many cases the result is majestic waterfalls; particularly notable is Dawson Falls with its drop of 18 metres and Bell Falls with a drop of 31 metres. But the gullies and gorges also make hiking tedious at times as some days are spent constantly going in and out of unbridged stream beds.

HISTORY

According to Maori myth the volcano was called Taranaki and was originally part of the central range of the North Island. Taranaki and Tongariro eventually came into conflict over the lovely maiden, Pihanga, and a battle ensued. Taranaki lost and was exiled from the range. The volcano retreated west, carving out the Wanganui River and, while resting near Stratford, forming Te Ngaere Swamp.

Mt Egmont

Finally he settled on the coast and when the Maoris saw the summit surrounded by mist they felt the volcano was weeping.

Egmont was a sacred place to the Maoris, a place where the bones of their chiefs were buried, and a place to escape from the terrorism of other tribes. The legendary Tahurangi was said to be the first person to climb the summit and when he lit a fire on it, he claimed the surrounding land for his tribe. The Maoris lived around the base until the Waikato invaders massacred them with muskets, despite their secret caves, in the 1820s and 1830s.

The first European to see Mt Egmont was Cook in 1770 and one of his ship's company later wrote it was 'the noblest hill I have ever seen'. Cook named the mountain in honour of Earl Egmont, First Lord of the Admiralty. The Dutch explorer Abel Tasman had actually been the first European to sail past the mountain in 1642 but the cone had been shrouded in clouds and was passed by unnoticed. Two years after Cook's visit, Mt Egmont was the first thing French explorer Marion du Fresne saw of New Zealand. He thought it was an islet until he noticed snow on the summit.

Both Cook and du Fresne recorded seeing fires of Maori settlers but never made contact with them. Naturalist Ernest Dieffenbach did, however, in 1839. Working for the New Zealand Company, he told the local Maoris of his plans to climb the summit. The native tribes tried passionately to dissuade him but Dieffenbach set off in early December anyway. Although the first attempt was unsuccessful, the naturalist set out again on 23 December and after bashing through thick bush he finally reached the peak. His Maori guides did not go beyond the snowline as the upper slopes were 'tapu' to them.

By boiling water and using thermometers, Dieffenbach calculated the height of the mountain to be 2694 metres. In 1850, a trigonometrical survey of the peak was performed by the crew aboard HMS *Acheron*, anchored in New Plymouth. They measured the height as 2520 metres and it wasn't until 110 years later in 1960 when a theodolite was carried to the summit that the present height was determined at 2517 metres.

The volcano early became a popular spot for trampers and adventurers. The second European ascent of the mountain took place in 1848 and the first woman, Jane Maria Richmond, reached the peak seven years later. By the 1870s a track and bridle path had been cut over the Pouakai Range to the final slopes at Holly Flats and organised climbs to the summit became a popular summer activity. In 1885 Thomas Dawson discovered the falls that now bear his name and pushed for the development of a track and campground in the area of Dawson Falls Tourist Lodge.

Fanny Fantham became the first woman to climb the parasite cone on the south side of Mt Egmont in 1887 and Panitahi was quickly renamed Fanthams Peak in her honour. A year later the summit route from Stratford Plateau was developed while in 1901 Harry Skeet completed the monumental task of surveying the area for the first topographical map. After that, development went ahead at a feverish pace with the construction of huts, access roads and additional tracks around the mountain.

Tourism boomed and to protect the forest and watershed from clearing for farms the Taranaki provincial government set aside an area of roughly 9½ km in radius extending from the summit. The national park – only the second one in New Zealand – emerged in October 1900 when an act of government set up the first park board.

CLIMATE

Mt Egmont has a maritime climate. February is the warmest month with an average reading of 18°C while the temperature slides down to an average of

10°C in July. The air temperature decreases 6°C for every 1000 metres you climb and the freezing level in winter is at 1750 metres. Snow is rare in the summer but not rain. Egmont and surrounding mountains force the moist westerly winds from the Tasman Sea to rise, cool and release their moisture. The average rainfall at the 1000-metre level is 6500 mm a year and at 2000 metres it is a soaking 8000 mm.

Mt Egmont's high altitude means trampers are exposed to strong winds, low temperatures and foul weather. The mountain is notorious for weather that can suddenly change from being clear and fine to a storm or a squall. Throw together the winds, possible freezing temperatures at night and heavy rains and you have the alpine dangers that have taken more than 40 lives.

NATURAL HISTORY

Volcanic activity began building Mt Egmont some 70,000 years ago and in about 30,000 years produced a good size cone of 150 metres. Geologists believe the mountain then entered a dormant stage that ended a mere 3000 years ago with a series of eruptions. When they were over, Egmont was left with its near perfect cone of today.

Activity continued with the Newall eruptions in 1500 AD, which destroyed much of the surrounding bush with gas-charged clouds. The most recent eruptions occurred in 1755, only 15 years before Cook sighted the summit. There is debate among geologists whether Mt Egmont is still active. Some point to dormant periods that have lasted for several thousand years and say the last eruption was too recent to be sure that it is inactive. Others believe its days of lava and streaming ash are over and gradually, due to erosion by rain and ice, Egmont will wear down as have Kaitake and Pouakai.

The very high average rainfall and its isolation from the other mountainous regions of New Zealand have led to

Egmont having a unique vegetation pattern. Species such as tussock grass, mountain daisy, harebell, koromiko and ourisia, have developed local variations and about a hundred of the common New Zealand mountain species are not found here. In particular trampers will notice the complete absence of beech. The lush rainforest that covers nine-tenths of the park is predominantly made up of broad-leaf podocarps. In the lower altitudes you find many large rimu and rata while further up kamahi is dominant and with its tangled trunks and hanging moss this formation is often referred to as 'goblin forest'.

MT EGMONT ROUND-THE-MOUNTAIN TRACK

The popular Round-the-Mountain (RTM) track is a 55-km journey that takes the average tramper 20 hours spread over four days to complete. It's a scenic walk but not, as many visitors imagine it to be, all above the bushline. Much of the track drops into forested areas of the park then climbs across scree slopes and herbfields. More climbing will be encountered when the track works around numerous bluffs, deep gorges and massive lava flows. The track is well cut and easy to follow.

In 1987, a low-level, all-weather Round-the-Mountain Track was completed with 16-bunk huts placed a comfortable day's tramp apart. The new circuit takes about five days to walk and lies almost entirely in the bush. Although the two routes share many of the same tracks, the trip described here will be the traditional high-level walk which offers trampers spectacular alpine scenery and the best views of Mt Egmont.

All trampers, both novice and experienced, should be well aware of the dangers of Mt Egmont before embarking on the RTM track. The mountain often gives a false appearance of being safe and the high altitudes reached on the track means that inexperienced people are within easy reach of icy slopes. Each year

Top Left: Tramping to hot springs, Great Barrier Island Trek (JD)
Top Right: Kauri dam along Great Barrier Island Trek (JD)
Bottom Left: Arriving at Port Fitzroy, Great Barrier Island (JD)
Bottom Right: Hot springs on Great Barrier Island (JD)

Top: Above the clouds, Tongariro NP (IK)
Bottom: Mt Egmont at sunrise, Mt Egmont NP (IK)

there are numerous accidents in the park that with more thought could have been avoided. More so than in other alpine areas, weather on Mt Egmont can suddenly change from being fine and warm to being stormy with rapidly dropping temperatures. Make sure you are prepared with enough warm clothing, preferably of wool, to avoid suffering from exposure.

Access

New Plymouth, the coastal city that has the volcano as a backdrop, is often the best departure point for trampers. The city can be reached from either Wellington or Auckland by NZRRS buses or Newman's Coachlines. Supplies can be easily obtained in New Plymouth and there is a DOC district office (tel (067) 80-829) in the Atkinson Building on Devon St West.

There are more than 30 roads that lead to or go near the park and most of them have a track from the road end into it. Three of them – Egmont Rd, Pembroke Rd and Manaia Rd – take you 900 metres up the mountain and close to the bushline. These roads are the most common access points into the park and all of them terminate near the RTM track.

The best one for most trampers is usually Egmont Rd. It is the closest to New Plymouth, departing from SH3 13 km southeast of New Plymouth and it is then another 16 km to North Egmont.

Pembroke Rd extends for 18 km from Stratford to Stratford Plateau at 1140 metres on the east side of the volcano. There's a ranger station halfway up the road and three km below the plateau is the Mountain House.

Manaia Rd is 15 km southwest of Stratford and goes for eight km to Dawson Falls. There is a National Park Interpretation Centre at Dawson Falls, open daily, as well as backpacker accommodation at Konini Lodge.

Those without transport will find the

hitching easy to Egmont Village, the turn-off to Egmont Rd on SH3, but harder after that to North Egmont. It's a $3.50 ticket for New Plymouth to Egmont Village on a NZRRS bus, or groups of two or more trampers can make arrangements with Dick Mercer (tel (067) 511-034) of New Plymouth who runs scenic tours of the park and will also run trampers up to the North Egmont visitor centre. The cost is only $15 per person and that includes being picked up when you complete the tramp.

Many trampers beginning at North Egmont will hike only as far round as Stratford Plateau and then hitch down Pembroke Rd to SH3. This cuts a day off the tramp and at Stratford you can pick up a NZRRS bus to New Plymouth, $6.50 one way. This is a better alternative than ending the trip at Dawson Falls as Manaia Rd can be very, very quiet, especially in the middle of the week.

Places to Stay

North Egmont Accommodation is available at the *Camphouse*, a 32-person bunkhouse with electricity and showers. The nightly fee is $7 per adult and bookings, which are advisable at the height of the summer, can be made by calling the visitor centre or writing to the Manager, North Egmont Visitor Centre, Egmont Rd, RD 6, Inglewood. You can also camp near the bunkhouse at no cost and pay $2 for a shower.

Stratford Plateau The *Mountain House* licensed tourist hotel (tel Stratford 6100) at RD 21, Stratford, about three km below the Stratford Plateau on the Pembroke Road, has rooms for $60 to $70 and also hires out tramping equipment.

Dawson Falls There is backpacker accommodation at *Konini Lodge* (tel Stratford 5457) for $7 per adult. Much more expensive rooms can be obtained at *Dawson Falls Tourist Lodge* (tel Stratford

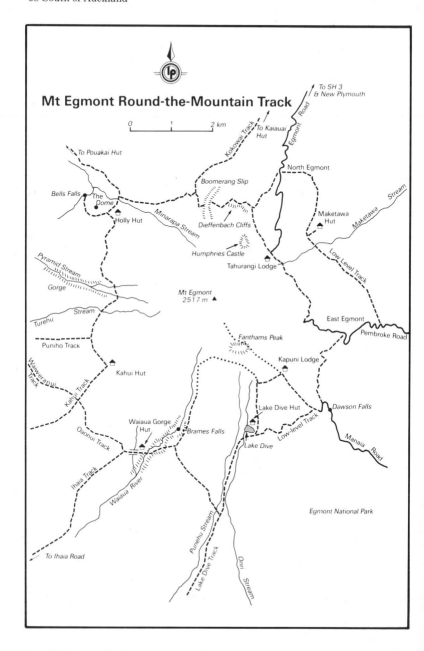

Mt Egmont Round-the-Mountain Track

To SH 3
& New Plymouth

To Pouakai Hut

Egmont Road

Kokowai Track

To Kaiauai Hut

North Egmont

Boomerang Slip

Bells Falls

The Dome

Holly Hut

Minarapa Stream

Dieffenbach Cliffs

Maketawa Hut

Maketawa Stream

Humphries Castle

Tahurangi Lodge

Pyramid Stream

Gorge

Turehu Stream

Mt Egmont
2517 m

Low Level Track

Puniho Track

East Egmont

Pembroke Road

Fanthams Peak

Waiwerangui Track

Kahui Track

Kahui Hut

Kapuni Lodge

Oaonui Track

Waiaua Gorge Hut

Brames Falls

Lake Dive Hut

Dawson Falls

Low-level Track

Ihaia Track

Lake Dive

Manaia Road

Waiaua River

Egmont National Park

To Ihaia Road

Punehu Stream

Lake Dive Track

Onri Stream

5457) which will send a courtesy car to pick you up in Stratford.

Information & Maps

Most huts in the park, including those on the RTM Track, are $7 a night and have an honesty box for payment. The track is covered on the NZMS 169 map of Egmont National Park or the metric Infomap 260 series in which the park is covered on quads P20 and P19.

At the end of Egmont Rd there is the North Egmont visitor centre (tel Egmont Village 710) that is open daily from 9 am to 5 pm and has an excellent set of displays on the life of a volcano and its impact on the surrounding countryside. There are also large viewing windows of the cone and a small theatre with a short slide presentation. Maps, books and the latest weather outlook can also be obtained here.

The Track

The trip can be hiked in either direction and, though a fair bit of climbing is involved, it is rated medium as the track is well cut and easy to follow. By heading counterclockwise you spread out the climbing fairly evenly over the four days.

Stage 1: North Egmont to Holly Hut

Walking Time: three hours
Accommodation: Holly Hut (26 bunks)
The trip begins on the Razorback Track near the Camphouse. The track climbs steadily for 240 metres past a monument to Tahurangi Trig at 1181 metres. It continues beyond the trig and up Razorback Ridge, ascending another 100 metres before reaching a junction with the RTM Track. Head northwest (right) on the well-marked RTM Track as it climbs around Waiwhakaiho Stream and along the base of Dieffenbach Cliffs near the bushline where there are excellent views of New Plymouth. You then descend slightly, cross a branch of Kokowai Stream and then pass Boomerang Slip

which is signposted with warning signs. From the slip the track works around the head of Kokowai Stream and then arrives at a junction with Kokowai Track.

Head west (left) and follow the RTM Track as it crosses two streams and then descends 244 metres over 2½ km to the junction with Ahukawakawa Track. The RTM continues south (left) and quickly crosses two branches and gullies of the Minarapa Stream before reaching Holly Hut. This is a popular place to spend a night in the park and from its verandah there are good views of the Pouakai Range. From the hut it is another two-km or 30-minute walk around the Dome to Bells Falls, a spectacular sight where water cascades down a 31-metre cliff. (The map of the Pouakai Track shows this section of the track in detail.)

Stage 2: Holly Hut to Waiaua Gorge Hut

Walking Time: 5½ hours
Accommodation: Kahui Hut (six bunks), Waiaua Gorge Hut (16 bunks)
The RTM heads west across Holly Flats, passing the junction to Bells Falls and descending into the gully of Peters Stream, named after Harry Peters, a well-known guide and Camphouse caretaker. It climbs out the other side and then begins a steady ascent for the next two km past Hook and Skinner Hills to the side of Pyramid Gorge. The erosion caused by Pyramid Stream has left the gorge so unstable that the track alongside it must climb up to tussock grassland above it before crossing branches of the stream. Poles point out the route around the gorge and at one point you climb to 1160 metres and are rewarded with excellent views of Stony River and Pouakai Range off in the distance.

The route descends from its high point through tussock and tall scrub, becomes a track again and passes the junction with Puniho Track. From here it's 1 km to Kahui Hut at 880 metres, one of the older huts in the park. This makes a good halfway point for lunch if you intend to spend the night at Waiaua Gorge. Or you could save a few dollars and spend the night here as the Kahui Hut is only $3, though the location is not nearly as scenic as Waiaua Gorge.

The RTM now becomes the Kahui Track as it makes a gentle descent through forest for two km to a major junction with Oaonui and Waiweranui Tracks. The RTM continues to the southeast (left) along the Oaonui Track, crossing numerous streams for the next 2½ km until it fords the Oaonui Stream and arrives at the junction of the Ihaia Track. This was the site of the old Oaonui Hut. The Ihaia Track heads southwest for four km where it ends at Ihaia Rd.

The RTM continues along Brames Falls Track, quickly crosses a footbridge and reaches Waiaua Gorge Hut. The new hut, built in 1984, is situated on the cliffs above the deep Waiaua Gorge and provides excellent views of the western slopes of Egmont.

Stage 3: Waiaua Gorge Hut to Lake Dive Hut

Walking Time: five to seven hours

Accommodation: Lake Dive Hut (16 bunks)

From the hut the Brames Falls Track immediately descends into the gorge, via an aluminium ladder and steep track, to Waiaua River and climbs up the other side. It then follows the steep edge of the gorge for half a km before arriving at the junction with the Taungatara Track. Trampers now have a choice of routes to Lake Dive Hut: through the forest or along an alpine route.

If you follow Taungatara Track to the southeast (right), it will be a five-km walk or three-hour stroll through thick forest and across eight streams until you reach the junction with the Lake Dive Track, one of the lowest points of the trip at 535 metres. The RTM continues north (left) on the Lake Dive Track as a steady climb of 400 metres over three km. It takes two hours to walk this stretch and along the

way the track swings close to Punehu Canyon for good views of the steep gorge. After that the track sidles around the Beehive Hills and then arrives at Lake Dive. The hut is at the far end. Built in 1980, it is in a scenic location along the lakeshore and on a windless day is graced with a reflection of Fanthams Peak in front of it.

The alternative route is to continue from Waiaua Gorge on the Brames Falls Track, passing the falls and emerging on tussock slopes where a route of snow poles replaces the track. It's a climb of 700 metres from the junction with Taungatara Track to Mangahume Stream and along the way you sidle below bluffs just before dropping to the stream bed and crossing it. Don't bother looking for Mangahume Hut on the other side of the stream as it has been removed. The route continues east and ascends sharply around the steep head of Punehu Gorge. From here it drops just as quickly to a major junction. One track leads south (right) quickly descending 1½ km to Lake Dive Hut. The other track heads east (left) to Kapuni Lodge (locked) right above Dawson Falls.

Choose carefully which track or route you hike. The Mangahume Route to Lake Dive Hut is shorter and much more scenic on a clear day but involves a great deal more climbing and should not even be considered during foul weather. Taungatara Track, though it makes for a longer day, is an easier and safer walk.

Stage 4: Lake Dive Hut to North Egmont

Walking Time: six to seven hours via alpine route; seven to eight hours via low-level tracks

From Lake Dive Hut you begin the day with a climb towards Fanthams Peak. It's a steep ascent, made easier by numerous steps and 13 short wooden ladders. You pass the signposted Mangahume Route junction and then sidle the slopes beneath Fanthams Peak for 30 to 40 minutes to reach the Kapuni Lodge Track. To the northwest (left) is the route to the peak, to the southeast (right) the infamous 'Egmont Steps' which quickly descend 360 metres over a span of a km to Hooker Shelter, a three-sided day shelter. The steps continue to drop for 240 metres in 1½ km before reaching the Dawson Falls parking lot and the visitor centre there. Plan on three hours for this leg of the journey.

If the weather is bad, take the low-level route, which departs from Lake Dive Hut and works its way through the forest before joining the Hasties Hill Track from Dawson Falls and ending at the visitor centre, a three to four-hour walk.

From Dawson Falls follow the Wilkies Pool Track as it climbs away from the car park along an extremely well-benched and maintained track. You start walking in a goblin forest, climb into mountain totara and cedar and emerge in sub-alpine scrub near the car park, where you'll find Anderson Shelter and a lookout tower nearby. It's an hour or so from Dawson Falls to this point where trampers again have a choice of following an alpine route or dropping down to a safer low-level track.

The alpine route is much more scenic but harder, as you begin it by strolling up the ski field road and then following the track from its end down into and back out of Manganui Gorge to the public shelter facing the ski field. The track ascends the tussock slopes, passing the old lava flow known as Ngarara Bluff and the noticeable Warwick Castle, and in an hour reaches Tahurangi Lodge (locked) and the huge TV transmitter near it. From here there is a 4WD track down to North Egmont but for better views continue along the poled route that descends beneath Humphries Castle to the top of Razorback Track. It is a 30-minute descent on Razorback Track, mostly on steps and stairs, to the Camphouse.

The low-level track begins further down Pembroke Rd, across from the Stratford Mountain House. You follow Curtis Falls Track to the new Maketawa Hut, a walk of 1½ hours. From the hut a new track descends through the forest to North Egmont, reached three to four hours after departing from the Mountain House. Keep in mind that Waipuku Hut no longer exists.

THE POUAKAI TRACK

For those who can't spare four or five days for the RTM trip, this is a shorter but equally scenic walk in Egmont National Park. The overnight trip includes spectacular views from the top of the Pouakai Range, which at one time was a volcano of similar size to Mt Egmont, before natural erosion reduced it to a rugged area of high ridges and rolling hills of sub-alpine bush. The night can be spent at spacious Pouakai Hut, where from the verandah you get panoramic views of New Plymouth and the Tasman Sea. See the Egmont Round-the-Mountain Track section for places to stay and sources of information.

Access

The trip is best begun from North Egmont (see the Egmont Round-the-Mountain Track for transportation) and walked as a two-day loop, ending back at the visitor centre. You can also depart from Pouakai Hut and hike the Mangorei Track to Mangorei Rd. This will take you back to New Plymouth but keep in mind that there is usually very little traffic on Mangorei Rd.

Maps

The most common map used is NZMS 169 map of Egmont National Park.

The Track

This walk is a two-day loop that follows the RTM track for part of the way. The track is well marked and benched and is rated medium. It can be walked in either direction.

The Pouakai and Holly huts are $7 but well worth the money as their sub-alpine locations and views from their verandahs

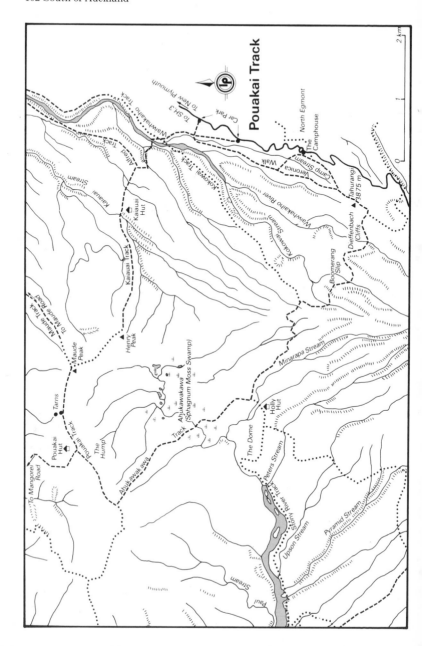

Pouakai Track

are superb. The other hut on this route is Kaiauai, an older four-bunk facility that costs only $3 a night.

Stage 1: North Egmont to Pouakai Hut via Holly Hut

Walking Time: five to six hours
Accommodation: Pouakai hut (16 bunks)
Begin at the Camphouse and hike the Razorback and RTM tracks to Holly Hut (see Stage 1 of the Egmont Round-the-Mountain Track for description). Those getting an afternoon start from North Egmont should plan on staying at Holly Hut, a 2½ to three-hour walk from the visitor centre, in which case you would bypass the junction to Ahukawakawa Track and ford Minarapa Stream to the 16-bunk facility a short distance away.

Trampers hiking on through would follow the Ahukawakawa Track which departs north (right) just before the stream. You make a gentle descent through bush until you come out at the southwestern end of Ahukawakawa Swamp. The track crosses the open swamp and then begins a long climb up a forested ridge. You ascend 304 metres to the junction with the Pouakai Track which should take you a little over an hour. At the junction you head east (right) following the track as it climbs gradually, sidles around the Hump (elevation 1295 metres) and then makes a short descent to a saddle. Pouakai Hut, a 2½ to three-hour walk from Holly Hut, is located on the saddle five minutes down Mangorei Track.

If you're planning to return directly to New Plymouth along the Mangorei Track, it's a 2½-hour walk to the end of Mangorei Rd. Once you reach the road, you will most likely have to continue walking as there is little traffic this far up. However, it is mostly downhill to New Plymouth.

Stage 2: Pouakai Hut to Egmont Rd

Walking Time: four hours to Egmont Rd
Accommodation: Kaiauai Hut (four bunks)
Hope for clear weather on this day for the views on the first half of the trek, as you traverse the backbone of the Pouakai Range, are superb. Head northeast along the Pouakai Track as it descends 100 metres before levelling out at the Pouakai Plateau, marked by a pair of tarns, a km from the hut. The track, marked by snow poles, traverses the flat land and often uses boardwalks to cross fragile bog areas. On a clear day, photographers will be able to capture reflections of Mt Egmont in the tarns. The track sidles Maude Peak, and from the junction with Maude Track right before it, the peak can be climbed in 10 to 15 minutes for more views. The route then drops into a low saddle to begin a steep 152-metre climb to the top of Henry Peak (elevation 1222 metres). Needless to say, there are more good views from here, including ones of the ridges and plateaus of the Pouakai Range.

From the top of Henry Peak the track

Common Room inside a typical NZ hut

begins a long steady descent until it reaches and follows the gorge cut by Kaiauai Stream, a 520-metre drop from the summit. The track eventually drops into the gully, climbs back out, and on the other side sits Kaiauai Hut. The hut is only a little over an hour from Egmont Rd as Kaiauai Track continues east and within a km reaches a junction with Alfred Track, the first of three tracks to Egmont Rd. From the signposted junction the track drops off a terrace, crosses a stream a couple of times and arrives at a wire bridge across the Waiwhakaiho River.

On the other side you will be on the Waiwhakaiho Track. Head north (left) and within a km you'll come to Mangaoraka Walk, a short track that leads to Egmont Rd, four km from the visitor centre. Head south (right) and the track leads to a car park that is two km from North Egmont. From here you can also cross a branch of the Waiwhakaiho River and pick up the signposted Veronica Walk that leads back to the Camphouse.

Whanganui National Park

In contrast to Egmont is Whanganui National Park, a lowland forest that lies between Egmont to the west and Tongariro to the east. The park was gazetted in December 1986 and covers an area of 742 square km. Its dominant feature is the Wanganui River, which splits the park in half. It is the longest navigable and second longest river in New Zealand at 315 km. Whanganui doesn't have an impressive skyline of volcanoes and peaks, but it still attracts a number of trampers as it is the largest lowland forest remaining in the North Island and some say the only true wilderness in this part of the country. Access is difficult but the park offers a rare experience of remote wilderness.

The Matemateaonga Walkway is a

four-day walk through Whanganui's remote interior and one end of the track can only be reached by boat. The track was opened up in 1980 by the New Zealand Walkway Commission as the first major stage of a proposed east-west walk from Cape Egmont to East Cape. The track runs along the crest of the Matemateaonga Range and is extremely well graded and is rated easy to medium. On each day's walk there are vantage points that will give you impressive views of the rugged countryside or even a glimpse of the peaks of Tongariro National Park, but this is a forest walk and its overwhelming feature is lush bush in an unbroken, natural wilderness where the track itself and an occasional hut are the only artificial elements.

HISTORY

Although much of the present Matemateaonga Walkway was originally an important Maori route, the native tribes never permanently settled the Matemateaonga Range. On the other hand, the Maoris first settled the Wanganui River more than 600 years ago and quickly established a chain of villages up and down the river valley. Food was plentiful along the river and there were many steep bluffs and ridges that were suitable as sites for pa (fortified villages). These were needed bcause inter-tribal warfare was common in this well-populated region, as it was around Mt Egmont in the 1830s.

The Maori conflicts only ceased with the arrival of European missionaries in the 1840s. Reverend Richard Taylor of the Church of England may have been the most influential minister to travel up the Wanganui but numerous churches and missions were built along the banks of the river. The ministers persuaded the tribes to abandon their fortified pa and begin cultivating wheat, especially in the lower reaches of the river where several flour mills were established.

The Europeans brought the first steamer onto the river in 1891. It originally was used to ship passengers, mail and freight to the villages on the upper reaches of the river. The steamer, however, quickly created a thriving trade taking tourists up the river. It was a remarkable era in the history of the Wanganui River. By the early 1900s, there was a fleet of 12 riverboats that plied past the traditional Maori canoes with the largest riverboat capable of carrying 400 passengers. The tourists stayed at the Pipiriki House, a grand hotel that was known world-wide and which in 1905 registered a total of 12,000 guests.

The hum of human activity along the river was not felt elsewhere in the park. In the early 1900s it was decided to cut a road from Makahu to Raetihi along the Matemateaonga Range and surveying began for the Whakaihuwaka Rd in 1914. The post-war demand for primary products in the 1920s increased the interest in building a road so the area could be opened up for farming; however, the rugged land and thick bush defeated the attempt. A dray road three metres wide was built to a point just beyond Pouri Hut, where work was suspended. The Ammon brothers – the only people to try and farm the land – cleared 160 acres on the western side of the range but abandoned the project during the Depression of the 1930s.

In 1912, the Wanganui River Trust was set up and by 1980 had increased to 350 square km. During the same year a national park assessment began and Whanganui National Park, the country's 11th, was gazetted in December 1986.

CLIMATE

Whanganui has a climate that is mild with few extremes. Annual rainfall ranges from 1000 mm towards the coasts to 2500 mm on the high country inland. Frost and snow occur only occasionally on high ridges in winter, while early morning mist is common in summer and usually the forerunner of a fine day.

NATURAL HISTORY

Whanganui is predominantly covered by a broadleaf podocarp forest, but several species of beech are also present, including black beech which often crowns the crests of ridges. The central area of the park, its most isolated section, is also a noted haven for birdlife. The more commonly seen species are the fantail, tui, North Island robin, tomtit and wood pigeon. Brown kiwis are present throughout the park and may be more numerous here than any other region of the North Island.

MATEMATEAONGA WALKWAY

The 42-km Matemateaonga Walkway is one of two major tracks in Whanganui National Park and by far the most isolated and wilderness-bound trip in the North Island. The walkway follows old Maori tracks and a settler's dray road across the broken and thickly forested crest of the Matemateaonga Range. The track ranges in altitude from 400 to 730 metres. Surprisingly, the walk is easier than the rugged nature of the countryside suggests, as the old graded road line reduces the amount of steep climbing encountered.

Total walking time is around 15 hours and it can easily be done in two days by experienced trampers. Most people, however, allow four days for the trip as arranging transportation in and out of the track is complicated, even if you have a vehicle.

Access

The eastern end of the walkway is at Tieke Reach, an isolated bend on the Wanganui River, 25 km up river from Pipiriki. A half-hour's ride on board a commercial jet boat is the only way to get to this end of the track. The western end of the track is at Kohi Saddle, 60 km from Stratford by way of SH43 to Strathmore and then right on Brewer Rd to Mangaehu Rd.

Stratford is easily reached from either New Plymouth or Wanganui on a NZRRS bus. There are also a couple of private individuals who are now running trampers out to the end of Mangaehu Rd. Make arrangements with C Dreaver in Whangamomona (tel 856) or Francis Ford (tel (0663) 23-895). In 1988 Ford was charging $30 per trip to pick up trampers at the Kohi Saddle and drop them off in Stratford in time to meet the 1.45 pm bus to Wanganui. Keep in mind these services may change and the best way to discover what is available is to call the DOC regional office in Wanganui.

Pipiriki Jet Boat Tours (tel Raetihi (0658) 54-733) at RD 6, Pipiriki, Wanganui, will take parties of at least three people up the river from Pipiriki to the start of the track, or bring parties back to Pipiriki, for $34 per person. For an additional charge the company will also arrange mini-van transport from Wanganui to Pipiriki, or you can jump on the mail bus. John Hammond (tel (064) 54-635) drives the mail bus and stops at the youth hostel in Wanganui at 7 am Monday to Friday for Pipiriki. One-way fare is $8.

Wanganui is a good place to stage this trip even if you plan to start from the western end of the track.

Information & Maps
The DOC regional office (tel (064) 52-402) is located on the corner of Victoria and Dublin Streets in Wanganui and is open weekdays 8 am to 4.30 pm. The office has all the brochures, maps and books you will need as well as displays on the history of Wanganui River. If you need to rent some equipment contact Rivercity Tracks (tel (064) 58-395) at 418 Victoria St. They specialise in arranging canoe trips, the most popular way to the see the national park, but you can rent a sleeping bag or backpack for $5.50 a day from them.

Being a newly created national park, there is no recreational map of Whanganui yet though that will probably change in the future. Quad R20 of the Infomap 260 series covers the entire walkway, however. The three huts along the track are $7 a night and fees can be paid at the DOC

office in Wanganui or at the ranger's office in Pipiriki (tel Raetihi 54-631).

The Track
The Matemateaonga Walkway can be hiked in either direction. Departure from either end must be carefully coordinated and timed in order to meet pre-arranged jet boat pick-up on the river or vehicle transport at Kohi Saddle. This trip, which is rated easy to medium, will be described west to east. By walking in this direction you leave the greatest physical feature of the park, the Wanganui River, and the jet boat ride down it, as a highlight for the end.

Take good raingear on this tramp. The prevailing winds along the Matemateaonga Range are westerlies and they often bring heavy rainstorms to this upland region of the park. Annual rainfall along the range is 2500 mm a year. The track can be walked year round though occasionally in the winter and early spring snow may be encountered.

Stage 1: Kohi Saddle to Omaru Hut
Walking Time: two hours
Accommodation: Omaru Hut (12 bunks)
Kohi Saddle and the walkway are well signposted from Brewer Rd and are located at the end of Mangaehu Rd, 15 km east of Makahu. There is a large car park at the saddle and a large track sign that marks the beginning of the walkway. The track begins by climbing through regenerating bush along a spur towards the crest of the Matemateaonga Range. Within 30 minutes, however, you move into a thick forest of kamahi and tawa that will be the dominant feature for the rest of the trip.

The track eventually becomes a three-metre wide trail as it follows the remains of the original dray road that was cut all the way to Pouri Hut. You sidle the narrow valley of Tanawapiti Stream and follow it to the signposted junction with the track to Puniwhakau Road (three hours), reached 1½ hours from the car park. Up

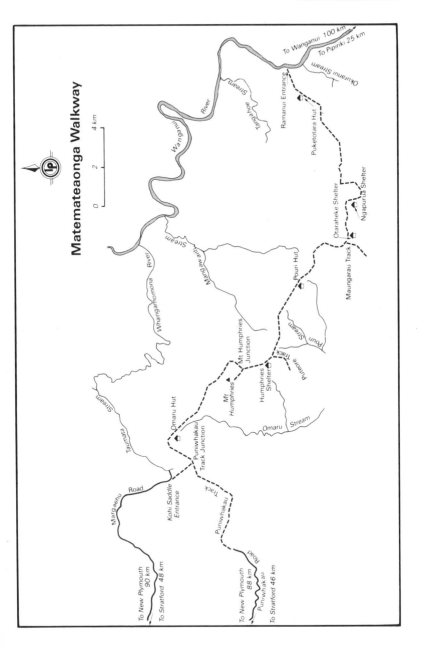

Matemateaonga Walkway

until 1983, this track served as the western access onto the walkway. At the junction the walkway has reached the crest of Matemateaonga Range and heads east (left) then north to descend steadily for 30 minutes. It levels out at a small saddle where Omaru Hut is located in a clearing. The hut is surrounded by forest but just behind it are some ladders that can be used to scramble down to pools near the source of the Omaru Stream.

Stage 2: Omaru Hut to Pouri Hut
Walking Time: 4½ hours
Accommodation: Humphries Shelter (two bunks); Pouri Hut (12 bunks)
The track heads southeast from the hut and continues in this direction for practically the rest of the journey. It follows the Matemateaonga Range on its southwest slopes where there will be few views through the thick forest of mostly kamahi and rata.

After two hours you cross over to the northern flank of the range and if the day is clear there is an occasional glimpse of the Tongariro National Park volcanoes through the trees. The track, muddy in places, continues through the forest until it reaches the junction to Mt Humphries, 3½ hours from the hut. The side track is signposted and climbs steeply for 100 metres over a km until it reaches the summit at 787 metres. The views are excellent, well worth the 1½ hour round-trip to the peak, as King Country is seen to the north and Mt Egmont to the west.

The walkway continues roughly southeast from the junction and in 30 minutes or so passes through Humphries Clearing where there is a two-bunk shelter, water tank and campsites. Just beyond the clearing the track arrives at the junction with Puteore Track, a route that heads southwest into the Waitotara forest. From here it is just another hour to Pouri Hut which is situated in a large clearing at the end of the dray road.

Stage 3: Pouri Hut to Puketotara Hut
Walking Time: seven hours
Accommodation: Otaraheke Shelter (two bunks); Ngapurua Shelter (two bunks); Puketotara Hut (12 bunks)
This is the longest leg of the trip, a distance of almost 20 km between huts, but it is an easy walk along a well-graded track and is broken up by a number of good views along the way. Also the forest here is the most pristine in the national park. Before taking off from Pouri Hut make sure your water bottle is full as often the only water source along the ridge will be the water tanks at Otaraheke and Ngapurua shelters.

The track remains on the crest of the ridge at an altitude of about 640 metres for most of the day with very little climbing involved. Within three hours the track passes a junction with the Maungarau Track, which heads south while the walkway continues southeast and quickly descends to a clearing where Otaraheke Shelter is located. If you're not ready to break for tea, it's less than an hour to Ngapurua Shelter in another clearing.

At Pipipi, 30 minutes beyond Ngapurua shelter, it's possible to see fossilised shells embedded in the track and at this point the ridge begins a northeast swing. The track continues in this direction and within 1½ hours the final descent towards Puketotara Hut begins. It takes an hour to descend the 200 metres to the ridge-top clearing where the hut is located. This is a fitting place for a final night on the walkway. Just beyond the hut there are sweeping views of New Zealand's second longest river while crowning the skyline to the east are the Tongariro volcanoes.

Stage 4: Puketotara Hut to Wanganui River
Walking Time: one hour
The final day is short, which is good if you are meeting a jet boat for the trip back to civilisation. The track quickly drops 100 metres to a lookout along the crest of a spur and then descends steeply again for

another 250 metres until you reach the large walkway sign above the sandy banks of the Wanganui River. It's about an hour down and 1½ hours up. Make sure you reach the river bank well before the jet boat does.

OTHER TRACKS
Mangapurua Track
Located in the Whanganui National Park, this track is a 40-km walk from Whakahoro up the Kaiwhakauka Valley, pass the Mangapurua Trig and down the Mangapurua Stream to the Wanganui River. Whakahoro can be reached by road from SH4 while the southern end of the track is accessible only by river transport, usually through a jet boat operator. The three-day trip is rated medium as the track follows an old road line. There is a 14-bunk hut at Whakahoro but trampers will need a tent for the rest of the trip. Highlight of the trip is crossing The Bridge to Nowhere.

Tararua State Forest Park

North of Wellington there is a place where the wind whips along the mountain sides and the fog creeps silently in the early morning. It's where gales sometimes blow through steep river gorges, snow falls lightly on sharp greywacke peaks or rain trickles down both sides of a ridge tightrope narrow.

Tararua State Forest Park and Wellington go hand and hand. For years it was almost an exclusive weekend retreat for hikers and tramping clubs from the windy city and surrounding area. Today trekkers from around the country are attracted to the park's broken terrain and the sheerness of its features that present a challenge to the most experienced backpackers. But being only 50 km north of Wellington, the Tararuas will always remain the quick escape for those who live in the Capital City.

The park is centred on the Tararua Range, which stretches for 80 km from Featherston north to the Manawatu Gorge, a natural gap that separates it from the Ruahine Range. The tallest peak is Mitre at 1571 metres, in the eastern central region, but there are many more close to that height throughout the park. Between the peaks there are ridges and spurs above the bushline that are renowned for being narrow, steep and exposed.

Tramping has had a long history in the park, resulting today in an extensive network of tracks and routes with more than 60 huts and shelters. Because of the capricious weather and the broken terrain, trampers who undertake the longer treks that go into the heart of the park should be both experienced and well prepared. Keep in mind that tracks in this park are not as well marked as in most of the national parks and it's easy to lose them. Once on the open ridge tops there are usually no signposts or poles marking the routes, only the occasional rock cairn.

The trips described in this section are less demanding than most routes through Tararua and thus undertaken by a greater number of trampers. The Mt Holdsworth Circuit is a two to three-day loop over the 1470-metre peak, beginning and ending at the Holdsworth Lodge, the eastern gateway to the park. The trip through Totara Flats also begins at the lodge and is perhaps the best tramp for less experienced trampers as it involves no open ridges or alpine areas at all. The three-day walk covers 40 km that involves climbing three low saddles.

HISTORY
The range was probably too rugged for any permanent Maori settlements but the native tribes did establish several routes through it to the West Coast. And it was Maori guides who lead J C Crawford to the

top of Mt Dennan in 1863 for the first recorded ascent in the range by a European. From the 1860s to late 1880s prospectors struggled over the ridges and peaks in search of gold but little was ever found.

Government surveyors were the next group to enter. They began charting the area in the late 1860s and by 1881 had produced a map of the range. From 1880, even though the region had yet to be fully explored, tramping clubs were formed to provide access into the wilderness. One of the earliest was the Greytown-Mt Hector Tourist Track Committee, which was active in cutting tracks and constructing huts. More tracks and huts came into existence during the next 30 years and by 1919 the Tararua Tramping Club, New Zealand's first such club, had been formed by enthusiastic Wellington-area trampers to promote trips into the Taraua Range.

But more than a place to tramp or search for gold, the importance of the Tararua range as the source of the town's water supply was recognised early by Wellington residents. In the late 1880s, much concern was expressed to the Department of Lands and Survey over forest fires, while Coleman Phillips, a Wairarapa station owner, urged the government in 1896 to reserve the area as a watershed. Today scars of past fires are barely visible except for the 1938 fire on Marchant Ridge. This blaze left a mass of black stumps that can still be seen today around Dobsons Hut.

When the State Forest Service was established in 1919, a move began to reserve a section of the Tararua Range. There was a proposal in 1936 to turn the area into a national park as a memorial for the Wellington Province centennial but it lost out to setting aside Petone Beach. Popularity of the range, especially among trampers, picked up after WW II and in 1952 another proposal to turn Tararua into a national park was submitted. This time the government chose a new system

of land management and reserved the area as New Zealand's first state forest park along with seven others in 1971.

Today Tararua State Forest Park covers 1166 square km of the range and is administered by DOC.

CLIMATE

Wind, fog and rain are the park's trademarks. The entire park is exposed to westerly winds that funnel through the gap between the North and the South Islands. The range is often the first thing the air streams hit and they hit it with full force, smacking against the high ridges and peaks. At times it's almost impossible to stand upright in the wind, especially with a pack on.

Calm afternoons and days of gentle breezes do occur during the summer, along with cloudless evenings that give way to glorious views of the sunset from the mountain tops. But, on average, the summits and peaks are fog bound two days out of three.

Rain averages around 1500 mm in the lowlands, 2500 mm in the foothills and often exceeds 5000 mm above the bushline. Snow may lie above 1200 metres three to four months of the year and a snow storm can be expected at any time in the alpine region.

It is the sudden storms – fierce and full of rain – that set the Tararuas apart from other parks in the country. They arrive with little warning and have dumped as much as 333 mm of rain in a single day. Trampers have to be prepared to spend an extra day in the hut if such storms blow in as they quickly reduce visibility in the uplands and cause rivers to flood dangerously in the lowlands.

NATURAL HISTORY

The sediments that would later form the Tararua Range were laid down in a deep sea basin some 200 million years ago. Earth movements along a series of faults that extended through the Upper Hutt Valley and the Wellington region resulted in a complicated uplifted mass of folded and faulted rock. This mass was subsequently eroded by wind, rain and ice, resulting in this rugged range that separates the rolling Wairarapa farm district from the West Coast.

There is a good variety of flora in the park and many plants reach their southern limits here. The forest is predominantly beech with scattered rimu and northern rata in the lowlands. Silver beech is the species along the bushline. Above 1200 metres the forest gives way to open alpine vegetation of tussock, snowgrass and scree.

MT HOLDSWORTH CIRCUIT

The Mt Holdsworth recreation area is a beautiful spot to begin any trip in the state forest park. Surrounded by rugged hills and graced by the rushing waters of Atiwhakatu Stream, this is a popular starting point for both trampers and day-users. There are no shops at Mt Holdsworth but any last minute items can be picked up at Masterton – the last town reached before turning off SH2 into the park.

Access

You can reach the town of Masterton either by NZRRS buses out of Wellington or the Wellington-Masterton train that departs from Wellington at 4 pm and 5.33 pm weekdays, 4.35 pm on Saturday and 5.20 pm Sunday.

Once in Masterton, the only way to Mt Holdsworth, if you don't have your own vehicle, is by taxi, which is expensive, or hitching. The recreation area is reached from SH2 by turning west onto Norfolk Rd, just south of Masterton. Norfolk leads into Mt Holdsworth Rd which ends at the recreation area, 15 km from SH2. The roads aren't quite the hitchhiker's nightmare they appear on the map. There are a number of sheep stations along the way and between the farmers and the day visitors to the park, you can usually pick up a ride if you're patient.

Places to Stay

You should plan on spending at least one night at Mt Holdsworth either at *Holdsworth Lodge*, a 32-bunk hut, or at a campsite. The roomy lodge has a hot point and a wood-burning stove but no gas rings. The charge is $7 a night for adults and $3 for children and in March it's a good practice to call ahead as school groups often reserve the entire hut. To camp in the grassy flats around the hut costs $3 a night.

Information & Maps

There is a year-round caretaker (tel Masterton 80-022) at Mt Holdsworth recreation area whose office serves as an information centre and is stocked with maps and brochures on the park. He also collects hut and campsite fees. The walk is covered on quad S26 of Infomap 260 series or you can obtain the recreation map to Tararua State Forest Park, NZMS 274/2, which includes all the tracks and huts within the range.

There is also a DOC district office (tel (059) 82-061) at Masterton in the Government Building on Chapel St that is open 8 am to 4.30 pm Monday to Friday.

The Track

The trip, rated medium to difficult, can be walked in either direction though most people tend to hike up to Powell Hut and return via Jumbo Hut.

Stage 1: Holdsworth Lodge to Powell Hut

Walking Time: three to four hours
Accommodation: Mountain House (20 bunks); Powell Hut (24 bunks)
The track begins as a wide gravel path, departing from the lodge, crossing Atiwhakatu Stream and immediately passing a track to Holdsworth Lookout (30 minutes one way). In another couple of hundred metres you come to the junction with Gentle Annie Track that heads west (left). The name is misleading as you depart the wide and level path and begin

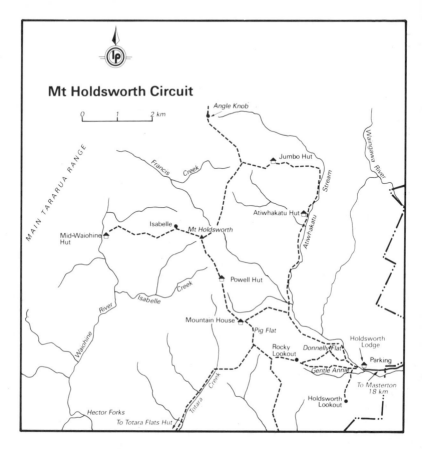

Mt Holdsworth Circuit

steeply climbing up a track criss-crossed with tree roots. The track soon swings left to sidle the ridge for a while before resuming its climb. This is an easy section to miss as the track is not well defined apart from a few orange blazes. More than one tramper has unknowingly continued up only to realise suddenly that he or she has strayed off course.

Eventually the track comes to a junction with the other route from Donnelly Flat just before it reaches Rocky Lookout, an hour's walk from the lodge. From the lookout there are good views of

Powell Hut and for those with sharp eyes even the trig on Mt Holdsworth can be seen. The track continues along the open ridge until it climbs to the signposted junction to the Carrington Ridge route. From here it's a short descent to a second signposted junction with one track heading south (left) to Totara Flat. The main track continues north (left) into Pig Flat and across it to a track to Mountain House. Along the way you pass a sidetrack that follows the ridge to the same hut.

Mountain House was built by the Wellington Tramping Club and is listed as holding 20 people. A two-hour walk from the lodge, the hut is badly run down with no mattresses and a shabby interior. Powell Hut is only another hour's walk and a much more pleasant place to spend the night.

The track begins a steep climb to Powell Hut but it is well cut and marked. It stays in bush the entire ascent except for the final 15 minutes when it emerges from the bushline into sub-alpine scrub. Powell Hut was built in 1981, replacing an older one that was constructed in 1939. It sleeps a dozen comfortably, 24 if necessary, and has gas rings and an excellent view from its verandah of the surrounding mountains and valleys. If the night is clear you can watch the lights of Masterton slowly appear after sunset.

Stage 2: Powell Hut to Jumbo Hut

Walking Time: 3½ to four hours

Accommodation: Jumbo Hut (10 bunks)

The rest of the climb to Mt Holdsworth is technically a route and there are very few markers or cairns. But the trip is so popular that a track has been worn to the peak and most of the way to Jumbo Hut. Before leaving Powell, fill your water bottle as there is little water along the ridge.

The track begins next to the hut and climbs steeply for 15 to 20 minutes until you reach a small knob with a battered sign on top. Below is Powell Hut, while above you the trig on Mt Holdsworth can clearly be seen in good weather and the route should be obvious. It takes another 30 to 45 minutes to follow the ridge that leads to the trig. The 1470-metre summit is a 210-metre climb from the hut but the views are excellent and include Mt Hector, the main Tararua Range and small towns along SH2.

Mt Holdsworth is the high point where three ridges come together. The track from Powell Hut follows one ridge and another ridge is marked by an obvious route that heads northwest at first then west towards Mid-Waiohine Hut (two

hours). Those heading to Jumbo Hut need to follow the ridge directly east that begins with a sharp descent. You almost have to backtrack a few steps from the trig to pick up a partially worn track that drops quickly to the ridge below.

Once on the ridge, it takes 1½ to two hours to reach Jumbo Hut. The route climbs a number of knobs. The first is marked with a rock cairn near the top indicating a route to Atiwhakatu Stream, while the second involves working around some rock outcrops on the way up and the third climb is towards Jumbo, which is really a pair of knobs with several small tarns between them. The knob to the south has a small cairn at one side and a track begins here which runs along the ridge that slopes east. By continuing on the main ridge you would reach Angle Knob in 40 minutes or so.

Within 15 to 20 minutes the route to Jumbo Hut comes to a spot on the ridge where it's possible to spot the hut far below by its bright orange roof (even the loo has an orange roof). From here it's a steady descent to the hut, reached in 30 minutes from Jumbo Peak. Built in 1982, the hut is another alpine shelter with an excellent view from its verandah. At night you can view the town lights of Masterton, Carterton and Greytown and, if you get up early on a clear morning, the sunrise is spectacular.

As it is less than a four-hour walk from one hut to the next, an enjoyable afternoon can be spent exploring the ridges to the north to view such prominent features as Broken Axe Pinnacle or the Three Kings.

Stage 3: Jumbo Hut to Holdsworth Lodge

Walking Time: five to six hours

Accommodation: Atiwhakatu Hut (10 bunks)

The day begins with a steady descent to the Atiwhakatu Stream. Just north of Jumbo Hut are three wooden stairs that mark the beginning of the track that quickly drops into the treeline and makes a steady descent of 600 metres along a ridge. The track is well worn and marked by orange discs and it takes about 1½ hours to reach the stream. Once within sight of the stream there is a track that heads south (right) along a river terrace but the junction sign is actually next to the stream bank.

Follow the track along the terrace. It will take almost an hour to reach Atiwhakatu Hut as the track is difficult to pick up especially when it swings inland to avoid steep embankments. When the water level is normal, a quicker route is simply to follow the stream, fording it when necessary. The hut was built in 1968 and is clean and well maintained though its location is less than inspiring. Just upstream from it there are some shaded river flats that are occasionally used for campsites.

The track continues from the hut – very level and distinguishable in some sections, hard to find in others. Again trampers often choose simply to follow the river itself but keep in mind there is a track the length of the Atiwhakatu on its true right (west) side. An hour from the hut, the track swings inland and climbs away from the stream before descending to ford Holdsworth Creek. It quickly crosses a second branch and then arrives at a signposted junction. The trail to the west (right) climbs steeply to Mountain House (one hour).

The main track is well formed at this point and runs along the stream, past a small gorge to Donnelly Flat, a km from the junction. Donnelly Flat is a traditional camping area in the park and only a km from the Holdsworth Lodge. Along the way the track passes two junctions that climb towards Rocky Lookout.

TOTARA FLATS TRACK

This is a three-day walk from Holdsworth Lodge down the Totara Flats in Lower Waiohine Valley and then along Tauherenikau Valley to exit at the Kaitoke car park, four km north of the Upper Hutt on SH2. It is a good trip for less experienced parties unsure about crossing open, unmarked alpine ridge routes. The walk traverses open river flats and three low saddles but never really climbs above the bushline.

Access

The northern end of the track is the Mt Holdsworth recreation area (see the Access section for the Mt Holdsworth Circuit). The southern end is a car park and day shelter located up Marchant Rd, a 20-minute walk from SH2. At the corner of Marchant Rd is a youth hostel.

NZRRS buses depart from the Kaitoke Post Office, 100 metres from the hostel, for Wellington on weekdays at 8.30 am, 1.45 pm and 5 pm; on Saturdays at 8.30 am and 1.45 pm; and on Sundays at 9.15 am. You can also catch the Hutt Valley suburban train which departs Upper Hutt, an easy hitch from the youth hostel, about every half-hour on weekdays and only a little less frequently on Saturday and Sunday. The one-way fare to Wellington is $4.20.

In recent years vandalism has become a problem at the Kaitoke car park and there are now posted signs warning you of this. For this reason, trampers with their own vehicles would probably be better off starting out from the Holdsworth Lodge where there is a caretaker to keep an eye on the car park.

Places to Stay

Conveniently located at the corner of Marchant Rd and SH2 is the *Kaitoke Youth Hostel* (tel (04) 267-251), a small and pleasant hostel that is run by a non-resident manager from the house next door. The cost per night for YHA members is $8.

At Holdsworth recreation area there is the *Holdsworth Lodge* and a campground (see Places to Stay for the Mt Holdsworth Circuit).

Maps & Information

The recreation map for Tararua State Forest Park, NZMS 274/2, is fine for this walk or else pick up quad S26 of Infomap 260 series. There is a visitor centre at Mt Holdsworth with a caretaker who collects the hut and campsite fees, and where maps and brochures on the park are sold.

There is also a DOC district office (tel (059) 82-061) at Masterton in the Government Building on Chapel St that is open from 8 am to 4.30 pm Monday to Friday.

The Track

This three-day walk, rated medium, is described from Holdsworth Lodge to Kaitoke.

Stage 1: Holdsworth Lodge to Totara Flats

Walking Time: four to five hours
Accommodation: New Totara Flats Hut (24 bunks)

The trek begins by climbing Gentle Annie Track past Rocky Lookout to the signposted junction to Totara Flats, a 1½ to two-hour walk from the Holdsworth Lodge (see Stage 1 for Mt Holdsworth Circuit for description). Take the track that heads south (left), which begins with a steep descent along a well-worn track – so worn in some places that it appears as a gully. The track drops 400 metres in 45 minutes to an hour before reaching the edge of Totara Creek which it immediately crosses, an easy ford most of the time. On the true right (west) side the track becomes a level walk, only occasionally climbing to avoid a steep embankment. Keep an eye out for discs and rock cairns to help you stay on the track.

In 2½ km (about an hour's walk) the track reaches the confluence of Totara Creek and the Waiohine River where it climbs to a cage and cable crossing. This is an interesting way to cross the river if you have never used one before. Once on the other side the track heads south and immediately comes to Old Totara Flats

Cable car crossing on Totara Flats Track

Hut, surrounded by bush and long since fallen into disrepair.

The track descends near the river and then emerges onto the grassy areas of Totara Flats. Across the flats and 20 minutes from the old hut the track leads around a stand of trees to the New Totara Flats Hut situated on the edge of the bushline. The hut is only a four to five-hour hike from the lodge but this is by far the most pleasantest place to stay along the route. It has a sweeping view of the flats and has not been vandalised like other huts closer to the track ends.

Stage 2: Totara Flats to Tutuwai Hut

Walking Time: 4½ to five hours
Accommodation: Cone Hut (12 bunks); Tutuwai Hut (20 bunks)

The flats are a scenic spot with a fine view of Mt Holdsworth to the north and the foothills you'll soon be climbing over to the south. An interesting side trip is to hike up the Waiohine River Gorge, best done through the water when the river is at a normal level. If the New Totara Flats Hut is too crowded there is always Sayers Hut, located on the opposite side of the river halfway down the flats. It's an older hut with an interesting interior but look carefully for it as it is easy to miss.

Totara Flats are two km long and easily the largest clearing in the Tararuas. Cut

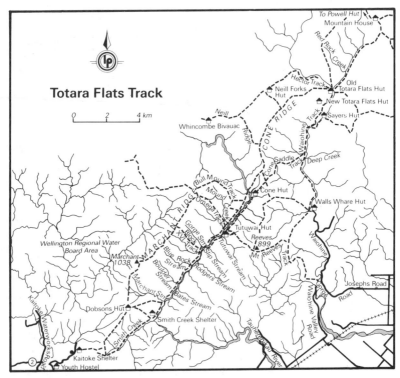

Totara Flats Track

0   2   4 km

across the grassy area to the bluff at the south end where a track ascends it to the right. You return to the river where the track immediately climbs another bluff. When water levels are normal, this extra climbing can be avoided by simply following the Waiohine and fording at appropriate places.

Within 1½ hours of the hut, the track swings inland and crosses Makaka Creek, identified by its sharp descent and the distinctive S-curve of the Waiohine at this point. You cross the stream several metres up from the river and then pass through a dry creek bed and climb a short distance up a steep embankment. On top of the embankment it swings right and climbs again where it quickly comes to the signposted junction with Cone Saddle

Track to the southwest (right) and the track to Walls Whare Hut which continues along the river south (left).

The Cone Saddle Track begins with a steep climb of 300 metres to a roundish knob and then sidles down to Clem Creek where the track reappears on the other side and is marked by a large rock cairn. It then makes a gentle ascent to the saddle where there is a major junction of four tracks with a signpost located high on a tree trunk. Head for Tauherenikau River along a track that descends 240 metres in 30 minutes to arrive at Cone Hut, a historic slab hut that is still used occasionally by those who like to reminisce about tramping in days gone by. For those with a tent, excellent campsites lie just a short way downriver.

Cone Hut on Totara Flats Track

The last segment of the day is a three km walk across grassy flats towards Tutuwai Hut. Most of the time the track remains just below the bushline but it is easy to make your own way across the flat for a much more scenic walk. Eventually a weathered sign that says 'Mt Reeves' points to a hut that sits on a terrace above the river, an hour's walk or less from Cone Hut. Tutuwai Hut has a nice view of the river flats but in 1988 was filled with graffiti and lacked mattresses.

Stage 3: Tutuwai Hut to Kaitoke

Walking Time: five to six hours
Accommodation: Smith's Creek Shelter
Twenty minutes after leaving the hut you arrive at the swingbridge across the Tauherenikau River. An all-weather track lies on the true right side of the river and will keep you away from a flooded Tauherenikau by ascending the bluffs that surround most sidestreams. There are some steep climbs around Gorge, Blue Rock and Boulder Streams in six km to Smith Creek but once on top the views of the valley are impressive. The alternative is to follow the river all the way to Smith Creek Shelter and in normal conditions this would involve following the flats most of the way with only an occasional ford to avoid the steep bluffs.

As the track nears Marchant Stream it swings inland. The stream is easily identified by the cable strung across it to assist trampers during flooded conditions. During normal water levels you can cross it without getting your boots wet. Smith Creek Shelter is reached in 10 to 15 minutes from the stream but it is strictly a shelter (no mattresses, table or water) and one in sad shape due to its close proximity to the road.

The track from the shelter, a popular day-walk, is a wide path most of the way that soon passes a track to Dobsons Hut. It crosses Smith Creek in an hour and then begins a steep climb to the saddle, reached after the track sidles the ridge the last few hundred metres. From the saddle there are impressive views of the sheep stations and farms in Hutt River Valley. From here it's a 30-minute descent to the car park with more views along the way as well as passing a signposted track to Dobsons and Alpha Huts.

From the car park, you pick up a metalled road and in 10 minutes arrive at Kaitoke Shelter, a three-sided building with benches inside. It takes another 20 minutes of walking to arrive at SH2 where the Kaitoke Youth Hostel is located.

OTHER TRACKS
Southern Crossing

This is the classic crossing of the Tararua Range, usually from near Otaki to Kaitoke, climbing along the way Mt Hector (1529 metres). It is an extremely challenging trip that should not be undertaken by trampers without extensive alpine experience. The route is usually walked in two to three days following Fields Track to Mt Hector, crossing Dress Circle and descending by way of Marchant Ridge.

SOUTH ISLAND

Nelson Region

Abel Tasman Coastal Park

In the early 1980s, the Abel Tasman Coastal Track, an easy walk around bays and along sandy beaches, was hardly known outside the Nelson region. Today overseas hikers arrive at the Nelson visitor centre almost daily, point to a page in their guidebook and speak the only two words they may know of the local language: 'Abel Tasman'!

It's remarkable the change that has taken place in less than a decade. This is now the most widely used recreational track in the country, easily surpassing such favourites as the Routeburn and Milford. Those tracks draw between 8000 and 9000 trampers a year. The Abel Tasman Coastal Track averages 2000 to 3000 a month, or more than 30,000 a year. The heavy use has changed it dramatically. It's still an easy and beautiful walk but now Bark Bay is something of a place for day-trippers instead of an isolated bay; the huts usually fill before noon each day; somebody is selling pizza and scones in the middle of the track; and the garbage left by visitors is such an immense problem that the park officials are considering flying it out by helicopter at a cost of $2000 a trip.

If you feel inexperienced as a tramper but desperately want to try one trek, the Coastal Track is perfect. It is not your typical New Zealand track as it is easier and better serviced than any other track in the country. It is a well-cut, well-graded and well-marked path that is almost impossible to lose, although I'm sure somebody has managed. It can be hiked in tennis shoes, there are no alpine sections to cross and there are always people just up the track in case a problem arises.

HISTORY

In 1642 Abel Tasman anchored his ships off Separation Point and that night four Maori canoes appeared but no contact was made. The next day eight Maori canoes put out and they eventually rammed a small boat that was ferrying between Tasman's two ships. Four crewmen were killed in the incident and the Dutch quickly departed.

Cook stopped briefly in 1770 but recorded little about the coastal area and nothing of its inhabitants. It wasn't until Dumont D'Urville sailed into the area in 1827 that Europeans met the Maoris on peaceful terms. The French navigator made friends with the villagers as he studied flora and wildlife and charted the bays and inlets of the northern coast.

European settlement of the area began in the early 1850s. The new settlers ranged from farmers and fishermen to shipwrights and loggers but by far the most enterprising was William Gibbs. The estate and mansion he built at Totaranui and the innovations he implemented there were ahead of their time. Visitors arrived at this isolated spot to find running water and porcelain sinks in every bedroom, hand-painted wallpaper in the main reception rooms, a glasshouse that provided grapes and other fruits, and smooth lawns and flower beds surrounding the two-storey home.

Gibbs also bought land between Wainui and Totaranui, including Separation Point and areas around Awaroa River. In 1870, he entered politics by becoming a member of the House of Representatives in Wellington before retiring in 1892 and moving to Nelson, leaving his glorious estate forever. Several other families purchased the home and farm and lived in high style from the late 1800s until the economic depression of the 1930s when the pastures reverted to ferns. In 1948, the estate passed to the Crown and was incorporated in the Abel Tasman National Park which had been formed in 1942 to mark the 300th anniversary of Tasman's ill-fated visit.

At Awaroa in 1855, Ambrose Ricketts, a shipbuilder from Nelson, purchased land, recognising the value of the site, with its fresh water, good timber and well-protected bay. He was quickly followed by other shipwrights. In just a few years, Awaroa was a settlement, with several boat-building ventures taking place. In 1875 the town produced, among other ships, a 50-ton topsail schooner, appropriately named *Awaroa*. Farming and logging also had an impact on the local economy but, as with other areas of the coast, once the main stands of timber were gone by the early 1900s the shipyards and the sawmills went also. Today only one farm remains in Awaroa, run by members of the Hadfield family, descendants of one of the original settlers.

CLIMATE

Clearly one of the main attractions of the park is not so much its bush, or even its beaches, but its exceptionally mild and sunny climate. Protection by mountain ranges from southerly and westerly winds gives Abel Tasman some of the best weather in New Zealand. Extreme temperatures are rare and in Totaranui the average daytime reading during January is 25° C. The coastal region averages 1800 mm of rain annually but over a span of only 125 days, resulting in long dry spells from summer through into autumn.

NATURAL HISTORY

Abel Tasman is the smallest New Zealand national park, covering 221 square km and rising to a maximum of only to 1134 metres at Mt Evans. Although it's small in size, the park contains a wealth of natural features including the well-known bays, lagoons and sparkling beaches that look like something out of the tropics and the not-so-well-known rugged interior that includes marble gorges and a spectacular system of caves. Along the coast, where it is moister and warmer, the park is characterised by a lush rainforest with vines, perching plants and tree ferns along with an abundance of the country's national plant, the silver fern. On the drier ridges and throughout much of the park's interior the bush is beech forest and all five New Zealand species of the tree are found here.

ABEL TASMAN COASTAL TRACK

There is a widespread belief among trampers that the Coastal Track ends at Totaranui. But the track is a 50-km walk between Marahau and a car park near Wainui Bay and those who continue north of Totaranui will discover the most dramatic viewing point (Separation Point), the least crowded hut (Whariwharangi Homestead) and some of the best beaches (Anapai and Mutton Cove) in the park. The entire trek takes only three to five days though you almost always meet a deeply tanned tramper who has been on the track for two weeks, sleeping on the beaches and living off mussels.

This track is unlike any other in the country. It has been best described as a relaxed walk, due to the easy nature of the track, the excellent weather and the beaches, lagoons and bays that make up most of the scenery. There is some climbing involved, but the coastal track is rated easy and can be attempted by most trampers, even those with little or no experience in the bush.

The preferred footwear is tennis shoes not hiking boots and occasionally you even see somebody heading down the track in sandals or flip-flops though park rangers strongly discourage it. You still need a backpack (shoulder bags just won't do), some raingear and a warm jersey or sweater as the nights can get chilly even in summer. But also pack along sunglasses, a swimsuit and a hat of some kind to keep the midday sun off the eyes and face. Make absolutely sure you have a bottle of insect lotion as well as suntan lotion.

Another piece of equipment that is very useful on this track is a tent. There are five huts, each an easy day's walk apart, but from November to February they fill rapidly. You must arrive at the next hut before noon to get a bunk or plan on sleeping on the floor or a bench. A tent, however, guarantees you shelter and allows you to sneak away from the crowds and spend a relatively peaceful evening at a small bay or beach.

There is one other way to enjoy the route and avoid much of the summer overcrowding. For those with sea touring kayaking experience, you can rent a kayak and paddle the intriguing coastline. Many of the small bays and beaches cannot be reached on foot, including Observation Beach which has developed campsites. Contact Ocean River Adventure Co (tel (0524) 88-823) in Motueka or Marlborough Sounds Adventure Company (tel (057) 42-534) in Picton to rent a kayak. Rates range from $20 to $25 a day for a single kayak.

Access

Nelson is the main departure point for the track but only one of several towns from which you can organise the trip.

Transport to and from the track has improved remarkably over the years. The southern end of the track is at a road's end (well signposted) just beyond Marahau and can be reached from Nelson either by Newmans Coachlines or Skyline Travel. Newmans (tel (054) 88-369) has a terminal at 220 Hardy St and offer a backpacker special. From mid-December to mid-February a bus departs Nelson at 8 am, passes through Marahau at 10.10 am and reaches Takaka at 11.45 am. At 3 pm it departs Takaka, returns to Marahau at 4.35 pm and arrives in Nelson at 6.45 pm. A round-trip ticket is $20, even if you are only going to Marahau. Skyline Travel (tel (054) 80-285) has an office at Achilles

Ave and its buses depart Nelson for Motueka at 8.30 am daily and again at 10.30 am on the weekdays. Its 8.30 am run continues on to Takaka and then Totaranui. The fare to Marahau is $8 way and $15 to Totaranui.

At Takaka, you can get a ride to Totaranui on a Skyline Travel bus that departs at 11 am daily and charges $8 one way. There is also Bickley Motors (tel (0524) 58-352, or 58-189 after hours) which charges $50 for groups of up to six trampers and $56 for larger parties. If you are leaving the track at Totaranui, the Skyline bus departs the ranger station at 1 pm daily and will take you to Motueka ($16.50) or all the way to Nelson ($22). Or you can call Bickley Motors if you're with a party of trampers. Keep in mind that there are no park huts or motor camp cabins at Totaranui.

A pleasant alternative means of reaching the track is on board a launch service. Abel Tasman National Park Enterprises (tel (0524) 87-801) leave Kaiteriteri daily from December 26 to March 31 at 9 am for a 6½-hour cruise up to Totaranui and back. Trampers can be put ashore or picked up at a number of locations including Torrent Bay ($13), Awaroa ($23), Tonga Bay ($16), Bark Bay ($16) and Totaranui ($23). The tour company does an excellent job and you get a view of the park from the sea that you miss along the track. The company also runs its own mini-van service to Nelson, picking up those with reserved passages at a number of locations in town, including the youth hostel.

It is unfortunate that there is no transport available from the Wainui car park. For those without a vehicle, there is no alternative at this point but to hike across the tidal flats of Wainui Bay at low tide and hitch a ride towards Clifton and Takaka from the traffic departing Totaranui. Many trampers turn around at the Whariwharangi Homestead Hut and return to Totaranui.

Places to Stay

There is a wide variety of accommodation in and around Nelson including the *Nelson Youth Hostel* (tel (054) 88-817) and *Tasman Towers* (tel (054) 87-950). These two are located opposite each other on Weka St and both offer beds for $13 a night. The only problem is securing a bed. It is best to book lodging in Nelson for both before and after you tramp the track. Arrive late afternoon in the summer without a reservation and you will have a tough time finding a reasonably priced place to stay.

At Motueka, only 20 km south of the national park, there is a *Youth Hostel* (tel (0524) 88-962). There is also *Takaka Summer Hostel* (tel (0524) 59-067) at Takaka as well as the *Shady Rest* (tel (0524) 58-133) at 141 Commercial St that offers backpacker-style accommodation for $12 a night.

Information & Maps

Information, maps and books on any track in the area can be obtained from the DOC regional office (tel (054) 69-335) in the Munro Building at 186 Bridge St, Nelson. The office is open weekdays 8 am to 4.30 pm. You can also get information on tracks at the Public Relations Office (tel (054) 82-304) at the corner of Trafalgar and Halifax Sts, open from 8.30 am to 5 pm weekdays.

Headquarters for Abel Tasman National Park (tel (0524) 58-026) is in Takaka at 1 Commercial St and the Waimea DOC district office (tel (0524) 89-117) is at the corner of Edward and High Sts in Motueka and is open from 9 am to 5 pm weekdays. Finally there is a ranger station (tel (0524) 88-083) and visitor centre (more of a waiting room for the bus) at Totaranui.

Huts along the coastal track are $4 a night and that's $4 even if you end up sleeping on the floor. There is usually a hut warden to collect the fees. For those with a tent, there are a number of developed campsites scattered along the track with fireplaces, pit toilets and reliable water sources. There is an honesty box near the sites and the fee is $1 per person per night. The developed sites are mentioned in the following description but in practice you can camp on any non-private bay or beach. If you plan to stay in a tent, keep in mind that in recent years possums have become a problem. The animals are so bold around trampers that they often end up stealing food. Keep all food and equipment in your tent.

The Abel Tasman National Park Map NZMS 183 is more than adequate for this trip or you can purchase quads N26 and N25 of Infomap 260 series.

The Track

The Coastal Track from Marahau to Wainui car park, a journey of approximately 50 km, can be walked in either direction and is rated easy. The following description begins at the southern end as this is still the popular direction to travel in.

The track can be hiked at any time of the year and the peak summer season runs from early November to February with January being the worst month. During this month Bark Bay looks more like a beach at a seaside resort than one in a national park as there could easily be a couple of hundred trampers with packs, as well as boaties with beer, families with picnics and retired couples who have just arrived for the afternoon. The best time for the Coastal Track may be from the end of February to May, when the crowds thin out but the weather is usually still pleasantly warm.

When walking the track take notice of the tides. The tidal differences in Abel Tasman are among the largest in the country, often between three and four metres. At many of the bays (Torrent, Tonga and Bark Bay) it's far easier to wait for low tide and then cross, than to follow the all-tidal track. At Awaroa Bay, you have no choice but to wait. Plan on crossing during the two hours before or after low tide. There are current tidal

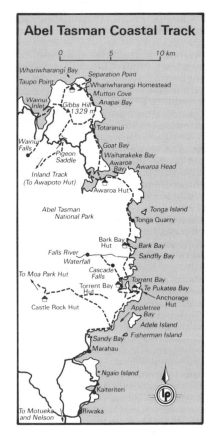

Abel Tasman Coastal Track

charts in all huts, or at a Nelson bookshop you can purchase a book of tide tables for $1. Usually only high tide is listed but by adding six hours you can determine low tide.

Stage 1: Marahau to Torrent Bay

Walking Time: four hours to Anchorage Beach; 4½ hours to Torrent Bay via tidal flats

Accommodation: Anchorage Hut (24 bunks); Torrent Bay Hut (eight bunks)

The track begins at a turnoff one km

outside of Marahau where there is a car park and information board. It crosses the Marahau estuary on an all-tide causeway, climbs gently to a clearing above Tinline Bay and then passes Tinline campsite, 2½ km from the start. Just beyond it there is another information board, marking one end of the Inland Track. The Coastal Track continues around dry ridges, hugging the coast and opening up to scenic views of Adele and Fisherman Islands and Coquille and Appletree Bays. Signposts indicate sidetracks leading down to the beaches and refreshing swims in the surf. There are also scenic campsites at Appletree.

After passing Yellow Point and its spur track, the track turns inland and climbs along ridges lined with silver fern. At the top, the trees thin out and the track splits off in two directions. The track to the east (right) descends quickly to Anchorage Beach, 30 minutes away, and then down the beach to Anchorage Hut, a very popular spot during the summer. Those with a tent can escape the crush of humanity usually found around the hut by following the short side track at the east end of the beach to a campsite on Te Pukatea Bay or backtracking to a developed campsite at Watering Cove.

The fork to the west (left) leads to the Torrent Bay Hut, which is much smaller than Anchorage Hut. This track descends towards the bay and then splits again with one track heading for the arm of the bay that separates Anchorage Beach from the Torrent Bay tidal flats. If the tide is right (or the water low enough), you can follow the short track down to the flats and across to the hut in 30 minutes or so. The other route, the all-tidal track, heads west and circles the bay through bush to arrive at the hut in 1½ hours.

There are more campsites beside Anchorage Hut and just north of Torrent Bay. They are very popular sites, however, which raises the question, why do people haul in a tent just to camp next to a crowded hut?

An interesting side trip from the all-tidal track is Cleopatra's Pool, a 15-minute walk one-way from the main track. The pool, fed by the Torrent River, is a metre deep and surrounded by smooth rocks that lend themselves quite well to sunbathing. The cold, fresh water is an invigorating change after a day in the sun and sea.

Stage 2: Torrent Bay to Bark Bay

Walking Time: three hours
Accommodation: Bark Bay Hut (28 bunks)

Those staying at Anchorage Hut, can head west (left) on the beach and take the short track over a headland to arrive at the Torrent Bay tidal flats, easily crossed at low tide. From Torrent Bay, you can cross the lagoon in front of the hut and south of the summer cottages and then turn left up the beach in front of the private residences for half a km before the track heads inland.

For those who want to see the various falls and pools of Tregidga Creek and Falls River, stay on the all-tidal track from Torrent Bay Hut and head northwest (left) at the sign posted junction. A good benched track follows Tregidga Creek to modest Cascade Falls after an hour walk. You can stay on the track and end up at the Falls River, 15 minutes downstream from its main falls. It's a boulder-hopping scramble with help from an occasional marker to see the impressive cascade.

Once the main track moves inland beyond the summer homes, it climbs 90 metres and sidles around Kilby Stream before reaching a low saddle where a side track takes you to the first of two lookout points that are passed. The Coastal Track descends to a swingbridge over Falls River where its possible to climb down to the river and scramble upstream for 20 minutes to view some waterfalls. From the swingbridge you climb to a spur track to the second lookout which can be followed for views of Bark Bay to the north and the coastline to the south. From the

junction it's a 20-minute descent to the bay.

Bark Bay is now a major access point for the track with a launch arriving at 11 am and then swinging back through at 2 pm, picking up trampers and day visitors at both times. The hut is the newest one on the track and situated on the edge of the lagoon, a short walk from the beach. Best camping is right on the sandy spit overlooking the bay but there are only a few sites here. More sites have been developed in the bush near the hut and all are $1 per person per night. If you don't mind the people, this bay is beautiful.

Stage 3: Bark Bay to Awaroa Bay

Walking Time: three hours
Accommodation: Awaroa Hut (24 bunks)

The track follows the spit and at its north end crosses the tidal lagoon, an easy ford most of the time except near high tide. The all-tidal track near the hut avoids this but takes an extra 20 to 30 minutes to hike. Entering the bush, the track begins an immediate ascent and in a km reaches the junction of the signposted Stony Hill Track that heads northwest (left) to Awaroa Hut. This track through the interior of the park (four hours) is no longer maintained. A challenging route, it should be tackled by experienced trampers only.

The Coastal Track departs the junction and winds over several inland ridges before dropping sharply to Tonga Quarry, 3½ km from Bark Bay. There is a metal plaque describing the quarry operations that took place here and several large and squarish stones near it. What remains of the wharf can be seen in the sand. The most interesting feature of the bay can only be reached at low tide, give or take 90 minutes on either side of it. Follow the rocky shore at the south end of the beach and in a 10-minute scramble you come to the sea arches of Arch Point, a set of impressive stone sculptures formed by the repeated pounding of the waves.

The track continues by climbing the

head that separates Tonga Quarry and Onetahuti Beach. It's a km walk until you come to a clearing overlooking the graceful curve of the long beach. This is another classic Abel Tasman beach and there are developed campsites at the south end for those who packed a tent. Near the sites a sign points the way to the freshwater pools, two delightful, deep pools that are cold and clear underneath a small waterfall – ideal after a day in the sun and sea.

The beach is more than a km long and you follow it to the north end where, on the other side of the lagoon, a track marked by an orange disc departs into the bush. Before heading up the track you can view some rare Maori carvings not usually seen in this part of the country. They are located in a pair of caves just beyond a small stream at the north end of Onetahuti Beach. The spiral, abstract carvings are in the left cave – the one not half-filled with water.

The Coastal Track departs the beach by gently climbing above the swamp formed by Richardson Stream to provide a nice overview of Tonga Roadstead. Eventually the track crosses Tonga Saddle at 260 metres and you get a quick glimpse of the beaches in the distance before descending into a private pasture that doubles as an airstrip.

Occasionally a sign here advertises pizza and scones, encouraging trampers to leave the track and head to a nearby farmhouse. After crossing the airstrip, the track comes to Venture Creek and crosses it, a difficult feat at high tide. From here orange signs lead you past private cottages on the beach and to Awaroa Hut on Awaroa Bay. The hut is large but lies on a small beach and has very little space around it for tents.

Stage 4: Awaroa Bay to Totaranui
Walking Time: 1½ to two hours
Accommodation: motor camp
There is no all-tidal track around Awaroa Bay, which has to be crossed within the

two hours before or after low tide. Check the tide chart in the hut then plan your day. You cross the bay directly in front of the hut where large orange discs lead you to Pound Creek. The track follows the creek until it passes a signposted junction to the Totaranui-Awaroa Rd and then quickly arrives at Waiharakeke Bay, another beautiful beach and a great spot for those with a tent as it is only 30 to 40 minutes north of Awaroa.

The track climbs away from the beach across a rocky ridge and then descends into Goat Bay. From here you are only 20 minutes from the ranger's station, the walk to which involves climbing over Skinner Point. Near the top is a scenic viewpoint complete with a pair of benches that provide an excellent overview of Totaranui.

The ranger station sells maps, books and brochures on the national park and has a few historical displays in one room. There is also a public phone outside which you can use to arrange transport or book a room in Nelson if you are planning to end your tramp. If not, remember, there is no hut here nor cabins at the motor camp. The next and final hut is at Whariwharangi Homestead, a 2½-hour walk from Totaranui.

Stage 5: Totaranui to Wainui Car Park
Walking Time: 4½ hours
Accommodation: Whariwharangi Homestead (15 bunks)
Follow the tree-lined avenue in front of the ranger station and turn north (right) at the intersection, passing the Education Centre. At the end of the road the Anapai Bay Track begins and quickly passes a junction with Headlands Track right before Kaikau Stream. Both tracks head for the bay but the left-hand fork is a more direct route that climbs a low saddle and then descends along a forested stream to Anapai Bay, a scenic beach that is split in two by unusual rock outcrops. Some older maps show a park hut here, but it's been gone since the early 1980s.

The Coastal Track continues up the sandy beach then heads inland and in two km reaches the first beach of Mutton Cove, where there are developed campsites. Just beyond it, before you reach the second beach, the old farm road to the Whariwharangi Homestead starts and goes inland from Mutton Cove. Halfway to the farmhouse, the vehicle track crosses a low saddle with a junction to Separation Point (30 minutes). The new side track heads east (right) directly to the granite headland that separates Tasman Bay from Golden Bay. The views are worth the extra walking to Separation Point as often the North Island is visible, along with the Farewell Spit to the northwest. The point is also a haul-out site for migrating fur seals but they are usually seen only in autumn and winter.

From the saddle the farm road continues through regenerated scrubland and two km from Mutton Cove reaches Whariwharangi Bay, another beautiful curved beach. The hut, a restored two-storey farmhouse that was last permanently occupied in 1926, is at the western end of the bay, half a km inland.

At this point trampers have three choices. You can make the final leg of the journey to the Wainui car park, a four-km walk along the farm road that takes about 1½ hours, and if it's within two hours of low tide, you can cross the estuary off Wainui Inlet and continue on to Clifton. Or by taking a track that leaves the farm road about halfway between the homestead and the car park you can return to Totaranui by way of Gibbs Hill. This is a waterless route. Or you can turn around at the homestead and backtrack to Totaranui (three hours) where there is public transportation out of the park.

OTHER TRACKS
Abel Tasman Inland Track

A network of tracks and five huts cut across the interior of the national park and offer a tramp that is a direct contrast to the Coastal Track. Here the walking is harder with few encounters with people and no beaches. Many begin this route at the end near Marahau and hike to Castle Rock or Moa Park the first day. You can reach Awapoto Hut the second day and from there it's a four-hour hike to Totaranui, Wainui car park or the Whariwharangi Homestead hut. The track, rated medium to difficult, can easily be combined with a portion of the Coastal Track for a five to six-day loop.

North-West Nelson State Forest Park

Situated due west of Abel Tasman National Park, North-West Nelson is the largest state forest park at 3765 square km. It includes the Tasman Mountains, a chain of steep and rugged ranges with a high point of Mt Snowden at 1856 metres.

The best known walk in North-West Nelson is the Heaphy Track. The four-day trek stretches 76 km from Aorere Valley near Collingwood to the West Coast north of Karamea. It is one of the most popular tracks in the country and averages between 3000 and 4000 trampers a year.

The Heaphy is just one walk, however, as the forest park contains more than 650 km of tracks. Included in this section are two others which are less used but many trampers feel are just as interesting.

The Wangapeka Track is a more challenging walk spanning 65 km from the West Coast, south of Karamea, to its eastern end on Rolling River. The five-day walk is often linked with the Heaphy by trampers who want to loop back towards Nelson. Perhaps the most remote walk in the park is Leslie/Karamea Track which traverses its namesake rivers for 48 km from the Tablelands area to the middle of the Wangapeka Track.

HISTORY

The legendary moa thrived in the north-west region of the South Island and this important food source led to the establishment of a significant Maori population. Maori occupation along the Heaphy River has been dated at least as early as the 16th century when they had already established a route up the river and over the Gouland Downs to Aorere. Cook sailed along the coast in 1770 but wrote little about it and it wasn't until the French explorer Dumont D'Urville sailed into the area in 1827 that the coast was thoroughly explored.

In 1846 Charles Heaphy, a draftsman for the New Zealand Company, and Thomas Brunner became the first Europeans to hike up the West Coast to the Heaphy River. During the four-month expedition on the coast the pair were told by their Maori guides of open tussock grasslands (Gouland Downs) and of the Maori route across the interior to Golden Bay. Neither Heaphy nor his partner, however, made it up the Heaphy River to search for the route. That was left to James MacKay and John Clark who completed the inland portion of the Heaphy Track in 1860 while searching for gold between Buller and Collingwood. A year later gold was discovered at Karamea, inspiring prospectors to struggle over the track to search for it.

The Wangapeka Valley was also opened up when gold was discovered in the Rolling, Wangapeka and Sherry rivers in the late 1850s. Dr Ferdinand von Hochstetter was believed to be the first to travel the entire route of the Wangapeka Track in 1860 when he carried out a geological exploration of the valley. A pack track was established from Nelson to the valley's eastern end for packhorses to carry supplies into the goldfields and the metal out.

The mining activity led to the establishment of Bush End though it was little more than a general store at the end of the cart road built in 1896 from Nelson.

The road, however, was never completed and stopped 16 km short of Rolling River. The biggest improvement in the route came in the early 1870s when surveyor John Rochfort cut a track along the Wangapeka River, over the saddle and down to the Karamea River.

Miners also had a hand in developing the Karamea River Track as they progressed from gold diggings at Mt Arthur Tablelands to the river. By 1878 a benched track had been formed and diggers were active in the Leslie, Crow and Roaring Lion rivers.

The Heaphy was improved when J B Saxon surveyed and graded the track in 1888 for the Collingwood County Council. The sought-after gold deposits were never found, however, and the use of both the Heaphy and the Wangapeka Tracks declined considerably in the early 1900s. But the unique flora of the Heaphy area attracted visiting scientists who, among other things, reported the track's quickly deteriorating condition and managed to push for setting aside Gouland Downs as a scenic reserve in 1915.

The Heaphy and Wangapeka tracks were improved dramatically in the late 1960s after the North-West Nelson State Forest Park was established in 1970 and the NZFS began to bench the routes and construct huts. But the real popularity of the Heaphy did not occur until plans for a road from Collingwood to Karamea were announced in the early 1970s. Conservationists, deeply concerned about the damage the road would do to the environment, especially to the nikau palms and other delicate flora, began an intensive campaign to stop the road and to increase the popularity of the the track. New plans for the controversial road pop up now and then but it's hard to believe that with 3000 to 4000 trampers on the Heaphy every year the authorities would ever go through with the project.

Top: Gushing geysers (IK)
Bottom: Bubbling mud pools (IK)

Top: Bark Bay, Abel Tasman Coastal Track (JD)
Bottom: Sea-sculptured arches, Abel Tasman Coastal Track (JD)

CLIMATE

All the rivers of the park are fed and occasionally flooded when the westerly winds that blow off the the Tasman Sea bring up to 5000 mm of rain to the mountainous areas. The rest of the park also experiences large doses of rain while frost is possible in the higher more exposed regions, particularly the Gouland Downs, in winter, spring, early summer and autumn. The Wangapeka Saddle, where a rain gauge is maintained, recorded more than 500 mm of rain in January 1964. The yearly average for most of the track is 2540 mm.

NATURAL HISTORY

The park stretches from the palm tree lined beaches of the Tasman Sea to an interior of alpine herbfields, rocky peaks and rolling flats of red tussock, the most spectacular being the Gouland Downs. About 85% of the park is bushclad with beech forest covering most of the hills while rimu and other podocarps are found on the lower slopes in the western fringes of the park. Here an understorey of broadleaf, ferns and toro, thick and dark green, create a jungle-like forest. Five major river systems drain the park; Aorere and Takaka into Golden Bay, Motueka into Tasman Bay and Karamea and Heaphy into the Tasman Sea.

HEAPHY TRACK

The popular Heaphy Track is an historic crossing from Golden Bay to the West Coast and offers one of the widest ranges of scenery of any walk in New Zealand. Along the 76-km track, you pass through native forest, across red tussock downs, along secluded river valleys to a beach lined by nikau palms. It's a considerably easier trek than any other extended tramp in North-West Nelson State Forest Park, having been upgraded in recent years. The four to five-day trip is rated easy to medium.

Access

The only major problem with the Heaphy in the past, besides some muddy sections of track, was transport to and from the track but that has improved. Collingwood is the staging area for the northeast end and can be reached from Nelson on Newmans Coachlines (tel (054) 88-369). Buses depart weekdays at 8 am and again from Monday to Saturday at 3 pm for Takaka. The second run connects with a Collingwood Bus Services (tel (0524) 48-188) coach which departs Takaka at 6.15 pm and arrives at the Collingwood Post Office in 30 minutes. A one-way fare on Newmans is $16; it's $4.40 for the ride with Collingwood Bus Services.

If you have to stay overnight there is Collingwood Motor Camp. Otherwise the journey continues with Collingwood Bus Services who run trampers out to Brown Hut, at the start of the track. The service is on request but there are usually a couple of runs daily during the summer. The fare is $10 per person with a minimum charge of $50.

At Brown Hut there is a phone and local calls are free. Trampers can ring up Collingwood Bus Services for the 35-km ride back to Collingwood. The company also runs a bus from Collingwood to Takaka at 7.10 am and again at 5.30 pm from Monday to Saturday. The morning run connects with a Newmans bus at 7.45 am which drops you off in Nelson at 10.20 am. The fares are the same as those for the reverse direction.

At the West Coast end of the track is a day shelter on the Kohaihai River, 15 km north of Karamea. There is also a phone there so trampers can ring up Karamea Motors (tel (028026) 757) which charges a flat rate of $25 per trip (four to five people) back to Karamea.

At Karamea, Cunningham Coaches (tel (0289) 7177) departs weekdays at 7.55 am for Westport. Newmans (tel (0289) 7709) can provide transport from Westport to Nelson with a bus departing at 11 am from Monday to Saturday. The one-way fare for Karamea to Westport is $13.75, and for Westport to Nelson it's $28.50. For those beginning the track on the West Coast, Cunningham Coaches depart Westport at 3 pm weekdays for Karamea.

Trampers with their own vehicles often use a short flight to return to the other end of the track. Heaphy Track Aerotaxi (tel (0524) 48-262) of Takaka provides flights between Karamea and the Bainham airstrip, located five km from Brown Hut. In Karamea, bookings can be made at the Karamea Tavern (tel (028926) 800) for the 25-minute flight.

Places to Stay
In Collingwood there is the *Collingwood Motor Camp* (tel (0524) 48-149) which offers tent sites and cabins. For accommodation in Nelson and Takaka see the Places to Stay for the Abel Tasman Coastal Track.

Information & Maps
Information on the track or the state forest park can be obtained at the DOC district office (tel (0524) 58-026) in Takaka on 1 Commercial St or at a forest service office in Karamea (tel (028926) 852). Hut fees are $4 and are paid on an honesty system at each hut. Best map for the track is the recreation map for Heaphy Track, NZMS 245.

The Track
The following description is for walking the Heaphy Track from east to west, which means that most of the climbing is done on the first day and the scenic beach walk is saved for the last day. For those trekking west to east, more time should be allowed for ascending the spur from Lewis Hut to Mackay Hut and less for the walk from Perry Saddle to Brown Hut. The walk is rated easy to medium and features 12 huts and shelters along the way, and four of the huts (Perry Saddle, Saxon, Mackay and Lewis) have gas rings.

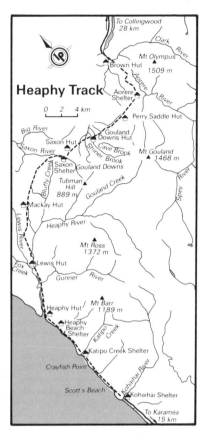

Heaphy Track

Stage 1: Brown Hut to Perry Saddle
Walking Time: five to six hours
Accommodation: Brown Hut (20 bunks); Aorere Shelter; Perry Saddle Hut (40 bunks)
Brown Hut, a km from the car park at Walsh Creek, is at the northeast end of the Heaphy Track. The hut was built to enable trampers to get an early start on the first leg of the journey – the steep climb to Perry Saddle. The hut has 20 bunks but during summer there are often quite a few people sleeping on the floor.

From the hut, the track follows the

Brown River for 180 metres and then crosses it on a swingbridge. From the other side the long climb to Gouland Downs begins as the track, often marked with poles, ascends steeply through a grass slope before moving into bush. Beech forest with scattered podocarps and rata now surround the track as it begins a gradual climb along monotonous switchbacks.

At one point the track passes the junction with the Shakespeare Flat Track that descends south (left) to the Aorere River. Just beyond the junction is a well-marked shortcut that climbs the ridge in a more direct route, a tough climb that saves about 30 minutes. The main track swings uphill in a wide loop and in about three hours, or after a seven-km climb, from Brown Hut, reaches Aorere Shelter. In another two km of climbing, the track takes a sharp turn and begins a gentle ascent past Flanagan's Corner, the high point of the trip at 915 metres.

From here it's another 40 minutes or two km before the track breaks out of the bush into the open tussock and patches of beech found on Perry Saddle. The hut is nearby and features 40 bunks, gas rings and, at 880 metres, views of the Anatoki Ridge across Aorere Valley.

Stage 2: Perry Saddle to Saxon Hut

Walking Time: 3½ to four hours
Accommodation: Gouland Downs Hut (14 bunks); Saxon Hut (16 bunks)
A well-formed track quickly reaches Perry Saddle and descends through low scrub on the true left (south) bank of Perry Creek. Within three km the track opens up to the bowl of the Gouland Downs, a wide expanse of rolling tussock that is broken up by patches of stunted silver beech and pygmy pine. Sheep Creek at the edge of the downs is crossed and from there the track continues over the red tussock until it reaches a swingbridge over Cave Brook, a stream within sight of Gouland Downs Hut. Although the hut is small and old, built in 1932, it has a nice atmosphere

about it and there are some interesting caves to explore behind it. Most trampers push on, however, as it is only a two-hour walk from Perry Saddle.

The track leaves the terrace of bush in which the hut is located and emerges onto the red-tussock downs again. You cross a footbridge over Shiner Brook and then a second one over Big River. Within a km you cross a third bridge over Weka Creek and at this point you follow the fringe of scrub and bush along the northern part of the downs. Right before crossing the Saxon River the track arrives at Saxon Hut, the newest one on the Heaphy and a five-km walk from Gouland Downs Hut. The hut has 16 bunks and gas rings. You can also cross the Saxon River and in two km reach Saxon Shelter.

Stage 3: Saxon Hut to Mackay Hut

Walking Time: three hours
Accommodations: Saxon Shelter; Mackay Hut (40 bunks)
The track begins with three km of level trekking as it passes Saxon Shelter and crosses Blue Duck Creek where it swings north. Eventually you enter the bush and begin one final climb, regaining all the height lost in the descent to Gouland Downs. From here the first glimpse of the Tasman Sea and the mouth of the Heaphy River may be possible.

From this high point you move steadily downhill through numerous grass clearings. You cross several small bridges and boardwalks over boggy patches as you skirt the southern edge of Mackay Downs. Seven km after entering the downs the track reaches Mackay Hut, situated on the fringe of dense bush. From the hut the views of the Tasman Sea and Gunner Downs are excellent, the sunsets on a clear evening extraordinary. The mouth of the Heaphy is only 10 km to the west.

Stage 4: Mackay Hut to Heaphy Hut

Walking Time: six to seven hours
Accommodation: Lewis Hut (40 bunks); Heaphy Hut (40 bunks)

The track leaves the hut and descends into bush as it works steadily downhill toward the West Coast. Gradually the valley closes in and through the dense bush only an occasional glimpse of the Heaphy River is possible. There is a pleasant change in flora when the first nikau palms appear 100 metres above the junction of the Lewis and Heaphy Rivers. The long 12-km descent is over at Lewis Hut which is situated at the confluence of the two rivers and is only 15 metres above sea level. The hut, a three to four-hour walk from Mackay Hut, has gas rings and 40 bunks.

The track heads southeast after the hut and in half a km crosses the Heaphy on a swingbridge to follow the true left (south) bank where it remains until it reaches the Tasman Sea. Limestone bluffs keep the track close to the river and in three km it arrives at a swingbridge over Gunner Creek. The track crosses a large river flat just after the bridge over Murray Creek and from there cuts through one last stand of bush. From the bush and hills, the track unexpectedly opens up to Heaphy Hut and the lagoon beyond, an eight-km walk from Lewis Hut.

Next to the new hut is the old Heaphy Hut with six bunks. Both are only a short hike from the beach on the Tasman Sea.

After struggling over much of the track, many trampers are inclined to spend a full day at Heaphy Hut. There is good swimming in the lagoon but the Tasman Sea should be avoided due to vicious undertows. To the north, it's possible to cross the Heaphy River at low tide and scramble through a hole in Heaphy Bluff to see if any remains of a wrecked Japanese squid boat are still around. There is also a blazed route over the bluff which leads up the coast for about an hour and from which fur seals occasionally can be seen. To the south, the McNabb Track begins from the hut and climbs the Bellbird Ridge to Gunner Downs, a full day side trip.

Stage 5: Heaphy Hut to Kohaihai River
Walking Time: five hours

Unquestionably one of the most beautiful walks in the South Island, the final segment of the Heaphy works its way south along the West Coast, always near the pounding Tasman Sea. The track itself remains along the edge of the bush most the way but in many places well-worn paths show where trampers have decided to forego the track and hike along the edge of the beach.

The track departs from the huts, passes a small pond and reaches the sand and surf of the Tasman Sea at Heaphy Beach Shelter. It continues south along the coast, crosses a bridge over Wekakura Creek and then a second bridge over Katipo Creek, generally regarded as the halfway point in the 15-km journey from the mouth of the Heaphy River to the end of the road. Just on the other side of the stream is Katipo Creek Shelter.

Still further south the track crosses a third bridge over Swan Burn and arrives at Scott's Camp where the first signs of civilisation, in the form of private huts, greet trampers. Scott's Camp is a grassy clearing near a good beach, about two km from the end of the track. From the clearing, the track makes a gentle climb over a saddle and descends to the Kohaihai River where a long swing bridge brings you to a shelter, a public phone and the end of the road.

WANGAPEKA TRACK

The Wangapeka Track is a 60-km journey along the southern border of North-West Nelson State Forest Park. There are no beaches or pounding surf on this tramp, but to many backpackers its rugged scenery and isolation make it a pleasanter alternative to hiking the Heaphy. The track could be walked in four days though due to its rough terrain most trampers tend to spread it over five or six days.

Access
The one thing the Wangapeka does share

with the Heaphy is the need for complicated transport arrangements to reach its remote beginning and end. The track can be hiked in either direction but it is described here from east to west as this means easier climbs over the saddles. The east end is Rolling Junction Shelter, reached by following a 4WD track for nine km from the ranger's house on Wangapeka River Rd, after fording the Dart River. You reach the ranger's house via the towns of Tapawera, Tadmor and Matariki.

Wadsworth Motors (tel (054) 34-248) departs Nelson from the Montgomery Square from Monday to Friday at 1.15 pm, Monday, Wednesday and Friday at 4 pm and Sundays at 8 pm for Tapawera, where the bus line is based. The one-way fare is $4.20. The company also has a five-seater taxi that it runs out to Rolling Junction Hut for $50 per trip. You can also catch a Newmans Coachlines bus (tel (054) 88-369) which departs Nelson at 8.45 am and 9.35 am and stops at Kohatu, a town just south of Tapawera. From here the Wadsworth taxi ride to the beginning of the track is $55.

The western end of the track is a shelter at the end of Little Wanganui River Rd, 25 km south of Karamea. It's three km down the road to a public phone and a total of eight km to SH67 where it's possible to flag down a bus. Cunningham Coaches (tel (0289) 7177) out of Westport passes the Little Wanganui River Rd junction on weekdays at 5.05 pm for Karamea and at 9.30 am, heading south for Westport. The one-way fare in either direction is $13.75 and the 9.30 am run connects with a Newmans bus to Nelson, at $28.50 a ticket.

If walking west to east, just reverse the transportation arrangements but keep in mind it's a nine km walk out to the ranger's house where you can phone for the Wadsworth taxi service. Trampers who are moving directly from the Heaphy to the Wangapeka, using the two tracks to form a semi-circular route back towards Nelson, can arrange for a ride between Kohaihai Stream and Little Wanganui River Rd junction through Karamea Motors (tel (028926) 757). The cost for the 47-km trip is a flat rate of $55.

Maps

The best map to use is Wangapeka Track NZMS 318, the recreational guide, that sells for $5.50. Otherwise you have to purchase three quads of Infomap 260 series.

The Track

The Wangapeka Track is rated medium to difficult and is described here from east to west. For those who choose to walk it in the opposite direction more time is needed from Little Wanganui Hut to Little Wanganui Saddle and less time for the downhill segment from Stag Flat to the Taipo Bridge.

Stage 1: Rolling River to Kings Creek Hut

Walking Time: 3½ hours

Accommodation: Kings Creek Hut (30 bunks); Kings Hut (eight bunks)

Near the Rolling Junction Hut a swingbridge crosses the river and the track begins on the south bank of the Wangapeka. The track is well defined and the Wangapeka River is almost always in sight as the track winds in and out river flats of grass and low scrub. Three hours (nine km) from the start of the track it passes Kiwi Shelter, an old bivouac, and then crosses a footbridge to the north bank of the Wangapeka, passing a signposted junction. The side track crosses Kiwi Stream and heads north (right) up the valley to the six-bunk Kiwi Saddle Hut (3½ hours).

In another 30 minutes along the main track Kings Creek Hut is reached via a short side track to a grass bank above the Wangapeka Forks. The hut, one of the newer ones on the track, is a 3½-hour walk from Rolling River. Another 10 minutes up the river is Kings Hut, more an historic site than a place to spend a night. The old miner's hut was built in 1935 by Cecil

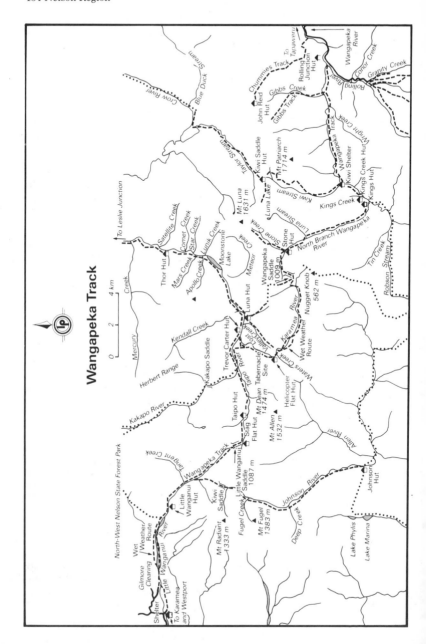

Wangapeka Track

King who prospected in the area right up to the 1970s.

Stage 2: Kings Creek Hut to Helicopter Flat Hut

Walking Time: six to seven hours
Accommodation: Stone Hut (six bunks); Helicopter Flat Hut (six bunks)

Just beyond Kings Hut, the track passes the junction of the North and South Branches of the Wangapeka. It continues along the true left side of the North Branch and gently climbs towards Stone Hut, passing a deep gorge along the way. It's a 2½-hour (8½-km) walk to the six-bunk hut and 30 minutes before reaching it the track fords Luna Stream and then immediately crosses a footbridge to the true right side of the North Branch. The hut, which features an open fireplace, is located on a grassy flat opposite the Stone Creek Junction.

The track departs Stone Hut in bush but soon comes to an open landslip, the result of the 1929 Murchison earthquake. You follow the Wangapeka River to its source and then ascend sharply to the Wangapeka Saddle along a well-marked route until it reaches the pass at 1009 metres. At the bushclad top there is a signposted junction with one track heading northwest (right) along a steep and rough route to Luna Hut and another east (left) to a clearing on Nugget Knob. The main track heads southwest (straight) towards Helicopter Flat Hut.

Following the main track you descend gently from the saddle, ford Chime Creek and then begin a more rapid descent along the infant Karamea River into the valley. You cross several side streams before working steadily along the true left (south) bank of the Karamea. The river is crossed twice not far from Helicopter Flat Hut and the fords are easy if the weather is good. If not, then there is an alternative all-weather route marked with poles that continues along the true left bank. The flood route takes an extra 20 minutes to walk. Both rejoin on the south bank and

continue on to Helicopter Flat Hut, just past Waters Creek. If the creek is flooded, there is a wirewalk 30 metres upstream.

Helicopter Flat Hut has only six bunks and there is little camping in the area. Trampers should avoid pitching their tent on the helicopter pad.

Stage 3: Helicopter Flat Hut to Taipo Hut

Walking Time: 3½ to four hours
Accommodation: Taipo Hut (10 bunks)

This is a short three to four-hour day to one of the newest huts on the track. Trampers can continue past Taipo Hut and in another 1½ hours reach Stag Flat Hut, but this is a smaller and older hut with poor campsites around it.

From Helicopter Hut, the track follows the Karamea and sidles up through bush and away from the river. The track gradually climbs to Tabernacle Lookout while the Karamea carves its way through a deep and rugged gorge far below. The Tabernacle is the site of an old shelter, now long gone, that was built by Jonathan Brough when he was surveying the original track. The views from up here are excellent as you can see most of the Karamea Valley below.

The track leaves the lookout and after 100 metres passes a side track that descends sharply east (right) to Luna Hut. The main track heads west (left) and descends steeply for 30 minutes to a swingbridge over Taipo River. On the true left (north) side of the river there is a junction with one track heading east (right) to Trevor Carter Hut. It is possible during fair weather to hike both the track to Luna Hut from the Tabernacle and this track as a round trip, adding two hours to the day's walk.

The main track is well marked as it heads west (left) and follows the north bank of the Taipo. You climb gently for several km and in two hours from the bridge reach Taipo Hut. This is a pleasant 10-bunk hut and there are also good campsites below the nearby helicopter pad.

Stage 4: Taipo Hut to Little Wanganui Hut
Walking Time: 5½ to six hours
Accommodation: Stag Flat Hut (four bunks); Little Wanganui Hut (16 bunks)
Soon after leaving the hut you cross a bridge over Pannikin Creek and then begin a steady climb towards Stag Flats, a tussock area of many creeks, much bog and mud. The climb steepens just before you reach the flats. The track cuts across the flats for 200 metres to reach Stag Flat Hut. After leaving the hut you enter the bush and begin another steep climb towards Little Wanganui Saddle, an open clearing of snowgrass. The climb is a knee-bender but the views from the top are the best of the trip. The saddle is the highest point of the track at 1087 metres and overlooks the Little Wanganui River to the West Coast or the Taipo River to the east.

The track descends past Saddle Lakes and drops steeply to the valley floor, re-entering bush and finally crossing a bridge over Little Wanganui River to its true right (north) side. The track fords Tangent and McHarrie Creeks and then climbs steeply around the Little Wanganui Gorge, returning to the river just above the bridge to Little Wanganui Hut. If the water level is normal, you can skip the track around the gorge and follow the river, fording it when necessary. Little Wanganui Hut is located in a clearing on the true left (south) side of the river.

Stage 5: Little Wanganui Hut to Road's End
Walking Time: two to 2½ hours
The final seven km of the journey to the end of the Little Wanganui Road is usually considered to be a pleasant stroll by most trampers, as the hardest walking of the trip is over. Return across the bridge and follow the track on the true right (north) side of the river. In about 20 minutes, you come to the junction with the all-weather track.

The river route is well marked and criss-crosses the Little Wanganui four times as

it follows the river flats to the road's end. If the water level is normal, you won't have difficulty crossing the fords, which are clearly signposted. Two km before the end of the track you pass through Gilmore's Clearing.

If the river is in flood, follow the all-weather track along the true right (north) side of the river all the way to the end. This track eventually joins an old logging road which after a km merges with Little Wanganui River Rd. The all-weather route is a longer walk as there is considerably more climbing involved.

LESLIE-KARAMEA TRACK
The best tramp into the wilderness heart of North-West Nelson State Forest Park is the Leslie-Karamea Track. Two river routes are combined for a 48-km trek but the actual journey is closer to 86 km as hikers need to walk in and out of each end of the track. With this in mind, plan on five to seven days for the trip, which will include tramping half of the Wangapeka Track.

The highlights of the track are interesting huts and campsites, a little gold-mining history along the way and the best trout fishing in the park. Just about every river in the state forest park has fish but the Karamea River is renowned for its stocks of brown trout, especially where the Leslie empties into it at Karamea Bend. If departing east along the Wangapeka Track, the Wangapeka River is also worth exploring with a rod in hand.

Access
This trip is described from north to south and there two ways to reach the northern end of the track. The start of the Leslie River Track is technically near the high point of Tableland on Starvation Point though many people consider Salisbury Lodge as its beginning. You can reach it by way of Cobb Valley, which lies 110 km northwest of Nelson and 28 km from the Upper Takaka turn-off. Follow the service road along the valley to Mutton Hut near

the end of Cobb Reservoir and then take the track to Balloon Hut. Tableland Peak is an 11½-km (four-hour) hike.

The most popular approach is from the Graham Valley on the west bank of the Motueka River. From SH61 cross the river on bridges at Woodstock, Ngatimoti or Pangatotara to the West Bank Rd and then follow AA signs to the valley. It's an hour's drive from Nelson and then four km up Graham Valley to the end of the road. You then tramp Flora Track over the saddle of the same name and follow signposts toward Salisbury Lodge (30 bunks). The 14-km tramp takes about four hours.

The southern end of the Karamea Track ends at the Wangapeka Track and trampers can depart either eastwards or westwards. Although the Karamea end is 12 km closer, most trampers need two additional days to cover the final segment of the journey regardless of which way they head down the Wangapeka Track. Transport can be arranged at either end of the Wangapeka Track (see preceding Wangapeka Track section) but it's rough going to reach the car parks at the northern end if you don't have a vehicle. Large parties can rent a taxi from Collingwood Bus Service in Takaka to Cobb Valley (see Heaphy Track section) or Wadsworth Motors in Tapawera for Graham Valley (see Wangapeka Track section). All others just have to hoof it or hitch it.

Maps

There is no recreational map for the track. Most of the route is covered by quad M27 of the Infomap 260 series.

The Track

The following track is rated medium and begins from Salisbury Lodge in the Tablelands. It is described here going from north to south.

Stage 1: Salisbury Lodge to Karamea Bend

Walking Time: five hours

Accommodations: Leslie Clearing Hut (six bunks); Leslie Hut (20 bunks)

Just beyond the lodge is a signpost that points the way to the Leslie River. The track begins as a series of snow poles and a well-worn path that cuts through the snowgrass to a junction on Tableland Plateau (altitude 1280 metres). The track to the west heads off to Balloon Hut (30 minutes) and the Cobb Valley while the main track descends south into the bush. The drop is steep as the benched track descends 360 metres over a span of four km. Within an hour, after passing two good lookout points, you arrive at Splugeons Rock. The campsite is a platform that was blasted out of rock and makes for an unusual but very scenic place to spend the night.

The benched track, really an old pack track, continues to descend, emerges on the true left side of Peel Stream and in three km from Splugeons Rock arrives at the confluence of the stream and Leslie River. A swingbridge crosses the Leslie here to its true left bank. If you want a little adventure, you can hike up the Leslie from the bridge and reach Arthur Creek in 30 minutes. Along the creek there are dozens of flume pipes that were hauled in by pack horse as this was one of the best gold-bearing streams of the Tablelands.

Downstream from the bridge, the track moves through beech forest and along flats and terraces and in five km reaches Leslie Flats, the site of a six-bunk hut. Leslie Clearing Hut is only the latest in a succession of shelters that have been built on the flats since the 1890s. It is an easy four km from the hut to Karamea Bend, where the Leslie and Karamea Rivers meet and the river swings towards the West Coast. There are two huts here but only one, the newer Leslie Hut, which was built in 1975, is open to the public. The river here is a noted spot for trout fishing.

Stage 2: Karamea Bend to Venus Hut

Walking Time: 4½ to five hours

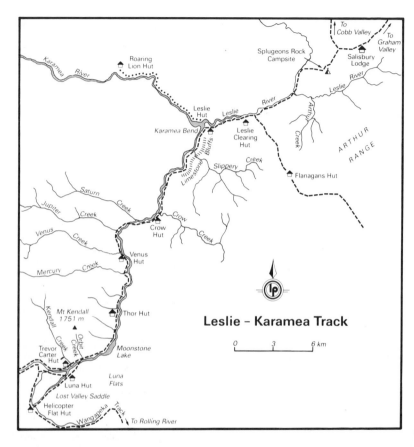

Leslie – Karamea Track

0   3   6 km

Accommodation: Crow Hut (six bunks); Venus Hut (six bunks)

The track heads upriver along the Karamea working its way through forest and over terraces and across flats. The track fords several creeks, the first being Slippery Creek, before arriving at Crow River where there is a swingbridge. It is a 10-km (about a three-hour) walk through mostly beech forest to Crow Hut, just across the bridge. When the water levels are normal or low, a pleasant alternative (if you don't mind wet boots) is to hike up the river bed. Fords are numerous and range from knee to waist deep but the scenery is much more interesting.

The track follows the Karamea for the first 30 minutes from Crow Hut, passing pools that will tempt any angler carrying a rod and reel. You then swing away from the river and climb a terrace for the next km before you emerge from the forest to a view of the Karamea swingbridge below, which is located just upriver from Saturn Creek. Once across the bridge the track remains on the true left side of the river for the rest of the trip.

You remain mostly on the bush terraces

as you continue towards the Karamea headwaters, crossing bridges over Jupiter and Venus Creeks. It's about three km from the Karamea Bridge to Venus Hut, located on the south side of Venus Creek.

Stage 3: Venus Hut to Trevor Carter Hut
Walking Time: 5½ to six hours
Accommodation: Thor Hut (four bunks); Lunar Hut (four bunks); Trevor Carter Hut (four bunks)
From Venus Hut you continue to work your way through bushclad terraces and in two km (30 minutes) from Venus Hut you come to the footbridge over Mercury Creek. The next major side stream is Atlas Creek, 2½ km further up the Karamea River. From here the track hugs bluffs above the river until it crosses Thor Creek and arrives at Thor Hut situated on a small promontory overlooking the Karamea River.

Beyond the hut you begin climbing undulating bush slopes, where it's easy to get tangled up in the tree roots that crisscross the track, and you ford more creeks. Mars Creek is about 30 minutes from Thor Hut and Apollo Creek 10 minutes beyond that. The debris and loose rocks that surround the track are the result of a 1929 earthquake that was also responsible for the rubble that spilled down Apollo Creek and the dam that formed Moonstone Lake. The lake extends three km beyond Apollo Creek and the track skirts it by climbing onto the bushclad slopes above it.

Beyond the head of Moonstone, the track returns to the Karamea at Orbit Creek where the valley opens up and the trek becomes an easy walk along river beaches. In normal conditions, the Karamea is easily forded here and by crossing it just beyond Orbit Creek, you can pick up a track on the true right (east) bank that is cut across scrub and tussock flats to Luna Hut (30 minutes).

An all-weather track continues up the true left (west) side of the Karamea,

crosses bush flats and in three km from Orbit Creek fords Kendall Creek. The best ford of the braided stream is near its mouth. The track continues from Kendall, rounds the scrub end of a spur opposite Luna Hut and then enters rubble flats to arrive at Trevor Carter Hut in 30 minutes.

Stage 4: Trevor Carter Hut to Wangapeka Track
Walking Time: 45 minutes to 1½ hours
There are several ways to reach Wangapeka Track. The most recently built track departs from Trevor Carter Hut and follows the true left (north) side of the Karamea and its tributary, the Taipo, before reaching the Wangapeka Track at the Taipo Bridge. The 2½-km walk takes about 45 minutes and from here it takes about another two hours to reach either Taipo Hut to the west or Helicopter Flat Hut to the east. From Luna Hut, you can also follow a track on the true right (south) side of the Karamea and cross the river below Saxon Falls. There is a short spur track to the impressive falls but the main track climbs steeply for 15 to 20 minutes before it reaches the Wangapeka Track at Tabernacle Lookout. Helicopter Flat Hut is less than an hour away to the east.

A poorly marked track also departs up the rubble banks of Lost Valley Creek and in 2½ km the track emerges at a bushclad saddle with a large tarn. From here it's a quick drop back to the Karamea near Helicopter Flat Hut.

Once on the Wangapeka Track, most trampers need an additional two days to reach either the western or eastern start of the track (see preceding section on the Wangapeka Track).

OTHER TRACKS
Tableland Walk
This is a two to three-day trip in North-West Nelson State Forest Park from Flora Track car park in the Graham Valley to Mytton Hut at the end of the service road along the Cobb Reservoir (see the Access

section of the Leslie-Karamea Track). The 25-km trek could include nights spent at Flora Hut, Salisbury Lodge, Balloon Hut or a number of unusual shelters passed along the way. The trip is rated easy to medium and includes good views along the way.

Mt Richmond State Forest Park

Often overlooked by trampers rushing off to Abel Tasman, Mt Richmond State Forest Park is right on Nelson's doorstep. The Richmond Range forms the backbone of the 1820 square km park which covers most of the steep bushclad mountains between Nelson and Blenheim as well as reaching north to the Tasman Sea near Whangamoa Head.

There are 250 km of cut and marked tracks in the park with 34 huts scattered along them. The tracks range from challenging alpine routes to easy overnight walks suitable for families.

As they are so close the climate of the park is very similar to that of the North-West Nelson State Forest Park.

HISTORY
Within the Mt Richmond area, Maoris had a number of argillite quarries where they mined the very hard mudstone for weapons and tools.

NATURAL HISTORY
All of the park is covered by forest with the exception of small patches of alpine tussock around the summits of taller peaks. The bush includes all five species of beech as well as the podocarp species of rimu, miro, totara, matai and kahikatea.

PELORUS RIVER TRACK
One of the more popular walks in the Richmond State Forest Park, especially with trout fishermen, is the Pelorus River

Track, a three-day walk of 40 km that begins just 27 km from Nelson.

Access
The east end of the track is 13 km up the Pelorus River Valley from the Pelorus Bridge Scenic Reserve along the Pelorus River and Maugatapu Roads. The reserve, which has a campground, a caravan park with five cabins, a small store and tearooms, is eight km south of Rai Valley on the SH6 (Nelson-Blenheim Hwy).

The western end of the track is at the Hacket picnic area at the confluence of Hacket Creek and Roding River in Aniseed Valley. The picnic area is 27 km from Nelson and reached by driving 1½ km south of Hope on SH6 and turning off onto the Aniseed Valley Rd.

Pelorus Bridge can be reached by either a Newmans or Delta Coachlines bus from Blenheim or Nelson. Newmans has a depot on Grove Rd in Blenheim (tel (057) 85-189) and departs for Nelson 11.45 am Monday to Saturday and 2.20 pm daily, passing the campground within 1½ hours. From Nelson, Newmans (tel (054) 88-369) departs for Blenheim at 8.30 am daily. Delta has a depot in Blenheim (tel (057) 81-408) and departs for Nelson at 7.50 am on weekdays and 2.15 pm daily. Delta (tel (054) 80-285) departs Nelson from Skyline Travel on Achilles Ave at 5.05 pm daily and at 11 am on weekdays for Blenheim, passing the Pelorus River Bridge a little over an hour later.

If you are coming from the North Island and are eager to begin tramping right away, Newmans and Delta buses greet all ferries at Picton and can provide an immediate ride straight to the Pelorus River Bridge. Getting up to the start of the track, however, is a different story as hitching or walking the 13 km is the only way for those without a vehicle. But you can walk from the bridge to the first hut in a day without too much difficulty, as it is only a 2½ to three-hour walk from the start of the track.

You can get to the Roding River Rd on a Newmans bus which departs Nelson at 8.45 am from Monday to Friday and passes the turn-off about 30 to 40 minutes later. From there it is 11 km up the metalled road to the picnic area and the start of the track. If you have a vehicle, you can easily turn the trip into a loop by hiking the side tracks to the new 20-bunk Rocks Hut. The best loop, the one with the least amount of backtracking, would be to begin at the western end of the track and hike into Roebuck Hut, a six-hour walk. The second day would be another six-hour walk to Rocks Hut. The third day would be a tramp to Totara Saddle and a return to Hacket picnic area.

This area receives some of the highest rainfall in the park and when there are extremely heavy falls of rain some of the streams might become impassable. But if you wait for a day, or sometimes for just a few hours, the water levels will drop enough for you to ford safely. Flooding should not be problem on the Pelorus River as the track runs high above it. Where the track does cross the river there are cable swingbridges.

Information & Maps

Books, maps, brochures and information on the tracks in the area can be obtained at the DOC offices. In Blenheim, there is a DOC district office (tel (057) 88-099) located at 68 Seymour St. The DOC regional office (tel (054) 69-335) is in the Munro Building at 186 Bridge St, Nelson. There is also a DOC district office (tel (057) 37-582) in Picton in the Picton Harbour Board Building on Auckland St. Or for those who just jumped off the ferry, a short walk from the terminal is the Picton visitor centre which has good information on most tracks in the area. Two quads, O27 and O28, of the Infomap 260 series are needed to cover the park, or you can purchase NZMS 274/6, the recreational map to Mt Richmond State Forest Park with a scale of 1:100,000.

The Track

This trip is a one-way, three-day walk from Pelorus Valley over the Bryant Range into Aniseed Valley and is rated medium. For those who want to turn the tramp into a loop, you can set off from Totara Saddle and hike northeast to

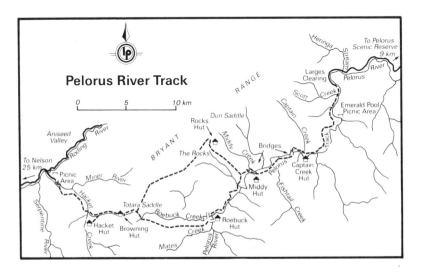

Pelorus River Track

Rocks Hut and then southeast back to Middy Hut on the Pelorus River.

Stage 1: Road's End to Middy Hut
Walking Time: 4½ to five hours
Accommodation: Captain Creek Hut (six bunks); Middy Hut (six bunks)
You start the walk at the signpost in the car park at the end of Maungatapu Rd. The track begins in private property and follows the edge of the Pelorus River on the true left (west) side. It's two km to the boundary of the state forest park and along the way you cross a swingbridge over Scott Creek.

Once inside the park, you continue through native forest and begin to follow the valley above the river only quickly to drop in 15 minutes to a terrace above a sandy river beach and a deep pool. This is the Emerald Pool picnic area, a popular day-walk as the track up to this point is well benched and graded. The pool is an excellent swimming hole and marks the start of the good trout waters up the Pelorus.

The track leaves the river and climbs 100 metres from the terrace through a thick forest of rimu, tawa, matai and beech. It arrives at the crest of the main ridge, then levels out until it reaches the edge of a bluff. The track follows the bluff for an hour and then begins descending towards the river, gradually at first but ending with a series of switchbacks. Before reaching the Pelorus, the track swings to the west and crosses a bushclad terrace to reach the short side track to Captain Creek Hut located in a clearing well above the river, a three-hour walk from the car park.

From here the main track continues to follow the valley above the river and soon crosses Captain Creek. In another five minutes, the track crosses a swingbridge to the true right side of the Pelorus with some accessible pools down below for anglers to fish. Once on the true right bank the track begins to climb steeply and then follows the narrow valley through open forest and sparse scrub before crossing a swingbridge over Fishtail Stream upstream from its confluence with the Pelorus.

The track continues to stray from the river as it crosses an undulating terrace where the Pelorus has formed a loop in the valley. You walk along this forested terrace the rest of the way to Middy Hut, an hour's walk from Fishtail Stream or two hours beyond Captain Creek Hut, a distance of six km. Middy Hut is opposite the junction of the Middy Creek and Pelorus River and has screened windows as the area is a haven for mosquitoes.

Stage 2: Middy Hut to Browning Hut
Walking Time: seven hours
Accommodation: Roebuck Hut (six bunks); Browning Hut (six bunks)
A swingbridge crosses the Pelorus to its true left side 150 metres upriver from Middy Hut and from here you climb sharply up to the junction with a track that continues up the spur to Rocks Hut (three hours). The main track heads southwest (left), working its way to a saddle above Rocks Creek, and then drops steeply to a creek some distance upstream from the Pelorus River. After crossing the creek, the walk becomes more difficult for the next four km as the track goes through thick forest where you are constantly stepping over protruding tree roots. The forest is lush here, a mixture of beech and rimu along with tree ferns, pepper trees and an understorey of ferns.

Eventually the track descends to Roebuck Creek and a pair of swingbridges. The first crosses the creek and the second one extends over the Pelorus River, 200 metres upriver. Roebuck Hut is situated on an open terrace directly across from the junction of the creek and the Pelorus, which at normal water levels can be forded here.

From Middy to Roebuck Hut is a three-hour walk. To continue on, you return to the swingbridge over the Pelorus River where, on the true left side, the track immediately climbs the ridge that separates Roebuck and Mates Creeks. It's a steep 30-minute climb for the first 150 metres and then the track ascends at a more gradual rate to Totara Saddle at 670 metres. Before reaching the saddle the track works its way across the slopes of the Roebuck Catchment. There are some good views of Mt Fell and Mt Richmond from here.

At the saddle is the junction with a new track to Rocks Hut (20-bunks) which goes northwards (four hours). The main track heads west (left) and quickly descends, dropping 180 metres in a km, over an open slip and through a beech forest before reaching Browning Hut. This hut is in a large open area on the edge of the bush and can sleep six, with mattresses placed on a communal shelf.

Stage 3: Browning Hut to Hacket Picnic Area

Walking Time: two hours
Accommodation: Hacket Hut (six bunks)
The track immediately crosses to the true right (north) side of Browning Stream. For the next hour it's an easy 2½-km walk through forest and across several eroded stream beds. During high water, you follow a steep alternative track around these streams and slips. Just before crossing the Browning for the last time, a side track is passed that leads south (left) over a low saddle to Hacket Hut. The main track crosses the stream five minutes later near the confluence with Hacket Creek which is immediately forded as well.

Once on the other side of the Hacket, you are on private farmland but you do not need permission to walk through it. An easy, benched track follows the creek on its true left (west) side for an hour almost to the Hacket picnic area. A km before the area, the track crosses a swingbridge over Hacket Creek and then joins a 4WD track to a wooden footbridge over the Roding River right off Roding River Rd.

OTHER TRACKS
Wakamarina Track

This is an easy two-day walk in Mt Richmond State Forest Park that originally was an old gold-miner's track. The track begins at the end of the Wakamarina Rd, 19 km from Canvastown, and crosses the Richmond Range to a car park off Kiwi Rd in Onamalutu Valley. Most people undertake it as an easy weekend trip with a two-hour walk the first day to Devil's Creek Hut (six bunks) and a five-hour walk the second day.

Mt Richmond Alpine Route

This is a three to four-day circuit, rated difficult, along the exposed alpine ridges and peaks of Mt Richmond State Forest Park. There are numerous entry and departure points but the trip generally involves leaving Mt Starveall and crossing Slaty Peak, Pelorus Tops, Ada Flat and Old Man to reach Mt Rintoul. The easy way to hike the route is from Lee Valley Rd. A new track that was marked from Bishops Cap to the Lee River allows trampers to walk a loop of the Alpine Route, starting from Waterfall Creek Hut (six bunks) in the valley.

Nydia Track

Part of the New Zealand Walkway system, this track is a two-day tramp in the Marlborough Sounds. The southern end of the track is at the end of Kaiuma Bay Rd, 32 km north of Havelock, and the northern end is at Duncan Bay, 21 km northeast of Rai Valley. Both ends can be reached by road but you can also arrange to be dropped off and picked up by the mailboat through Glenmore Cruises (tel 42-276) in Havelock.

The track was completed in 1979 and most of it passes over old bridle paths through pastures, virgin forest and scrubland. The walk is rated easy but does climb over two low saddles. There are no huts on this track but there is excellent camping along isolated Nydia Bay. For more information call the ranger in Havelock (tel 42-159).

Nelson Lakes National Park

Some say the Southern Alps end in Nelson Lakes National Park. The great mountain range of New Zealand rises out of Fiordland and forms a crest along the South Island until it diminishes in height and importance here, merging with the ranges to the north in North-West Nelson and Mt Richmond State Forest Parks.

The reason most visitors come to the park, located 103 km southwest of Blenheim, is to see the two lakes Rotoiti and Rotoroa. But once beyond the shores of the lakes, trampers soon discover that this is a land of long valleys and numerous passes, with alpine routes that are not nearly as demanding as those found elsewhere in the Southern Alps.

Long to climb a mountain and stroll along a ridge? Nelson Lakes is a good place to begin adventuring above the bushline. It is a true mountain region and many of the peaks rise well above 2000 metres, but the tracks are well benched and the routes well marked with cairns or snow poles.

There are a number of round trips possible in the park with most requiring four to six days of walking and climbing of one, if not two passes. The most popular one, and the best round trip for trampers with limited experience on alpine routes, is the Travers-Sabine Circuit. The five to six-day walk begins and ends at St Arnaud and includes tramping over Travers Saddle and the Mt Robert skifield. These are not easy climbs but they are well marked and within the capabilities of most fit trampers during good summer weather. More remote and more challenging is the D'Urville Valley Track described here as a round trip out of

Rotoroa utilising Sabine Valley and Moss Pass. Without a water-taxi drop-off, this is usually a seven-day journey for most trampers which could end at Rotoroa or St Arnaud.

The Nelson Lakes National Park is connected to St James Walkway by two challenging alpine routes. Experienced trampers can hike from Bobs Hut on the West Branch of the Matakitaki River over a very challenging route to Ada Pass Hut on the walkway in a single day. Or it's possible to hike from Blue Lake Hut on the West Branch of the Sabine River over Waiau Pass into Waiau River Valley. This trip requires two to three days and joins the walkway near the privately owned Ada Homestead.

HISTORY
The Maoris believed that a giant named Rakaihaitu created the lakes after arriving at Nelson in his Uruao canoe. Exploring the land to the south by foot, he picked up a digging stick in upper Buller Valley and gouged out Rotoiti and Rotoroa before continuing down the Southern Alps and creating other lakes.

Though they rarely settled here, the native tribes did pass through this region as there were important routes that crossed it between the Tasman Sea and Canterbury. The lakes were an important place for travelling parties to stop as the waters were rich in easily obtained eels and mussels.

The arrival of Europeans and the gun altered the patterns of Maori warfare. Armed with muskets, the Ngataiapa tribe from the North Island, led by Te Rauparaha, began settling the South Island. They massacred the people of the settlements around Marlborough Sounds and the region north of Nelson. Many of the survivors fled but later returned as the Maori guides who led the first Europeans into the area.

One such guide was with John Cotterell and a companion when they pushed their way through more than 300 km of trackless terrain to the Tophouse and the Clarence River in 1842. The following January, the party retraced their journey and continued on to become the first Europeans to see to Lake Rotoiti. Cotterell, a Quaker who refused to carry a gun, died later that year at the hands of Te Rauparaha at the Wairau tragedy of 1843 when the Maori tribe killed a party of 22 settlers from Nelson who had come to arrest their chiefs.

Three years later another Maori guide, named Kehu, from the Ngatitumatakokiri tribe lead William Fox, Charles Heaphy and Thomas Brunner on one of the best recorded exploration trips in the South Island. With Heaphy keeping the diary and Fox using a paintbrush to record the scenery, the group struggled down to Rotoiti under the weight of 34-kilogram packs. From the lake, Kehu took the party up the Howard River where they 'discovered' Lake Rotoroa. By September of 1846, Fox had sent a pair of surveyors to cut a track towards Rotoiti and by 1848 a Scot named George McRae had driven 400 sheep from his Rotoiti run to Nelson.

More exploration of the area followed with Christopher Mailing and William Thomas Locke Travers becoming the first Europeans to explore the Lewis Pass area. Later Travers returned to take up his own pastoral station in the upper Waiau. The year before the Nelson Provincial Council had commissioned German naturalist and geologist Julius Von Haast to explore the areas south and west of their city and to keep a sharp eye out for traces of gold. Haast did find a little evidence of the metal around Rotoiti and Rotoroa but it was clearly the beauty of the area that overwhelmed him. 'I am sure that the time is not far distant when this spot will become the favourite . . . resort of those whose means and leisure will permit them to admire picturesque and magnificent scenery,' he commented in what was to prove an astute prophecy.

The gold discoveries on the Buller River and in the West Coast region quickly overshadowed the small amount Haast had discovered near the Nelson lakes. The excitement of the finds gave the push needed to replace the rough track with a dray road from Nelson to the West Coast goldfields, which touched the fringes of the national park along the way. It was continually upgraded; the present highway, SH6, was in place by the 1920s. Within the next 10 years a road to the edge of Lake Rotoiti was built and by the 1930s the automobile was a common sight and St Arnaud was born. Initially it was a collection of boatsheds on the water, huts in the hills and one store.

Nelson Lakes was gazetted in 1956 as a national park of 575 square km; It was brought to its present size in 1982 with the addition of 430 square km which included the Spencer Mountains.

CLIMATE
Nelson Lakes possesses a surprisingly moderate climate for an alpine region. Ranges to the west, south and east protect the park, preventing many storms from arriving and reducing the intensity of others. As rain is brought by the prevailing westerlies that blow in from the Tasman Sea, the western side of the park is wettest. In the popular tramping area of Travers Valley in the east of the park, the average rainfall is only around 2000 mm a year and at the park headquarters at Rotoiti it drops to 1600 mm.

You still have to be prepared for the sudden weather changes that alpine areas are noted for. A warm, clear day on a mountain pass can become a whiteout with heavy rain or even a blizzard in no time at all. Above the bushline, snow may fall throughout the year and all trampers should carry warm, preferably woollen, clothing and windproof and waterproof gear. But overall the climate of the park is pleasantly moderate and characterised in summer by long spells of settled or even clear weather.

NATURAL HISTORY

The landscape of Nelson Lakes was created by the Alpine Fault and carved by glaciers. The fault, where the edges of two great plates in the earth's crust meet, is the major geological feature of the South Island and splits the park almost in half. Movement along the fault created the mountainous terrain millions of years ago but it was the glaciers of the last ice age that gouged out the land to give the mountains their present shape. Long valleys were carved out by the glaciers which, when they reached the area of St Arnaud, were finally stopped by the hard rock of Black Hill. They forked at this point, pushing up a rocky moraine in the middle. When the glaciers finally retreated some 8000 years ago, deep holes at the head of Travers and Gowan Valleys were left that filled with the water of the melting ice and turned into Lake Rotoiti and Lake Rotoroa. The moraine that surrounds Black Hill became the peninsula that today separates West Bay from Kerr Bay in Lake Rotoiti.

The forests of Nelson Lakes are predominantly of beech and all five New Zealand species can be found here. In the lower valleys, where the conditions are warmer and more fertile, you'll find red and silver beech interspersed with such species as kamahi, toetoe, kowhai and southern rata, with its mass of bright flowers when in bloom. In high altitude habitats, above 1050 metres, or where there are poor soils in the lowlands, mountain and silver beech become dominant.

As for birdlife, the dominant species is the kea, though in character rather than numbers. Dark olive-green with scarlet feathers under the wings, which can be seen in flight, this inquisitive alpine parrot is often encountered above the bushline. It's not uncommon to take a rest stop in the mountains and soon have four or five perch themselves on large boulders around you.

Another animal of the park many visitors would like to encounter – those who are anglers anyhow – is the trout. Brown trout are the predominant species caught and can be found in both lakes as well as in the main rivers of Travers, D'Urville, Sabine, Matakitaki and Buller. Both spinners and flies are used to entice the fish.

TRAVERS-SABINE CIRCUIT

Unquestionably the most accessible and popular tramping area of Nelson Lakes is Travers Valley. It provides easy tramping along good tracks with excellent alpine scenery, plenty of huts and a bridge just about every time you need to cross a stream. Though Nelson Lakes does not receive a fraction of the number of visitors and trampers that Abel Tasman or many of the well-known tracks in Fiordland do, Travers Valley is the one area in the park

Waterfall on Travers-Sabine Circuit
in Nelson Lakes NP

where the huts will be filled on public holidays and long weekends.

When it is combined with the route in the Sabine Valley next to it, via the Travers Saddle, the trip is ideal for those new to the alpine areas of New Zealand. The passes above the bushline are well marked but are still part of a 'route' where you wander through meadows, up steep scree slopes and along a winding ridge. The views on a clear day – and there are usually many such days in February – are of spectacular alpine scenery.

Access

The departure point for this trip is St Arnaud, the site of the park headquarters near the north end of Lake Rotoiti. The village can be reached from Greymouth or Picton on a Delta Coachlines bus. Trampers who take the 10 am ferry from Wellington can catch the Delta bus at the Picton terminal. It departs daily at 1.35 pm for Greymouth, arriving at St Arnaud at 3.35 pm. You can purchase the ticket at the Mt Cook office at the Picton Terminal or at Travel Stop (tel (057) 37-925) at 27 High St. A one-way fare to St Arnaud is $19. In the other direction, a Delta bus departs Greymouth from the Revingtons Hotel (tel (027) 7055) on Taunui St daily at 7.30 am, arriving at St Arnaud at 11 am before continuing on to Picton.

You can also reach the park headquarters from Nelson. A Wadsworths Motors (tel (054) 81-462) bus leaves Nelson from Montgomery Square on Monday, Wednesday and Friday at 4 pm and arrives at St Arnaud at 6.45 pm. On the same days the bus departs St Arnaud at 8 am for Nelson. A one-way fare is $7.50. There is also daily transport by Nelson Lakes Service Car (tel (054) 36-858) which departs St Arnaud at 11 am and arrives at Nelson at 1 pm. It then turns around and departs Nelson from Skyline Travel on Achilles Ave and returns to St Arnaud by 3 pm. The Service Car runs connect with Delta buses to and from the West Coast and the one-way fare from Nelson to St Arnaud is $11. All buses depart and arrive St Arnaud at the Lake Rotoiti Service Centre.

The described trip is usually walked in six days but you can cut out two days and one alpine crossing by utilising the water-taxi service on each lake. St Arnaud Transport (tel (054) 36-840) will run you up Lake Rotoiti from the boat ramp on Kerr Bay to either Coldwater or Lakehead huts at the south end. The one-way charge is $36 for less than four or $11 per person for up to six with packs. For transport on the other lake, contact Lake Rotoroa Water Taxi (tel (054) 39-195). Rates range from $40 for two persons to $72 for six with packs. Keep in mind that by ending the trip at Sabine Hut on the south end of Lake Rotoroa, you skip the challenging climb over the Mt Robert skifield. But at the same time you also miss out on spending a night at Angelus Hut, easily the most scenic one of the tramp.

Places to Stay & Eat

All buses depart and arrive at St Arnaud at the Lake Rotoiti Service Centre, which serves as the village's only store, tearoom and post office. The store stocks a good selection of food and supplies though, as might be expected, it's cheaper to purchase your supplies in Nelson or Greymouth.

Just up SH63 from the store is the *Yellow House* (tel (054) 36-850), a private hostel that has beds for $12 a night along with kitchen facilities, showers and even TV in the lounge. This is a popular spot for trampers before or after their trek. Book ahead if you can.

There is other hotel and motel accommodation in the village or if you have a tent the national park runs two excellent campgrounds on the edge of Lake Rotoiti. The one off Kerr Bay is closer to the park headquarters and the more popular of the two. The other on West Bay has the showers. For either it's $3.30 a night.

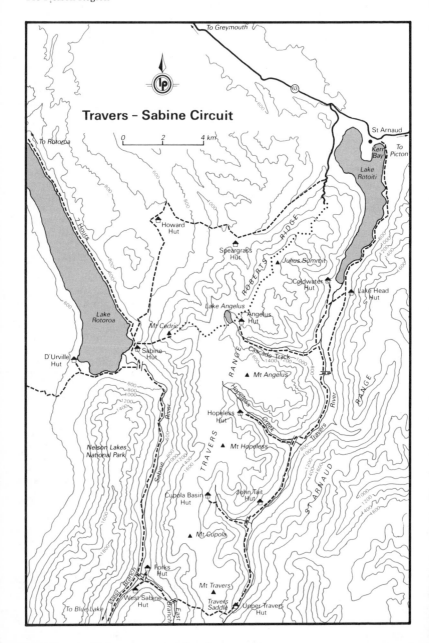

Travers – Sabine Circuit

Information & Maps

The park headquarters and visitor centre (tel (054) 806) is a five-minute walk from the store in St Arnaud. This is the place to ask questions, gather maps and books, leave intentions and pay your hut fees. It's $4 a night for John Tait, Upper Travers, Blue Lake and Angelus Huts, all other are $2. You can also purchase a fishing license here or store your extra gear free of charge. The centre is open daily from 8 am to 5 pm and its worth taking a moment to review the interesting displays on the park's natural and human history.

Look for the metric quads of the Infomap 260 series for this trip (as of 1988 they hadn't been published). Quad S33 of NZMS 1 covers the entire trip except the Travers Saddle crossing which is on S40. Or you can get away with the recreational map for Nelson Lakes National Park, NZMS 273/5.

The Track

The following trip is a six-day walk, which is rated medium, but it can be shortened by using water-taxis on the lakes (see the Access section). It begins with the Lakehead Track along the east side of Lake Rotoiti. You can also follow the Lakeside Track along the west side but this is a longer walk to the south end.

Stage 1: Kerr Bay to John Tait Hut

Walking Time: six to eight hours
Accommodation: Lakehead Hut (16 bunks); Coldwater Hut (10 bunks); John Tait Hut (16 bunks)

The Lakehead Track is clearly signposted and begins just beyond the toilets at Kerr Bay Campground. The first km to the junction of the Loop Track is a wide and level path. Beyond the junction it resembles more of a true track but remains an easy walk through the forest on the edge of Lake Rotoiti. At four km the track passes a gravel clearing where there are good views of the northern half of the lake including the peninsula between the bays and in another 2½ km it passes a

second clearing. This time the southern half of the lake can be seen.

Lakehead Hut is nine km (about a 2½ to three hours) from Kerr Campground and is situated on a grassy bank overlooking the mouth of Travers River. There is good trout fishing in the river here and especially in the lake near the mouth. If the hut is full, Coldwater Hut, smaller and not as pleasant, is about 1½ km and a ford of Travers River away on the other side of the lake.

At Lakehead Hut, there are signposts that direct you across Travers River and through a grassy flat to the walking track on the true left (west) side of the river. The alternative during high water is to follow the true right (east) side of the river for five km to a swingbridge across the Travers. The true left side is more scenic however as it swings close to the river in many places.

Once on the track along the true left side, you soon pass a signposted junction for Cascade Track, which leads to Angelus Hut (4½ hours), and then the track meanders between stands of beech and grassy flats until it reaches the footbridge across the Travers. The track continues to follow the river closely in the forest until it emerges onto another flat in 3.2 km where Mt Travers dominates the view. Just beyond the end of the flat you arrive at a footbridge over Hopeless Creek and on the other side is the signposted junction to the track to Hopeless Hut (2½ hours).

The sign also says John Tait Hut is two hours away but most trampers cover the remaining five km in less time. The track begins gradually to climb now and in the final two km has been relocated the path shown on most maps and definitely swings away from the river. The hut is located on a small grassy clearing with good views of the peaks at the head of the valley.

Stage 2: John Tait Hut to Upper Travers Hut

Walking Time: two to three hours

Upper Travers Hut in Nelson Lakes NP

Accommodation: Upper Travers Hut (16 bunks)

The track continues to climb the valley and within a km of the hut passes the junction with the track to the Cupola Basin Hut (two hours). The climb steepens at this point and within another km the track passes the side track to Travers Falls. It's well worth dropping the pack and descending to this beautiful cascade of water, a three-minute walk away. The falls, about a 20-metre drop of rushing water, are encased in a large rock bowl and have created a sparkling clear pool at the bottom.

From the falls the track climbs gently and soon crosses a bridge over Summit Creek. You cross a second bridge in 1½ km and at this point you begin a much steeper climb to the bushline. The edge of the bush is reached a little over two km from the second bridge and trampers are

greeted here with good views of the peaks of both the Travers and St Arnaud Range.

The Upper Travers Hut is in a grassy clearing before the last stand of mountain beech towards the saddle. It's a beautiful spot, surrounded by gravel and scree slopes that can be easily climbed for better views.

Stage 3: Upper Travers Hut to West Sabine Hut

Walking Time: five to six hours
Accommodation: Forks Hut (eight bunks); West Sabine Hut (eight bunks)

The route over Travers Pass is well marked with rock cairns and snow poles. The ascent begins when you emerge from the final stand of trees into an area of tussock-covered slopes decorated by large boulders. From here you are technically following a route but, due to its popularity, a track exists most of the way. The route climbs gently towards the saddle for a km until you reach a 'Travers Saddle' sign pointing up a steep gravel slope. The stiff climb lasts several hundred metres and it's best to take your time, stopping often to admire the fine views below.

Once at the top of the slope, the climb to the true saddle is easy and done with the sharp-edged Mt Travers (2338 metres) looming overhead to the north. The saddle is marked by a huge rock cairn and it is a nice spot but for an awe-inspiring view you should scramble to one of the nearby ridges. From the saddle, you begin descending rapidly, first passing through tussock slopes, then over a rock slide before returning to the grass. At one point, about 1½ km from the saddle, there is a superb view of the Mahanga Range just before you descend into the treeline and return to the track.

You remain in the stunted mountain beech only momentarily as the track quickly swings onto a scree-covered gully and embarks on a very rapid descent – some 600 metres over a span of three km.

This is probably the hardest section of the day and care has to be taken on the steep sections of loose rock. Halfway down, at the treeline, the track reappears and you follow it as it levels out next to the East Branch of the Sabine River.

Shortly after you cross a small bridge over a gorge where it's impossible to see the water but where it can certainly be heard roaring between the narrow rock walls. The best view is from the river bank upstream from it. Once on the other side, the track follows the steep valley for the next four km and in many places is a maze of tree roots. The final leg of this long day is a very steep drop down the East Branch to where a swingbridge crosses the river to Forks Hut on the other side. West Sabine Hut, in a slightly more scenic location, is another 10 minutes along a side track, past a second bridge on the Sabine River.

Stage 4: West Sabine Hut to Lake Rotoroa

Walking Time: five to six hours

Accommodation: Sabine Hut (12 bunks)

Return to the swingbridge over the Sabine River where the track follows the true left side (west) of the river along a very level route for the first two km. This is a very pleasant stretch as the track remains close to the water and an easy start for those who still ache from the climb over Travers Saddle. The track remains in the wooded fringe along the river for seven km until it breaks out onto a grassy flat.

The track crosses the flat for the next two km, climbs steeply at its north end, only to descend onto another one. At the north end of this flat is a climb to a small knob that overlooks Deep Gorge. This is the steepest ascent of a relatively easy day. Once the track descends to the other side, it follows the river to the junction with the track to D'Urville Hut. If heading for Sabine Hut, cross the bridge that is built high above a deep rock gorge. From the middle of the bridge you can look down into the pale green water and occasionally even spot large trout swimming along the bottom. The gorge is impressive

from either end and it is easy to scramble down to the water level. Trampers have even been known to float through it for a refreshing dip on a hot day.

From the bridge the track climbs up and out of the narrow valley and then spills out onto a grassy flat. You are now less than a km from the hut along a wooded and level path. Sabine Hut has 12 bunks but when filled is a rather crowded place. There are lots of sandflies here but there are also excellent sunsets over Lake Rotoroa that can be enjoyed from the hut's jetty.

Stage 5: Lake Rotoroa to Angelus Hut

Walking Time: six to eight hours

Accommodation: Angelus Hut (16 bunks)

Before embarking on the alpine trek to Lake Angelus, fill the water bottles as there is no water along the way. Also keep in mind that this route is very exposed and there is little shelter once you climb above the bushline.

The track to the alpine hut is signposted 'Mt Cedric' and begins right behind the hut. Beware – the first portion is extremely steep, as you gain well over 900 metres in four km. You get a partial view of Lake Rotoroa on the way up. This section ends once you break out of the bushline. Here you are greeted with an immense view of the entire lake, Sabine Valley and the surrounding mountains. Now a route, you follow the poles to a high point which gives way to a view of Mt Cedric to the north and the rounded ridge to it.

Mt Cedric (1532 metres) is 2½ km from the bushline and appears as a rounded dome. The snow poles continue from the peak along a ridge to the northeast where you reach the high point of the day at 1650 metres and then skirt the flank of Peak 6150. For most of this ridge walk, you almost circle a basin below marked by a small tarn which feeds Cedric Stream. Once the route goes around the peak, it returns to the crest of a ridge and soon Hinapouri Tarn comes into view below.

In a short distance the poles direct you off the ridge and you begin to descend towards Lake Angelus. This section involves hopping over huge rocks – good footing is important. At one point you'll spot Lake Angelus, and even the top of the hut, while still a good 20 minutes away. Lake Angelus, actually two lakes, lies in a beautiful basin surrounded by ridges and peaks. This is a good spot to spend a spare day if you have one. The roomy hut was built in 1970 (the old one is now the loo) and there are plenty of ridges to scramble along for a scenic day-hike.

Stage 6: Lake Angelus to St Arnaud
Walking Time: five to seven hours
There are two ways to return to the park headquarters. If the weather is clear the route along the ridge past Mt Robert skifield is a spectacular walk. But keep in mind the whole length of the ridge is exposed to southeast winds and there are few places for shelter on the lee side. In poor weather with poor visibility it is easy to become disorientated and wander off the route. During poor weather, follow Cascade Track, which drops quickly into the safety of the valley. Plan on five to six hours to reach the park headquarters combining this track with the Lakehead Track.

The ridge route begins as a series of metal poles that head east from the hut and climb a scree slope to a saddle on the rim of Angelus Basin. The route drops down a scree slope on the other side into a saddle and then climbs up the western side of the main ridge over a knob of 1814 metres. Follow the ridge in a northeast direction, scrambling over or sidling the steep rock outcrops that are encountered. The route comes to a basin below the Julius Summit (1794 metres), passes under the peak on the western side, and returns to the main ridge by first climbing a small saddle immediately north of it.

The well-marked route continues along the ridge past the Third Basin and ascends Flagtop (1690 metres) from which

you can view the skifield and shelters. You drop 160 metres over 1½ km along a well-worn track before reaching the Mt Robert skifield, one of the oldest in New Zealand. From here you continue along the poled route that follows the ridge to Mt Robert (1141 metres) and then pick up Pinchgut Track. The trail drops steeply to the skifield car park and shelter, which is still a seven-km walk from the park headquarters.

D'URVILLE VALLEY TRACK
Most people find the tramp through D'Urville Valley an easy stroll; it's the alpine pass that makes this five-day trek a much more challenging one than the Travers-Sabine Circuit. It's better to drop into D'Urville Valley from Moss Pass than to climb out as it is a steep ascent of 1500 metres.

Access
The trip described here starts from Rotoroa and goes along the east shore of Lake Rotoroa into Sabine Valley and over Moss Pass to the D'Urville River. It ends at D'Urville Hut near the shores of the lake and from here there are several ways to exit. You can backtrack along Lake Rotoroa (an eight to nine-hour walk) or follow the Howard and Speargrass Tracks, an 11-hour walk to St Arnaud that most people accomplish in two days. There is the route to Lake Angelus and over the Mt Robert skifield to the park headquarters (see Stage 6 of Travers-Sabine Circuit section) or the Tiraumea Track to the village of Tutaki.

To complete the circuit in five days, or even to reduce it to a four-day trip, you can arrange a drop-off to Sabine Hut and a pick-up from D'Urville Hut through Lake Rotoroa Water Taxi (see Access for Travers-Sabine Circuit). There is no bus service in or out of Rotoroa. The closest spot you can reach by public transport is the Gowan Bridge, 11 km to the north on SH6, on a Newmans bus. If hiring the water-taxi, the operator will arrange to pick you up there. For transport to or from St Arnaud you can hire a taxi through Nelson Lakes Service Car (tel (054) 36-858). There is a park campground at the north end of the lake as well as Lake Rotoroa Tourist Lodge (tel Murchison 121), a 60-year-old historic guest house with 10 rooms and a restaurant.

Maps & Information

Information can be obtained or intentions left at the ranger station (tel Murchison 369) which is open 8 am to 5 pm daily. The maps for this trek are the same as the ones for the Travers-Sabine Circuit.

The Track

This five-day trip, rated medium to difficult, is described from Sabine Valley to D'Urville Valley, the easiest way to cross Moss Pass.

Stage 1: Rotoroa to West Sabine Hut

Walking Time: two days (11 to 13 hours)
Accommodation: Sabine Hut (16 bunks); Forks Hut (eight bunks); West Sabine Hut (eight bunks)
The Rotoroa Track begins at the northern end of the lake at the picnic area and campground and follows the eastern bank for 18 km to Sabine Hut. The track, which stays in the forest, makes for a tedious day of crossing many small ridges and gullies. It's a six to seven-hour tramp to the hut.

For those coming from St Arnaud, you can also reach the hut by hiking the Speargrass and Howard Tracks. The Speargrass Track begins at the car park for the Mt Robert skifield where it descends to Speargrass Creek and then follows the true right bank until it crosses a footbridge right before Speargrass Hut. It's 2½ hours to the hut (six bunks) and another three hours to Howard Shelter (four bunks). From the shelter you head south on Howard Track and reach Sabine Hut in three hours.

There is a well-benched track that departs up Sabine Valley (see the description for Stage 4 of the Travers-

Sabine Circuit but here you walk it in the reverse direction). After crossing a deep ravine, most of the day is spent walking through grassy meadows and beech forest to the confluence of the East Branch and West Branch of the Sabine River where there are two huts located across swingbridges. If you don't hire a water-taxi, plan on two days to reach the river forks either from Rotoroa or St Arnaud.

Stage 2: West Sabine Hut to Blue Lake

Walking Time: three to four hours
Accommodation: Blue Lake Hut (16 bunks)
Return to the true left (west) side of the river over the swingbridge and continue south (left) along the track. From the river fork the track climbs over roots of stunted beech and scree slopes, gaining 400 metres over the next six km. It traverses forest and clearings, many of them made by avalanches, until it enters a basin encircled by mountains. At this point the track veers left and climbs the forested hillside for a km until it reaches Blue Lake Hut just at the treeline.

The hut is set back from the lake and camping is discouraged near the shores because of the impact on the delicate terrain. Although it's only a three to four-hour walk to Blue Lake, this is a popular place to spend a day resting up before tackling Moss Pass. The lake itself is enchanting with its vivid colours of turquoise and emerald green. There is an even better view if you take the track that climbs the remaining km through one last stand of stunted beech to an excellent view of Lake Constance as well as a good overview of Blue Lake. This is truly one of the most scenic spots in the park.

Stage 3: Blue Lake to Ella Hut

Walking Time: five to seven hours
Accommodation: Ella Hut (16 bunks)
The route over Mahanga Range is well marked but good visibility is necessary for a safe crossing of the pass. Snow poles mark the route, beginning behind Blue

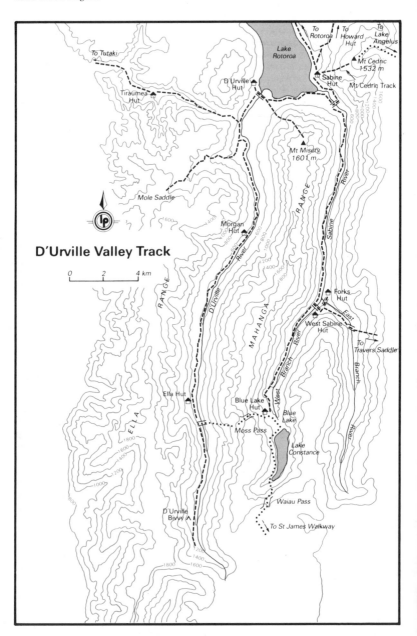

D'Urville Valley Track

Lake Hut, and head in a southwest direction through tussock and beech forest to a small creek. The route quickly climbs along the creek to a shingle scree and then makes a steep ascent northwestwards to an obvious shoulder that extends to the north.

From the shoulder you can spot Moss Pass, a gap to the northern (right) side. Follow the snow poles as they traverse across the scree slopes to the base of the steep gully. It's a hard climb up to the pass at about 1800 metres but once on top you are greeted with a view of Mt Ella across Upper D'Urville Valley. The pass often has snow well into summer.

On the D'Urville side follow the snow poles carefully if visibility is poor. This section has many bluffs and waterfalls that need to be avoided. The route is a long and steep descent that first swings to the south then curves back to a westerly direction, passing two small tarns and finally reaching the bushline.

Here a well-marked track departs through the beech forest, descending steeply until it levels out at a swingbridge across the D'Urville River. Cross to the true left (west) side of the river and follow the track north (right) as it stays close to the river. Ella Hut is reached within a km.

Stage 4: Ella Hut To D'Urville Hut

Walking Time: eight hours

Accommodation: Morgan Hut (14 bunks); D'Urville Hut (10 bunks)

After a challenging day over Moss Pass, it's easy going down D'Urville Valley and most trampers have no problem reaching Lake Rotoroa in a day. The track remains on the true left (west) side of the river the entire way and close to the water for the first five km. Two hours from the hut, however, it departs from the river and passes through forest to an outcrop of rock above a gorge. Here, if you inch carefully to the edge, there is a great view of the river below, a swirl of whitewater thundering through huge boulders.

The track descends from the high point and returns to being a gentle valley walk. In another six km you pass Morgan Hut, a four-hour walk from Ella Hut. The trout fishing improves from this point on until you reach to the mouth of the D'Urville at Lake Rotoroa, a haven for anglers. The tramp downriver crosses beech-clad terraces and river flats for the next six km where it passes a signposted junction with Bull Creek Track to Mole Saddle outside the park.

At this point you are only two or three km from D'Urville Hut and in a km will pass a second junction with the Tiraumea Track heading west (left) over the saddle of the same name. In about 1½ km the valley track ends at a junction. The north (left) fork is the short spur to D'Urville Hut, while the east (right) fork leads around the end of Lake Rotoroa and then inland a short way before returning to the lake at Sabine Hut. It's a two to three-hour walk between the two huts.

Lewis Park National Reserve & Others

The St James Walkway begins in the Lewis Pass National Reserve that borders Nelson Lakes to the south. It is a 66-km trek, making it the longest walkway in the country. For most people, it's a five-day journey. The track is well benched and marked, and has an excellent series of huts. It winds through pastoral land and beech forests but is labelled a sub-alpine tramp as the trip involves climbs over Ada Pass (998 metres) and Anne Saddle (1136 metres). Still it is not as challenging as most round-trip tramps in Nelson Lakes and well within the abilities of moderately fit trampers.

Though the St James Walkway was built by the New Zealand Walkway Commission and is administered by DOC, it runs through a variety of public and private land, including Lewis Pass National Reserve, St James Station, Lake Sumner State Forest Park and Glenhope Station. The heart of the track, from the upper Boyle River along the Anne River to the Ada, runs through the St James Station, one of the largest in New Zealand, and along this section of the walkway trampers must not deviate from the track or interfere with livestock in any way. Stiles have been erected over fences so all gates should be left alone.

If you plan to tramp from Nelson Lakes National Park to the walkway through Waiau Valley (via the Waiau Pass from Blue Lake) then you should contact the owner at the St James Station as it involves crossing additional private property. Write for permission to Mr J Stevenson, St James Station, 48 Scarborough Terrace, Hanmer; or call (tel Hanmer 7066).

HISTORY

As part of the same region, the Lewis National Reserve and the other reserves and private land along the St James Walkway share the history of the Nelson Lakes area.

Though the region was only sparsely settled, the native tribes did pass through it, particularly along a portion of the St James Walkway that was part of a popular route from the Tasman Sea to Canterbury. The Ngatitumatakokiri tribe was the most powerful to use the route but it was constantly warring with a rival tribe, the Ngai Tahu. The rivalry ended in a particularly grisly manner when a Ngai Tahu party was trapped in a gorge along the Maruia River by the Ngatitumatakokiri and ended up being the main dish of a victory meal. That spot, of course, is the Cannibal Gorge passed on the walkway.

The Lewis Pass area was first explored by Europeans in the 1860s and in the late 1970s the area was chosen as the site of the first long-distance walkway in the South Island. The St James Walkway, named

after the historic sheep station it runs through, was opened in November 1981.

CLIMATE

Extreme weather can be encountered in this sub-alpine area with heavy rain or even snow occurring almost any time of the year. Pack warm clothing (mittens, hat) as well as the usual good raingear.

ST JAMES WALKWAY

The St James Walkway is a well-benched and marked track with five huts spaced evenly along the way a reasonable day's walk apart. But the track should not be underestimated as 66 km is a long journey. The trek from Nelson Lakes over Waiau Pass to the walkway is definitely for experienced trampers only.

Access

Both ends of the walkway are located off the SH7 which crosses Lewis Pass from North Canterbury to the West Coast. Transport to and from the track is easy as there are buses that run along the highway whose drivers are used to dropping off and being flagged down by trampers. Both Newmans and NZRRS buses pass the start and finish of the track on SH7.

Many trampers arrive at the walkway from Christchurch, a three-hour drive away. NZRRS runs a Christchurch-Westport bus that departs at 10.40 am Monday to Friday, passing the ends of the track around 2.30 pm. There is also a 6 pm departure the same days, that reaches the ends of the track at about 9 pm. One-way fare from Christchurch to the track is $26. When returning to the Garden City, a NZRRS bus departs Westport at 9 am on weekdays, passing the track ends at 12.15 pm and arriving at Christchurch at 3 pm. There is also a 7.40 pm bus out of Westport the same days that passes the ends of the track at 10.30 pm.

Newmans also passes the track on its Nelson to Christchurch run. The bus departs Nelson at 9.35 am Monday to Saturday, reaching the track ends around

2 pm. In the opposite direction, Newmans departs Christchurch at 9.40 am the same days and passes the track ends between 12.30 and 1 pm. By picking up a bus in the morning, you can easily hike into the first hut that day. When departing the walkway, arrive at SH7 30 to 60 minutes before the bus is due to to ensure you catch it if it is running early or late.

The buses are also used by those with their own vehicles to return to the car park they departed from. There is a a car park at both ends but it is best to leave a vehicle at the Boyle area as vandalism has been a problem at Lewis Pass.

Information & Maps
As well as DOC regional offices in Nelson and Christchurch, information about the track can be obtained at ranger stations in Hanmer Springs (tel 7210) and in Maruia (tel 873). It takes four quads, S46, S53, S47, and S40, of the NZMS 1 series to completely cover the walkway. Or if you're not up to investing $35 on maps, just purchase the recreational maps to Lake Sumner State Forest Park, NZMS 274/16, and Nelson Lakes National Park, NZMS 273/5. The two maps include the entire walkway at a slightly smaller scale but cost only $11 together.

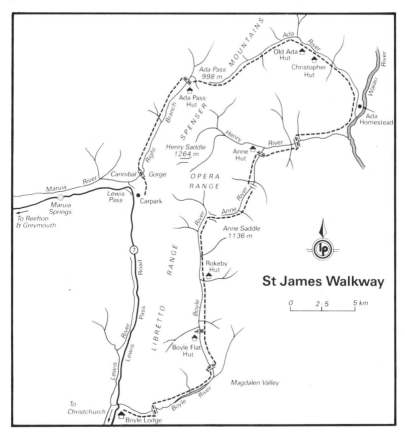

St James Walkway

The Track

The walkway can be tramped in either direction but it is described here from the Lewis Pass to the Boyle River. Lewis Pass is the most popular starting point and there is less climbing when the track, rated medium, is begun from this end. For most trampers it is a five day walk.

Stage 1: Lewis Pass to Ada Pass Hut

Walking Time: five hours

Accommodation: Ada Pass Hut (20 bunks)

From the car park and picnic area located just south of Lewis Pass, follow the Tarn Nature Walk as it immediately passes the Rolleston Pack Track and then comes to the junction with the walkway. The St James track heads northeast (right) and is actually a continuation of the old pack track. It begins a sharp descent into beech forest and in 30 minutes the track drops 170 metres to a swingbridge over Cannibal Gorge with the Right Branch of the Maruia River below.

From the bridge the track continues along the true right (west) bank of the gorge and in 30 minutes passes Phil's Knob, an excellent lookout point. A staircase assists you around the knob and you continue along the gorge, climbing in and out of numerous gullies. This is not the easiest tramping but the walkway is well marked and much work has been done on it with chainsaws to cut log steps over fallen trees.

Two hours beyond the knob the track passes through Windfall Flat and then soon begins a steep but short climb up a bushclad terrace and then around a slip. Just minutes from the hut, you enter Ada Pass Flats where there are views back down the valley and Gloriana Peak to the north. Right before reaching the hut, the track crosses a swingbridge over the Maruia River once again. Ada Pass Hut, like most of them along the walkway, is a roomy facility that has 20 bunks.

Stage 2: Ada Pass Hut to Christopher Hut

Walking Time: four to five hours

Accommodation: Old Ada Hut (two bunks); Christopher Hut (20 bunks)

The track departs from the east end of the hut and gently ascends to the Ada Pass, 998 metres, fording the Right Branch of the Maruia River (now a stream) once more along the way. The bushclad pass will be recognised by the large sign marking the border between Lewis Pass National Reserve and the St James Station. The walkway now descends into Ada Valley along the true right (south) side of the Ada River. A small alpine clearing is passed through and then a much larger tussock grassland with a few patches of bush on it.

It's a km across this one and orange discs are used to point out where the track resumes in the beech forest. The birdlife is good in this area or you might spot cattle or a few wild horses along the edges. Looming overhead are the peaks of Faerie Queen, a beautiful sight on a clear day. Two hours from Ada Pass, the track emerges from beech forest again to the wide expanse of the station. Shortly the flats (and the track) turn the corner, swinging from northeast to southeast where the Christopher River flows in from the north.

At the junction of the Christopher and Ada rivers is Old Ada Hut, also known as Historic Hut. Built in 1956 for deer hunters, the two-bunk hut is now more a monument to the old New Zealand Forest Service than a place to stay. Another km down the track is Christopher Hut, another roomy 20-bunk facility with a good view of the Waiau Valley.

Stage 3: Christopher Hut to Anne Hut

Walking Time: five hours

Accommodation: Anne Hut (20 bunks)

The third day of the journey is spent almost entirely on grazing land and during the summer this can be a hot walk as there is little shade to escape the sun. Often the track is simply a 4WD track or a route marked by cairns and posts with orange discs. After leaving Christopher Hut, you cut across grassy flats along the true right bank of the Ada River. You follow the open flats until they converge with the river at Federation Corner, about 1½ km above Ada Homestead, a St James outstation. The homestead, on the opposite side of the Ada River, is private property and should not be entered by trampers.

The track keeps west of the river and is well benched as it hugs the hillsides and passes the wide flats of Waiau Valley to enter the valley of Henry River. The track continues to hug the lower slopes of Mt Federation through matagouri thickets and eventually sidles up a terrace and comes to a junction with a 4WD track. The walkway heads west (right) on the 4WD track and within 30 minutes fords Jackson Stream. Here you leave the vehicle track and cross a swingbridge over the Henry River to its true right (south) bank. In another km the track rejoins the 4WD track as it gently climbs to Irishman Flat and then descends it to swingbridge over Anne River.

Anne Hut and an old shelter are just on the other side of the bridge. If the weather is good and water levels normal, you can save some time and climbing by following the vehicle track all the way to the hut, bypassing the track and bridge near Jackson Creek.

Stage 4: Anne Hut to Boyle Flat Hut
Walking Time: six hours
Accommodation: Rokeby Hut (two bunks); Boyle Hut (20 bunks)
The track winds up the Anne River for two km where it climbs a bushclad spur to a swingbridge that takes you to the true left (east) side. It continues up the valley towards Anne Saddle, not a difficult climb and only 4½ km from the swingbridge. About half way up, or 45 minutes after crossing Anne River, the track fords Kia Stream, where just before

the creek you get a final view of the Valley.

Anne Saddle is still bushclad at 1136 metres but a short climb up the ridge north (right) of it brings you to a clearing for good views of the mountains at the head of Boyle Valley. The descent off the saddle is steep, dropping 210 metres over two km which takes about 30 minutes. The Boyle is followed for the next 3½ km with the track remaining on its true left (east) side all the way to Rokeby Hut. At several places the track climbs high above the river to avoid flood conditions. If the water level is normal, it is far easier and quicker to ford the river and remain along its banks.

Rokeby Hut is an old shelter with two bunks and not a very desirable place to stay. The track remains on the true left (east) side of the Boyle as it continues south. Boyle Flat Hut is only another 3½ km and is reached in 60 to 90 minutes. It lies on the true right (west) side of the river and is reached by a swingbridge across the Boyle.

Stage 5: Boyle Flat Hut to Boyle Car Park
Walking Time: four hours
Accommodation: Magdalen Hut (12 bunks)
Return and cross the swingbridge and head south along the track, now a series of red and white markers through the tussock grass of Boyle Flat. At the edge of the bush is the border between St James Station and Lake Sumner State Forest Park. The track will shortly descend into the Boyle River Gorge where it stays 150 metres above the river as a wide, well-benched path. It traverses the gorge and then drops down to the river's edge.

An hour from the hut, the track arrives at a swingbridge over the Boyle. If you skipped the bridge and continued along the true left (east) side of the river in a km the track would lead to Magdalen Hut. Cross the bridge instead and the track on the true right (west) leads down into Magdalen Valley. Once the track enters the valley it's seven km through river flats and patches of bush along the true right (now north) side of the Boyle to a swingbridge. The track crosses the bridge and shortly joins the St Andrews Station Rd on the opposite bank.

It's about 1½ km along the road until you reach Boyle Lodge, a three-side shelter and the car park.

Top: Mt Cedric on Travers-Sabine Circuit, Nelson Lakes NP (JD)
Left: Hiking along Travers River, Nelson Lakes NP (JD)
Right: Mt Travers, Nelson Lakes NP (JD)

Top: Travers River, Nelson Lakes NP (JD)
Left: East branch of Sabine River, Nelson Lakes NP (JD)
Right: Swingbridge over Travers River, Nelson Lakes NP (JD)

West Coast & Southern Alps

Paparoa National Park

Travelling down the isolated West Coast between Westport and Greymouth, most tourists are enthralled by the rugged seascape while hitchhikers lament the lack of traffic. The region usually receives little attention from trampers passing through as the common notion is that there's no reason to stop other than to take a quick walk through the Pancake Rocks Reserve.

New Zealand's newest national park, however, is slowly changing that opinion. Paparoa National Park was officially opened in December 1987 as part of the country's national parks centennial celebration. Paparoa includes the rugged granite peaks of the Paparoa Range and the lowlands and river valleys west of it. It does not include, ironically, the spectacular seascape seen along SH6.

But the park doesn't lack beautiful scenery. Within an easy walk inland lie river valleys made tropical by groves of nikau palms; there are also spectacular limestone formations, narrow gorges, and interesting caves to explore. All these features remain hidden from most travellers but can be seen by trampers who take the park's most noted tramp, the Inland Pack Track.

The 25-km walk extends from Punakaiki to the spot where the SH6 crosses the mouth of Fox River. There are no huts along this track, only the Ballroom, one of the largest (if not the largest) rock bivvies in New Zealand. There are no alpine passes to negotiate or excruciating climbs above the treeline but the tramp is no easy stroll. There is mud to contend with and a couple of rivers to hike. (That's right: in places the track is the river.) Dilemma Creek flows through a gorge so steep and narrow, trampers just walk down the middle of it. Occasionally you can follow a gravel bank but much of the trek involves sloshing from one pool to the next. During normal water levels, the stream rarely rises above your knees and if it's a hot, sunny day this can be the most pleasant segment of the trip.

HISTORY

Most historians doubt if the Maoris ever settled this rugged section of the West Coast as no fortified pa sites have been uncovered in the Punakaiki area. But middens (rubbish heaps) have been recorded at Barrytown which suggests that the native tribes made seasonal

Maori

161

excursions to the bays and rivers of Paparoa to gather food. The coastline, as rugged as it may appear, also provided a trade route for the Maoris who most likely carried greenstone north through here from the Arahura district near Hokitika.

New Zealand's earliest explorers, Abel Tasman, James Cook and Dumont D'Urville, undoubtedly sailed past the Paparoas but never landed. The first European explorers to walk through the area were most likely Charles Heaphy and Thomas Brunner who, in 1846, were led by the Maori guide Kehu on a five-month journey down the West Coast. The three men passed 23 Maoris heading north but the first native settlement they came to was at Kararoa, 20 km south of Punakaiki.

Heaphy was impressed by the Paparoa region and he devoted a dozen pages of his diary to it. But he also wrote about the 'incessant rain', delays caused by swollen rivers and of climbing rotting rata and flax ladders up the steep cliffs of Perpendicular Point at the urging of his Maori guide. Later that year Brunner and Kehu would make a return trip to the area. It was an epic journey, one that lasted 18 months, in which they completely circumnavigated the Paparoa Range, traced the Buller River from source to mouth and travelled as far south as Paringa. An epic journey but not an adventure Brunner ever wanted to repeat. He often faced starvation, was forced to shoot and eat his dog, and spent Christmas huddled under a blanket waiting out a snow storm. During his long absence, most people in Nelson presumed he was dead.

Gold was discovered on the West Coast as early as 1864 but the hunt for the precious metal really only gained momentum two years later when famed prospector William Fox and a companion chartered the SS *Woodpecker* and landed it on the lee side of Seal Island in May 1866. The area, where the Fox River empties into the Tasman Sea, became known as Woodpecker Bay and miners by the thousands stampeded to this stretch of the coast. They scattered around Charleston to the north and then formed the town of Brighton near the Fox River. Many historians estimate that by 1867 Charleston had a population of 12,000 and Brighton, where there is almost nothing today, was a booming town of 6000.

Reaching the areas along the 'beach highway' was extremely challenging for miners. Despite the Nelson Provincial Government replacing the Maori flax ladders up Perpendicular Point with chains that had saplings forced through the links, miners still looked inland for a safer route. In 1866 work began on the Inland Pack Track which headed south from Brighton, thereby avoiding the hazardous Perpendicular Point. It was cut through the western lowlands of the Paparoa Range and in 1868 was used to extend the Christchurch to Greymouth telegraph line north to Westport. The line, which passed through Brighton and Charleston as well, was one of the most expensive ever installed in New Zealand, costing 'about 104 pounds, 10 shillings and 8 pence per mile' due to the wet weather and the thick jungle-like bush.

After the miners left, tourism was the main activity in the region. A coastal track being cut by the early 1900s would eventually become SH6. When passenger cars first travelled the Westport-Greymouth Rd in the 1920s, few rivers had bridges and the tourists often had to ford a stream to a vehicle waiting on the other side. By the 1930s most rivers were bridged and today an estimated 400 vehicles pass through Punakaiki daily.

Nearby Pancake Rocks has long been a popular tourist sight but the Paparoa Range and lowlands were thrust into the consciousness of the nation only in the 1970s when there was interest in logging the area. This sparked a heated conservation campaign that lead to the establishment of the national park in 1987.

CLIMATE

Trampers have to be prepared for the rainy weather the West Coast is renowned for; gentle streams can quickly turn into raging rivers. The park's lowlands are a lush, almost subtropical, forest because of the warm ocean current that sweeps past the coast and the moist westerlies that blow in off the Tasman Sea. The effect is a wet but surprisingly mild climate.

Average rainfall in the western lowlands is between 2000 and 3000 mm a year, much of it falling in late winter and spring. Mid-summer to autumn, on the other hand, can be exceptionally sunny with long spells of settled weather. Both Westport and Punakaiki average almost 2000 hours of sunshine annually.

NATURAL HISTORY

The Paparoa Range is composed mainly of granite and gneiss peaks that over time have been carved by glaciers and weathered by rain, snow and wind into a craggy chain of pinnacles and spires. This is a low but extremely rugged set of mountains of between 1200 and 1500 metres. Routes over the alpine areas of the Paparoas are only for experienced backpackers willing to endure the impenetrable bush, the consistently cloudy weather at the top, and the rough terrain of a true wilderness area.

The western lowlands area, which lies between the ocean and the mountains, is totally different in character. This is a karst landscape – a limestone region where the soft rock has been eroded by rivers and underground drainage. What remain are the deep canyons and gorges whose limestone walls may rise 200 metres above the river. There are blind valleys, sink holes, cliffs, streams that disappear underground, overhangs and, perhaps most intriguing to trampers passing through, numerous caves.

The nikau palms, which line the beaches and cliffs along the coast and give SH6 its tropical nature, extend inland and together with a profusion of black mamuku tree ferns, smaller ferns and supplejack vines form a jungle-like canopy. Still further inland the lowland forest becomes a mixture of podocarps, beech and broadleaf trees with rimu and red beech often the most dominate species.

The size of the forest and the fact that it's been left relatively unmolested by man has led to the park's profusion of bird life. Commonly spotted along the tracks are bellbirds, tomtits, fantails, grey warblers, New Zealand pigeons, riflemen and tuis. One of the favourites often encountered is the western weka, the brown flightless bird often spotted in the Fossil Creek area. There are also good numbers of great spotted kiwis, but trampers will hear them at night more often than seeing them.

The other resident of the park that attracts attention is the trout. Anglers planning to walk the Inland Pack Track should take a rod and reel with them as they will be passing enticing trout pools along the way. The first two miles of the Pororari River from the SH6 can be an especially productive stretch.

INLAND PACK TRACK

Even without a tent, the Inland Pack Track can be walked by using the Ballroom, the giant limestone bivvy, for overnight shelter. This would involve a long day from Punakaiki to the huge bivvy located north of the junction of the Fox River and Dilemma Creek and then a short two to three-hour tramp the next day out to SH6. It is better to carry a tent, however, as a precaution against rapidly rising streams which can delay trips or prevent you from crossing Walsh Creek to the Ballroom. A tent also allows the tramp to be divided more evenly into two days or walked at a more leisurely pace over three days.

Access

Punakaiki serves as the departure point for this trip and many tramping parties spend a night here at the beginning or end of their adventure.

Newmans Coachlines provides bus transportation to Punakaiki on a route that begins in either Nelson or Greymouth. From Nelson the bus departs the Newmans depot (tel (054) 88-369) on Hardy St at 8.45 am from Monday to Saturday, arriving at Westport at 1.35 pm and at Punakaiki around 3 pm. In the opposite direction, the bus departs Greymouth the same days from the Newmans office (tel 6118) on Herbert St at 8.05 am and reaches Punakaiki at 9.20 am. A one-way fare from Nelson to Punakaiki is $29.

Along the way the Newmans bus crosses the bridge over Fox River, the north end of the Inland Pack Track. Trampers can use this service to get to and from the ends of the track or to move up the coast. Trampers heading south to Punakaiki should be at SH6 around 2 pm or so, ready to flag down the bus that will usually pass within 40 minutes. You can also be dropped off at the same spot and have enough time that day to hike easily to the Ballroom.

Places to Stay & Eat

DOC runs the *Punakaiki Motor Camp* (tel (02721) 893) an exceptionally pleasant place to camp. Every site is overshadowed by the towering limestone bluffs across SH6, surrounded by nikau palms and only a short walk to the beach on the Tasman Sea. Tent sites are $6 a night for adults and caravan sites $13.50 for two people. Roomy cabins are also available for $22 a night for two people and $9 for every extra adult. The motor camp contains a communal kitchen, showers and washing machines.

One km south along the highway is the Pancake Rocks area where there is a tearoom and store with limited supplies that is open daily until 5 pm.

Information & Maps

There is a DOC office (tel (02721) 893) at Punakaiki, right off the highway, which is open weekdays from 8 am until 4.30 pm. On the outside there is a box that contains the intentions book and brochures on tracks and walks in the area. There is also a DOC visitor centre at the Pancake Rocks area with displays and exhibits on the national park. The centre is open daily from 8 am until 4.30 pm and until 9 pm during the summer holidays.

The only map that covers the track is quad K30 of the Infomap 260 series. It is usually best to purchase it on your way through Nelson, Westport or at the DOC regional office in Hokitika (tel (0288) 58-301) and not wait until you are at Punakaiki where it might be hard to find.

The Track

The Inland Pack Track is rated medium. Trampers should not wander off the actual track as this is a karst limestone country and there are a number of hidden sink holes and underground streams in the area, some quite near the track.

The track can be walked in either direction and many parties, arriving in the afternoon, start at the Fox River end, from which it is a shorter walk to the Ballroom. But the track will be described here from Punakaiki, the direction trampers should follow if they don't have a tent. By staying overnight at the motor camp you can get the latest report on the weather conditions and water levels from the DOC office or visitor centre before departing the next morning.

If the forecast is poor, wait another day or move down the coast. To be trapped out on the track by rising rivers with no tent makes for a very long night. On the other hand, if the forecast is good you can take the longer walk with no problems and be safely at the Ballroom by nightfall.

Stage 1: Punakaiki to the Ballroom

Walking Time: seven to eight hours
You can begin the track either at a farm road near the Punakaiki River 1.2 km

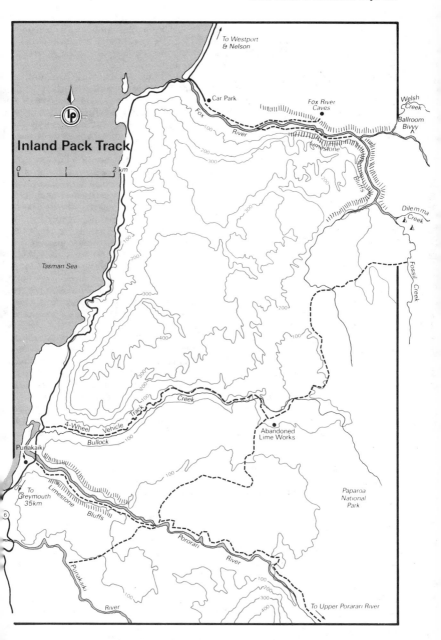

To Westport & Nelson

Car Park

Fox River Caves

Welsh Creek

Ballroom Bivvy

Fox River

Limestone Bluffs

Dilemma Creek

Inland Pack Track

0   1   2 km

Tasman Sea

Fossil Creek

Creek

4-Wheel Vehicle Track

Bullock

Abandoned Lime Works

Punakaiki

To Greymouth 35km

Limestone Bluffs

Paparoa National Park

Pororari River

Punakaiki River

To Upper Porarari River

south of the Pancake Rocks visitor centre or at the Pororari River Bridge on SH6 just north of the motor camp. Punakaiki River is part of the original track but many feel the route along Pororari is more scenic. It follows the river closely along the true left (south) bank through a spectacular landscape of towering limestone cliffs graced by nikau palms and tree ferns. Within 15 minutes it passes Punjabi Beach. Keep an eye on the deep green pools of the river, as often it's easy to spot trout or even a freshwater eel early in the morning.

In 3½ km, the track comes to a junction with the loop back to Punakaiki River and SH6 (which would take two hours to walk) and then, in another 100 metres, to a signposted ford of the Pororari River. In normal conditions, it's an easy crossing to the junction on the other side. The Pororari River track continues along the true right (north) side of the river to a fine viewing point over the Pororari Gorge (two hours one way). The Inland Pack Track heads north (left) and for the next four km works it way through a silver beech forest. The track can become muddy in places and there is little to look at here except the bush around you and an occasional signposted sink hole.

The track is easy to follow. In 1½ hours you enter a clearing and then join a 4WD track. To the east (right) are good views of the rugged Paparoa Range while to the north pairs of white posts direct you through the private property. The route passes the shacks of the abandoned lime works, some farm sheds and the signposted vehicle track along Bullock Creek to SH6 before arriving at the creek itself. This is a nice spot and the first decent place to set up camp for those who got off to a late start.

After fording Bullock Creek, the track resumes as a rough vehicle route for almost a km and then enters bush again. The track stays in the beech forest but sidles an open area and passes some immense patches of flax. After two km the

track begins its climb to a low saddle. There's a lot of mud here but the climb is easy and the descent on the other side rapid.

The track remains fairly level until it emerges at Fossil Creek, which is 2½ hours from Bullock Creek and marked by a large rock cairn and a small sign. There is no track at this point – you simply follow the creek downstream towards its confluence with Dilemma Creek. You may want to change into tennis shoes to follow the river but if your boots are already caked in mud it is a good way to clean them. The walk, which is about one km, takes you under a thick canopy of trees and through pools that are gentle in normal conditions.

It takes about 30 minutes to reach the junction with Dilemma, marked by another rock cairn and a small sign. There are grass flats around this area and it is a good place for camping. Even larger flats are reached several hundred metres further up the Dilemma.

The next stretch is a walk through the Dilemma, which is the most spectacular segment of the trip. You follow the creek bed beneath massive limestone walls and there is no room for a track of any kind. You make numerous fords to avoid deep pools or to follow short gravel bars. The Fox River can probably be reached in well under an hour but most trampers, so overwhelmed by the stunning scenery, take 1½ to two hours to cover this short stretch.

A very small sign is located on the true left side of the Dilemma, just before the confluence with the Fox River indicating where the track resumes. The confluence is an easy spot to recognise as a sharp rock bluff separates the two canyons. Occasionally someone will scale this bluff during high water to continue up the Fox to the Ballroom. The easier way is to drop down the river and then ford it. Once on the true right side of the Fox, follow it back up past the confluence (left branch facing upstream) to reach the Ballroom. The bivvy is about a km up the river and is easy to spot. It takes about 20 minutes and three or four fords to reach it.

The rock overhang is properly named as it is about 100 metres long with a cavern and towering arched ceiling in the middle. The roof is a hanging garden of sorts with grass, vines, rows of ferns and even small trees growing out of it. Its popularity has lead to benches and a large fire pit being built but there is little firewood in the immediate area. There is good swimming in the Fox nearby.

Stage 2: The Ballroom to SH6

Walking Time: two to 2½ hours

Return to the small track sign on the Dilemma Creek right before its confluence with the Fox. A rough and very bushy track begins here and follows the true left (south) side of the Fox. It is rough at first but turns into a pleasant walk along the gorge high above the river. It follows the valley for three km before dropping down to the Fox River and fording it to the true right (north) bank.

On the other side is a junction with the track to the Fox River Caves heading east (right). With the exception of the final 100 metres it's a gentle climb to the caves – it takes about 30 to 40 minutes to reach them. The entrances to the three impressive caves are inside a huge rock overhang. The best one to enter is at the upper left-hand corner where stone steps lead to the opening. A few metres inside you'll encounter stalagmites and stalactites.

An alternative route to the caves is a side track that runs straight up a moss-covered stream from the Fox River to the caves. It's difficult to find when travelling downriver but it can save you from backtracking up the Fox from where the main track fords the river. For the adventurous, the shortest route down to the ford from the caves lies in the Fox; you follow it in the same way you followed Dilemma Creek. This should be done only in good weather – even then some fords will be almost waist deep.

After returning to the main track where

it fords the Fox to the true right (north) side, you take the track to the west (left) and follow the river, crossing numerous gravel bars and using the little footprints designed to keep wandering trampers on course. This section takes about 40 minutes. You emerge at a car park where the Inland Pack Track is signposted. SH6 is another 200 metres down the metalled road.

OTHER TRACKS

Kirwans Track

Located in Victoria Forest Park on the east side of the Paparoa Range, the track is a three-day loop that includes nights at two huts and travel across river flats as well as climbs to open tops of tussock. The highlights of the trip for many are the rusting artifacts – from ore buckets and giant return wheels to tools and boots – that remain from the quartz mining operation that took place here in the late 1890s. The start of the track is located at Capleston, a mining ghost town at the end of Boatmans Rd off the SH69 between Reefton and Inangahua Junction. For more information stop at the DOC office (tel (02728) 390) in Reefton on Crampton Rd.

Arthur's Pass National Park

They arrive by the train-loads, on buses and in cars; or, if they're low on funds, by hitching. They're trampers and walkers headed for a small alpine village in the middle of the Southern Alps.

They come from all over New Zealand and around the world, they want to see the mountains, and maybe experience them on foot or even strap on a backpack and do a little 'pass hopping'. Arthur's Pass National Park is the destination. From the moment visitors step out of the train depot in the village of Arthur's Pass they are surrounded by mountains.

Arthur's Pass is an alpine park, located 154 km northwest of Christchurch. The reserve is 984 square km and stradles both sides of the Southern Alps with two-thirds of it on the Canterbury side of the Main Divide and the rest in Westland. It's a rugged mountainous area cut by deep valleys and ranging in altitude from 245 metres at the Taramakau River to 2402 metres at the highest peak.

Mountain climbers, hunters and, in the winter, skiers all arrive at this noted alpine area to pursue their activities, but most of all Arthur's Pass is a tramper's park. It's easy to get to by public transport, there is a good network of huts and bivouacs, and many tracks are semi-loops that begin and end at the SH73. You can arrive at the village and use it as a base for dozens of walks through valleys and over alpine passes.

There are many tracks for day-walks, especially around the park headquarters, but the longer trips are generally routes rather than tracks and involve following the valleys and then climbing the saddles that link them. For the most part a cut track is provided only when needed and much of the time you will be boulder hopping along a river bed. Where tracks do exist they are usually only marked with rock cairns and are rarely signposted, while most streams are unbridged. Here and there you'll find unofficial paths, formed by repeated usage around a bluff or up a sidecreek, but they soon fade.

Park rangers refer to as trampers' tracks, those routes in the heart of the park where segments connect valleys and passes to form a loop off SH73. These are not benched walkways like the Heaphy, Routeburn or Abel Tasman Coastal Tracks. Here a topographical map and a compass are essential equipment.

Arthur's Pass Village can be used as the departure point for all three trips described here as well as for the Cass-Lagoon Saddle Track described in the next section. It's even worth scheduling some extra days at this one-road town hemmed in by towering mountains. Day walks to spectacular vistas abound in the area and there are some interesting displays at the national park headquarters, including one of the horse-drawn coaches that used to travel through the park at the turn of the century.

HISTORY

There is no evidence that the Maoris ever settled the area that is now the national park. The highly prized greenstone did lure them across Arthur's Pass but only occasionally as the easier route over Harper Pass was preferred. Arthur's Pass had long been abandoned by the time Europeans were settling Canterbury in 1850.

The first settlers had little interest in venturing into the Southern Alps and it wasn't until September 1857 that Edward Dobson travelled up the Hurunui River as far as Harper Pass and possibly into the Taramakau Valley before turning back. But it was 20-year-old Leonard Harper, with the aid of four Maori guides, who became the first European to cross the swampy saddle and then descend the Taramakau to reach the West Coast. Within two years the route was surveyed and a track cut to Harper Pass by Dobson himself.

Dobson didn't get a pass named after him but his son, Arthur, did. The first person to spot the famous pass was Samuel Butler. In 1860, he looked up Bealey Valley and saw the saddle but as he was travelling alone, and unwilling to leave his horse unattended, he turned back. In March of 1864, Arthur Dobson and his younger brother, Edward, journeyed up the same valley and camped above the treeline. The next day they crossed the pass and descended a short distance into Otira Gorge. By February 1865 Arthur's other brother, George, had been commissioned to select the best route from Canterbury to the West Coast gold-fields.

He re-examined the alpine crossing and declared 'Arthur's pass is the best route'. The name stuck.

At the same time that George Dobson was selecting the 'best' route, two parcels of gold had been sent from Hokitika to Canterbury. Gold fever and a stampede followed and regardless of what was determined to be the best route, the diggers chose the easiest route. In one week in March 1865 a thousand men poured over Harper Pass on their way to the West Coast; some 4000 made the trip between February and April. The traffic was so heavy – not only were there the miners but also the herds of cattle and sheep needed to feed them – that the route became almost impassable with mud. Along the track stores and liquor shanties sprang up, including one on the pass itself.

The gold rush and the poor condition of the Harper Pass track intensified the efforts of Christchurch citizens to build a dray road to the West Coast. Work began on the Arthur's Pass road and by 1866 the first coach drove all the way from one shore of the South Island to the other. The coach era thus began and the horse-drawn service over Arthur's Pass continued for 57 years.

In 1923 the Otira Tunnel was finally completed after work had dragged on over four decades. Tunnels were dug from both ends and when they finally met, in July 1918, there was less than a three-cm error in their alignment. Trains quickly ended the era of horse-drawn coaches and today the run from Greymouth to Christchurch through Arthur's Pass National Park is the most spectacular train ride in the country.

The train brought tourists, of course, and it wasn't long before there was a growing push to make the area the country's first national park in the South Island. In 1929, only six years after the Otira Tunnel was opened, Arthur's Pass became New Zealand's third national park after Tongariro and Egmont.

CLIMATE

The mountains of Arthur's Pass not only attract bad weather, they create it. Like all alpine areas in New Zealand, the mountains of Arthur's Pass make the park colder, windier and wetter than the nearby lowlands. The wettest areas are on the western side of the Main Divide and Otira Township averages 5000 mm of rain a year. While at Bealey Spur, just down the road from Arthur's Pass on the eastern side of the mountains, the annual rainfall is about 1500 mm. Rain falls on Arthur's Pass Village 150 to 175 days of the year with the most unsettled weather occurring in spring and autumn.

The best weather is experienced in February and March but bring raingear and warm clothing whenever you visit the park. The high altitudes mean that temperatures fluctuate widely. The average maximum for Otira in January is 28° C while the average minimum for the same month is only 10° C.

NATURAL HISTORY

The Main Divide also marks a sharp contrast in the park's flora. The Westland slopes, with their greater rainfall and milder temperatures, are covered with lush forests of tall podocarp and higher up kamahi, rata and totara. On the eastern side, however, trampers encounter mountain beech forests with less understorey and drier conditions on the forest floor. The thick bush on the western side of the park also contains more birdlife; commonly seen are the tui, bellbird, South Island tomtit, rifleman and grey warbler.

The bird to watch out for, literally, is the kea. This alpine parrot is naturally inquisitive, a trait essential for its survival in the harsh alpine environment but also the cause of its many encounters with trampers. The kea, easily recognised by its olive-green plumage and piercing 'keaa' cry, will search huts for food and just for amusement. Its most notorious traits are stealing shiny objects, including metal cups, knives and car keys, and dissecting boots and backpacks with its strong, curved bill. It's an entertaining bird, however, sighted often above the treeline and even occasionally in the village itself.

With the possible exception of Harper Pass, keas can be encountered on any of the tramps in this section.

KEAS

CONSERVATION

Arthur's Pass National Park

The world's only alpine parrot

GOAT PASS

Goat Pass – also referred to as the Mingha-Deception Track (the two rivers the route follows) – is a two-day walk that is one of the least complicated routes to follow in the park. It's rated medium and is a popular trip – making it an excellent introduction to tramping in the park.

Access

Arthur's Pass is reached from either Greymouth or Christchurch by train or bus. The train is known as the Tranz-Alpine Express and is an enjoyable way to travel to the park. It departs Christchurch Railway Station (tel (03) 794-040) daily at 7.30 am and arrives at Arthur's Pass at 10.30 am. On the same day it departs Greymouth at 1.15 pm passing through the park again at 3.50 pm on its return to Christchurch. A one-way fare to Arthur's Pass from Greymouth is $16 and from Christchurch $23.

NZRRS buses for Arthur's Pass Village depart Christchurch from Monday to Saturday at 8 am, reaching the village at 10.45 am. There is a second run at 1.45 pm that arrives in the park at 4.25 pm. These are the same buses that continue to Greymouth. In the other direction buses depart Greymouth at 8.15 am and reach Arthur's Pass at 10.30 am before continuing to Christchurch. A second run leaves Greymouth at 1.15 pm and arrives in the park at 3.50 pm. There is little difference in fares between the buses and trains.

The Chalet Restaurant, just north of the youth hostel, serves as the bus depot. Tickets can be purchased here daily from 10 am to 4.30 pm and 6 to 7.45 pm. The best part about the NZRRS buses is that they can be used by trampers who are just heading down the SH73 a short distance to the start of a track. They can also be flagged down when you emerge from the track. The small cost of a bus fare saves a lot of hassle hitching in and out of town.

Places to Stay & Eat

Good accommodation is available at the *Arthur's Pass Youth Hostel*, a 10-minute walk north of the train depot. The hostel (tel (0516) 89-230) is well-organised for

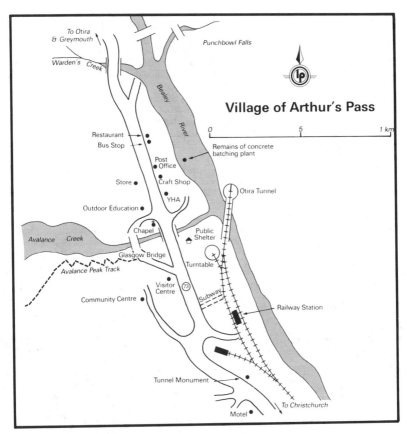

Village of Arthur's Pass

To Otira & Greymouth

Punchbowl Falls

Warden's Creek

Bealey River

Restaurant
Bus Stop

Post Office

Remains of concrete batching plant

Store

Craft Shop

Otira Tunnel

YHA

Outdoor Education

Avalance Creek

Chapel

Public Shelter

Glasgow Bridge

Avalance Peak Track

Turntable

Visitor Centre

73

Community Centre

Subway

Railway Station

Tunnel Monument

To Christchurch

Motel

tramping with lots of information on walks, a limited amount of equipment that can be rented, and even a potbelly stove in the common room perfect for drying out your boots. The cost is $11 per night for YHA members. It is even cheaper to pitch your tent, free of charge, at the public shelter, which doubles as a communal kitchen for campers. Also in town are a tearoom, a restaurant and motels. Then there is the Arthur's Pass Community Centre up the hill behind the park headquarters. On Thursday nights it turns into a pub. Lots of good tramping information there.

Equipment
This track is not a place for tennis shoes. The best footwear is the traditional all-leather hiking boot. Trampers with the new ultra-light hiking boots will survive but should anticipate sore feet at the end of the day due to long periods of boulder hopping along rivers.

Arthur's Pass is one place you don't want to be carrying any excess gear. Free storage is available at the park headquarters and the youth hostel. Remember that the headquarters closes at 5 pm; if you plan to arrive later, store your your excess gear at the YHA. On the other hand, the YHA doesn't open until 5 pm so if you are passing through at mid day leave your gear at the headquarters.

Also in town is a store (open daily from 8 am to 6 pm), with a good but expensive selection of supplies.

Information & Maps

Hut fees in the park are $7 per adult for Casey, Hawdon, Edwards, Goat Pass, Carrington and Carroll Huts. All others are $3. The fees can be paid at the park headquarters (tel (0516) 500) which is open daily from 8 am to 5 pm. You can also purchase maps, brochures and books here, notify them of your intentions (very important), and receive the latest weather forecast, which comes in at 9 am.

Use the recreational map to Arthur's Pass National Park, NZMS 273/1 or quad S59 of the NZMS 1 series.

The Track

Goat Pass is a 25-km walk, rated medium, that most people accomplish in two days, spending the night at the popular Goat Pass Hut. The hut is above the bushline and an extra day can be spent scrambling the surrounding ridges. The track can be walked in either direction but the following description is from the Mingha to the Deception River, allowing trampers to undertake the shorter day first. The southern end of the track is the confluence of the Bealey and Mingha rivers near Greyneys Shelter on SH73, five km south of Arthur's Pass. The northern end is the confluence of the Otira and Deception Rivers, six km up the road from Otira.

Stage 1: Greyneys Shelter to Goat Pass

Walking Time: four to five hours
Accommodation: Mingha Bivvy (two bunks); Goat Pass Hut (20 bunks)
If you are travelling by bus, the driver will drop you off at Greyneys Shelter as this is the first place the bus can pull over. It's a 10-minute walk north along the road to the junction of the Bealey and Mingha

Rivers, easily spotted from SH73 as it is a huge gravel plain.

Ford the Bealey and then round the point into the Mingha Valley and head up the valley along the true right (west) side of the river. In about a km you have to ford the Mingha to the true left (east) side where the easy walking continues for another three km. In about 1½ hours a huge rock cairn appears on the true right (west) side of the river with a small red marker on a tree near it. Ford the river again and follow the track which very soon comes out of the trees and crosses a wide rock slide.

On the other side of the rock slide is another large rock cairn and a 'Mingha Track' sign. At first the track runs level with the river but then makes a steep ascent to the top of Dudley Knob. It's a good climb but once on top you'll be able see both sides of the river valley. The track descends the knob a short way and then begins a gentle climb towards Goat Pass. This stretch can be especially boggy at times but the park service has planked much of it. A little more than two km from the knob the track passes Mingha Bivouac, a two-bunk hut.

For the next 1½ km you follow the river and ford it a number of times before a large rock cairn and red sign appears on the true left bank. This marks the final climb. The track passes the impressive bowl of Mt Temple and then follows the gorge to Goat Pass, though you rarely see it. This tussock slope is quite wet and boggy in places and there are long sections of boardwalk. The climb is easy and from the pass you can look down on its north side and spot the hut below.

Goat Pass Hut is a great place to spend a night or two. It's a roomy hut and it has a radio link with park headquarters that can be used to receive the latest weather report. An excellent climb for a layover day is to ascend to the east and follow the ridge to Lake Mavis.

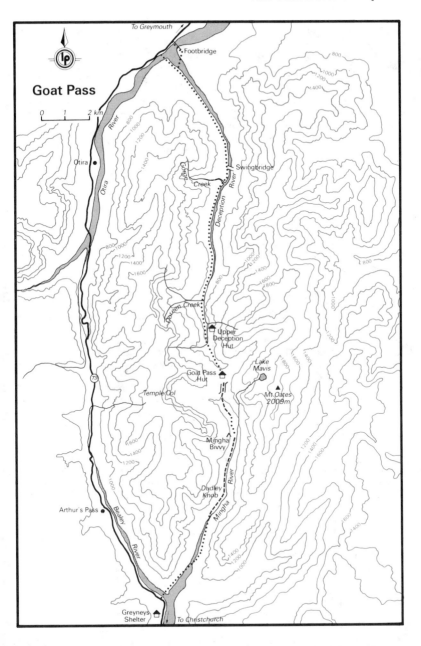

Goat Pass

0 1 2 km

Stage 2: Goat Pass to SH73
Walking Time: five to seven hours
Accommodation: Upper Deception Hut (six bunks)
The day begins at the stream behind the hut where a couple of snow poles have been placed. Follow the small stream, stepping from boulder to boulder, and you soon emerge at Upper Deception River. Here a huge rock cairn and equally large pole alert trampers walking towards the pass to leave the river and avoid the gorge just ahead.

Those heading down the valley continue boulder hopping along the river on the true left (west) side most of the time, though a series of cairns alert you to when to cross over to the other bank. There are also short sections of unmarked track that can be used if found. In about two km, you pass the Upper Deception Hut on the true right (east) bank, but you need to watch for it carefully as it is easy to miss.

In less than two km you break out into a wide section of the valley. The walking becomes considerably easier and again most of the track encountered will be on the true left (west) side of the Deception. In two hours you enter a gorge, pass the junction of Gorge Creek at the north end and then in two km enter another small gorge that, like the first one, is easy to walk through with only one or two fords of the river.

At the end of the second gorge, 10 km from Goat Pass, you arrive at a swingbridge across the river. Continue under it and soon Deception Valley swings to the northwest and begins to widen. It's about 5½ km from the bridge to SH73 with the final two km being a track on the true left side of the river through grazing land. Watch out for the cows.

Under normal conditions the Otira River is easily forded to reach the road just on the other side. But if recent rain has flooded the river, you should ford the Deception to its true right side and use Morrison swingbridge located just above the confluence of the two rivers.

If the Deception is flooded, it is also possible to follow its true left bank (rather than crossing it at the cairns) all the way from Goat Pass to the swingbridge at the end of the second gorge, though this would require negotiating a number of bluffs along the way. You would then cross the river here and follow the true right (north) bank to the Morrison swingbridge.

WAIMAKARIRI-HARMAN PASS ROUTE
This is an excellent five to six-day tramp, which crosses two alpine passes and covers a variety of terrain. It is rated difficult as much of it involves trackless river valleys where long stretches of boulder slogging will quickly tire out ankles and calves, while crossing the two passes involves steep routes that are only lightly marked with rock cairns. Part of this track crosses the neighbouring Taipo State Forest.

It is a walk for experienced trampers, but a rewarding one. Highlights include excellent views from Harman Pass and Kelly Saddle, superb trout fishing in the Taipo River and an evening soak in the hot springs at Julia Hut. If short on time or experience, you can shorten this tramp by hiking up the Waimakariri River and spending two nights at the roomy Carrington Hut before backtracking to SH73. The spare day can be used to climb Harman Pass, the more scenic and easier of the two alpine crossings.

Access
The trip begins at Klondyke Shelter, the next day-use facility south of Greyneys Shelter on the SH73, just before the road crosses the Waimakariri River. It terminates to the north at Kelly Shelter, also on the SH73, three km north of Otira Township. Neither shelter is set up for overnight use and both can be reached by NZRRS buses out of Arthur's Pass Village (see Access for the Goat Pass section)

Information
In 1988, there were hut fees for the

national park huts of Carrington and Carroll (see Information & Maps for Goat Pass for details) but not as yet for huts in the Taipo State Forest. Purchase a fishing licence if you plan to drop a line in the Taipo River.

The Track

This five to six-day trip, rated medium to difficult, is described from the Waimakariri River north to Taipo River and then over the Kelly Saddle, the easiest direction to cross the alpine pass.

Most trampers hike into Carrington Hut the first day and climb Harman Pass the next, spending the second night at the new Julia Hut. It is difficult, however, to know where to spend the third night. The natural destination is Seven Mile Hut, but in 1988 this was in bad shape. To continue to Carroll Hut makes for a 12-hour walk, which is beyond the capabilities of most trampers. Even if you stop at Mid-Taipo Hut – the one before Seven Mile Creek – you still face a nine-hour walk to Carroll Hut.

A small stove is almost a necessity on this trip as Carroll Hut does not have gas rings or a stove of any kind, while starting a cooking fire in Seven Mile Hut is nearly impossible.

Stage 1: Klondyke Shelter to Carrington Hut

Walking Time: five hours
Accommodation: Anti Crow Hut (six bunks); Greenlaw Hut; Carrington Hut (50 bunks)
In normal conditions, the Waimakariri River can be forded in most places using a degree of caution. This makes the shortest and easiest walk to Carrington Hut the route along the riverbed where trampers cross the Waimakariri and many side streams numerous times. If the river is flooded, however, you can use the all-weather track that runs along the south bank. This track can be very muddy at times and there is little to see except the trees around you. The average tramper

can follow the river to Carrington Hut in around five hours but would need six to seven hours to hike the all-weather route.

Begin at the 4WD track opposite the Klondyke Shelter on SH73 and follow it west to the small car park at the end. The route continues along the open grassy flats of the Waimakariri River catchment area. You will save time here if you avoid the meanderings of the braided river by hiking it 'from corner to corner'. Most trampers stick to the true left (north here) bank until they reach the confluence with the Crow River about 4.8 km from the highway. Fording the Waimakariri can be avoid along this stretch except where Turkey Flat forces the river to swing into the forested banks to the north of it.

As you near Crow River, the easiest route is often to cross the Waimakariri to the true right (south) bank and cut across the flats between the knobs and the mouth of Anti Crow River. If planning to stay at Anti Crow Hut ford the Waimakariri early and keep an eye on the treeline for the shelter. Once past Anti Crow River, ford the Waimakariri again to the true left (north) bank and follow this side to the distinct forested 'corner'. The river swings sharply around this corner so it is best to ford back to the true right (south) side before reaching it.

From the true right bank it is easy to reach Greenlaw Creek, recognised by a large two-metre log sticking out of a pile of rocks. You can look up the creek to see a portion of Greenlaw Hut sticking out among the trees. The hut belongs to the New Zealand Alpine Club but is open to the public. Beyond Greenlaw Creek a series of poles swing north across the flats for a km to Harper Creek. Stay on the true right side of the river after crossing the creek and quickly the bushy knob that marks the confluence of the White River should become visible.

It's roughly 3.2 km from Greenlaw Creek to the knob, at which point a well-beaten track heads west for five minutes

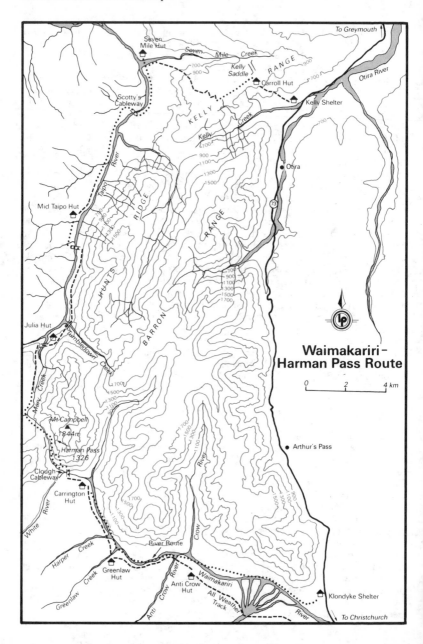

Waimakariri–
Harman Pass Route

to Carrington Hut. The hut is massive with four separate sleeping areas and two common rooms. This facility can easily sleep 50 people without anybody having to endure the floor. It also contains a radio that can be used in the morning to receive the latest weather report from park headquarters in Arthur's Pass. The hut is named after Gerald Carrington who in 1925 proposed to his friends around a campfire that they form a club and promote this valley for tramping. The Canterbury Mountaineering Club was formed but before the original hut was built here, Carrington drowned at the Waimakariri Gorge. The present hut was constructed in 1975 after the river changed its course.

Stage 2: Carrington Hut to Julia Hut

Walking Time: five to seven hours
Accommodation: Julia Hut (six bunks)
A track departs west from the large hut and in a little more than a km through the forest reaches Clough Cableway. It's an interesting device if you've never used one before and definitely easier if there are people cranking the car from both banks. If that's the case then all the passenger has to do is to keep away from the spinning handle inside the car and enjoy the great view of White River Gorge below. Once on the true left (north) side of the gorge a short track runs from the cableway to the Taipoiti River.

For most of the climb to Harman Pass, you follow the river up, hopping from one boulder to the next. There are a few rock cairns (but never when you need one) and even a few segments of beaten path. But during most of the climb you have to pick and choose your own route. It is probably easier to follow the true left (west) bank of the river for the first 1.3 km until a rock bluff forces you to the other side. More bluffs force you back to the true left side and eventually you climb towards what appears to be a granite bowl with steep walls and a waterfall. There is only one route up from here and that's on the true

right (east) side of the river where several large cairns mark the way up an easy rock and tussock slope.

Once on the slope, a distinct track appears and crosses two gullies before making the final ascent to Harman Pass. From the pass you can see up into Whitehorn Pass to the west or, more importantly, the three branches of Mary Creek to the north. Study the creeks and the gorge below. On the bluff opposite the pass there is an obvious route up it (the only one possible) that will allow trampers to skirt the gorge.

Also take time to study the route from the pass down to the branch of Mary Creek. Cross the stream and then ascend the bluff before the gorge. There are rock cairns to assist you but make sure you climb the bluff high enough to avoid the gorge totally. You then drop back down to the creek. Descend through the tussock grass and rocks (not as easy it appears) until you reach Mary Creek quite near the junction of its third branch. Ford the creek to its true left (west) side and begin boulder hopping down the stream.

The quickest route is to ford the creek from corner to corner and stay along the banks. Eventually within an hour or so from the pass you reach the bushline. Continue along the stream banks until you pass a rock slide on the true left (west) side and see a huge rock cairn (the biggest since crossing the pass); this is the start of the Julia Track which is marked by white metal tags. The track is three km long and twice climbs steadily up the side of the valley and then descends again. The first time you get an excellent view of Mary Creek. The second time involves a quick descent to the swingbridge, from which the hut is just a few minutes away. Be aware that at one point the track comes to a rock slide five metres above the river and resumes on the other side 30 metres up the scree.

Julia Hut was rebuilt in 1987 and is a very pleasant six-bunk facility with views of peaks all around it. The feature of this hut is the nearby hot springs that can be reached in 10 to 15 minutes by passing the old Julia Hut and continuing down the valley. Once you pass a tarn, look for a side track with white metal tags marking it. The track drops steeply to a swingbridge across the Taipo River. Don't cross the river, but rather hike downstream 150 metres or so and look for the greyish pools on the true right (east) bank.

During a dry spell, the water might be too hot to enter. If there has been too much rain, the pools could be impossible to locate in the swollen river. But if conditions are right, you can scoop them out and then soak away in the warm water with the Taipo rushing by an arm's length away. After climbing Harman Pass, nothing could be more pleasant. Bring the bucket from the hut to scoop out the gravel and deepen the pools.

Stage 3: Julia Hut to Seven Mile Hut

Walking Time: 5½ to six hours
Accommodation: Mid-Taipo Hut (six bunks), Seven Mile Hut (five bunks)
A track leaves the new hut, climbs a terrace and passes the old Julia Hut before heading down the valley along the true right (east) side of the Taipo River. In a km it crosses a wirewalk over Tumbledown Creek and continues as an easy walk although it tends to get boggy in places. It reaches a swingbridge five km from Julia Hut and crosses it to the true left (west) side of the Taipo. From the middle of the bridge it's possible to see a portion of the Mid-Taipo Hut although it's still a 15 to 20-minute trek away through grass and scrub flats. The six-bunk hut is a 2½ to three-hour walk from Julia Hut but it is in much better shape than the one at Seven Mile Creek.

From the hut a track continues through the open flats for 20 minutes and then climbs steeply up and around a gorge that the Taipo flows through. After descending to the riverbed the track becomes a route more or less through open flats for the next four km as it works it way towards the

noticeable knob located right before Scotty's Cable. This is a good stretch for anglers to look for pools in the river that might hold trout.

Eventually you reach the north end of the flats with the knob looming overhead and find a white metal marker pointing to a track leading up into the bush. If the weather is clear and the river easy to ford, parties should seriously consider continuing through the gorge instead of using the cableway to cross it. The track to Scotty's Cable involves an extremely steep climb, part of which is along an old stream bed, and an equally steep descent.

Either way you emerge from the gorge on the true right (east) side of the Taipo and continue down the river where the terrain quickly changes into grassy flats and terraces that make for easy walking. It's about 3.2 km from the cableway across the flats and past One Mile Creek to the Seven Mile Creek. Cross the creek (do not head upstream) and look for the hut in the open flats but near the bushline. The hut is old and rapidly deteriorating but still keeps out the weather. It's in a crucial location, however, and presumably it will be replaced someday soon.

Stage 4: Seven Mile Hut to Kelly Shelter

Walking Time: to Carroll Hut five to six hours; to Kelly Shelter six to eight hours
Accommodation: Carroll Hut (eight bunks)
You begin the day by recrossing Seven Mile Creek to its true left (south) side and hiking upstream to the distinctive white pole high on a bank. Go just beyond the pole (a 15-minute walk from the hut) and look for white metal tags and the start of a track. Once on the track you climb steeply and soon pass through an old mining trace, almost eerie to walk through. You then ascend sharply to the bushline, climbing 800 metres in four km. It's about a 2½ to three-hour hike from the hut to the small knob, marked by a large cairn just beyond the last stand of mountain beech. There are good views in

almost every direction, even of Seven Mile Hut where the day began.

From the knob a well-defined track climbs up the ridge through scrub and flax but quickly becomes obscured. There are a few white metal markers and segments of worn track here and there but basically you make your own route up to the top of the ridge where a large cairn and pole with a yellow disc are located. This is a very important marker for trampers walking in the opposite direction as it puts them in line with the start of the track at the bushline.

Once on top, a couple of cairns point the way along the most northern ridge, the lower of the two viewed running east. There are very few markers up here but try to stay to the north keeping the Seven Mile Creek in view below. Hike east up the ridge and over small knolls until you emerge at a series of small tarns. The route continues northeast from the small ponds over a tussock basin and up the main ridge of Kelly Range. When you reach the crest of the range you will be able to view at least a portion of Otira Valley.

From the tarns it's a km to the main ridge if you follow a direct route and then another 1½ km to Carroll Hut. You will actually see the hut soon after reaching the main ridge but stay on the crest of Kelly Range as the southeast side is very steep with rugged bluffs. The ridge will lead to slopes that you can easily descend to the hut, which is reached in five to six hours from Seven Mile Hut.

Carroll Hut, rebuilt in 1981, has eight bunks but no gas rings or heat of any kind. It's a very pleasant spot with excellent views of the surrounding mountains and a great place to spend an extra day. The hut is named after Patrick Carroll who died in the mid-1930s from a mountaineering accident. There is a chilling newspaper account of the mishap framed on the wall.

Beyond Carroll Hut, it is only 1½ hours to Kelly Shelter, maybe two hours if it's raining. The first km is above the bushline, the rest in the forest.

HARPER PASS

This is a five to six-day walk along a historic route that served as the main gateway for diggers in the 1864-65 gold rush to the West Coast. The track runs from Arthur's Pass National Park in the west to Lake Sumner State Forest Park in the east and crosses the Main Divide over Harper Pass, a low saddle of only 963 metres. The segment in the national park is a valley route along the Taramakau River, but in the state forest the track is well cut and marked which, combined with the low alpine pass, makes crossing the Harper Pass an easier trip than many others in the area, including Waimakariri-Harman Pass route.

Trampers have to be cautious with the Taramakau, however. It is a large and unruly river located in a high rainfall area, making it prone to sudden flooding. Because of the wild nature of the river, it's debatable in which direction it is best to walk the track. The easiest way is from east to west as less climbing is required when crossing from the valley of the Hurunui River to the Taramakau River. But the trip will be described here from west to east.

The track is easier to reach from Arthur's Pass and by following the Taramakau first you won't get blocked halfway along the track if a sudden rainfall makes the river impassable. Unlike the Taramakau below Locke Stream Hut, there is a well-defined track along the Hurunui and Hope Rivers and bridges at all major crossings. Once you cross Harper Pass into the state forest park, the track can be walked during most foul weather.

Access

At the western end of the track is a forest-service base hut, 1½ km north of Aickens on the SH73. It can be reached from Greymouth or Christchurch by NZRRS bus or on the Tranz-Alpine train which drops you at Aickens (see Access section of Goat Pass for details). At Arthur's Pass, an NZRRS bus departs the restaurant at 10.45 am from Monday to Saturday for Greymouth, passing the base hut along the way.

The eastern end of the track is Windy Point on SH7, seven km north of the Hope Bridge across the Boyle River, almost half way between the turnoff to Hanmer Springs and Maruia Springs. Current bus schedules are usually posted in Hope-Kiwi Lodge, the last hut for most trampers, but, as a rough guide, an NZRRS bus passes Windy Point between 2 and 2.30 pm weekdays for Westport and at 12.30 pm for Christchurch. The fare from Boyle River to Christchurch is $21.

The walk from Hope-Kiwi Lodge takes most trampers five hours, so an early start is necessary if you hope to catch one of the buses. It is best to be at the highway, ready

to flag down the bus, 30 to 40 minutes before it is due to arrive.

Information & Maps
Information, intentions and hut fees for national park huts can be left at the Arthur's Pass visitor centre and park headquarters. There is also a DOC office in Hanmer Springs (tel 7218). The entire track is covered by combining the national park recreational map, NZMS 273/1, with the national park recreational map for Lake Sumner Forest Park, NZMS 274/16.

The Track
This trip, rated medium, begins at the forest service base hut north of Aickens. If the Otira River is flooded, think twice about embarking on the tramp. A walk confined to the true left (south) side of the Taramakau, using the Morrison swing-bridge over the Otira near Deception

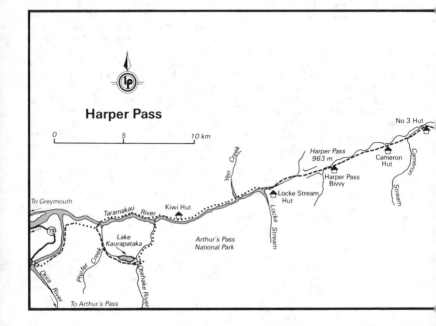

River and the Otehake Bridge and side track below Lake Kaurapataka would take 10 to 12 hours to reach Locke Stream Hut.

Stage 1: SH73 to Locke Stream Hut

Walking Time: six hours
Accommodation: Kiwi Hut (eight bunks); Locke Stream Hut (18 bunks)
From behind the forest service hut follow the paddock fence to the Otira and ford it to head for the obvious gap in the bushline directly across the river. A track leads through scrubby bush to grassy flats that provide an easy walk to Pfeifer Creek. Near the creek is a junction with a track that leads south (right) to Lake Kaurapataka, a beautiful body of water in the Otehake Wilderness Area. This is also a flood track as it connects with a route along the Otehake River, which joins the Taramakau. The high water alternative would take two to three hours to walk.

The main route continues from Pfeifer Creek with a ford of the Taramakau to the true right (north) bank where the travel is easier. It's about six km from the creek to Kiwi Hut and 1½ km before reaching it

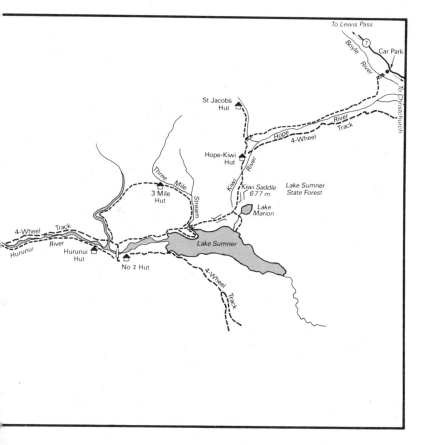

you pass the confluence of the Otehake River. Stay on the true right (north) side of the Taramakau River and keep a sharp eye out for an old track that departs for a grassy clearing. Trampers have been known to miss the hut as it sits well back from the river but the track to it is now well marked.

In places you might find remnants of an old vehicle track, but beyond Kiwi Hut the route is mostly boulder slogging along the true right (north) side of the river. It's nine km from Kiwi Hut to Locke Stream and the riverbed begins to narrow halfway up near Townsend Creek and steep northern banks force you to ford to the true left (south) side. Continue along the gravel beds until Locke Stream is reached. A track on the other side leads through the bush for 10 minutes to Locke Stream Hut, a national park 18-bunk facility with a radio link to the headquarters in Arthur's Pass. You can use the radio to pick up the latest weather report every morning around 9 am.

Stage 2: Locke Stream to No 3 Hut
Walking Time: seven hours
Accommodation: Harper Pass Bivvy (two bunks); Cameron Hut (four bunks); No 3 Hut (18 bunks)
Above Locke Stream the valley continues to narrow and the Taramakau appears more like a mountain stream. Signs of recent floodings, slips and fallen logs, mar the banks of the stream. Harper Pass Track begins at the hut and winds in and out of the forest as it climbs towards the alpine crossing. Keep a sharp eye out for trail markers that will indicate when the track moves back into the bush. This section is challenging and slow but within 1½ hours you should reach the footbridge located three km above Locke Stream.

After crossing the stream you swing to the true right (north) side and follow the Taramakau (though it's rarely visible through the bush) to the headwater gorges. Here the track begins a steep 280-metre ascent through forest to Harper

Pass, which is reached three hours from the hut. You never enter the tussock grasslands on the pass but drop quickly on the eastern side to the headwaters of the Hurunui River. Within 15 minutes of the stream, Harper Pass Bivvy is reached, a pleasant place to spend an evening.

The track departs the creekbed into lush subalpine scrub and follows terraces along the true right (south) side of the stream. It's a steady descent from the Harper Pass Bivvy for 6½ km until the track enters the first substantial flat with Cameron Hut half way down on the edge of the forest. From the small hut, it's a short walk to No 3 Hut. The track crosses the flat to a wirewalk over Cameron Stream and then stays in the fringes of the forest for the next 1½ km until it breaks out into a flat opposite Waterfall Creek.

No 3 Hut, which looks like a deserted schoolhouse, stands in the middle of the grassy clearing. The old building has a large wooden porch and an open fireplace.

Stage 3: No 3 Hut to No 2 Hut
Walking Time: four to five hours
Accommodation: Hurunui Hut (20 bunks); No 2 Hut (18 bunks)
A 4WD track departs from the hut and crosses the flats, reaching a signposted junction in a km. The main track veers to the south (right) and stays on the true right (south) side of the Hurunui River the entire day. The track undulates as it bypasses steep embankments the river has cut into the hillsides. If you want flat, easy travel, veer to the north (left) at the junction and follow the vehicle track all the way along the true left (north) side. If you plan to stay at the new Hurunui Hut, it's best to stick to the walking track.

From the junction the walking track is marked by a series of poles as it crosses the flats and then enters the forest. The track sidles up and down along the forested hillsides for two km, crosses another flat and then makes a long descent to the signposted hot springs, a two-hour walk from the hut. The thermal water emerges from rock 30 metres above the Hurunui and forms a cascade of hot water to the riverbed below. It's possible to soak in a small pool.

The track departs the hut and returns to the forest for a km before emerging onto a flat. The route cuts across the flat, returns to the bush and in 1½ hours from the hot springs arrives at the site of the new Hurunui Hut. The hut was built in 1987 as alternative accommodation for trampers who dislike sharing with people who drive vehicles to No 2 Hut.

The walking track continues and in 30 minutes arrives at the swingbridge across the Hurunui River, a km below the confluence of McMillan Stream. A vehicle track leads to No 2 Hut from here, another 15 minutes downriver. The hut features 18 bunks in two rooms with an excellent view across the lower flats to Lake Sumner and Mt Longfellow. Unfortunately it's a popular destination for vehicle users.

Stage 4: No 2 Hut to Hope-Kiwi Lodge via Kiwi Saddle

Walking Time: four to five hours
Accommodation: Hope-Kiwi Lodge (24 bunks)
Resist the temptation to cut across the flats and to ford the Hurunui River directly in front of No 2 Hut to avoid backtracking to the swingbridge. This route includes boggy areas and clumps of matagouri that can make the walk tedious and in the end more time consuming. Return to the swingbridge and follow the vehicle track on the other side to where it swings sharply to the west. A route marked with poles heads east (right) from here and crosses the valley along the forest edge. To avoid some cliffs, the track dips into the bush once before reaching the head of the lake.

On the northern side of Lake Sumner, the track enters forest again for an easy climb to Three Mile Stream, crossed by a swingbridge. There's a junction here with one track heading north towards Three

Mile Stream Hut and another south to Charley's Point on the lake. The main track departs east across the stream and begins the steepest climb of the day, gaining 150 metres before levelling off and finally reaching Kiwi Saddle, bushclad at 677 metres.

It's a quick descent through bush to the open tussock country along Kiwi River. The track follows the edge of the beech forest along the true left (west) side of the river and it's an hour's walk through the cattle flats to the Hope-Kiwi Lodge situated near the western edge of the forest. This hut is large – five rooms, two stoves and 24 bunks. There is more modest accommodation 1½ hours up the Hope River, at St Jacobs Hut.

Stage 5: Hope-Kiwi Lodge to SH7

Walking Time: five hours
Accommodation: Hope River Shelter (no bunks)
Begin this day early if you are intending to connect with an NZRRS bus on SH7. A vehicle track departs the hut and follows the true right (south) side of the Hope River, reaching the highway at the Hope Bridge. The walking track heads north through beech forest and grassy flats and in 45 minutes reaches a swingbridge over the Hope River. A side track continues north towards St Jacobs Hut (a 45-minute walk) but the main track crosses the swingbridge to the true left (north) side of the river.

The track immediately enters a large open flat and it's an easy walk for the next hour as you follow poles for four km until a bend in the river forces the track to climb into the forest. The track sidles between bush and more flats and in two km arrives at the Hope River Shelter, a three-sided hut with a stove and benches. The shelter marks the halfway point to SH7 as seven km remain of the journey.

The track remains in beech forest for the next two hours with few views of the Hope River. Eventually it breaks out onto a series of grassy terraces and follows the farmland for two km to a swingbridge over the Boyle River gorge. On the other side the track leads past service huts to a picnic area and a small shelter. A metalled road covers the remaining half km from the picnic area to the SH7.

OTHER TRACKS
Casey Saddle-Binser Saddle
This is an easy-to-medium two-day tramp in the drier southeast corner of Arthur's Pass National Park. The loop begins and ends near Andrews Shelter, reached from the SH73 by turning on to Mt White Station Rd and following it for five km to where it crosses Andrews River. There is a track most of the way and no difficult fords of large rivers. The well-cut track crosses two easy saddles, winds through open beech forest and follows the grassy terraces along the Poulter River. You can spend the night at Casey Hut, a modern 16-bunk facility, or at one of the good campsites you will find all along the route. Keep in mind that this track can often be walked when wet weather makes other routes marginal.

Three-Pass Trip
This is a challenging alpine route for experienced trampers through Harman, Whitehorn and Browning Passes. The trip can be walked in four to five days. From Arthur's Pass National Park you hike up the Waimakariri River to Carrington Hut. You cross Harman and Whitehorn passes to Park Morpeth Hut on Wilberforce River on the second day and climb over Browning Pass to Harman Creek Hut on the third. The east-west route ends at the Lake Kaniere-Kokatahi Rd where most trampers must continue the walk into Kokatahi. There are many steep climbs on this trip but the alpine scenery is spectacular.

Waimakariri Col
This is yet another trek that begins with a tramp along the Waimakariri River to Carrington Hut. From the hut, trampers continue along the upper portions of the river to Waimakariri Falls Hut. The three-day journey ends with a challenging climb over Waimakariri Col (1753 metres) and down Rolleston River to the SH73. This trip is rated difficult and the routes are only lightly marked over most of the alpine region.

Craigieburn State Forest Park

CASS-LAGOON SADDLE TRACK
One of the easier alpine routes in the Arthur's Pass region is a well-developed track over two saddles that actually lies just south of the national park. Cass-Lagoon Saddle Track is a 34-km walk in Craigieburn State Forest Park that has become a particularly popular weekend trip for Christchurch trampers. Although part of the tramp is technically a 'route', the entire trek is well marked and the alpine saddles easy to climb. This trip is rated medium and is usually walked in two days with a night at Hamilton Hut, one of the nicest huts in the South Island.

The track can be reached from Arthur's Pass Village (see the Goat Track section for information on getting to the village). As the state forest park is so close to the Arthur's Pass National Park, its history, climate and natural history are very similar.

Access
There is good transport to and from each end of the track along the SH73. The Tranz-Alpine train will stop at Cass Railway Station where there is also a car park. From here it is half a km down a road to the signposted track off the SH73. There is no station near the other end of the track at Bealey Hut but NZRRS buses

run in both directions along the highway and can be flagged down between 10 and 11 am from Monday to Saturday.

Information & Maps

The state forest has a park headquarters (tel Springfield 790) and small visitor centre in the southeast corner of the preserve, two km from the SH73 and 110 km from Christchurch. The visitor centre is open daily during the summer and contains displays on the park's features as well as information on the recreational opportunities, which range from tramping and hunting to skiing and caving. You can also pick up brochures and maps on the state forest park at the national park headquarters in Arthur's Pass.

Maps that cover the track include quad S66 of the NZMS 1 series or the cheaper recreational guide to Craigieburn State Forest Park, NZMS 274/17.

The Track

The track can be walked in either direction but will be described here from the Cass end to Bealey Hut, which is a 15-minute walk from SH73. You must almost run along the track from Hamilton Hut to meet any of the buses passing on the SH73. The more sensible alternative is either to end the second day at scenic Lagoon Saddle, two hours from SH73, or spend the night at Bealey Hut and catch the bus the next morning.

Stage 1: SH73 to Hamilton Hut

Walking Time: five to seven hours
Accommodation: Cass Hut (three bunks); Hamilton Hut (20 bunks)
From the signposted car park near the Cass railway station, follow the road back to the marked start of the track on the SH73, about a half km south of Cass River Bridge, and cross the stile into farmland. The route is well marked with poles and crosses the paddock to arrive quickly at a large state forest display sign that contains a box with an intentions book. The Cass River is just beyond and you

head upstream along the gravel flats fording from one side to the other when necessary.

If the river is flooded, there is an all-weather route that is signposted on the Grasmere Station access track near the display sign. Or within two km up the Cass River you will see flood route signs on the true right (south) side. But in normal conditions the Cass is easily forded and its gravel beds make for a much more pleasant walk than the flood route.

After travelling up the riverbed for four km (about 1½ hours) from SH73, a 'Craigieburn State Forest Park' sign appears on the true right (south) side and next to it is a well-defined track. You make an immediate climb, steep in some parts, and in three km you cross the Cass River on a bridge made of a huge log. The track then climbs another 90 metres in the next km to reach Cass Hut. As far as bivvies go – most being little more than a mattress in a tin box – this one is not bad. It's near the bushline, has some space inside, a small table and a nice stove.

Within minutes from the hut, you begin climbing towards Cass Saddle, and then break out of the trees to good views all around. During the winter this area is avalanche-prone and in the summer it's easy to see why. There are steep scree slopes on both sides of the alpine route. Poles lead through open tussock the remaining 1½ km from the hut to Cass Saddle at 1326 metres. The pass is marked by an exceptionally large pole. You can look down into the Hamilton Creek valley and, on a clear day, can even see the light-brown roof of Hamilton Hut.

From the saddle, the route veers left for 100 metres and then begins a quick descent into the bush and down a narrow ridge. The track drops more than 300 metres before it levels out in the upper portion of Hamilton Valley where it crosses several streams. One km from the hut, the track emerges from the bush onto the grassy terraces along Hamilton Creek. The hut is on a ledge above the creek and

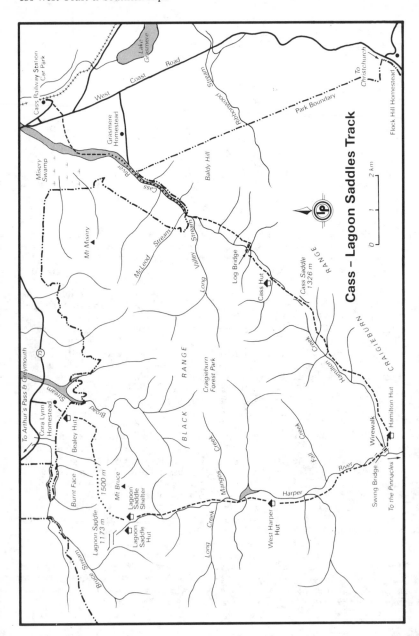

Cass – Lagoon Saddles Track

from its verandah you have a commanding view of the valley. Inside it's an impressive structure with 20 bunks, a wood stove, a huge stone fireplace and even a drying rack that can be lowered and raised.

Stage 2: Hamilton Hut to SH73

Walking Time: six to seven hours
Accommodation: West Harper Hut (five bunks); Lagoon Saddle Shelter (two bunks); Lagoon Saddle Hut (three bunks); Bealey Hut (six bunks)

The track heads west from the hut and almost immediately arrives at a wirewalk across Hamilton Creek (unnecessary in normal conditions). You continue up the Harper River on the true left (east) side and quickly come to a swingbridge. The track resumes on the true right (west) side and follows the valley through forest and open flats for 4½ km until it reaches West Harper Hut. Keep in mind that the track is well marked with red and white metal tags. Hunter's trails abound in the area, especially up side streams like Tarn Creek, and it's easy to mistakenly depart on one and not notice the main track resume on the other bank. West Harper Hut is 15 to 20 minutes beyond Tarn Creek and is strictly a hunter's bivvy with dirt floor, canvas bunks, fireplace and even an impressive set of antlers mounted on the wall.

From the hut the track soon arrives at a short gorge which it bypasses with a steep climb. In fine weather, it is easier to follow the river, fording it once or twice, and avoid the climb altogether. The track returns to the Harper and becomes more of a route along the riverbed with rock cairns marking the way. In about three km, you ford the river to a cairn on the true left (east) bank and pass a posted flood route before arriving at the confluence of the Harper and Long Creek.

At this point Long Creek usually looks like the major channel so a sign has been erected in the middle of the confluence that points the way to 'Lagoon Saddle'.

You continue to follow the riverbed for another half km until a track on the true left (east) side leads off into the bush and climbs to the saddle. The climb is steady but not steep and in 1½ to two hours from Long Creek you come to a sign pointing the way to the saddle or to the short spur track to Lagoon Saddle Shelter. The shelter is a clean A-frame with two mattresses, a wood stove and an inside loo. Nearby is Lagoon Saddle Hut that sleeps three.

The main track departs the junction and climbs steeply through beech forest for 120 metres until it reaches the bushline. Above the trees there is an excellent view of the saddle and the tarn in the middle, which is actually bypassed by the track. The climb continues but it is much easier and the views of the snow-capped peaks of Arthur's Pass National Park to the north get better and better. It's about three km across the alpine region with snow poles marking the route around Mt Bruce until you return to the forest edge at Burnt Face.

The final leg is a steep descent and in 2½ km the track reaches Bealey Hut. The hut is in surprisingly good shape considering how close it is to the road. It has a stove, table and canvas bunks. It's a five-minute walk to the car park and from there a 4WD road leads 1½ km through Cora Lynn Homestead to the SH73.

Mt Cook & Westlands National Parks

In a country as rugged and mountainous as New Zealand, where towering peaks are part of the everyday scenery, the Southern Alps still stand apart and boggle the mind. This great range, revered by climbers throughout the world, stretches along the length of the South Island, forming a backbone of greywacke and granite from Fiordland to the Nelson

Lakes. But the heart and the soul of the Southern Alps, and maybe of all New Zealand mountains, lie in a pair of national parks that straddle the Main Divide.

Mount Cook and Westland National Parks form a bastion of towering peaks and glaciers that is crowned in the centre by the monarch of mountains, Mt Cook, the tallest summit in New Zealand at 3764 metres. Surrounding the famous mountain are 18 other peaks that are over 3000 metres. Glaciers, including the Tasman that stretches for 29 km, cover 40% of Mount Cook, while Westland contains 60 named glaciers of which two, the Franz Josef and the Fox, are renowned trademarks of the West Coast.

It's not surprising then that, with so much rock and ice, these national parks are not trampers' parks. Mount Cook National Park is 70 square km of peaks, subalpine scrub, tussock, riverbed and permanent snow. Westland is 117 square km and rises dramatically from the Tasman Sea at Gillespies Beach to the Main Divide. Though the scenery is phenomenal and the day walks to fine viewpoints are numerous, the parks do not lend themselves to long-term tramps in the way Arthur's Pass to the north does. Most valleys west of the divide are extremely rugged, with steep gorges and thick bush, while to the east they inevitably lead to glaciers where experience and special equipment are needed to continue on the ice. Crossing the passes between the valleys is a major climbing feat.

This is a climber's world, not a tramper's.

The Copland Pass is an historic crossing of the Main Divide that is traditionally done in three to four days from east to west. Although 300 to 500 people make the crossing each year, it is an *extremely challenging* trek that demands more fitness and technical skill than any other popular walk in New Zealand. The walks up the Hooker or Copland Valleys are

Mt Cook

generally straightforward tramps – it's crossing the pass itself that is so challenging. Beyond Hooker Hut, the route involves a 1029-metre scramble up a loose rock ridge, while the final 150 metres is a climb up a 35° snowslope.

The second walk is an overnight trip to Mueller's Hut at the end of Sealy Range. The trek to the hut is still a stiff climb but it is not nearly as technical as the Copland, nor does it normally require the use of crampons and ropes. But the trip is, nevertheless, a journey into the alpine world of Mount Cook and, if the weather is clear, the views from the hut are spectacular. For most trampers this one-way track is the only opportunity to depart from Mt Cook Village and spend a evening among the peaks and the glaciers.

Even if you don't have the experience to continue onto the famous pass, you can make a very pleasant two to three-day journey from the West Coast up the

Copland Valley in Westland. A common trip is to hike into the Welcome Flats Hut, site of some very popular hot pools, and then spend a spare day exploring above the bushline around the Douglas Rock Hut. On the third day you tramp back out from Welcome Flats to the highway.

HISTORY

Only a small group of Maoris and a handful of European explorers lived or travelled in South Westland before the 1865 gold rushes brought miners to Okarito and Gillespies Beaches. Maoris knew of Mt Cook and called it 'Aoraki'. Tasman and Cook remarked on the rugged land as they sailed by, but it's doubtful they ever saw the towering peaks that now bear their names.

The first European to mention Mt Cook was Charles Heaphy. Travelling with Thomas Brunner along the West Coast in 1846, Heaphy made sketches of the mountain after learning about it from their Maori guides. In 1857 John Turnbull Thomas was the first non-Maori actually to explore the Mt Cook region from the east when he followed the west side of Lake Pukaki to its head and sketched the Tasman Valley with Mt Cook rising magnificently at the end.

Five years later Julius von Haast and Arthur Dobson spent four months exploring the rivers, valleys and glaciers of what is now the park and Haast wrote a colourful account of their findings for the Canterbury Provincial Government. 'Nothing I have previously seen,' wrote Haast, 'can be compared with the scenery, which certainly has not its equal in the European Alps.'

With such glowing reports, it didn't take long for climbers around the world to stage a race to its peak. The first serious attempt was made in 1882 by a young Irish clergyman and member of the Alpine Club of London. Reverend William Green saw photographs of Mt Cook and was so inspired he convinced Swiss guides Emil

Boss and Ulrich Kaufmann to sail halfway around the world to attempt the summit. Their first attempts, up an ice-ridge from the south and then up a route along Ball Glacier, were unsuccessful.

They then turned their attention to the north side and, following Haast Ridge, they came within several hundred metres of the top when the good weather broke and forced them back down. The three men spent a long night clinging to a narrow rock ledge at 3050 metres and listening to the boom of avalanches around them while trying to keep each other awake with song and political discussions to avoid slipping off. The next morning they retreated to their base camp. The climbers never reached the top but their story was widely publicised and this encouraged others, especially New Zealanders, to consider climbing the peak.

In 1894 Edward Fitzgerald, a famous English climber, announced his intention to become the first man to scale Mt Cook. Fitzgerald departed Europe with Italian guide Mattias Zurbriggen but soon after he arrived on the South Island the honour was swept from him by three New Zealanders. At 3 am on Christmas Day that year Tom Fyfe, George Graham and Jack Clarke launched a final assault on Mt Cook and by 1.30 pm reached the High Peak. Fitzgerald, who was quietly fishing near Christchurch at the time, was so infuriated that he didn't climb Mt Cook at all. Instead he made the first ascent of peaks all around the mountain – Sefton, Tasman and Haidinger.

The first Hermitage Hotel was built in 1884 near White Horse Hill (a fireplace is all that remains today) and it sparked interest in discovering an east-west route to the West Coast. In 1892, the Canterbury Provincial Government sent explorer and surveyor Charles Douglas to search for a pass over the Main Divide suitable for mule traffic. From the West Coast, Douglas went up the Copland Valley and explored several passes. He finally decided that the Copland Pass offered the best possibilities.

Fitzgerald and Zurbriggen made the first recorded crossing from east to west in 1895 when they climbed what is now Fitzgerald Pass and then spent three arduous days without supplies trying to find a way down the Copland Valley. Later that year Arthur Harper crossed the Copland Pass on his way to the West Coast after having accompanied Fitzgerald and Zurbriggen back to the Hermitage via passes at the head of Fox Glacier. Construction of the existing track began in 1910 and by 1913 the first Welcome Flats Hut was built. Its hot springs quickly made it a popular spot.

Climbs on Mt Cook continued to dominate the history of this region and give the Hermitage the unique status and aura of adventure that it still enjoys today. Much easier routes were pioneered after the first ascent which was not duplicated for 61 years. One by one the faces of Mt Cook were conquered, including the South Ridge in 1948 by a team of three headed by Sir Edmund Hillary. The last major approach, the hazardous Caroline Face, was finally conquered in 1970 by New Zealanders Peter Gough and John Glasgow.

CLIMATE

As might be expected, the weather in this region is harsh and extremely volatile. The Southern Alps are highest at Mount Cook and with the Main Divide, which averages 3000 metres here, form a major barrier to prevailing westerly winds. The mountains actually create a climate of their own. The annual rainfall in Mount Cook Village is 4000 mm and it rains on an average of 149 days a year.

The park experiences both long periods of fine weather and foul weather that lingers for days or even weeks. It is the latter that the park is most noted for; visitors often leave disappointed at not having viewed 'the mountain', while many arranged treks over the Copland

Pass never get further than the Hermitage Hotel.

Come prepared for strong winds, heavy rain and even snow, then rejoice if the skies clear and Mt Cook comes into view.

THE COPLAND PASS

The complete Copland Pass trek, from the Hermitage to SH6, offers an incredible cross-section of New Zealand terrain, from glaciers and steep snowfields to rock ridges, thermal pools and the lush rainforest near the West Coast. This is usually a once-in-a-lifetime adventure that can only be completed under good conditions and is only for those who are properly prepared.

For those who aren't properly prepared, it can turn into a life-threatening nightmare. It is a serious trip into an alpine area that experiences sudden changes in weather which can pin parties down for days with heavy snow, rain or gales. If you question your own physical stamina or alpine experience, don't even consider crossing the Copland Pass. Instead a modified trip, either heading to the Hooker or Welcome Flat huts for a night, would be a much more enjoyable tramp.

It is possible to hire guides from Alpine Guides. Since most parties employing a guide have considerable tramping experience, more than enough to handle Copland Valley, they usually hire a person for only 1½ days. The guide leads them over the pass to safe ground on the West Coast side and then returns to the Mount Cook Village with any equipment that was rented. The cost of a trip that includes a guide, hut fees at Hooker and equipment rental is $230 per person for a party of two and $190 per person for a party of three. It's best to write ahead (Alpine Guides, Box 20, Mount Cook; tel (05621) 834) if you're contemplating hiring a guide.

Access

The Copland Pass walk begins in Mt Cook

Village and finishes at the end of the Copland Valley on the SH6. The national park headquarters offers free storage but most people who cross the Copland Pass arrive carrying only what they need for the trek to avoid an expensive return to the village. The alternative is to catch an NZRRS bus from the Copland Valley end of the track to Fox Glacier and then a flight through Mt Cook Airlines (tel 812) back to the village. There is also a northbound NZRRS bus which passes the track end around 5 pm daily and reaches Franz Josef at 6 pm. A southbound bus reaches the track end at around 9 am daily and arrives at Queenstown at 4 pm. A one-way fare from the track to Franz Joseph, where there is a YHA, is about $10.

Equipment

The national park staff strongly recommend that every person attempting the pass has an ice axe to assist climbing in snow and crampons in case the snow is too hard for boots to grip. To hold a fall if somebody slips, there should be one rope in every tramping party and at least half the party should have enough mountaineering experience to be able to put in effective belays capable of holding a fall on snow or rock.

Trampers who have mountaineering experience but lack the proper equipment can rent ice axes and crampons from Alpine Guides who have a shop in Mount Cook Village. They will rent you the equipment necessary for four days for $43. This includes a fee to have it flown back after it has been dropped off at the Alpine Guides office at Fox Glacier so you don't have to return to Mount Cook Village after the trip.

The company can rent you just about any other piece of equipment, from climbing boots to headlamps. It will also sell camping and tramping gear. Food supplies can be obtained from a small store just up the street, though it's cheaper to bring your own.

Places to Stay

Besides the world renowned and very highly priced *Hermitage Hotel*, there are many places to stay in Mount Cook Village, including the *Mt Cook Youth Hostel* (tel (05621) 820), one of the nicest hostels in the country. A bed here costs YHA members $13 a night. It is well equipped and conveniently located within the village. Call ahead as it is heavily booked during summer.

The *White Horse Camping Area*, 1.8 km by road (about a 30-minute walk) from the village, is in a scenic location and has toilets, water and an eating shelter. Best of all, it's free.

Accommodation is also available at the *Franz Josef Youth Hostel*.

Information & Maps

Maps, books and brochures can be obtained from the national park head-quarters and visitor centre (tel (05621) 819), open daily from 8 am to 5 pm. The centre has a number of displays on the park as well as an interesting slide presentation that covers the mountain-eering history of the park in such a way that you want to start climbing the minute it's over. This is also the place to leave your intentions, check the weather which is recorded every day at 9 am and pay hut fees – $10 a night for Hooker Hut and $7 a night for Douglas Rock and Welcome Flat Huts in Westland. You can also pay the fees at the Fox Glacier visitor centre in Westland.

NZMS 180, the recreational map that covers both Mount Cook and Westland National Parks, is sufficient if you are only hiking the valleys of the Copland Pass track. For the entire crossing you need quads S79 of the NZMS 1 series, covering the track from the village to Welcome Flats Hut.

The Track

Crossing the Copland Pass from east to west is strongly recommended as it is the easier and safer route to follow. The

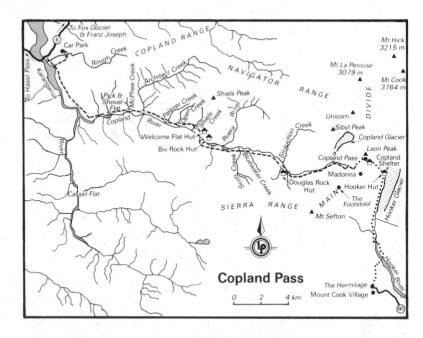

Copland Pass

0   2   4 km

following description is a four-day trip
with nights spent at Hooker, Douglas
Rock and Welcome Flats Huts. To save a
day, you can pass Douglas Rock and
spend the second night at Welcome Flats.
This trip is rated extremely difficult.

Stage 1: Mount Cook Village to Hooker Hut
Walking Time: three to four hours
Accommodation: Hooker Hut (12 bunks)
For most parties the first day is an easy
three-hour walk from the village to
Hooker Hut. The track begins in front of
the Hermitage on the Kea Point Nature
Walk and appears as a well-graded tourist
path before quickly branching off and
passing White Horse Hill, 30 minutes
from the hotel. It continues through old
moraines towards Hooker River and if the
day is clear, Mt Cook will dominate the
valley scene. Eventually the track reaches
the river, crosses over to its true left (east)

side on a swingbridge and then in 30
minutes crosses back over to the true right
(west) side.

About 1½ km from the second bridge
the track reaches an alpine meadow where
there is a shelter on the north side of
Stocking Stream. At this point the track
begins to climb and in 30 minutes reaches
the terminal lake of the Hooker Glacier.
This is the end of Hooker Valley Track. A
marked route takes over, following the
beach for 150 metres. The route then
heads diagonally uphill, crossing the
rocky bed of a side stream. From here rock
cairns show the way and even stretches of
track appear as the well-defined route
leads across a moraine terrace to a second
side stream. This is an avalanche path in
winter and spring.

The route crosses the gully and works
its way up a terrace. Once across the
terrace, the route zigzags through another
side gully and a section of rocky scree

Top: Wekas on Inland Pack Track, Paparoa NP (JD)
Left: Start of the Inland Pack Track, Paparoa NP (JD)
Right: Limestone bluffs along Inland Pack Track, Paparoa NP (JD)

Top: Lake Tekapo, Mt Cook NP (IK)
Bottom: Moeraki River, Mt Cook and Westlands NPs (IK)

before finally dropping to the grassy basin where the Hooker Hut is. The hut has 12 bunks but can be a very busy and cramped place during summer. It also has gas rings, a radio and a beautiful view of Mt Cook's southern face.

Stage 2: Hooker Hut to Douglas Rock Hut

Walking Time: 10 hours

Accommodation: Douglas Rock Hut (12 bunks)

Leave Hooker Hut early, as the 1020-metre climb to the top of the pass can take from three to six hours, depending on the fitness of the group. Most parties leave at 5 or 6 in the morning and work steadily towards the Copland Pass, knowing that even clear weather can deteriorate in as little as two hours. Cloud and mist often blow in from the west during the afternoon and obscure visibility.

The route, marked by rock cairns and poles at the beginning, heads up the valley and then climbs steeply along a deep rocky gully before crossing it. On the other side a well-formed path descends slightly and then climbs to the main ridge to Copland Pass. Rock cairns indicate the way along the main ridge through broken rock bands and scree slopes. It is safest to follow the ridge but you will be exposed to steep dropoffs here. If conditions become icy on the ridge, parties should put on crampons and rope up before continuing.

The ridge is easy to follow to a step, 152 metres below the pass, where there is an emergency shelter. The Silver Barrel Hut contains benches, a radio and a shovel that is attached to the roof for use when the door is buried in snow early in the season. The hut is reached by most parties in about three hours and is often used as a rest stop for the second breakfast of the day. Beyond the shelter the route to the pass is on permanent snow. The snow slope lies at an angle of about 35° and parties should rope up before continuing. Usually the snow is soft enough to 'kick' steps but late in the summer it might become icy and good cramponing

techniques are needed to negotiate the slope safely.

The snow slope lies on the right of a rocky ridge that makes a line from above the shelter towards the pass. The slope follows the ridge until it nears the top then veers further right to the actual pass, a small notch in the Main Divide. It takes about an hour to travel from the shelter to Copland Pass, reached at 2148 metres. If the weather is clear, the view from 'the roof of New Zealand' is immense. To the south is the Tasman Valley, to the west the Tasman Sea and all around are the peaks of the Southern Alps, dwarfed by Mt Cook's overpowering size.

The descent into Copland Valley begins with a steep and sometimes iced-up rocky gully that is followed for 45 metres. Again this is a section where many parties will rope up. The route continues through two rocky scree basins that are often filled with snow. Keep towards the bottom of the basins. The second will run into the rocky gully of a stream. A well-defined track begins on the true left of the stream at about 1300 metres.

This track is marked by rock cairns. It wanders through tussock to large rocks and a waterfall, from where it follows a series of switchbacks to the head of the Copland Valley, crossing a number of avalanche gullies before reaching the bushline. Five minutes after entering the bush, Douglas Rock Hut is reached, completing a 1430 metres descent from the pass. Douglas Hut has a radio link to the Westland National Park headquarters that provides trampers with weather reports every morning.

Stage 3: Douglas Rock Hut to Welcome Flat Hut

Walking Time: two to three hours

Accommodation: Welcome Flat Hut (50 bunks)

This easy walk of eight km to Welcome Flat Hut takes most trampers only two to three hours. But after the hard climb over Copland Pass many find a short hike and a long afternoon in the hot springs the ideal way to spend the next day. The well-defined track leaves Douglas Rock Hut, almost immediately crosses a bridge over Tekano Stream and works its way through forest around a ridge. It follows a broken Copland River and crosses a number of open slips before descending to Scott Creek.

Under normal conditions the creek is easy to ford and the track continues on the other side where it breaks out into the open tussock of Welcome Flat. This is a pleasant area along the river surrounded by peaks and snowfields. It's not hard to justify an extended break here even though you're less than an hour from the hut. The flats are marked with rock cairns that lead back into bush, and in 30 minutes the track arrives at the swingbridge. The hut is on the true right (north) side of the river.

Welcome Flat Hut was built in 1986 and is an excellent facility featuring a coal stove, a radio and enough platform bunks to hold up to 50 people. Nearby are the hot pools first noted by Charles Douglas in 1896. The water emerges from the ground at 60° C and flows through a series of pools towards the Copland River. Most bathers prefer the second pool. A midnight soak on a clear evening is one of the most memorable highlights of this trip; weary hikers can lie back in the heated water and count the falling stars streaking across the sky.

Stage 4: Welcome Flat Hut to SH6 Car Park

Walking Time: six hours

The track climbs for a km through a ribbonwood forest to the high point of the day and then makes a quick descent to the bridge across Shiels Creek. It's another 20 to 30-minute descent to Open Creek and the next footbridge and an even shorter walk to Palaver Creek where you cross the third bridge of the day. You continue to descend gradually and in two km you reach a swingbridge over Architect Creek,

a 300-metre drop from the Welcome Flat Hut.

The track swings towards the river's edge after crossing Architect Creek, forcing trampers to hop from one large boulder to another. From here the track alternates from the river bed boulders to bush. Trampers should keep an eye out for the orange markers where the track enters the forest again. It's a km to the bridge over McPhee Creek from Architect and then another two km to a bridge over an unnamed stream.

The track eventually departs from the Copland and crosses a forested terrace to a side track that leads to a view of the confluence between the Copland and the Karangarua Rivers. The track, well graded now, continues in a forest of rimu and totara for two km until it emerges onto open river flats. Poles mark the route across the flats where, on the other side, the track enters the forest for a short distance before coming to Rough Creek. There is a footbridge 30 minutes upstream but normally the creek can be easily forded.

On the other side is the car park with an intentions book where people can sign out. From the car park it is 200 metres to SH6.

MUELLER HUT

A round-trip walk to Mueller Hut can be done in a single day but to appreciate fully the scenic setting of the hut and its unique montaineering character a night should be spent on the alpine ridge. Mueller Hut also makes it possible to venture away from the bustling village and into the mountains unencumbered by mount-aineering equipment and without the many complications of the Copland Pass.

Equipment

Many trampers take an ice axe on this walk though crampons and rope are usually unnecessary during summer. Experienced trampers can easily handle

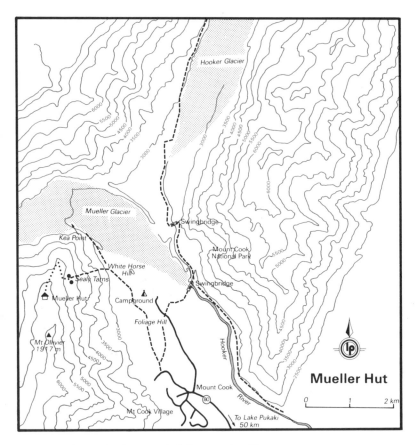

Mueller Hut

0   1   2 km

this overnight trek but keep in mind that this is still an alpine trip that should not be undertaken in poor weather.

See the preceding Pass section for information on places to stay, renting equipment or purchasing supplies in Mount Cook Village.

Maps & Information

Before heading out in the morning, stop at the national park headquarters to read the weather forecast for the day. Also leave your intentions there and pay your hut fees. The fee for Mueller Hut is $10 per

night. The best map for this trek is the quad S79 of NZMS 1 series which can be purchased at the visitor centre.

The Track

This trip is rated difficult because it involves a steep climb. Return along the same track but decrease the walking time from five hours to three hours.

Stage 1: Hermitage to Mueller Hut

Walking Time: five hours in good conditions

Accommodation: Mueller Hut (12 bunks)

The trip begins at the Hermitage by following the Kea Point Nature Walk, a very level and well-maintained path that heads up the open scrub of Hooker Valley towards White Horse Hill. Within 30 minutes you pass Foliage Hill and see two lodges and the campground shelter near the base of White Horse Hill. The track begins to climb gently, moves into bush and comes to the signposted junction of the Sealy Tarns Track. Kea Point is to the north (right fork), a 15-minute walk away. It is well worth the side trip as the viewing point sits on an old lateral moraine above Mueller Glacier with Mt Sefton overhead.

The route to Mueller Hut continues west (left fork) on the Sealy Tarns Track. It's a two-hour climb to the tarns, a knee-bender at times but overall not that difficult as the track was recently improved with steps much of the way. As soon as you begin climbing you are greeted with excellent views of the lower end of the

Hooker Valley

Hooker Valley to the south, including the Mount Cook Village. Higher still are views of the upper portions of the valley and the Mueller Glacier. The tarns, a series of small pools, make a natural rest stop as they are located in a narrow meadow on the ridge. Occasionally somebody even swims in the larger one.

Just south of the tarns look for a huge rock cairn that marks the route continuing to Mueller Hut. It begins as a well-worn track that involves a lot of scrambling and eventually fades altogether on a slope of rocky scree. At this point more rock cairns mark the way over boulders towards a large orange and black pole that is impossible to miss on a clear day. Take your time hopping from one boulder to the next to avoid any mishap.

Once at the pole, the route swings around to head in a more northerly direction and continues towards the end of the ridge. This section is often covered by snow – an ice axe comes in handy if conditions are icy. It's about a 15 to 20-minute scramble up the snow or scree slope to the end, from which there are excellent views of the upper portion of the Mueller Glacier and the peaks of the Main Divide. Rock cairns continue around the side of the ridge and lead south for about 20 minutes until the hut is reached on the crest of the ridge. Keep a sharp eye out for the hut as occasionally trampers miss its orange roof.

The original hut was built in 1915, closer to Kea Point than on top of the ridge. It was replaced in 1950 but was almost immediately destroyed by an avalanche. The present hut, at 1800 metres, has gas rings and a radio. Needless to say, the views are excellent and include not only its namesake glacier below but, if you are blessed with clear weather, the peaks of the Main Divide crowned by Mt Cook. It's possible to scramble up Mount Ollivier, the first peak Sir Edmund Hillary climbed, which at 1917 metres commands an even better panorama of the area.

OTHER TRACKS
Karangarua Valley

This is a much more remote valley than the popular Copland Valley just north of it. The track begins just south of the SH6 bridge over the Karangarua River, not far from the car park for the track to Welcome Flat. The first leg is a five-hour walk to Cassel Flat Hut (six bunks) through the dense, lush rainforest. The track to the hut is rated medium but to go beyond is a much more challenging trip because of the rougher terrain. The huts further up the valley at Lame Duck and Christmas Flats are in poor condition.

The Far South

Mt Aspiring National Park

Stand on the ridge to Cascade Saddle and when you look up you see snow, ice and the classic spire summit of Mt Aspiring. When you look down, the scene changes to wide tussock flats, beech forest and the pulsating current of the Matukituki River's West Branch. Climb the ridge in the early morning and there might be a mist blanketing the valley below; stay for the afternoon and the sun might be reflected by the snowfields and glacier, blinding you with brightness.

Mt Aspiring National Park is a fitting end to the Southern Alps. It has wide, rounded valleys with secluded flats,

more than 100 glaciers and mountain ranges with peaks of over 2700 metres, including 3027-metre-high Mt Aspiring, the tallest mountain in New Zealand outside Mt Cook National Park. The park is more than 2890 square km and stretches from the Haast River in the north to the Humboldt Mountains in the south, where it has a common border with Fiordland National Park.

From a tramper's point of view, the national park has a split personality. Although this is the country's second largest park, most trampers walk only the small portion of it around Glenorchy. Within this region there are several popular tracks including the Routeburn – second only to the Abel Tasman Coastal Track as the most heavily used trail in New Zealand. This three-day walk draws

Swingbridge in Mt Aspiring NP

about 9000 trampers a year, most of whom walk the track sometime between November and March.

The Routeburn is a tramp over the Main Divide from the Milford Rd in Eglinton Valley to the lower portion of the Dart Valley. It passes through thick rainforest with red, mountain and silver beech forming the canopy, and ferns, mosses and fungi covering everything below like wall-to-wall shagpile carpeting. But it's the alpine sections that most appeal to trampers. The tranquillity of a tussock meadow, sprinkled with giant buttercup and flowering spaniard, and the dramatic views of entire valleys or mountain ranges are ample rewards for the steep hike up and for the frequent encounters with other trampers.

The other tracks in this area, though not nearly as busy, also draw large numbers of trampers during the summer. The Greenstone is a two-day walk renowned for its trout fishing. It is a relatively level walk that draws between 2000 and 3000 hikers a year and is often combined with the Routeburn to form a circular walk. Nearby is the Caples Track which is a two-day walk just to the north of the Greenstone that shares its starting and finishing points. Both feature open river-flats of tussock grass along rivers with clear pools and rippling currents where it's often possible to spot the trout lying in their holes.

North of Glenorchy is the Rees-Dart Track. This is a walk along the valleys of the Dart and Rees Rivers, which are joined by the Rees Saddle. The Dart River separates the Forbes Mountains from the Southern Alps on the west while the Rees River separates them from the Richardson Range on the east. Both rivers drain into the head of Lake Wakatipu. The four to five-day trip is more difficult than the other three Glenorchy tracks but still draws about 1500 trampers a year.

In contrast to the popularity of the Glenorchy region, the other tramping areas of the national park near the towns of Wanaka and Makarora are little used. Though the Routeburn draws 9000 trampers a year, the equally beautiful Wilkin Valley near Makarora is walked by fewer than 500 trekkers each year. Much the same is true of the Matukituki Valley. These areas offer spectacular alpine scenery and more challenging trips but far fewer encounters with other people. The Wilkin River Track is a three-day trip that involves bush tracks, grassed valleys and a climb over 1460-metre Gillespie Pass.

Near Wanaka, there is the challenging but scenic Cascade Saddle Route – a two to three-day walk along the West Branch of the Matukituki River, over the 1500-metre pass and along Dart Glacier to the mid-point of the Rees-Dart Track. The entire trip, from Matukituki Valley to the end of the Rees-Dart Track is a four to five-day journey that many trampers believe is unmatched in alpine beauty, even by the Routeburn or Milford Tracks.

HISTORY

There are traces of a village at the mouth of the Routeburn and a moa-hunting site near Glenorchy but the real value of this area to the Maoris was as a trade route between South Westland and Central Otago and as a source of greenstone, highly valued for tools and weapons. The first people probably discovered the greenstone when wandering through in search of moa. Some tribes might even have settled portions of the Routeburn, lower Dart and Rees Valleys, but when the giant bird became extinct in the 1500s they quickly moved back to the coast.

Maori expeditions in search of greenstone are said to have been held as late as 1850 – about the same time the first Europeans began exploring the region. The veil of obscurity over the upper Wakatipu area was first lifted by W G Rees. In 1860, after establishing his sheep station near Queenstown, he sailed to the head of Lake

Wakatipu in September and discovered the Rees and Dart rivers draining into it. In 1861, he set up a sheep station near Glenorchy and was granted the lower flats of the Rees for stocking.

In the same year, David McKellar and George Gunn, part explorers and part runholders, shed some light on the Greenstone Valley when they struggled up the river and then climbed one of the peaks near Lake Howden. What they saw was the entire Hollyford Valley, but they mistakenly identified it as the George Sound in Fiordland. The great Otago gold rush began later that year and by 1862 miners were digging around the lower regions of the Dart and Rees as well as in the Routeburn Valley.

Prospector Patrick Caples made a solo journey up the Greenstone from Lake Wakatipu in 1863 and then discovered the Harris Saddle before descending into the Hollyford Valley and out to Martins Bay. Caples, brave enough to cross the Ailsa Mountains on his own, saw a native hut and smoke from a fire near a beach in Martins Bay and panicked. He returned to the bush where he hid, too afraid to approach the handful of Maoris despite being starving. Caples returned through the valley that now bears his name to end a three-month odyssey in which he became the first European to reach the Tasman Sea from Wakatipu. But, in all his walking, he never did turn up any payable gold.

Miners were mystified by the hidden valleys of the area and dreamed of a mother lode that was yet to be discovered. Much exploration and prospecting was done in the Humboldt Mountains and the Olivines and Rees Valley, but little was undertaken in the upper portion of the Dart.

The first person to cross the Barrier Range, late in the century, from Cattle Flat on the Dart to a tributary of the Arawata River was William O'Leary, an Irish prospector better known as 'Arawata Bill'. He roamed the mountains and

valleys of this area and much of the Hollyford River for 50 years, searching out various metals and enjoying the solitude of the open, desolate places. Unfortunately, Arawata Bill kept most of what he knew about the passes and routes to himself.

Mountaineering and a thriving local tourist trade began developing in the 1890s and was booming, even by today's standards, in the early 1900s throughout the Mt Aspiring area. Visitors were taken up to the Routeburn Flats by horseback and on the following day would climb to Harris Saddle for the view. Hotels sprung up in Glenorchy along with guiding companies who advertised trips up the Rees Valley by horse and buggy. Sir Thomas Mackenzie, Minister of Tourism, pushed for the construction of the Routeburn trail and hired Harry Birley of Glenorchy to establish a route. In 1912, Birley 'discovered' Lake Mackenzie and the next year began cutting a track.

The famous track reached Lake Howden by the outbreak of WW I but the final portion wasn't completed until the road from Te Anau to Milford Sound was built by relief workers during the Depression. Until then a tramp on the Routeburn had meant returning on the Greenstone.

Relief workers also cut a stretch of the Rees-Dart Track when they carved out a horse route from Cattle Flat to the junction of the Dart River and Snowy Creek. The last five km to Dart Hut, which finally connected the two river tracks, was constructed in 1939 by contract workers. That same year, Ernie Smith and A P Harper pioneered a route from Cascade Camp in the West Matukituki Valley to Tyndall Ridge and eventually down the Dart Glacier to Dart Hut.

The first move to make Mt Aspiring a national park came in 1935, but for all its beauty and popularity with trampers and tourists, the park wasn't officially preserved until 1964. Still some valleys such as the Greenstone, Caples and much of the Rees lie outside the park with little protection from road-building enthusiasts.

CLIMATE
Weather in Mt Aspiring varies dramatically from from one end to the other. A rain gauge just west of the Homer Tunnel measures 7110 mm a year while Glenorchy, 34 km to the east, receives only 1140 mm annually. In general, the Routeburn, the Dart River valley and the western half of the Greenstone and Caples Tracks receive about 5000 millimetres of rain a year and there is the possibility of snow above the 1000-metre level in almost any month. But the lower Rees, Matukituki and Wilkin Valleys are considerably drier, receiving on an average about 1500 mm.

The weather tends to be more settled from January to March and February is often suggested as the best month for walking. But keep in mind the park is a typical alpine region and you must be prepared for sudden changes in weather and unexpected storms regardless of what month it is. To tramp any but the Greenstone Track outside the November-to-May season requires much experience and special equipment.

NATURAL HISTORY
Much of the park is predominantly silver beech with red and mountain beech in the southern half. This makes for semi-open forests and easy tramping in most valleys, unlike in the Fiordland jungles where you rarely step off the track because of the thick understorey. West of the divide there is rainforest of rimu, matai, miro and kahikatea. Between the valleys are mountain meadows that support one of the greatest ranges of alpine plants in the world.

The distinctive character of the park is due to repeated glaciation between long warm periods. This has lead to an array of glaciers, hanging valleys and cirque basins among the mica-schist mountains. Glaciers gouged out the distinctive wide valleys and rounded the ridges, taking the sharpness off the terrain for trampers.

ROUTEBURN TRACK
Combine the well-cut track with the great alpine views and the notoriety the Routeburn enjoys in tramping and travel literature and you have the reason almost 9000 people walk it a year, the vast majority between December and February. Often if overseas visitors tackle no other track during their stay, they will walk the Routeburn.

During most of the summer, the huts along the track are full and many trampers are thankful just to get a spot on the floor. There will also be a constant flow of foot traffic between huts and probably a small gathering at Harris Saddle. You put up with the large numbers of people because the mountain scenery is truly exceptional or you go somewhere else to tramp.

Access
The track can be hiked in either direction and there is now a variety of public transport going to each end. The majority of trampers pass through Queenstown and begin the track from the Glenorchy side. They end up at the Divide where they can catch transport to Te Anau (after first viewing Milford Sound) or all the way back to Queenstown. Or you can loop back to the Glenorchy side of the Humboldt Mountains by walking either the Greenstone or the Caples Tracks.

The newest transport company is perhaps the most accommodating for trampers. Magic Bus was formed in 1986 primarily to transport walkers between the major tracks of the area and features numerous photo spots along the way, music in the buses, and generally very friendly and helpful drivers. A bus departs Queenstown in the morning from a variety of points including the post office at 8 am, the Queenstown Motor Camp at 8.15 am and the Youth Hostel at 8.30 am. It reaches the ranger station and visitor centre in Glenorchy at 9.30 am, where information and maps can be obtained, and finally arrives at the track at 10.15 am.

It departs the track at noon and is back at the Queenstown Youth Hostel by 1.40 pm. On the other side at the Divide, a Magic Bus reaches the track at 9.30 am daily and continues on to Milford Sound. It returns to the track at 2.45 pm and arrives at the Te Anau Youth Hostel at 4 pm. The one-way fare for Queenstown to Routeburn is $15; for the Divide to Milford Sound to Te Anau it is $25. The fare for Divide to Te Anau is only $15. It's best to book; tickets can be purchased at the Queenstown Youth Hostel (tel (0294) 28-413), the Te Anau Youth Hostel (tel 7847) or the Magic Bus office in Queenstown (tel (0294) 27-880).

Also providing a service to both ends of the Routeburn are buses from H & H Tours and NZRRS. H & H buses depart Queenstown daily during the summer from the company office (tel 149) on Camp St at 9 am, stop at Glenorchy at 10.45 am and reach the start of the track at noon. The bus then departs the track at 2 pm and is back in Queenstown by 4.15 pm.

NZRRS provides two buses daily between Queenstown and Milford that pass through Te Anau and can be used by trampers who want to depart from the Divide in either direction. The buses depart Queenstown at 8 am and 10.30 am and Milford Sound at 7.45 am and 3.30 pm, quickly passing the Divide. H & H charges $18 for its Queenstown to Routeburn run while a one-way fare on the NZRRS bus from Queenstown to Milford (including the Divide) is $49.

And finally, for those who absolutely have to be first on the track to ensure getting a bunk at Routeburn Falls Hut, Glenorchy Holiday Park (tel (0294) 29-939) offers an early bird package. This includes transport from Queenstown to Glenorchy – a beautiful little town surrounded by mountains – and a night's lodging at the holiday park. The next day

a mini-bus departs the motor camp at 8.30 am and reaches the track at 9.30 am. The cost of the package is $23 per person for a tent site or $28 for a bunk in one of their bunkrooms. This is not such a bad deal as it allows you to get ahead of the stampedes of walkers that the buses create. In addition, a night in Glenorchy, with its friendly little pub, is much more pleasant than staying in touristy Queenstown.

It's possible to hitch to and from the track but the 50 km from Queenstown to the Routeburn can be a challenging stretch to thumb, especially beyond Glenorchy. There is considerably more traffic on the Milford Rd.

Places to Stay

At Glenorchy, the *Glenorchy Holiday Park* offers tent sites for $5 per adult, cottages that hold one to four people for $40 and a large bunkroom with beds at $10 per night. These all include use of the communal kitchen and the showers. At Milford Sound there is now low-cost accommodation at *Milford Lodge*, which the park administers like a track hut. A bunk for the night is $15.

At Te Anau, there is the *Manapouri Holiday Camp* (tel 624) which is a km from the post office down the Te Anau Road and has sites for $12 for two and cabins from $22. On a stunning site adjacent the lake and river is the *Manapouri Glade Caravan Park* (tel 623) with sites at $12 per night, cabins at $18 and on-site caravans at $28.

There are also youth hostels in Queenstown and Te Anau, and a motor camp in Queenstown.

Equipment

Most equipment can be bought in Queenstown or even rented at Bill Lacheny Sports (tel (0294) 28-438) in the Mall where you can obtain a backpack for $6 a day or a sleeping bag or boots for $5 a day. The best food prices are found at the 4-Square Supermarket in the Alpine shopping area, but everything is expensive in this town.

It's also possible to outfit your trip in Glenorchy where there is a store with an excellent selection of tramping food – freeze-dried dinners, noodle dinners, cereal and fresh fruit – with prices not much higher than those you'd pay in Queenstown.

Although you occasionally see somebody tackle the track in running shoes, your feet will tire quickly in such footwear due to the rocky nature of the terrain. Boots are best.

Information & Maps

Maps, books and information can be obtained from the DOC district office on the corner of Ballarat and Stanley Streets across from the Queenstown public library. The visitor centre (tel (0294) 27-933) is open Monday to Friday from 9 am to 4.30 pm.

In Glenorchy there is a ranger station (tel (0294) 9) and visitor centre. The centre is open daily during the summer though not always manned and contains a number of displays including the bones of a moa leg from the Dart Valley that are over a metre long.

Do not pay hut fees or leave your intentions at the ranger station for the Routeburn Track. This will be taken care of by hut wardens. The best and cheapest map is the recreational map to the Routeburn Track, NZMS 316.

It's hard to avoid the crowded huts. Bunks cost $11 a night and there are hut wardens who collect the fees during the summer. All the huts have gas rings for cooking as well as a wood or coal stove. Bunks cannot be reserved like on the Milford and you still have to pay $11 whether you end up with a mattress or a spot on the floor. There is some restricted camping at Lake Mackenzie but it's at the discretion of the hut warden to permit it and then it's $7 a night per site.

The Track

The Routeburn is a classic alpine crossing over the Humboldt Mountains to the Divide on the Milford Rd. Most trampers take three days to walk the 39 km, but leave an extra day in case foul weather holds them up between the Routeburn Falls Hut and Lake Mackenzie or obscures the panoramic alpine views enjoyed along this stretch. The track is rated easy to medium.

The following description starts from the end of the track just north of Kinloch, and finishes at the Divide on the Milford Rd. One possibility for those who want to do a round trip on the Routeburn is to hike from Lake Mackenzie back to Routeburn Flats via Emily Pass. This is a difficult route that is poorly marked with stretches of untracked bush and scrub. Interested trampers should first consult the ranger at Glenorchy or the hut warden at Lake Mackenzie before attempting it.

There is a considerable amount of climbing involved with the Routeburn as you have to cross the Harris Saddle which is reached at 1277 metres. But the track itself is well benched and graded, in fact it's surprisingly wide in many places, and difficult to lose.

The two most popular places to spend the nights are at Routeburn Falls and Lake Mackenzie, two huts located near the bushline. The route between them is the most spectacular section of the walk and it's a shame to see some people hustling through just to get a bunk at the next hut. You can completely avoid the huts by camping but you are pretty much restricted to the free campgrounds at Routeburn Flats and another one 20 minutes from Lake Howden.

The Routeburn Falls Hut, which has only 20 bunks, is a bottleneck and is seemingly always crowded. To ease the problem, the Routeburn Flats Hut was recently upgraded and made considerably more pleasant to encourage more trampers to spend the night here. The views from the hut are nowhere near as dramatic as

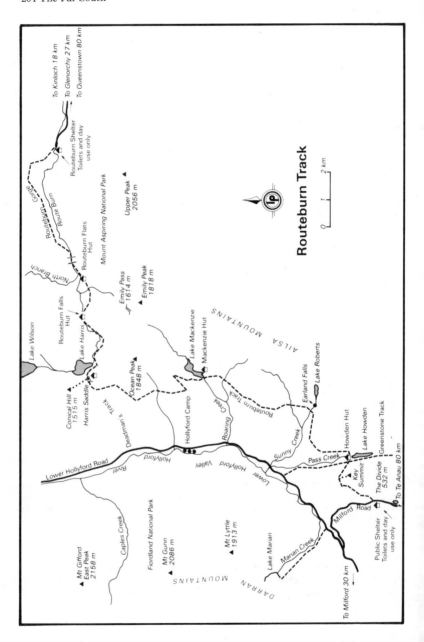

Routeburn Track

those from the porch of the Routeburn Falls Hut but it's only a 1½-hour walk between the two.

Stage 1: Routeburn Shelter to Routeburn Falls

Walking Time: four hours
Accommodation: Routeburn Flats (20 bunks); Routeburn Falls (20 bunks)

Next to the car park, or where the buses drop you off, is Routeburn Shelter and from here the track crosses the Route Burn on a swingbridge to its true left (north) bank and winds a km through beech forest to a footbridge over Sugar Loaf Stream. Once across the stream the track climbs gently for 20 minutes until it reaches another bridge over Bridal Veil Stream and then begins to sidle Routeburn Gorge.

The track follows the narrow valley around the gorge and then breaks out in beech and grass flats before crossing a swingbridge over the Route Burn and quickly emerging in Routeburn Flats, 6½ km from the shelter. From the flats you can clearly see Routeburn Falls Hut up the valley just above the bushline at 1005 metres. It's an easy 30-minute stroll through the flats to the junction where the right-hand fork leads to Routeburn Flats Hut, a 20-bunk facility that has been recently upgraded to encourage more trampers to spend the first night here.

The main track (left-hand fork) begins a sharp ascent towards Falls Hut. The track covers 270 metres over three km that takes about 1½ hours to walk before you reach the hut above the bushline. The view from the verandah of this hut is spectacular as it overlooks the flats far below and the surrounding Humboldt Mountains. There is no camping around this hut and the wardens are strict about enforcing the rule. If all the bunks are taken (normally the case) trampers either sleep on the floor, double up on bunks or even return to Routeburn Flats, an hour's walk going down.

Stage 2: Routeburn Falls to Lake Mackenzie

Walking Time: four to five hours
Accommodation: Lake Mackenzie Hut (40 bunks)

Right behind the hut are the impressive Routeburn Falls, which tumble down a series of rock ledges. A series of orange snow poles indicates the track which it cuts across an alpine basin to begin a steady climb to the outlet of Lake Harris. The track passes a square rock, ascends more sharply and suddenly Lake Harris is there. The lake takes away any other thought (even of sore legs), especially on a clear day when the water reflects everything around it.

The track works its way around the lake along bluffs and moraines. You get a second jolt 1½ hours from the hut when the grassy meadows of Harris Saddle come into view. At 1277 metres the view changes from that of Lake Harris to the entire Hollyford Valley all the way to Martins Bay if the weather is clear. If you are blessed with such weather, drop the packs and climb the side track to Conical Hill, about an hour's round trip. The 360° view from the 1515 metre peak includes Darren Mountains, Richardson Range in Otago and the Hollyford Valley.

There is an emergency shelter on Harris Saddle, which is a popular place for tea and lunch. From here the track descends a stone gully then turns sharply south. The following narrow stretch of track that clings to the Hollyford Face of the ridge high above the bushline is the best part of the trip. After 30 minutes the track arrives at the junction with Deadman's Track, an extremely steep route to the floor of the Hollyford Valley (five hours). The immense views continue and two km from the junction with Deadman's Track the track passes an emergency rock bivvy. The rock is huge but should not be used as a way to avoid a crowded hut at Lake MacKenzie or hut fees.

Two hours from the saddle, the track ascends and rounds a spur, exposing Lake Mackenzie, a jewel set in a small green mountain valley. The track begins a zigzag pattern down to the lake, dropping sharply for the final 300 metres. It then skirts the bush and arrives at Lake Mackenzie Hut, an impressive two-storey hut with a spiral staircase. Camping is tightly restricted around the lake because of the fragile nature of the ground and alpine plants. Trampers should also remember that the lake doesn't have a conventional outlet and if you wash yourself or clothes in it, the soap will be seen for weeks, even months.

Stage 3: Lake Mackenzie to the Divide

Walking Time: four hours

Accommodation: Lake Howden Hut (20 bunks)

The track begins in front of the hut, passes a private hut and cuts across a tussock meadow before climbing for an hour to a bridge over Roaring Creek. The climb is to make up for the height lost in the descent to Lake Mackenzie and at one point the track breaks out of the trees to fine views of the Hollyford Valley and the Darren Mountains on the other side. In another hour from Roaring Creek the track arrives at the thundering Earland Falls, an ideal spot for an extended break. The spray will fog up camera lenses and quickly cool off any overheated trampers. If it is raining, the falls will be twice as powerful, in which case there is a swingbridge nearby to cross the flooded stream.

The track steadily descends and in three km emerges at Lake Howden and a major junction, a three-hour walk from the last hut. Located on the beautiful lake is another split-level hut, or you can camp at the far end, reached by following the Greenstone Track. The Greenstone is the track to the south (right) while the track north (left) is a route to Hollyford Rd used by trampers heading directly to the Hollyford Track. To the west (straight ahead) is the remainder of the Routeburn Track and Key Summit.

The track swings by the flanks of Key Summit and a side trip (45 minutes) to the top on a clear day is well worth the energy spent if you're not racing down to catch a bus. From the 919-metre highpoint you can see the Hollyford, Greenstone and Eglinton Valleys. From the side track the Routeburn Track descends steadily to the bush, where thick rainforest resumes, before reaching the Divide, the lowest east-west crossing of the Southern Alps. It's three km (about an hour's walk) from Lake Howden to the Divide where there is a car park and a shelter for those waiting for the bus.

GREENSTONE TRACK

This two to three-day walk is the opposite of the Routeburn. Some trampers, just coming from the dramatic alpine scenery of the Routeburn or Milford, feel let down by the Greenstone but most trampers find it a pleasant change from the crowds of the more popular tracks. The Greenstone is an historic trail and at one time was the only way to return to Lake Wakatipu from the Routeburn. The track runs from Lake Howden to Elfin Bay along the almost dead-flat valley of the Greenstone River. This is the reason the tramp is rated easy.

Although more and more people walk the Greenstone every year, especially now that there is good public transport to the Greenstone car park, it's still nowhere near as popular as the Routeburn. Anglers will enjoy walking this track as the Greenstone River is renowned for its brown and rainbow trout, which average somewhere between 1½ and three kg. Access to the river's pools and holes is very good as the track remains quite close to the Greenstone from Lake McKellar to near its mouth at Lake Wakatipu.

Access

Glenorchy Holiday Park supplies transport between the Greenstone car park and Glenorchy, a 40-km trip along a dirt road. The service is provided on request but turns out to be a daily run most of the summer. The van leaves the motor camp at 11 am and reaches the car park at noon. It turns around at 1.30 am and returns to Glenorchy by 2.30 pm. The cost is $10 per person and parties of four can also arrange to be taken to Queenstown for an additional $11 each. It's essential to book ahead; call Glenorchy Holiday Park (tel (0294) 29-939).

H & H Tours (tel (0294) 146) also provide transport to the Greenstone car park on Monday, Wednesday and Friday throughout the summer. The bus departs Queenstown at 9 am from the company's office on Camp St, passes through Glenorchy at 10.45 am and reaches the car park at 12.15 pm. It then departs at 1.30 pm and is back in Queenstown at 4.15 pm. A one-way fare is $22. The west end of the track is at Lake Howden Hut on the Routeburn Track and transport can be picked up from the Divide on the Te Anau to Milford highway (see the preceding section). For accommodation in Glenorchy see the Places to Stay section of the Routeburn Track.

Information & Maps
From Lake Howden to Lake McKellar the Greenstone lies in the Fiordland National Park but the majority of it is in Wakatipu State Forest, which forms the southern border of Mt Aspiring National Park. Intentions can be notified and information obtained from either the Queenstown DOC office or the Glenorchy Ranger Station and visitor centre. A good map is the recreation guide to the Routeburn Track, NZMS 316.

There are two good huts on the Greenstone and the fee, $6 per night, can be paid at the Glenorchy Ranger Station.

The Track
The track, rated easy, can be walked in either direction but it is described here going from west to east. See the Routeburn Track description for details from the Divide to Lake Howden Hut. Trampers planning to loop back on the

Greenstone from the Routeburn can easily walk from Mackenzie Hut to Lake McKellar, a 5½ to six-hour day. Two more days would be needed to complete the track, with a six-hour walk to Mid-Greenstone Hut on the first day and then a 6½-hour tramp out to the car park. The track by itself can also be covered in two days or be combined with the Caples (see next section) to form a four-day loop.

Stage 1: Lake Howden to McKellar Hut
Walking Time: three hours from the Divide; two hours from Lake Howden
Accommodation: McKellar Hut (20 bunks)
From the signposted junction near Lake Howden Hut, the Greenstone is the southern fork which follows the west side of the beautiful lake. In 20 minutes the track passes the campsites at the south end of Lake Howden and then leaves the lake and very gently climbs to the Greenstone Saddle, though few trampers realise when they have reached the low pass. Less than an hour from Lake Howden Hut, the track emerges onto a grassy flat to the signposted junction to the McKellar Saddle and Caples Track.

The Greenstone Track departs south (right) and gently climbs the forested edges along Lake McKellar. Within an hour the track passes Lake McKellar Lodge (private hut for guided walks) and then shortly arrives at McKellar Hut, situated near the swingbridge that crosses the Greenstone River to its true left (east) side.

Stage 2: Lake McKellar to Mid-Greenstone Hut
Walking Time: six to seven hours
Accommodation: Mid-Greenstone Hut (12 bunks)
The track immediately crosses the Greenstone River to the true left (east) side and cuts through beech forest for about 15 minutes until it emerges onto Greenstone Flats. Here the track is well marked as it runs down the flats and

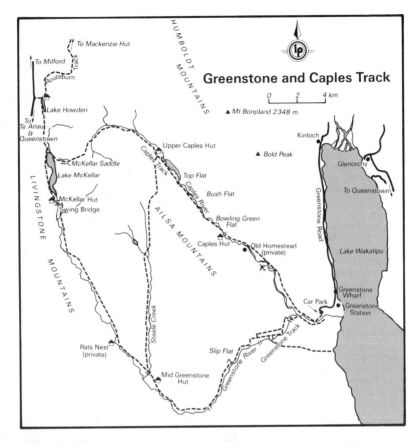

Greenstone and Caples Track

0   2   4 km

▲ Mt Bonpland 2348 m

patches of scrub and bush until Rat's Nest Hut is spotted across the river, a 1½-hour walk from the hut. Rat's Nest is a private hut for musterers.

A short way beyond the musterers' hut, the track climbs past a deep chasm where the river can be heard thundering below. The view is spectacular and the chasm makes a nice place for an extended break. An hour from Rat's Nest, the track leaves the river's edge to avoid swamps and bog areas and eventually comes to Steele Creek. Right before the swingbridge over the creek is a junction with a track heading north (left) to Steele Creek Saddle and Upper Caples Hut, a very difficult route (10 hours).

Once on the other side of the swingbridge, the Greenstone Track follows the flats for 20 minutes or so and passes the private Steele Creek Lodge before it reaches the Mid-Greenstone Hut, a km below Steele Creek. The 12-bunk hut is located close to the edge of the bush on a terrace.

Stage 3: Mid-Greenstone Hut to Greenstone Car Park
Walking Time: five to six hours

Top: Tramper on Routeburn Track, Mt Aspiring NP (IK)
Bottom: View from Routeburn Track, Mt Aspiring NP (IK)

Top Left: Routeburn Track, Mt Aspiring NP (IK)
Top Right: West Matukituki River, Mt Aspiring NP (JD)
Bottom Left: West branch – Matukituki River, Mt Aspiring NP (JD)
Bottom Right: Rainforest, Mt Aspiring NP (IK)

Accommodation: Slip Flat Bivvy (four bunks)

The track continues skirting the forest edge along the open flats for about an hour beyond Mid-Greenstone Hut until it enters the bush across from the junction with Pass Burn. The hut seen near the confluence on the true right (west) side of the Greenstone River is private. Once in the bush, the track begins to ascend above the Greenstone Gorge and comes to a junction to Pass Burn bridge. The swingbridge is only a short descent down the side track and is a good vantage point from which to view the narrow rock walls of the gorge.

Eventually the main track climbs high above the gorge and swings left along with the valley before emerging onto the western end of Slip Flat. The track quickly passes Slip Flat Bivvy on the edge of the forest and then re-enters the bush close to the river. In 20 to 30 minutes, the track crosses a stream and comes to a junction. The track to the east (right-hand fork) stays close to the river to cross a swingbridge and head for Rere Lake (one hour). The main track to the north (left-hand) remains on the true left (north) side of the river and climbs through the rest of the gorge.

In about 1½ to two hours, the track reaches a swingbridge over the Greenstone River and on the other side crosses Caples Flat. It takes about 20 minutes to traverse the grassy flats before a second swingbridge is reached with the signposted junction to the Caples Track just beyond it. The track to the west (left) heads up the Caples Valley to the Caples Hut (2½ hours). The track to the east (right) follows the Greenstone River for another 20 minutes before it ends at a car park.

CAPLES TRACK

The Caples Valley separates the the main body of the Ailsa Mountains from the Humboldt Range and is a smaller and, at times, steeper valley than the Greenstone. Many think the Caples is more scenic

however with its 'park-like' appearance of small grassy clearings enclosed by beech forest. There is also good trout fishing in the lower portions of the Caples River, from its confluence with the Greenstone to the Caples Hut.

Both ends of the Caples are located on the Greenstone Track with the eastern end of the track a 20-minute walk from the car park. The west end joins the Greenstone Track at the head of Lake McKellar, about an hour south of the Lake Howden Hut. Transport for the Caples is the same as for the Greenstone and the two tracks are often combined to form a four-day loop.

The Track

The Caples, which involves a climb over McKellar Saddle (945 metres) is rated medium and is described here starting from the Greenstone car park and going to Lake McKellar.

Stage 1: Greenstone Car Park to Upper Caples Hut

Walking Time: five hours
Accommodation: Upper Caples Hut (20 bunks)

The track departs the car park and ascends into the lower portion of the Greenstone Gorge for 20 minutes before it arrives at the signposted junction with the Caples Track, which is the fork to the north (right). The Caples Track continues along the true left (east) side of the Caples River but stays in the beech forest above the valley to avoid crossing grazing land of the Greenstone Station. At one point an airstrip and a woodshed might be spotted on the far bank.

It's a 2½-hour walk along the true left (east) bank before the well-marked track descends past a small gorge and crosses a swingbridge to Mid-Caples Hut on the other side. The hut is on an open terrace above the river near the edge of the forest. From the hut, the track remains on the true right (west) side of the river and crosses open grassy flats for the first hour.

You then ascend into beech forest to round a small gorge before quickly returning to the flats where there is a fence to protect the forest from station stock.

Eventually the track turns into bush before it emerges at the south end of Top Flat. It takes about 20 to 30 minutes to cross the flat and cut through more beech forest to Upper Caples Hut. Just before the hut is the signposted junction with the Steele Saddle route to the Greenstone Track, an extremely difficult walk. Upper Caples Hut is in a scenic setting in a grassy flat with the Ailsa Mountains rising directly behind it.

Stage 2: Upper Caples Hut to Greenstone Track

Walking Time: four to five hours to Greenstone Track

The track leaves the valley floor and begins ascending towards McKellar Saddle, climbing 150 metres to pass the junction of Fraser Creek and Caples River to a small boggy meadow. From here the track continues to climb and sidle past upland basins that are marked with snow poles, and in two hours from the hut you ford the Caples, now a mountain creek, to its true left side. The track crosses back to the true right side of the Caples and makes its final ascent through open alpine terrain to the saddle, a climb of 450 metres from the hut.

The saddle is free of bush at 945 metres but can be extremely boggy after heavy rain. After an especially bad summer in 1988, trampers were asked to stay off the Caples Track while Mt Aspiring National Park trail crews laid a planked trail across it. The views are good from McKellar Saddle and on a clear day the peaks and hanging valleys of Fiordland can be seen to the west.

The track is well signposted where it leaves the saddle and quickly descends 100 metres before swinging north. The track drops another 200 metres with a series of switchbacks and it takes about 1½ hours to descend the steep track from

the saddle until you break out of the bush near the head of Lake McKellar. Here the track swings north to bypass swampy lowlands and then crosses a bridge to the signposted Greenstone Track. To the north (right) the track leads to Lake Howden Hut, 45 minutes to an hour away. The south (left) fork can be followed to reach McKellar Hut an hour's walk away. Those trampers heading all the way to the Divide on the Te Anau-Milford Highway should plan on a 6½ to seven-hour day.

REES-DART TRACK

The track in the Glenorchy region that experiences the lightest use by trampers is the Rees-Dart, a four to five-day route that connects two splendid valleys and winds through a variety of scenery including grassy flats, lush forests, high bluffs and even over an alpine pass. Although the 70-km trip is rated moderate, it's longer and definitely more challenging than either the Routeburn or the Caples. But most of the track is well marked and maintained, making the Rees-Dart a journey within the capabilities of average trampers.

Access

For a long time, the only public transport was provided by buses that dropped you off at the Rees River Bridge on their way to the Routeburn Track. You were still faced with a two to three-hour walk to reach either end of the track along metalled roads that see very little traffic. H & H Tours and Magic Buses (see the Access section for the Routeburn) still drive this route but now Glenorchy Holiday Park provides a van service to the actual ends of the track.

The motor camp van departs Glenorchy at 11 am daily from December to March and reaches Muddy Creek, the Rees Valley end of the track, at 11.30 am. It then departs the car park at noon for Glenorchy. At 2.30 pm the van departs the motor camp and reaches Paradise, the Dart Valley car park, at 3 pm, waits 30 minutes and then returns to Glenorchy. The fare to either end of the track is $8 per person one way or $12 return. It's best to call the holiday park (tel (0294) 29-939) ahead of time and book a seat.

Occasionally trampers will go from the Dart Valley directly to the Routeburn by fording the Dart River, usually above Chinamans Flat. Here they follow the true right (west) side of the river and spend a night at an old hunter's hut on the south side of Rocky Burn. The next day they follow a track to Lake Sylvan and a tramline-walkway from there to a swingbridge across the Route Burn. The start of the Routeburn lies up the road to the west.

Before contemplating this adventure, keep in mind that the Dart is a glacial river that runs fast and deep. It's impossible to see the bottom, making the waist-deep crossing extremely dangerous. No less than four trampers at a time should attempt to ford the Dart.

Information & Maps

Information and maps can be obtained from either the Glenorchy ranger station or the DOC district office in Queenstown (see the preceding section). You can get away with the recreational map to Mt Aspiring National Park, NZMS 273 – though the detail is somewhat obscured. Otherwise, purchase quads S114 and S113 of the NZMS 1 series.

Hut fees are $7 a night and there is a warden at Dart Hut who collects fees for all the huts used on the trip.

The Track

The majority of people first hike Rees Valley and then return down the Dart – the easiest direction in which to climb the Rees Saddle – and this is the way the tramp will be described here. Nights are usually spent at Shelter Rock and at the Dart and Daleys Flat Huts, with an extra night at Dart Hut if you plan to undertake the side trip to Dart Glacier (see the next section). The trip is rated medium.

Stage 1: Muddy Creek to Shelter Rock Hut

Walking Time: seven hours
Accommodation: 25 Mile Hut (eight bunks); Shelter Rock Hut (10 bunks)
A 4WD track leads up the Rees Valley to 25 Mile Hut and you can even hire a jeep from Glenorchy Holiday Park to the old hut. But most cars can't go beyond the Muddy Creek car park, the traditional beginning of the track. From here you ford the creek and head up a bulldozed track reaching the private Arthur Creek Hut in two km. Grassy flats lie beyond Arthur Creek and it's four km of open travel on the true left (east) side of the Rees River until the track fords 25 Mile Creek. Right before the creek, sitting 60 metres up an open terrace, is 25 Mile Hut, which was built by the Otago Tramping and Mountaineering Club and is reached in two to three hours from Muddy Creek.

The route continues along open river flats for another 1½ hours until a track, marked by a park boundary sign, enters the bush. Within a km the track crosses a swingbridge to the true right (west) side of the Rees. The track continues on this side of the river, passes through Clarke Slip and over grassy flats and then begins a climb through beech forest. Within two km the track passes the site of the old Shelter Rock Hut, now used occasionally by those who carry a tent. From here it is another km along the true right (west) bank of the Rees and through stands of stunted beech before the track arrives at a swingbridge back to the true left (east) bank. The new Shelter Rock Hut is located just on the other side in a tussock flat, 30 minutes from the site of the former hut.

Stage 2: Shelter Rock Hut to Dart Hut

Walking Time: five to seven hours
Accommodation: Dart Hut (20 bunks)
The climb over the alpine pass of Rees Saddle begins by following the river on the true left (east) side for a short time to pick up a well-cairned track that rises through alpine scrub. The track gradually sidles

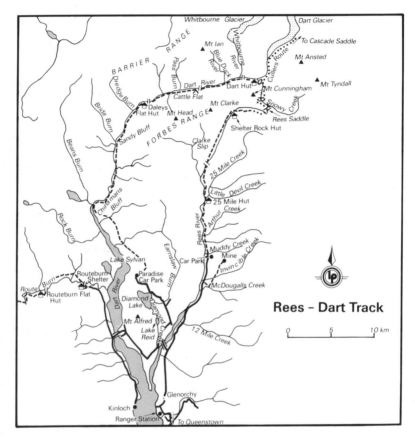

Rees – Dart Track

up the valley until it reaches a tussock basin below the saddle, about four km from the hut. Rees Saddle is the obvious lowpoint to the north and you keep to the stream bed before climbing up the steep slope to the top of the saddle. The final ascent is marked with poles and a well-beaten path. As to be expected, there are good views from the saddle (1447 metres) of the peaks and valleys around it, making it the natural place for lunch if the weather is clear.

Follow the orange poles from the saddle to Dart Hut. They quickly descend 90 metres to a terrace and group of tarns above Snowy Creek. The route stays on the true left (west) of the creek before dropping suddenly to a swingbridge to the true right (east) side. The track climbs above the bridge, passes some good views of upper Dart Valley and glacier and descends quickly across broken slopes of rock and shrub.

Dart Hut is visible on the true left bank during the final descent which ends at a swingbridge across Snowy Creek. There are some campsites here before you cross the bridge to the true left side of the creek, from where the hut is five minutes away. Dart Hut is the only one on the track that has gas rings as well as a wood stove. There are some excellent daytrips from here, including walks to view the Dart and Whitbourn Glaciers. The only problem is that this hut tends to be a bottleneck on the track and occasionally will be full at night.

Stage 3: Dart Hut to Daleys Flat Hut

Walking Time: six to eight hours
Accommodation: Daleys Flat Hut (20 bunks)

The track climbs away from the hut and along a bluff above the river where there is an occasional view of the rushing water below or of the valley in front of you. In two km, the track passes the junction to the swingbridge that crosses the river to the track for the Whitbourn Valley and the lower Whitbourn Glacier which takes three hours to walk. The main track continues along the valley through thick forest and you can often hear the river below but you can rarely see it.

Within 4½ km of the Whitbourn Bridge, the track climbs sharply but then drops into a rocky stream clearing, situated near the east end of Cattle Flat. The track quickly emerges from forest onto the flat, an almost endless grassy area where the trail appears as a path of trampled grass marked occasionally by a rock cairn. The Dart is seen all along the flat as is a portion of the Curzon Glacier high in the mountains across the river. The track follows the middle of the flat and in three km passes a sign to a rock bivvy. The bivvy, a three-minute walk up a side track, is a huge overhanging rock that can easily hold half-a-dozen people or more. If it's raining, this is an excellent place for lunch as it is almost at the halfway point to the next hut.

The track continues across Cattle Flat for another 1½ km, crosses a fence on a stile and finally returns to the bush. From here it's a steady drop towards the river until the track actually reaches the banks

of the Dart in 2½ km. Along the way the track passes another rock bivvy, though this one is much smaller than the one at Cattle Flat. Eventually the track breaks out at Quinns Flat, a beautiful stretch of golden grass surrounded by mountains, and then returns to the bush.

The track crosses a few more streams and in 30 to 40 minutes breaks out onto Daleys Flat at its top (eastern) corner. Again follow the trampled grass across the flat to reach Daleys Flat Hut on the other side.

Stage 4: Daleys Flat Hut to Paradise

Walking Time: six to eight hours

This last leg of the journey is not a difficult hike but at 26 km it makes for a long day. If you plan to catch the 3.30 pm van to Glenorchy, it's best to be out of the hut by 7 am, allowing yourself a full eight hours to reach Paradise. The morning begins in forest but within 15 minutes the track comes to a small grassy flat only to return to the bush on a high bank above the river.

Four km from the hut the track breaks out onto Dredge Flat and cuts across it. Use a pair of large white squares posted high in a tree to locate where the track re-enters the bush in the middle of the grassy flat. At the lower end of the flat, Sandy Bluff looms overhead and a white square directs you to the track.

As soon as the track enters the forest it begins climbing the steep bluff where at one point a ladder and steel cable are needed to get up a rock face. This is very adventurous but at the top you are rewarded with a fine view of Dredge Flat and the valley beyond. The track immediately descends to a grassy flat, crosses it and stays close to the river for the next seven km. Eventually the track enters an open flat where Chinamans Bluff is straight ahead and an impressive waterfall from Lake Unknown is visible high in the mountains across the Dart.

The track skirts the bluff with only a fraction of the climbing endured at Sandy

Bluff and descends onto Chinamans Flat to arrive at another sign for a rock bivvy. The bivvy, a rock overhang, is up in the bluff a short scramble away. It has enough room for two or three people. Once on the flats you come almost immediately to a 4WD track, where people occasionally arrange to be met by a jeep hired from Glenorchy Holiday Park. For those who are walking out to Paradise, it's about 6½ km to the car park, a good two-hour trek unless you're late for the van and have to start running down the track.

The 4WD track passes through Dan's Paddock and begins a gentle descent. At one point it comes to a junction with a vehicle track heading in one direction and a walking track to Paradise in the other. The walking track is shorter as it follows the cattle yards and ends at the start of the road where a sign tells you to 'Wait Here For Bus'.

CASCADE SADDLE ROUTE
Cascade Saddle is truly one of the most scenic alpine crossings in New Zealand that can be walked without the aid of mountaineering gear or climbing experience. It is still a very steep and hard climb to the pass and one that shouldn't be attempted in adverse weather conditions. Steep snowgrass slopes on the Matukituki side become treacherous when wet or covered by fresh snow.

By hiking the route from Matukituki to Dart Valley, you receive the latest weather report, via a radio in Aspiring Hut, on the morning before you attempt the steepest section, a four-hour climb from the hut to the Pylon at 1835 metres. The stretch from Aspiring Hut to Dart Hut on the Rees-Dart Track is a long 10 to 11-hour day for those without a tent. With a tent you can break the hike in half and spend a glorious night camping in an alpine meadow near the pass, with Mt Aspiring looming overhead.

Access
There is good public transport at the end

of both the Matukituki and Dart Valleys and the total trip, including a two-day portion of the Rees-Dart Track, would be a four to five-day adventure. But trampers should schedule an extra day or more to ensure that they have good weather to cross the Cascade Saddle. If not needed for the saddle, then a spare day can be spent at Dart Hut undertaking a number of side trips, including a climb of Rees Saddle.

The access point for an east-west crossing of Cascade Saddle is Wanaka, the scenic town on the edge of Lake Wanaka which is the site of Mt Aspiring National Park headquarters and visitor centre.

Wanaka can be reached from Dunedin or Queenstown on a NZRRS bus, from Christchurch on Mt Cook Coachlines, and from Invercargill by an H & H Lines bus. From Wanaka to the end of the track in the West Matukituki Valley, transport can be arranged through Matuki Services (tel (7587) 7135). From early December to March, the local van service departs Wanaka Booking Centre at 99 Admore St at 1.30 pm on Sunday, Tuesday and Friday and reaches the road end at 3 pm. On Wednesday the van departs at 4.30 pm and reaches the track at 5.45 pm, when there is still enough daylight to reach Aspiring Hut. A one-way fare is $15 to the road end and the scenic drive and interesting commentary by Dick William alone are well worth the price of the ticket. See the preceding section for transport out of the Dart or Rees Valleys.

Information & Maps
The recreational map of Mt Aspiring National Park, NZMS 273, is fine for the Dart or Rees Valley but it's reassuring to have quad S114 of NZMS 1 series that covers the route over Cascade Saddle to Dart Hut.

The visitor centre (tel (7587) 7660) of Mt Aspiring National Park headquarters is located on Admore St at the eastern edge of town and is open daily from 8 am to 5 pm from mid-December to mid-

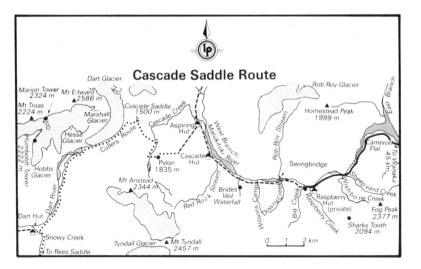

Cascade Saddle Route

January and weekdays the rest of the year. Inside there are natural history displays, audiovisual programs and, of course, loads of information and brochures for trampers as well as books, maps and the latest weather report.

Aspiring Hut was built by the New Zealand Alpine Club and is maintained by them through a park warden stationed there to collect the $7 a night fee. The hut is an interesting place to spend a night as there are usually a number of climbers with their piles of mountaineering gear to give it an atmosphere of high adventure. The huts on the Dart-Rees are also $7 and a warden is stationed at Dart Hut to collect fees.

The Track

The easiest way to climb Cascade Saddle, a route rated as difficult, is up the Dart Valley from the west. But the safest way is east to west to tackle the steepest and potentially the most treacherous segment in the beginning of the day when you can be assured of good weather, and this is the way it will be described here.

Stage 1: Road End to Aspiring Hut

Walking Time: 2½ to three hours
Accommodation: Aspiring Hut (24 bunks)
The Matuki Services van will take trampers to the road end, a car park at Big Creek 54 km from Wanaka. Ford the creek where on the other side a 4WD track cuts across the open valley of grassy flats. The scenery up the river includes Shotover Saddle and Mt Tyndall to the left (south), Cascade Saddle straight ahead (west) and an occasional sheep. Within two km the track passes the swingbridge built in 1987 as part of the country's centennial celebration of its national parks. The bridge provides access across the West Branch of the Matukituki River to the Rob Roy Glacier route (a five-hour round trip) and the hanging glacier can clearly be seen above it.

The 4WD track ends at the bridge and beyond it you can either follow the river bed and grassy flats, fording when necessary and enduring wet feet, or follow a marked track that climbs into the valley. In four km from the bridge, the track climbs away from the river a second time passing Brides Veil Falls and from the ridge Cascade Hut can be seen. At this point the track swings to the northwest along the valley floor, passes Cascade Hut and in another 2½ km (30 minutes) Aspiring Hut appears.

The stone and wood hut is a classic climbers' lodge that was built by the New Zealand Alpine Club. There is a huge floor-to-ceiling window overlooking Mt Aspiring and there is even a telescope to enable you to watch the climbers attempt various ridges. Also in the common room is a stone fireplace, surrounded by easy chairs, with a mantel that contains books, photos and other mountaineering memorabilia. There is a warden stationed here in the summer to collect fees and to receive weather reports every evening and morning.

Stage 2: Aspiring Hut to Cascade Saddle

Walking Time: four to six hours

The trip to Dart Hut is a long day so an early start is important. But ironically many trampers wait until 8.30 am or later until the hut warden receives the morning weather report from park headquarters in Wanaka. The track begins behind the hut and heads southwest into the trees where it is signposted. It immediately begins the steep climb through beech forest and within an hour or so you get views of Mt Aspiring to the north and the rest of the valley to the south.

The track continues a steady ascent, works around a waterfall and in two to three hours from the hut breaks out above the bushline. For most trampers this is a glorious moment. If the day is clear there will be stunning views the minute you leave the last few stunted beech trees.

The next section is difficult. The route is marked by orange snow poles and follows a steep snowgrass-tussock ridge upwards. Occasionally you're on all fours working from one pole to the next, as the route sidles a few ledges and outcrops and at times becomes very steep. From the bushline it takes a good two hours until the track swings well to the left and then,

veering right again, climbs an easy slope to Pylon, the marker at 1835 metres. Take a break – the views are wonderful and you've just climbed 1335 metres over four km.

From the marker, the track skirts the ridge to the south and then descends steadily through rock and scree to Cascade Stream. The route crosses the stream to its true left (west) side and climbs some slopes in an easy manner towards the saddle to the north. The route veers left just before the saddle but you can continue to the low point at 1500 metres where you can look from its edge (be careful!) straight down a sheer rock face of 1000 metres or so to a small valley below. It's an incredible feeling standing there looking at so much scenery, with Mt Aspiring to one side and the Dart Glacier to the other.

Right before you climb to the saddle there are grassy alpine meadows that provide a degree of protection for those who plan to pitch a tent. If the evening is clear, this is a once-in-a-lifetime camping experience as you watch the pink alpenglow on the peaks around you and then witness a blaze of stars emerge overhead.

Stage 3: Cascade Saddle to Dart Hut

Walking Time: four to five hours
Accommodation: Dart Hut (20 bunks)
For those heading to Dart Hut, you have only completed the first half of the walk. As soon as the route veers off the saddle you get your best view of the Dart Glacier, from its beginnings among the peaks right down to the gravel-covered ice of its snout in the valley. If it's fine weather, this is a good place to lie down, enjoy lunch and study this wonder of nature.

The snow poles continue down the tussock slope to a ledge on the top of a moraine and then descend quickly along the ledge. The glacier is an impressive sight but you are forced to keep one eye out for the next pole or, when they run out, for the next rock cairn. The cairns are hard to pick up at times as the route sidles a ridge of rock and stone that has very little flora anywhere.

You steadily descend slopes of loose rock as you head for the valley floor, finally coming to it near the end of the glacier, where the ice is black. The route continues down the true left (east) side of the river and eight km from the saddle it passes the hanging ice of Hesse Glacier as it drops out of the mountains towards the Dart. At this point the route departs the rocky moraine hills and it's an easy tramp for the next two km across grassy benches along the wide river bed.

Eventually the valley closes in and the route is forced to climb around a few steep banks. It also fords several side streams that come roaring out of the mountains before the Dart makes a wide swing to the west, a sign that you are only 30 minutes from the hut. Always stay on the true left side and the final half km is along a steep bank above the river until the hut comes into view. Hike a short distance up Snowy Creek to cross it on a swingbridge to reach the hut.

At Dart Hut, trampers have a choice on how to reach the road: either to continue along the Dart or to climb the Rees Saddle and follow Rees River. The Dart is actually a longer, two-day walk but the preferred choice of many who, after having seen its beginning at the glacier, want to follow the river all the way to its end at Lake Wakatipu.

WILKIN-YOUNG VALLEYS CIRCUIT

Wilkin Valley offers two features that are hard for most trampers to pass up once they 'discover' the Makarora region. The mountain scenery is outstanding, easily rivalling that of Matukituki Valley near Wanaka or even the tramps in the Glenorchy area. But the number of trampers is light. Compared to the 9000 who hike the Routeburn Track every year, probably less than 900 trampers use the huts and tracks of the Wilkin Valley and the same is true of the forested valley of

the Young River, another tributary of the Makarora River. The two valleys can be combined for a loop trip that offers superb scenery but no crowds, except during the brief holiday periods around Christmas and Easter.

Access

Makarora is located 60 km north of Wanaka or 192 km south of Fox Glacier. NZRRS has buses that run this route, departing Fox Glacier daily at 8.35 am and Wanaka at noon. Both buses pass through the small town between noon and 1 pm.

The easiest direction is first to hike the Young Valley and spend the night at South Branch Hut. The second day is spent climbing Gillespie Pass, a 1490-metre saddle. On the third day parties can return to Makarora with a jet-boat ride down the Wilkin River. The boat ride eliminates three to four hours of walking, as well as allowing trampers to spend the night at Siberia Hut and still make the afternoon NZRRS buses out of Makarora. Trampers with more than three days, however, should seriously consider spending a day or two hiking the upper portions of the Wilkin Valley, where the best mountain scenery of the park lies.

The jet-boat service has a much more important function than just saving some walking time. The most challenging part of this trip isn't crossing the alpine saddle but fording Makarora River. Although the braided river is often crossed, near its confluence with the Wilkin River, it is a very difficult ford. Most tramping parties avoid this ford by taking a jet boat from Kerin Forks back to Makarora. The jet boat can also be arranged to drop off trampers in Young Valley, and fording the Makarora here is not as difficult.

Haast Pass Tourist Service (tel (02943) 8372) runs the boats and charges $20 per person for the trip from Kerin Forks down the Wilkin and $80 for a boat load. The service is provided on request and can be arranged at the store in Makarora.

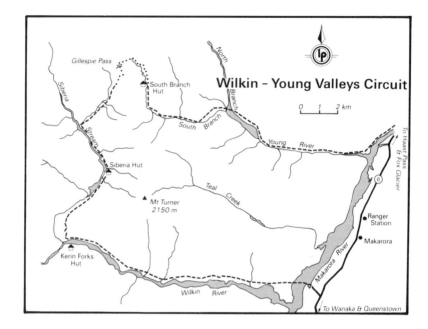

Information & Maps
Just up the SH6 is the Makarora Ranger Station (tel (02943) 8365) open weekdays from 8 am to 5 pm where information can be gathered and intentions left. You can also pay hut fees here which are $7 a night for huts in the Wilkin or Young Valleys.

The recreational map for Mt Aspiring National Park, NZMS 273, covers the entire route but doesn't supply much detail. The alternative is to purchase quad S107 of NZMS 1 series.

The Track
This three to four-day trip, rated medium to difficult, is described beginning with the Young Valley, the easiest way to cross Gillespie Pass.

Stage 1: SH6 to South Branch Hut
Walking Time: 6½ hours
Accommodation: South Branch Hut (10 bunks)

It is wise to check at the ranger station for the best spot to ford the Makarora River. To reach Young Valley, the river is generally forded at Sawmill Creek, four km north of the village on the SH6. Study the Makarora carefully and choose the best ford between its confluence with the Young River and Brady Creek. At this point the crossing is within the ability of most trampers when the water level is normal.

Once on the true right (west) side of the Makarora, you round the corner into Young Valley where you will find a good track leading up the river's true left (north) bank. The track remains close to the river and makes for an easy stroll up the valley. Within three hours, the track enters the flats below the junction of the North and South Branches of the Young River. Continue to just above the confluence and cross the North Branch.

A track on the other side continues on

the true left (north) side of the South Branch and immediately climbs and crosses three slips that are well marked with rock cairns. It then descends to the first flat along the South Branch where there is a small rock bivvy across the river, a little more than an hour from the forks. The track continues to climb through bush and small clearings until it reaches the alpine zone. The South Branch Hut lies another km up the valley on the true right (south) side, a 3½-hour walk from the forks. The hut has a small stove, 10 bunks and a scenic view of Mt Awful framed by the valley walls.

Stage 2: South Branch Hut to Siberia Hut

Walking Time: six to seven hours
Accommodation: Siberia Hut (10 bunks)

Continue up the valley along the true left (north) side of the South Branch for a little more than a km. Within 45 minutes a large rock cairn marks the start of a route up a northeast facing slope of scrub and tussock. By following the slope you skirt the bluffs that mark the end of a spur leading to Gillespie Pass. It's a steep climb of 400 metres up the slope and then along the crest of the spur where metal poles mark most of the route. Just before reaching the 1490-metre pass, the route swings left up a small gully. It takes three hours to reach the saddle from the hut and for many parties the alpine setting is a good spot for an extended break or lunch.

You leave Gillespie Pass by following the metal poles southeast along a ridge for a km until the route swings more to the west and follows a spur down through a stand of bush to Young Basin. Head to the end of the flats in the basin where a marked track enters the forest. It follows a stream on its true left (south) side for a short distance before descending into Siberia Flats.

The walk through the flats is an easy stroll and the mountain scenery surrounding you is spectacular. It takes about an hour to cross the grassy flats to Siberia Hut on the true left (east) side of Siberia Stream. Plan on three to 3½ hours to reach the hut from the top of the pass.

Stage 3: Siberia Hut to Kerin Forks

Walking Time: three to four hours
Accommodation: Kerin Forks Hut (10 bunks)

Head to the south end of Siberia Flats to reach a marked track that enters the forest. This is about a 30-minute walk. The track remains on the true left (east) bank of Siberia Stream and gradually descends away from the flats through bush. It sidles around a shoulder then follows a series of switchbacks the final 450 metres to the Wilkin River, a short distance upstream from Kerin Forks. The Kerin Forks Hut is located on the flats below the confluence of the Siberia Stream and Wilkin River.

It takes three to four hours to reach the hut, where most parties will have arranged to be picked up by a jet boat. To continue down the river, follow the well-marked track along the true left (north) side. The walk is easy and within four hours the track comes to the confluence on the Makarora River. Much caution has to be used if fording this river and it is best done upstream from its junction with the Wilkin.

OTHER TRACKS
Wilkin-East Matukituki Route

This is a very challenging route, for experienced alpine trampers only, from Wilkin Valley over the 1402-metre Rabbit Pass into East Matukituki Valley. A jet boat ride to Kerin Forks in Wilkin Valley and then a lift back to Wanaka at the end of the walk can be arranged (see Access for the Wilkin-Young Valleys Circuit).

Plan on five to six days and pick up the brochure to Wilkin Valley from the Makarora ranger station that explains the route over Waterfall Face, a dangerous segment unless the weather is good. There are no huts in East Matukituki Valley.

Liverpool Bivvy

Those without the time to complete the Cascade Saddle trip can enjoy a shorter tramp to this eight-bunk hut in the upper portion of the West Matukituki Valley and then return to Wanaka for a scenic three-day trip. Take the van service (see Access for the Cascade Saddle Route section) to the road's end and then hike into Aspiring Hut the first night. The next day is a four to five-hour walk up the valley to Liverpool Bivvy with its majestic views of Mt Aspiring and surrounding peaks. You can easily return to the road end on the third day to catch the van back to Wanaka. This trip is rated medium.

Shotover River

Trampers can retrace part of the great gold rush that took place on the Shotover River and end up in West Matukituki Valley where there is public transport back to Wanaka. You can get to the start of the track from Queenstown through Gray Line (tel 27-166) by joining a bus tour to Skippers Canyon. The road ends at Branches Flat and from there it's a four to five-hour walk to Sixteen Mile Hut and three more hours to 100 Mile Hut. The following day is a climb through Shotover Saddle and you end up near Cascade Hut in West Matukituki Valley.

Fiordland National Park

Anchoring New Zealand's national park system in the south is Fiordland, the largest park in the country and, at 12,000 square km, one of the largest in the world. It stretches from Martins Bay in the north to Preservation Inlet in the south with the Tasman Sea bordering one side and a series of deep lakes the other. In between are rugged ranges with sharp granite peaks, narrow valleys, 14 of the most beautiful fiords to be found, and certainly the best collection of waterfalls.

The rugged terrain, thick rainforest-like bush and abundant water have kept progress and people other than trampers out of much of the park. The fringes of Fiordland are easily visited and some tracks, like the Milford, are crowded during the summer. But most of the park is impenetrable by all but the hardiest trampers, making this corner of the South Island a true wilderness in every sense.

As rugged as the park is, the most intimate and personally rewarding way of experiencing Fiordland is the oldest: on foot. There are 500 km of tracks and more than 60 huts scattered along them. Unquestionably the most famous track in New Zealand is the Milford Track. Often labelled 'the finest walk in the world', the Milford is almost a pilgrimage to many Kiwis who, if they never do another walk, must hike this 55-km track. Right from the beginning the Milford has been a highly regulated and commercial venture, and this has deterred some. But in the end, despite the high costs, mileposts, sight-seeing planes buzzing overhead and the abundance of buildings on the manicured track, it's still a wonderfully scenic walk that is within the ability of most people.

There are, however, many other tracks in Fiordland. The Hollyford, stretching from the end of Lower Hollyford Rd out to isolated Martins Bay, is steeped in history and has good fishing holes. At the opposite end of the park the Dusky Track, an eight to 10-day walk from the West Arm of Lake Manapouri to Supper Cove, is the truest wilderness walk in the park. And in 1988, the park opened its newest track, the Kepler – a four-day alpine walk designed to take some of the pressure off the Milford and the Routeburn.

HISTORY

In comparison with other regions of the country, little is known of the pre-European history of the Maoris in Fiordland. There is evidence of a permanent settlement at Martins Bay and possibly summer villages at Te Anau and Preservation Inlet which were used for seasonal hunting expeditions into the area.

The most significant find, however, was made in 1967 when the remains of a Maori sitting burial were discovered in a small, dry cave on Mary Island in Lake Hauroko. It was the best preserved burial ever recovered and possibly one of the oldest. The body was that of a woman – presumably a high-ranking one – and dated back to the mid-1600s.

In 1770 Captain Cook arrived in the *Endeavour* and worked his way up the west coast, attempting to land at several of the sounds. He was unsuccessful: dusk arrived too soon in one instance, while in another he was doubtful about the direction of the wind. When the great sea captain departed he had put names on a map, but never a mark on the soil. Cook returned three years later, bringing the *Resolution* into Dusky Sound where the crew recuperated after three months at sea. Recorded in his log in 1773 was the crew's seal hunt – the first in New Zealand, along with what was probably the first written description of sandflies: 'most mischievous animals . . . that cause a swelling not possible to refrain from scratching'.

During Cook's second voyage he made contact with three parties of friendly natives, one member of whom was even bold enough to board the ship and fire a musket three times. But Cook never sighted any permanent settlements. Obviously Fiordland was an important hunting ground and a source of greenstone for the Maoris but not a place to linger.

Cook's midshipman, George Vancouver, returned to Fiordland in 1791, taking his ship up Dusky Sound as his former captain had. The following year a sealing gang of 12 men were left in the sound for a few months where they reaped a harvest of 4500 skins, constructed one of the first buildings in New Zealand and nearly completed a ship with the emergency iron work left behind. They were eventually taken away by the mother ship, but more

sealers returned, and by 1795 there were 250 people in Dusky Sound. By the turn of the century there was a regular sealing trade in the sounds and it took but a few more years for most of the seals in the area to be slaughtered, putting a quick finish to the industry.

Whaling followed sealing for a brief period and in 1829 the first station of any size in the South Island was built in Preservation Inlet. The two industries wiped out seals and whales but did promote exploration of the coast. The Welsh sealing captain John Grono was the first to sail into the Milford Sound, in 1823, naming it after his hometown in Milford Haven.

Fiordland continued to be explored from the sea until runholder C J Nairn reached Te Anau in 1852 from the Waiau Valley. Nine years later two more cattle drivers, David McKellar and George Gunn, climbed to the top of Key Summit and became the first Europeans to view the Hollyford Valley. It was Patrick Caples, however, who was the first to descend into the valley from the Harris Saddle in 1863. Caples reached Martins Bay but didn't stick around too long as smoke from some Maori fires scared him back into the bush. A few months later Captain Alabaster made his way from Martins Bay to Lake Howden and was followed by a prospector James Hector who worked his way up the Hollyford and eventually back to Queenstown to a hero's welcome from miners. Each man thought he was the first to make the journey as news travelled along a much slower path then.

Miners continued to move deeper into Fiordland in search of the golden stream that would make them rich. In 1868, the Otago Provincial Government added stimulus to the growth of the area when it decided to start a settlement at Martins Bay. The town was surveyed on the northeast corner of Lake McKerrow, named Jamestown, and many of its lots sold. But right from the beginning

Jamestown had to struggle to exist in the desolate region. The road down the Hollyford was never built as two attempts proved hopeless. Ships, meanwhile, had an extremely hard time navigating the river's entrance and many simply gave up during rough seas and sailed on without delivering their vital supplies.

The settlers who finally moved into the area found life hard and lonely. By 1870 there were only eight houses in Jamestown. Nine years later the settlement was completely deserted and only a handful of people continued to live in Martins Bay. The only other permanent residents of Fiordland at the time were two hermits who had settled in the sounds during the 1870s. One was William Docherty who, after earning his prospecting licence, settled in Dusky Sound in 1877 and stayed until the late 1890s. The other was Donald Sutherland, a colourful character who sailed 100 km from Thompson Sound into Milford Sound in 1877 and became known as the 'Hermit of Milford'.

In 1880, Sutherland and John Mackay struggled up the Arthur Valley from Milford in search of precious minerals. Instead they found a fine waterfall which MacKay left his name on after winning a coin toss. After several more days of labouring through the thick bush, they sighted a magnificent three-leap waterfall and it was only fair that Sutherland name it after himself. The pair then stumbled up to the Mackinnon Pass, viewed the Clinton River and returned to Milford Sound.

Gradually, as word of Sutherland's falls leaked back to towns and cities, the number of adventurers determined to see the natural wonder increased, as did the pressure for a track or road to the Milford area. In 1888 Quintin Mackinnon and Ernest Mitchell, with the financial support and blessing of the government, set out to cut a route along the Clinton River.

Moving up through the Arthur Valley at the same time was C W Adams, chief surveyor of Otago, and his party of 11. In October 1888, Mackinnon and Mitchell stopped track cutting, scrambled over the pass, spent an icy night above the bushline, and then made their way past the present site of Quintin Hut to meet Adams. A rough trail was finished, a few flimsy huts thrown up and by 1890 tourists, including the first woman, were using the route with Mackinnon as a guide.

The government continued to seek improvements to the track and huts and in 1903 the Government Tourist Department took over all facilities on the track, including the ferry that transported trampers to the trail.

While the Milford Sound was attracting people, Martins Bay was driving them away. By the turn of the century, the McKenzie brothers were the sole inhabitants of the area, using a rough track in the Hollyford Valley to drive their cattle out to the stockyards. In 1926, the brothers sold out to Davy Gunn, a Scotsman from Invercargill.

Gunn became a legend in his own time. He improved the track in the valley, constructed huts along the way and gradually went from runholding cattle to guiding tourists. Gunn's greatest achievement, however, was the emergency trip he undertook to get help for victims of an aircraft crash in Big Bay in 1936. Gunn tramped from Big Bay to Lake McKerrow, rowed up the lake and then rode his horse more than 40 km to a construction camp where he telephoned for a plane. The trip would take an experienced hiker three days, Gunn did it in 21 hours. He continued his single-handed promotion of the valley until 1955 when he drowned in the Hollyford River after his horse slipped on the track. Today at Gunns Camp there is a small museum dedicated to the man and to the early settlers of Martins Bay.

The Milford Track changed significantly in 1940 when trampers could walk through Homer Tunnel. Up to that point most hikers had to turn around at the sound and backtrack to Lake Te Anau. In

1954, the tunnel, which began as a relief project in the 1930s, was finally opened to motor traffic. Two years before that Fiordland National Park had been created, preserving 100 square km and protecting the route to Milford Sound.

Up to 1965, all the track and hut facilities were controlled by the Tourist Hotel Corporation and trampers had to take part in a guided (and costly) trip to walk the trail. A protest and demonstration in front of the THC Hotel in the sound brought about changes and the creation of huts for the so-called 'freedom walkers'. Today the freedom walkers are referred to as independent trampers and they share the track with the guided parties but use different huts along the way.

Fiordland National Park was finally rounded out to its present size in 1960 when the Hollyford Valley and Martins Bay were added. In 1988, during New Zealand's centennial celebration of its national park system, the Kepler Track was finished and officially opened. The track was first conceived in 1986 as a way to relieve walking pressure on the Milford and especially the nearby Routeburn Track.

In 1888, Mackinnon and Mitchell were paid $60 to cut half of the Milford Track; a century later the Kepler was completed at a cost of more than $1 million.

CLIMATE

Fiordland has come to mean waterfalls, lakes and fiords, and rain – buckets of the stuff. Weather is predominantly wet year round with storms and winds moving west from the Tasman Sea and dumping up to 8000 mm of rain on the coast and western portions of the park. Early morning mist and thick layers of fog are quite common in the southern region. Fiordland's weather is described by the park staff as 'violent and wet'. The area averages 200 days of rain a year, yet sitting in a rain shadow behind the mountains is Te Anau which receives only 1200 mm a year. When travelling to the park bring good raingear and expect the average summer temperatures in the lowlands to be around 18° C.

NATURAL HISTORY

One of the first impressions trampers gain of the park is of the almost overpowering steepness of the mountains. This impression is accentuated as the mountains are usually only separated by narrow valleys. The rocks and peaks of Fiordland are very hard – much harder than the ranges to the north – and they are only being very slowly eroded. The mountains in the Mt Aspiring and Arthur's Pass parks are softer, erode more quickly and consequently present walkers with a gentler topography of large shingle screes and wide, open river valleys.

Fiordland is the result of several geological processes. First, sediment gradually built up on the sea bottom more than 350 million years ago to form the oldest rocks. A period of mountain folding followed, resulting in the transformation of sediments into hard crystalline rocks such as granites and gneiss. The area was again flooded by the sea 40 million years ago.

The most important contributors to Fiordland's majestic mountain scenery were the glacial periods of the last ice age, which lasted some two million years and ended a mere 14,000 years ago. The glaciers shaped the hard granite peaks, gouged the fiords and lakes, and scooped out rounded valleys. The evidence of the ice flows can be found almost everywhere from the moraine terraces behind Te Anau and in Eglinton's U-shaped valley to the pointed peaks of the Milford Sound.

One result of the glaciers is Fiordland's trademark of lakes. Te Anau is the largest in the South Island and second largest in the country. It is 66 km long and has a shoreline of 500 km and a surface of 342 square km. It provides an avenue to most of Fiordland's scenic attractions. Lake Hauroko, one access point to Supper Cove in Dusky Sound, is the deepest lake in

New Zealand with a depth of 463 metres.

Other results of Fiordland's glacial beginnings are the waterfalls. The sheerness of the mountain walls and fiords (some sea-cliffs rise 1½ km out of the water) has created ideal conditions for waterfalls. There seems to be one at every bend of every track, cascading, tumbling, roaring or simply dribbling down a green mossy bluff.

The most famous by far is the Sutherland Falls on the Milford Track; with its three magnificent leaps and a total drop of 580 metres,it is the third highest in the world. By the end of any trip trampers become connoisseurs of falling water, viewing the shape, drops and force of falls with an artist's eye. Some may even secretly pray for rain which can double the size and the number of the waterfalls along the tracks.

The large amounts of moisture mean lush vegetation as well as waterfalls. On the eastern side, forests of red, silver and mountain beech fill the valleys and cling to the steep faces. In the northern and western coastal sections impressive podocarp forests of matai, rimu, northern rata and totara can be found.

Much of the forest can be seen growing on the surface of hard rock covered by only a thin layer of rich humus and moss, a natural retainer for the large amounts of rain. It is this peaty carpet that allows thick ground flora to thrive under towering canopies and sets western Fiordland bush apart from that of the rest of the country.

Fiordland stunned the ornithological world in 1948 when Dr Geoffrey Orbell 'rediscovered' the takahe, a flightless bird that stands 45 cm, has scarlet feet and bill and is brilliantly coloured with feathers of blue to iridescent green. The Takahe had not been seen in 50 years and was thought to be extinct when Dr Orbell sighted seven birds in what is now the Takahe Valley of the Murchison Mountains. An immense management programme was launched to save the species and in 1986 it was estimated that 181 birds lived in the park. The birds trampers will most likely spot, however, are the usual wood pigeons, fantails, bush robins, tuis, bellbirds and kakas. In the alpine regions you may see Keas; if you wander around at night you might occasionally come across a kiwi.

Backpackers will also encounter something else buzzing through the air: the sandfly. The insect is common throughout New Zealand but Fiordland has the distinction of being renowned for them. There seems to be an exceptionally high proportion of them around Martins Bay, at Supper Cove at the end of Dusky Track and at several points along the Milford, including the end which has been appropriately named Sandfly Point. In alpine regions or in wind, rain or direct sun, the sandfly's numbers are reduced significantly but rarely does it disappear completely. There are also mosquitoes in a few places.

One insect that delights trampers is the glow-worm. Their bluish light is most spectacular in the Te Anau Caves where they line the walls by the thousand. They can easily be spotted on most tramps, glowing at dusk or at night beneath the ferns and in heavy bush sharply cut by a benched track.

Fiordland offers first-class freshwater fishing for brown and rainbow trout and some excellent coastal fishing opportunities at Martins Bay and Supper Cove. The lakes are renowned for their trout populations but trampers, not having a boat at their disposal, do much better concentrating on rivers and the mouths of streams that empty into lakes. Almost any stream in the park will hold trout but the better ones near tracks include the Clinton off the Milford, the Spey on the Dusky Track, Hollyford River and its Lake Alabaster on the Hollyford Track and the Irish Burn off the Kepler Track. You need a licence and there are special regulations and seasons for some waters. Check with the park headquarters before you start casting.

Top: Hooker Valley from Mueller Hut route, Mt Cook NP (JD)
Bottom: Creek along Routeburn Track, Mt Aspiring NP (IK)

Top: Lake Wakatipu, Queenstown (IK)
Bottom: Steamer, Queenstown (IK)

Tree fern in Fiordland NP

MILFORD TRACK

The Milford is best enjoyed if you accept the fact that it is a highly regulated tourist attraction where every step is controlled. You *must* walk the track in one direction during the summer season starting from Glade Wharf. You *must* stay at Clinton Forks the first night, despite its being only two hours from the start of the track, and you *must* complete the trip in the prescribed three nights and four days. This time limit is perhaps the bitterest point with independent walkers as even if the weather goes sour you still have to push on and cross the alpine section. Unlike the Routeburn or Kepler or any other track in New Zealand, trampers can't wait a day or two for good weather and clear views on the Milford.

Independent walkers and guided parties are kept apart as they use separate huts and launch trips. Credit has to be given to the system, for rarely do the two groups see each other on the track. With careful segregation and the one-way travel, the Milford appears much less crowded than you might expect with 8000 trampers crossing it every year. The only problem on the track is the scenic flights which have become a nuisance in recent years. The planes have to follow the same valleys as walkers and on a clear day up to 24 planes will be buzzing around the Sutherland Falls.

Keep all this in mind when considering the Milford. If the regulations, high cost and non-wilderness atmosphere outweigh the outstanding scenic values, skip this track.

Making all the necessary arrangements for the Milford can often be harder than walking the track itself. The first and most important step for independent walkers is to secure a reservation. If your party is larger than two or three people and you want to walk during the period from mid-December to January, book way ahead if possible. Park officials recommend you send for reservations *a year in advance* to obtain one of the 40 spots open each day on the track.

If you are travelling alone or in a pair and can wait a few days, you have a reasonable chance of getting on the Milford without booking, as cancellations can make places available. By late February the summer rush is over and reservations are much easier to obtain. The walking season for the Milford is from early November to mid-April.

The cost of a booking is $41.50 for adults and $35.50 for children and must be paid before a reservation is confirmed. This includes three nights of hut fees, the launch from Sandfly Point (the end of the track) to Milford and a reservation fee. You can make a booking through any tourist agency or by writing to the Tourist Hotel Corporation, PO Box 185, Te Anau; or by calling THC (tel (0229) 7411). All payments must be made in New Zealand dollars if you book from overseas.

Access

Te Anau, a small version of Queenstown on the shores of Lake Te Anau, is the home of the Fiordland National Park visitor centre and the departure point for most tracks in the park. Within this town you will find everything you need to complete your preparations for walking in Fiordland, including gear rental at Te Anau Sports Centre (tel (0229) 8195). They charge $6 a day to rent packs, sleeping bags, boots or a fishing rod for up to four days. No stoves are needed on the Milford Track as all the huts have gas rings.

Once in Te Anau, you also need to arrange bus transport from the town to Te Anau Downs, the two-hour boat launch from the Downs to Glade Wharf (start of the track) and transport from Milford back to town. For most people (those who don't hitch) the total cost of walking the Milford is usually around $110 – not a cheap track by any means.

The launch departs daily at 2 pm from the Downs and you can book it at Fiordland Travel (tel (0229) 7416) on the Te Anau waterfront or at Mt Cook Lines Travel Centre (tel (0229) 7516) just a few metres down on Te Anau Terrace. The fare to Glade Wharf is $32. An NZRRS bus departs daily at 1.15 pm for the Downs and the fare is $8. Book it at Fiordland, Mt Cook Lines or the NZRRS centre on Milford Rd heading away from the lake.

Since you've already paid for the launch from Sandfly Point, the only transport left to arrange is the bus from Milford Sound back to Te Anau and here you have some choices. Traditionally only NZRRS ran the route. Their buses depart at 7.45 am for those who want to spend the night in the sound, and 3.30 pm for those who want to return to Te Anau right away. The fare for the trip is $26.50. But when the Magic Bus company began in 1986 things became competitive, with independent trampers emerging as the winners. Magic Bus departs the sound at 1.30 pm for Te Anau and offers a much more enjoyable ride back (free coffee, music,

plenty of photo stops etc). The best part is that the fare is only $20.

If you ride the Magic Bus, keep in mind that you have to spend the night at the sound. This is no longer the ripoff it used to be. If you do spend the night there, you can catch the scenic boat trip next morning through the sound, which really isn't seen on the 20-minute launch trip from Sandfly Point, and you'll be back in plenty of time to have a beer at the pub before catching the Magic Bus at 1.30 pm. Book passage for the Magic Bus at the Te Anau Youth Hostel (tel (0229) 7847) or the Te Anau Motor Park (tel (0229) 7457).

Places to Stay

At Milford Sound there is now low-cost accommodation at *Milford Lodge* which is administered by the park like a track hut. A bunk for the night is $15 and you should book it before you leave Te Anau at THC.

At Te Anau there is the *Manapouri Holiday Camp* (tel 624) which is a km from the post office down the Te Anau Road and has sites for $12 for two, and cabins from $22. On a stunning site adjacent the lake and river is the *Manapouri Glade Caravan Park* (tel 623) with sites at $12 per night, cabins at $18 and on-site caravans at $28. There is also a Youth Hostel at Te Anau.

Information & Maps

Information on the track can be obtained from the Fiordland National Park visitor centre, the newest and most impressive park centre in the country. The centre, which is also the park headquarters, is open daily from 8 am to 5 pm and 6 to 9 pm and has several rooms of displays and exhibits as well as a small theatre where audiovisual programmes are shown throughout the day. There are also racks of brochures, books and maps on the park, its summer activities and the tracks. The best map is the Milford Track Recreation Map, NZMS 299. You can also get good information on any track in the area and

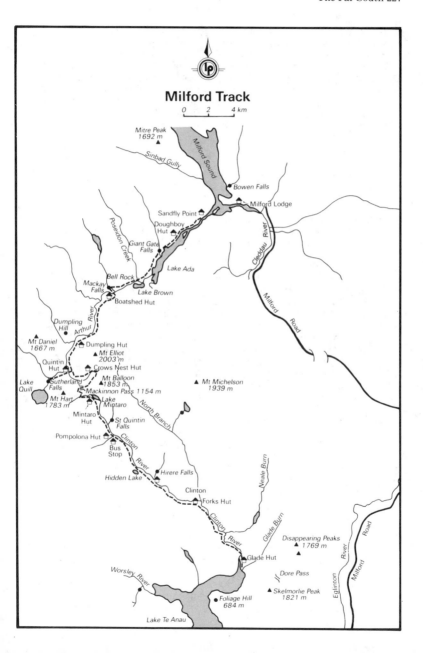

Milford Track

0   2   4 km

even a tramping partner at the Te Anau Youth Hostel. You can also store extra gear there for a small fee.

The Track

Most trampers take the launch across Lake Te Anau, a pleasant trip that is a good introduction to the area. One alternative to the lake cruise is to climb Dore Pass from Eglinton Valley to Glade House, which takes seven to eight hours. The route is a challenging one and should only be undertaken by experienced trampers. Milford, on the other hand, is rated easy.

Stage 1: Glade Wharf to Clinton Forks Hut

Walking Time: two hours

Accommodation: Clinton Forks Huts (40 bunks)

The track from the wharf is a wide 4WD trail which was once used by packhorses to carry supplies to the various huts. In 15 minutes it passes Glade House, first overnight stop for guided parties and the official start of the Milford Track. The track crosses the Clinton River here over a large swingbridge and continues along the true right (west) side as a gentle path where no stone or blade of grass appears out of place. The lower portion of the Clinton from here to past Clinton Forks Hut (the first hut for independent walkers) has excellent trout fishing.

At one point the track gives way to an impressive view of the peaks next to Dore Pass but most of the walk along the river is through beech forest. Clinton Forks Hut is reached two hours after departing the launch at the wharf. All independent walkers must spend the first night here.

Stage 2: Clinton Forks Hut to Mintaro Hut

Walking Time: four to 4½ hours

Accommodation: Mintaro Hut (40 bunks)

Beyond Clinton Forks the track heads up the West Branch of the Clinton River and in four km reaches the old 6 Mile Hut where the valley becomes noticeably narrower with granite walls boxing it in on both sides. The track remains in beech forest until it comes to the Prairies, the first grassy flat, which is reached in 30 minutes from 6 Mile Hut. There are good views from here towards Mt Fisher (2131 metres) to the west, and Mackinnon Pass to the north. A short side track curves west (left) to Hidden Lake where there is a towering waterfall on the far side.

The track re-enters bush again and begins a rocky climb to the first Bus Stop Shelter, nine km from Clinton Forks, and then to the deluxe Pompolona Hut, the second night layover for THC hikers. The track crosses a swingbridge over Pompolona Creek and continues its winding course over low scrub. The track ascends more steeply as it passes a sidetrack to St Quintin Falls and eventually works its way to Lake Mintaro and Mintaro Hut a short distance away. The Mintaro Hut is a 3½ km walk beyond Pompolona Hut.

If the weather is clear, you might want to stash your pack and continue to the pass to be assured of seeing the impressive views without hindrance from clouds or rain. The Mackinnon Pass is a 1½ to two-hour climb from the hut and offers a spectacular view during sunset on a clear evening.

Stage 3: Mintaro Hut to Dumpling Hut

Walking Time: six hours

Accommodation: Dumpling Hut (40 bunks)

The track leaves the hut, swings east with the valley and resumes its climb to Mackinnon Pass. It crosses Clinton River a second time and begins to follow a series of switchbacks out of the bush and into the alpine sections of the route. After four km at a knee-bending angle, the track reaches the large memorial cairn that honours the discovery of this scenic spot by Quintin Mackinnon and Ernest Mitchell in 1888.

The track now levels out and crosses the rest of the alpine pass and there are impressive views all around of the Clinton and Arthur Valleys and several nearby peaks. The two most prominent peaks on the pass are Mt Hart (1783 metres) and Mt Balloon (1853 metres) situated right behind the emergency shelter. If the weather is fair, the pass is a place trampers like to spend some extra time; if it isn't, they can't get off it fast enough.

The track passes several tarns and reaches the emergency shelter where it swings north for the descent. From the pass to Quintin Hut, the track drops 870 metres over a span of seven km. Soon the track arrives at Roaring Burn Stream, crosses it and re-enters the bush. Once in the bush the track passes Crows Nest, an emergency shelter for THC trips, and then continues toward Quintin Hut.

Quintin is a THC hut where there is an airstrip and several buildings for the guided trampers and a day-use shelter for independent walkers. You should seriously consider leaving your pack and following the spur to Sutherland Falls (a 1½ hour round trip). The falls – three leaps totalling 580 metres – are an awesome sight and often are the highlight of the trip for many. Trampers can also wait until the following day if weather is bad and hike an hour back up the track from Dumpling Hut. This allows you to catch the falls at sunrise when the early morning sun presents the cascading water in a different light.

The track leaves Quintin Hut and descends Gentle Annie Hill, re-entering the thick forest which is often slippery and wet. Within three km (an hour's walk) from Quintin the track arrives at Dumpling Hut, a welcome sight after a long day over the pass.

Stage 4: Dumpling Hut to Sandfly Point

Walking Time: 5½ to six hours

The last leg of the Milford Track is an 18-km walk to a shelter on Sandfly Point. The trek takes most people between five and six hours and if you plan to meet the 2 pm launch to Milford you should be out of Dumpling hut no later than 8 am.

The track descends back into bush from Dumpling Hut and soon the roar of the

Arthur River is heard as the track closely follows the true right (east) bank. Six km (about a two-hour walk) from the hut, the track reaches the THC Boatshed Hut and then crosses the Arthur on a large swingbridge. Just beyond the Boatshed Hut, the track crosses a bridge over MacKay Creek and then comes to the sidetrack to MacKay Falls and Bell Rock. Both natural wonders are a short walk from the main track and worth the time it takes to see them – especially Bell Rock, where water has eroded a space underneath the rock large enough to stand in.

The track begins to climb a rock shoulder of the valley above Lake Ada where at one point there is a view of the lake all the way to the valley of Joe's River. From here the track descends to Giant Gate Falls and passes the falls by a swingbridge six km from Bell Rock before continuing along the lake shore. It takes about an hour to follow the lake past Doughboy Shelter, a THC hut, and through wide open flats at the end of the valley before you reach the shelter at Sandfly Point.

Though it is important to be on time to meet the boat at 2 pm or 4 pm, Sandfly Point is not a place to spend an afternoon. The place is a haven for the insect after which it was so rightfully named.

HOLLYFORD TRACK

The Hollyford is the longest valley in Fiordland National Park, stretching 80 km from the Darran Mountains out to Martins Bay on the Tasman Sea. The upper portions of the valley are accessible by the Lower Hollyford Rd, which extends 18 km from Marian Corner on the Milford Rd to the start of the track. The track is generally recognised as extending from the road end to Martins Bay and includes a seven-hour segment from Lake Alabaster Hut to Olivine Hut on the Pyke River.

In recent years portions of the route have been upgraded, new transport services have emerged and more and more trampers have discovered the lush rainforest, extensive bird life and unique marine fauna (seals and penguins) at Martins Bay. The track now averages about 3500 walkers a year, both guided parties and independent trampers, which is a considerable increase since the early 1980s but still nowhere near the numbers using the Routeburn or Milford.

One reason the Hollyford will always lag behind its two famous counterparts to the south is the length of the trip. The track is basically a one-way tramp, unless a Big Bay-Lake Alabaster loop is followed through the Pyke State Forest, a nine to 10-day trip for experienced trampers only. Otherwise it's a four-day walk out to Martins Bay where you turn around and retrace your steps back to the road end for another four days.

Once out in Martins Bay, two things are needed: spare time and lots of insect lotion. The isolated bay is a great spot to spend an extra day as it offers superb coastal scenery and saltwater fishing as well as good views of a seal colony and penguins. The hut is pleasant, situated in a beautiful spot and usually stocked with handlines and hooks. But be prepared for the sandflies and mosquitoes that quickly introduce themselves to all trampers passing through.

Access

Many trampers will get around back-tracking all or a portion of the track by using the transport services of Hollyford Tourist & Travel Company (HTC), based out of Invercargill (tel (021) 4300). The company offers a number of possibilities including flying from an airstrip near Gunns Camp to Martins Bay or from Milford Sound to Martins Bay. The plane holds four people and their packs and costs $200 per trip. Most trampers prefer to hike out to Martins Bay so as to save the most scenic section for the end, and then return by plane.

The company also runs a jet boat along Lake McKerrow and will transport trampers from the head of the lake to Martins Bay in either direction for $120 per boat load for up to four people or $30 per tramper for five or more. This saves a day and eliminates walking the Demon Trail, by far the most difficult portion of the track. Arrangements can be made either by calling or writing to the company (Box 216, Invercargill) or by contacting HTC staff on the track at their Pyke Lodge or Martins Bay Lodge. You can also make arrangements in Auckland through NZ Adventure Centre (tel (09) 399-192) in the Victoria Park Market.

NZRRS buses will drop off or pick up trampers at the Marion Corners Shelter on its Te Anau to Milford run or you can pick up a ride all the way to Gunns Camp on a Magic Bus. The Magic Bus departs Te Anau at 8 am daily and arrives at Gunns Camp at 10.15 am. The cost is $18 one-way and tickets can be purchased at the Te Anau Youth Hostel (tel (0229) 7847) or the Te Anau Motor Camp (tel (0229) 7457). This still puts you about eight km short of the start of the track and the only way to reach it without a vehicle is to walk or try to hitch a ride.

Places to Stay

Many trampers, especially those coming directly from the Milford or Routeburn Tracks, will make their way to *Gunns Camp*, where there is a motor camp with cabins ($10 single, $16 for two) and tent sites ($3 per person). You can re-supply here from a small store well stocked with backpackers' food and items. The next day it's a two-hour walk to the road end and then another three hours to the first hut at Hidden Falls.

Information & Maps

Hut fees of $11 a night are payable at the Fiordland National Park visitor centre in Te Anau. Maps that cover the track include the recreation map of Fiordland National Park, NZMS 273/3, and quads S113 and S115 of NZMS 1 series.

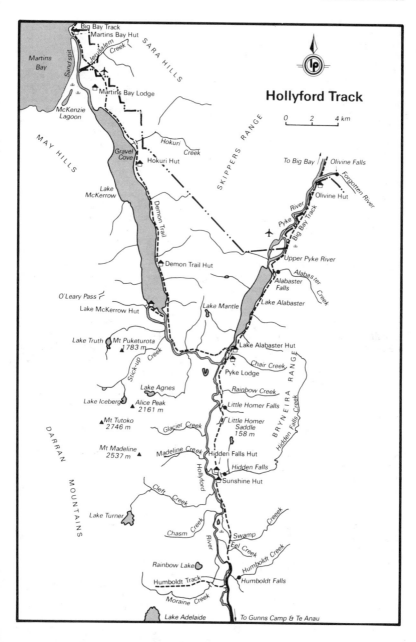

Hollyford Track

0   2   4 km

Big Bay Track
Martins Bay Hut
Jerusalem Creek
SARA HILLS
Martins Bay
Sandhill
Martins Bay Lodge
McKenzie Lagoon
MAY HILLS
Hokuri Creek
SKIPPERS RANGE
Gravel Cove
Hokuri Hut
To Big Bay
Olivine Falls
Olivine Hut
Forgotten River
Pyke River
Lake McKerrow
Demon Trail
Big Bay Track
Demon Trail Hut
Upper Pyke River
Alabaster Creek
O'Leary Pass
Alabaster Falls
Lake Alabaster
Lake McKerrow Hut
Lake Mantle
Lake Truth
Mt Puketurota
1783 m
Lake Alabaster Hut
Stick-up Creek
Chair Creek
Pyke Lodge
Lake Agnes
Rainbow Creek
BRYNEIRA RANGE
Lake Iceberg
Alice Peak
2161 m
Little Homer Falls
Hidden Falls Creek
Mt Tutoko
2746 m
Glacier Creek
Little Homer Saddle
158 m
DARRAN
Mt Madeline
2537 m
Madeline Creek
Hidden Falls Hut
Hidden Falls
Hollyford
Sunshine Hut
MOUNTAINS
Cleft Creek
Lake Turner
Chasm Creek
Swamp
Eel Creek
Humboldt Creek
River
Rainbow Lake
Humboldt Track
Humboldt Falls
Moraine Creek
Lake Adelaide
To Gunns Camp & Te Anau

The Track

The following description covers the Hollyford Track from the road end to Martins Bay. The five-day trip is rated medium and from Martins Bay trampers either backtrack, arrange to be flown out or continue on the Big Bay-Lake Alabaster loop (see the following Other Tracks section).

Stage 1: Lower Hollyford Rd to Hidden Falls

Walking Time: 2½ to three hours
Accommodation: Hidden Falls Hut (12 bunks)

From the end of the road a track departs and in a km crosses a swingbridge over Eel Creek and then continues sidling bluffs for another km to a second bridge over Swamp Creek. At this point the track closely follows the true right (east) bank of the river and offers an occasional view of the snow-capped Darran Mountains to the west. It's about a three-km walk until the track emerges on the open flat of Hidden Falls Creek and quickly passes Sunshine Hut, an HTC lunchtime shelter.

Just beyond the private hut, a side track leads to Hidden Falls Creek, which are two minutes upstream from the swingbridge. On the other side of the bridge, five minutes away, is Hidden Falls Hut, which includes gas rings as well as a wood stove and a good view of Mt Madeline.

Stage 2: Hidden Falls to Lake Alabaster

Walking Time: 3½ to four hours
Accommodation: Lake Alabaster Hut (12 bunks)

The track departs from behind the hut and passes through a lowland forest of ribbonwood and podocarp for two km before beginning its climb to Little Homer Saddle, the high point of the trip. It's about a 30 to 45-minute climb of 120 metres through beech forest before the track reaches the saddle of 158 metres where through the trees there is a view of Mt Madeline and Mt Tutoko to the west.

The descent is steeper than the climb until the track reaches Homer Creek in a km at the spot where nearby Little Homer Falls is thundering 60 metres down into the stream. It's another 30 minutes before the track swings back to the Hollyford and crosses a swingbridge over Rainbow Creek. The track stays with the river for two km before it reaches the confluence of the Pyke and Hollyford Rivers and in a grassy clearing passes Pyke Lodge, an HTC hut for guided parties.

The track quickly crosses a swingbridge over Chair Creek and then comes to the giant swingbridge over the Pyke River. If planning to stop for the night, skip the Pyke bridge and continue up the true left (east) side of the river for another 20 minutes until Lake Alabaster and its lakeshore hut are reached. There are no gas rings in this one but the lake makes it a scenic place to spend the night and a favoured spot for trout fishing.

Stage 3: Lake Alabaster to Lake McKerrow

Walking Time: four hours
Accommodation: Lake McKerrow Hut (12 bunks)

Backtrack to the swingbridge over the Pyke River and after crossing it continue beneath the rocky bluffs along the lower section of the river. Here the track enters a lush podocarp forest where all sights and sounds of the two great rivers are lost in the thick canopy of the trees. For two hours the track works its way through the bush before breaking out into a clearing next to the Hollyford, now twice as powerful as it was above the Pyke River junction.

Before reaching Lake McKerrow, the Hollyford River swings west around McKerrow Island while another channel that is usually dry rounds the island to the east. Near the dry river bed there is a sign pointing up the main track to Demon Trail Hut. This is also the start of an unmarked route across the east channel to a track on McKerrow Island. Follow the track around the north side of the island to reach Lake McKerrow Hut, pleasantly situated near the mouth of the main channel and partially hidden by bush.

If the rain has been heavy, it may be impossible to cross the eastern river bed in which case trampers can stay on the Demon Trail and in 1½ hours or so reach Demon Trail Hut. If you're at Lake McKerrow Hut and it rains, there's little you can do but wait until the channel can safely be forded. One of the better fishing spots for trout is usually around the mouth of the main channel. Check the log book for the most recent catches.

Stage 4: Demon Trail from Lake McKerrow to Hokuri

Walking Time: 6½ to seven hours
Accommodation: Demon Trail Hut (12 bunks); Hokuri Hut (12 bunks)
From the signpost on the main track it's 20 minutes to the clearing that was the site of an old hut and is the start of the Demon Trail. This portion of the track used to be called 'the most exhausting non-alpine track in New Zealand' but has been upgraded in recent years. Still, the trail is rocky, undulating and basically a tedious walk. It's three km (a good hour's walk) to the new Demon Trail Hut that sits on a terrace overlooking Lake McKerrow, a pleasant spot.

At Slip Creek, considered to be the halfway point, there is a rock bivvy nearby large enough to hold six people in case emergency shelter is needed. Most trampers, however, try to cover the 12 km from Lake McKerrow Hut to Hokuri Hut as fast as possible. For those who push on to Demon Trail Hut, plan on a five-hour walk the next day to Hokuri.

Stage 5: Hokuri to Martins Bay

Walking Time: 4½ to five hours
Accommodation: Martins Bay Hut (14 bunks)
It's about a 10-minute walk beyond the hut to Hokuri Creek, which can usually be forded near its mouth. If not, there is a wirewalk 15 minutes upstream. The track continues along the lakeshore for 1½ hours and passes the township of Jamestown, though little remains of the settlement today. In another 30 minutes you reach the signposted turnoff where the track leaves the lake for good and heads inland.

The track cuts through bush at this point and in about three km (an hour's walk) it breaks out into the grassy clearing where the Martins Bay airstrip is located. A sign points to Martins Bay Lodge, a HTC hut, while poles lead across the grassy clearing and around one end of the airstrip where the track enters tall tutu scrub for a km before fording Jerusalem Creek. After the normally easy ford, the track continues through windshorn forest and passes several views of the Hollyford River mouth and the sandy spit on the other side. Within three km the track emerges from the bush, passes some artistic rock formations and then swings north to Martins Bay Hut, situated in coastal scrub overlooking Long Reef.

Adjacent to the hut is a rocky point with easy access to deep pools where coastal fishermen do well. Consult the log book for details of the latest catches. The seal colony is only a 15-minute walk down the rocks of Long Reef and is one of the best in New Zealand. It is easy to spend an afternoon photographing them. You might also spot penguins along the shore as they shuffle from one boulder to the next. An old cattle track continues north of Long Reef and this is the track to take to Big Bay and the circular route to Lake Alabaster.

KEPLER TRACK

The Kepler is not only the newest but also the best planned track in New Zealand. It's a perfect loop, beginning and ending near the control gates where the Waiau River empties into the south end of Lake Te Anau. Park rangers can actually show you the start of the track from a window inside the visitor centre.

It's an alpine crossing, designed to take

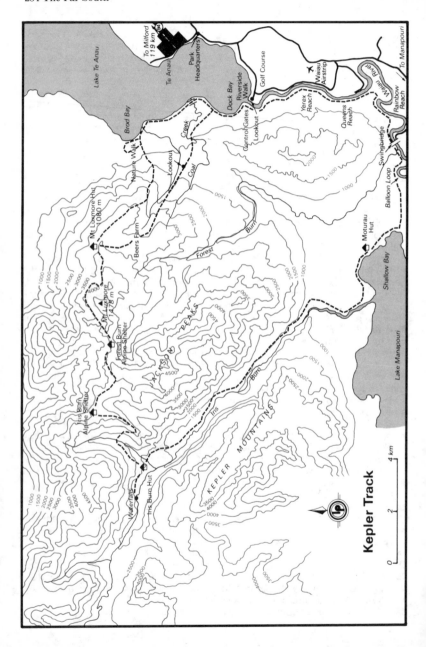

Kepler Track

pressure away from the Routeburn and the Milford, and includes an all-day trek above the bushline with incredible panoramas of Lake Te Anau, its South Fiord Arm, the Jackson Peaks and, of course, the Kepler Mountains.

The 40-bunk huts will undoubtedly be needed in a few years and possibly even be overflowing as more trampers discover this new, hassle-free walk. The only question is whether this track will ever attract the numbers the Routeburn does.

Access

The start of the track is about five km from the Fiordland Park visitor centre (a good hour's walk). Follow the Manapouri-Te Anau Rd south and take the first right turn that is clearly marked by a yellow AA sign. Continue past the golf course and take another right-hand turn, go past a car park and walk across to the control gates to reach the track.

Maps

The track is so new that it's not on the recreation map of Fiordland National Park or any quads. The best bet is to purchase quads S140 and S149 of NZMS 1 series which show the first leg of the journey to Mt Luxmore Hut. The warden at the hut can then outline on your map the alpine route covered the second day.

The Track

The Kepler track begins by ascending to Mt Luxmore Hut on the first day. This means there is almost no climbing on the second day when trampers are faced with the long alpine crossing.

The track was finished in 1988 and it's a cut and well-marked trail, passing three 40-bunk huts with gas rings. The huts are so large and comfortable it's hard to dispute the $11 nightly fee the wardens collect.

But the Kepler is considerably more difficult than the Routeburn and doesn't even compare with the Milford. It's rated difficult and the first day involves a gruelling climb of 850 metres from the shores of Lake Te Anau to Mt Luxmore above the bushline. If you have trouble handling the first day then return because the second day is even longer and more difficult.

The track is designed to be walked in four days but this can be reduced to three days by eliminating the night in the final hut on the shores of Lake Manapouri. It's a 5½-hour walk down the Iris Burn Valley to Moturau Hut. In another 1½ hours along the track you pass the swingbridge over the Waiau River at Rainbow Reach. Cross the river and in 15 minutes you'll be on the Manapouri-Te Anau Road, 11 km south of Te Anau.

Stage 1: Control Gates to Mt Luxmore Hut

Walking Time: six to seven hours
Accommodation: Mt Luxmore Hut (40 bunks)

The track begins by skirting the lake to Dock Bay, staying on the fringe of the mountain and red beech forest. Within 30 minutes the track begins to wind through an impressive growth of tree ferns with crown ferns carpeting the forest floor and then reaches the signposted junction to Beer's Farm, a more direct but tougher climb to Mt Luxmore that takes 4½ hours. You pass Dock Bay as the track continues to skirt the lake's western shoreline, mostly a pebbled beach at this point, and

Mt Luxmore Hut on Kepler Track

within a km crosses the swingbridge over Coal Creek.

In another three km (1½ hours) from the control gates, the track crosses another stream and arrives at Brod Bay, a beautiful sandy beach on the lake. There are pit toilets, a table and a barbecue here and for those who made a late start and have a tent this would make a scenic place to camp. The track to Mt Luxmore is signposted near the beach and you now begin the steepest climb of the trip. The original track climbed sharply, levelled out briefly and then climbed even more steeply and in three km reached a set of towering limestone bluffs. But in 1988 there were plans to re-route this stretch with switchbacks that would make the climb less demanding.

At the bluff, the track swings more due west, skirts the rock and then swings north and resumes climbing through stunted mountain beech. Within a km the track breaks out of the bushline and you get the first glorious view of the trip, a panorama of Lake Te Anau, Lake Manapouri and the surrounding mountains. From here the track becomes a marked route through the alpine scrub with planking crossing the wet sections. The track climbs a couple of small rises and within an hour of breaking out of the bush skirts a small bluff where, on the other side, Mt Luxmore Hut can be seen, with its namesake peak right behind it.

This hut, like all huts on the track, was built in 1987 and features two levels, gas rings, great views from the common room and even toilets that flush. From here Mt Luxmore can be easily climbed without packs (a two to three-hour round-trip). The warden who collects the fees also receives a weather report every morning around 8 am.

Stage 2: Mt Luxmore Hut to Iris Burn Hut

Walking Time: seven to nine hours
Accommodation: Iris Burn Hut (40 bunks)
Most trampers will find this a long day. Wait around for the weather report in the

Iris Burn Hut on Kepler Track

morning to be sure of good conditions for the alpine crossing and then head out immediately to make full use of the day on the track. Carry a full litre of water as there are only a few runoff streams along the way, which could be dry during the summer.

The track departs from the hut and climbs towards the unnamed peak east of Mt Luxmore but ends up sidling its northern slopes. Mt Luxmore looms overhead. Within three km of the hut the track swings to the north to skirt the ridge that runs north from the summit. For those interested in climbing the peak, very distinguishable with its large trig, it's best at this point to scramble to the top of the ridge and drop the packs. From here it's an easy 15 to 20-minute climb to the trig of the 1478-metre peak. If the weather is clear the view is perhaps the finest of the trip, a 360° panorama that includes the Darran Mountains 70 km to the north.

Backtrack to your packs. From the ridge you can easily see the track and its snow poles on the west side. The track resumes on the other side of the ridge by skirting a bluff on steep-sided slopes for the next three km until it reaches a high point on the ridge. Below you can see the first emergency shelter (1235 metre). The track swings away from the ridge, sidles along the slopes around it to make the final descent to Forest Burn Alpine Shelter, reached 2½ to 3½ hours from Mt Luxmore Hut.

From the shelter the track skirts the bluffed end of a ridge where there are great views of the South Fiord. The slopes are extremely steep and you look straight down into the valley. Before the track was cut, in 1988, this was unquestionably the hardest part of the route as it was necessary to take a firm handful of grass or scrub before each step. Eventually (in 3½ km) the track rounds the bluffs onto a ridge crest and the walk becomes considerably easier. You follow the ridge, skirt two knobs and then climb another one. Once on this high point, you can see the second emergency hut, Iris Burn Alpine Shelter.

The shelter sits on a ridge at 1341 metres and is usually reached in three hours from the first shelter or 5½ to six hours from Mt Luxmore Hut. The views are great from the shelter and if it's still early in the day, spend some extra time here: it only takes two to 2½ hours to reach the Iris Burn Hut, and as most of the walk is through bush, this view is much more inspiring than anything you'll see along the way.

The track departs the second shelter and follows a ridge to the south for two km or so. The ridge crest is sharp and at times you feel like you're on a tightrope. Eventually the track drops off the ridge with a sharp turn to the west and descends into the bush. The descent is a quick one down an endless series of switchbacks. The track drops 390 metres before crossing a branch of the Iris Burn. Once on the other side, the track levels out as it skirts the side of this hanging valley and at one point becomes a boardwalk across the steep face. The views of the Iris Burn below are excellent and there's a seat here, so you can lean back, put your feet on the guard rail and enjoy the scenery.

The final segment of the day covers more switchbacks as the track drops 450 metres. Just when it levels out, Iris Burn Hut comes into view, a welcome sight for many.

Stage 3: Iris Burn Hut to Moturau Hut

Walking Time: five to six hours

Accommodation: Moturau Hut (40 bunks)

After the long alpine crossing, this is a very easy, level and enjoyable segment of the track. Since the entire walk to Moturau Hut usually takes less than six hours, many trampers begin with a side trip (20 minutes) to see the impressive waterfalls near Iris Burn Hut.

The valley track is right behind the hut and begins with a short climb before levelling out in the beech forest. Within three km it crosses the Iris Burn and immediately breaks out into a wide open area. The cause of the clearing, a huge landslide that occurred in January 1984, is to your right. Piles of rocks and fallen trees can be seen everywhere as the track passes through the clearing. Once at the other end, the track returns to the bush and continues down the valley, at times following the river closely, to the delight of anglers.

The track crosses several small branches of the burn and remains almost entirely in the bush (one section is through an incredibly moss-laden stand of trees) until it reaches a rocky clearing 11 km from the hut, where the boulders are bright orange. This is the result of a healthy growth of red lichen. At this point the track climbs and follows a bluff above the burn and at times it is a boardwalk hanging from a sheer face from which there are excellent views of the river below.

Four km from the red lichen clearing, the track descends away from the bluff and swings south and in another two km passes a view of Lake Manapouri at the mouth of Iris Burn, a popular spot for anglers. The track swings east and in a km returns within sight of the lake. In the final leg, the track skirts the shore of Shallow Bay until it arrives at Moturau Hut.

This is a pleasant hut with a kitchen view of Lake Manapouri. Much of Shallow Bay features a sandy shoreline. Unfortunately many trampers skip this hut and continue onto the Rainbow Reach bridge to save $11.

Stage 4: Moturau Hut to Control Gates

Walking Time: 4½ to five hours

For the first two km the track heads south through bush until it reaches a junction with a short track to Shallow Bay. The main track heads east (left) and within a km comes to a large swamp known as Amoeboid Mire, which is crossed by a long boardwalk. The track then skirts the south side of the grassy swamp, passes a small lake in the middle, before leaving it and reaching an old river terrace that overlooks Balloon Loop, five km from the hut.

The track bridge crosses Forest Burn, which meanders confusingly before emptying into Balloon Loop. From here it's 30 minutes to the swingbridge at Rainbow Reach or 1½ hours from the hut. Along the way the track skirts bluffs that overlook the wide Waiau River. If you choose to cross the Rainbow Reach bridge, it's a 15-minute walk up the metalled road to the Manapouri-Te Anau Rd, where its easy to hitch a ride in either direction.

Otherwise the track continues in an easterly direction and within an hour begins to swing due north to pass Queens Reach. From the reach the track climbs onto a river terrace where there are views through the trees of a set of rapids, and then moves into an area of manuka scrub. At Yerex Reach, two hours from the swing-bridge, the track passes a few old posts and a quiet segment of the river known as

Beer's Pool. At this point you're only 30 to 45 minutes from the control gates.

DUSKY TRACK

Starting on two of Fiordland's largest lakes, ending at its longest fiord and traversing three major valleys and two mountain ranges, the Dusky Track offers trampers the widest range of experiences and scenery of any track in the park. It also offers the most remote wilderness setting. Due to the remoteness and the high cost of transportation in and out of the area, the Dusky Track, for all its beauty and variety, draws less than 500 trampers a year.

It's basically a Y-shaped track that goes to Supper Cove, with its end points on relatively isolated arms of Lake Manapouri and Lake Hauroko. Supper Cove is the scenic eastern end of Dusky Sound, at 44 km the longest fiord in the park. In recent years the track has been re-routed, upgraded and the huts improved but this walk is still a challenging one, even for parties with some previous tramping experience.

It's also a long walk. Traditionally many trampers would begin the trip by taking a launch across Lake Hauroko, then trek across Pleasant Ridge to Loch Maree Hut. From here they would head out to Supper Cove, backtrack to Loch Maree and then exit at the West Arm of Lake Manapouri, taking another launch to Manapouri. This is the cheapest way to walk the track and involves the least amount of backtracking. Lake Hauroko can get very rough at times, stranding trampers waiting for a scheduled launch.

This trip requires eight to nine days. To reduce the number of days required and to avoid all backtracking, many now utilise a float plane pick-up or drop-off in Supper Cove. Following a launch trip across Lake Manapouri, parties hike down the Spey River to Loch Maree Hut where a spare day is often spent in a climb to scenic Pleasant Ridge. The trip ends with the walk out to Supper Cove and float plane transport back to Te Anau. This walk requires only four to five days and is the one described here. Additional notes at the end of the section are given for the trek to Lake Hauroko.

Access

Te Anau is still the departure point for the majority of trampers attempting the Dusky Track.

The launch across Lake Manapouri is offered through Fiordland Travel (tel (0229) 7419) on Te Anau Terrace just down from the park headquarters. The trip is offered twice daily from September to March at 10 am until Christmas and then at 9 am and again at 2 pm. The fare for adults is $22.60 one way to the West Arm or $35 for the round trip if you decide to backtrack and depart by water. There is also a $4 charge for the bus from Te Anau to Manapouri.

The float plane service is also organised in Te Anau, through *Waterwings Airways* (tel (0229) 7405), who are conveniently located between Fiordland Travel and the park visitor centre, on Te Anau Terrace. The fare to be dropped-off or picked-up in Supper Cove is $120 per person, with a minimum of two passengers. It is wise to book ahead for the plane (write to them at PO Box 222, Te Anau) as they often get busy during the summer with scenic flights.

If including Lake Hauroko in the trip, depart from Tuatapere. The town is reached through Invercargill by H & H Travel (tel (021) 82-419) which departs at 4 pm weekdays. The Tuatapere Hauroko Boat Service launches travel to the end of the lake. This is an unscheduled service so prior arrangements must be made through V McKay at PO Box 13, Tuatapere, or by calling (tel (0225) 6475/6681). Also in Tuatapere is Borland Saddle Scenic Tours (tel (0225) 6681/6475) which has a permit to run the Manapouri Transmission Line Rd. It may be possible to arrange to be dropped off at the Dusky Track starting point, off the West Arm of Lake Manapouri.

Equipment

Among items needed for this trip are good raingear, both parka and pants, and lots of insect lotion.

Information & Maps

Just up the road from Manapouri, at Clifden, there is a ranger station (tel (0225) 6607) where information can be obtained and intentions left.

Although the track is well marked, it's best to purchase quad S148 and S157 of NZMS 1 series as opposed to using just the recreation map of Fiordland National Park.

The Track

The following four-day trip is rated as difficult and described from the West Arm of Lake Manapouri to Supper Cove.

Stage 1: West Arm to Upper Spey Hut

Walking Time: five to 5½ hours from the Jetty

Accommodation: Mica Burn Hut (12 bunks); Upper Spey Hut (12 bunks)

From the jetty on West Arm the trip begins on the Wilmot Pass Rd which crosses a bridge over Mica Burn and comes to a junction with a secondary road on the true right (west) side. Just down the side road is Mica Burn Hut, a 30-minute walk from the jetty. Those trampers heading to Upper Spey Hut for the first night continue on Wilmot Pass Rd and in 20 minutes come to the signposted start of the Dusky Track.

The track enters a forest of ribbonwood and beech along the true left (west) side of the Spey River. It is well graded at the beginning and in little more than a km comes to a wirewalk over Dashwood Stream. The track gently climbs the valley, passes through a couple of small clearings and four hours from the jetty fords Waterfall Creek. A short distance beyond the creek, the track crosses a

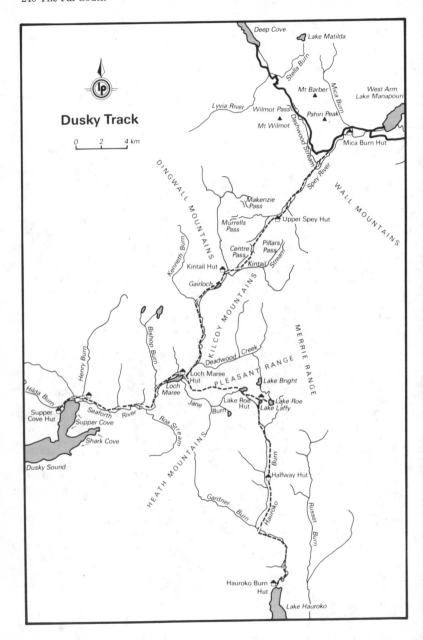

Dusky Track

0 2 4 km

Top: Milford Sound, Fiordland NP (IK)
Bottom: Eglington River, Fiordland NP (IK)

Top: Rainbow trout caught along Kepler Track, Fiordland NP (JD)
Bottom: Rainbow trout (JD)

second wirewalk to the true right (east) side of the Spey.

It's a short climb from the wirewalk to the edge of a large but swampy clearing. Yellow poles lead you across the clearing to the Upper Spey Hut at the top end.

Stage 2: Upper Spey Hut to Kintail Hut

Walking Time: five to six hours

Accommodation: Kintail Hut (12 bunks)

The day begins with a steep climb along Warren Burn, the headwaters of the Spey, before levelling out somewhat. The track then leaves the stream and departs the bush to climb steeply again towards Centre Pass, one of three saddles that lead into the Seaforth Valley. The route up through the alpine scrub, and then tussock slopes, is marked by snow poles. Snow may be encountered on the pass as late as November but after that it's usually clear till April. Looming over the pass to the northeast is Mt Memphis (1383 metres) and occasionally trampers drop their packs and climb it.

The descent on the west side to the Seaforth River is considerably longer and steeper than the climb on the east side. It begins on alpine slopes where there are excellent views of Gair Loch, Tripod Hill and the Seaforth Valley. When it enters the bush the drop steepens as the track descends to the true right (north) side of Kintail Stream and follows it to a wirewalk over the Seaforth right above its confluence with the stream. After crossing the wire, there is a short side track that heads upstream (right) and in five minutes reaches Kintail Hut. There are also good campsites along the river's edge near its confluence with Kintail.

Stage 3: Kintail Hut to Loch Maree

Walking Time: four to five hours

Accommodation: Loch Maree (12 bunks)

Return to the wirewalk but remain on the true right (west) side of the river. The walking is easy as the track heads southwest towards Gairloch, the first of two lakes that are passed. At the top end

of the loch, the track crosses a boggy area and then skirts the shoreline to its outlet where it begins to descend a gorge to Kenneth Burn. The tramping is rougher here until you arrive at the wirewalk across the burn.

The valley flattens out after Kenneth Burn and the travel becomes easier again. Halfway (about three km) to Deadwood Creek, the track crosses a wirewalk over an unnamed stream. Several clearings are crossed and track markers indicate where the track re-enters bush. The track also crosses a number of small gullies that fill with water when the Seaforth is swollen.

Right before the confluence of the Seaforth and Deadwood Creek, the track climbs over a knob and continues to sidle the steep valley on the true right (west) side. This is difficult walking, along a stretch that is prone to flooding during heavy rains. It ends about five minutes before Loch Maree Hut when you emerge at the six-foot track that was built in 1903 by 60 West Coast miners. The miners' track was never completed to Lake Manapouri as originally planned and you can still see picks, crowbars and a hefty anvil along the side of the track just below Loch Maree.

For many, Loch Maree is one of the most scenic spots along the track. The loch is a flooded lake caused by a landslide; fallen tree trunks still decorate the area and stumps can be seen above the water. In early morning this can be a most unusual sight. A layer of mist lies over the lake, silhouetting the stumps and making the loch appear like something from prehistoric times. The Loch Maree Hut is actually on a little peninsula at the head of the lake.

Near the hut is a wirewalk across the Seaforth which begins the overland route to Lake Hauroko. A common day trip for those not planning to exit at this lake is to hike up Pleasant Ridge to Lake Roe. The ridge is an alpine area of numerous tarns and it offers the best overview of Dusky Sound from anywhere on the track. Lake

Roe Hut is on Lake Laffy, while another 20 minutes brings you to Lake Roe itself, a beautiful body of water in a setting of granite outcrops. A round-trip tramp to the lake without packs would be a seven-hour walk.

Stage 4: Loch Maree to Supper Cove

Walking Time: six hours

Accommodation: Supper Cove Shelter (no bunks), Supper Cove Hut (12 bunks)

The route around Loch Maree was upgraded to an all-weather track but occasionally the lake still rises enough to make it impassable for a day or two. The track departs the hut and climbs above the north shore before it descends to a wirewalk across Bishop Burn. At this point it swings onto the two-metre wide miners' track for an easy stroll down the Seaforth Valley.

The valley is flat and trampers are aided with a wirewalk over Macfarlane Stream and a cable ladder over a cliff. About four hours from Bishop Burn, the track passes several heavily bushed flats, where 10 Canadian moose were released in 1910 (moose were last seen in 1970), and arrives at the old Supper Cove Hut, built in 1903 and reconditioned by park authorities in 1955. It still provides shelter today.

It takes another hour to reach the present hut as the track crosses wirewalks over Henry and Hilda Burns and then climbs around the hillside into Supper Cove. Some undulating terrain is covered before the track descends to a wirewalk across a small stream with the hut on the other side. At low tide this segment of climbing can be avoided by simply following the beach. There is a small boatshed next to the hut with a dinghy for public use. You have to row some distance out into the Sound to catch groper, but if you have a line it's easy to land a few blue cod in the cove itself or even from shore.

Lake Hauroko to Loch Maree

For most trampers it is a three-day walk from the lake to Loch Maree Hut. There is Hauroko Burn Hut (eight bunks) near the jetty on the lake for those who are dropped off late. Otherwise it's a six-hour walk to the next facility, Halfway Hut (12 bunks). The next day the track follows a gentle grade until it reaches the forks of Hauroko Burn where it climbs steeply out of the bush to Lake Roe Hut (12 bunks). The hut is actually on Lake Laffy and scenic Lake Roe is a 20-minute climb to the east. The walking time from Halfway to Lake Roe Hut is five hours.

The final leg is the most scenic. Snow poles mark the route around the outlet of Lake Horizon and then across Pleasant Ridge, where there are good views of Dusky Sound. At the end of the ridge the track drops steeply to the Seaforth River and Loch Maree Hut. The walking time from Lake Roe Hut to Loch Maree is four to five hours

OTHER TRACKS

Big Bay – Lake Alabaster Loop

Most of this route is in the Pyke State Forest but access to it is primarily from the Hollyford Track in Fiordland National Park. When the two tracks are combined they form a wilderness loop that continues from Martins Bay along the coast at Big Bay, inland to Pyke River and then down the shore of Lake Alabaster to return to the Hollyford. The entire loop is a nine to 10-day trek that is rated difficult. Tents and stoves should be carried but there is a series of old shelters and bivvies that could be utilised in a pinch. Ask for *Pyke Forest Route Guide* at the Fiordland National Park visitor centre.

George Sound

The marked route extends from the Northeast Arm of the Middle Fiord on Lake Te Anau to George Sound. There is a series of three huts along the track. There are rowboats on Lake Hankinson and it is a three-hour row to the other end where the track resumes. The second day is a 10-hour trek from Thompson Hut over Henry

Saddle to George Sound Hut. The round trip is a four to six-day walk that is rated difficult. The dinghys are locked up and must be hired through the Fiordlands National Park visitor centre.

Lake Monowai

This is a two to three-day trip from the end of Monowai Rd to the western end of Lake Monowai. The first leg is a 6½-hour walk around Green Lake to Green Lake Hut (four bunks), followed by a four-hour trek to Clarke Hut in Grebe Valley. The track ends at Monowai Hut in another 2½ hours. From here either you arrange for a launch trip through Hauroko Boat Service (tel (0225 6475) or follow a difficult route over a saddle near Cleughearn Peak down to the Roger Inlet where a track leads back to the road end.

Waitutu Tramway

This is a one-way track from the end of Blue Cliffs Beach Rd, running along the edge Te Waewae Bay south of Tuatapere. The track begins after the bridge over Track Burn and extends 44 km to Big River. Most trampers tackle only the first half, which includes an old logging tramway and four impressive viaducts to the mouth of Wairaurahiri River. There are three huts along this section and one more beyond it at Waitutu River. A round-trip walk to Wairaurahiri River and back would be a three to four-day trip rated easy.

Stewart Island

Going to Stewart Island is going to extremes: it is the southernmost point of New Zealand and is off the South Island below Invercargill. It's a most remote area with only one small village of 400 residents and vast tracts of wilderness that rarely feel the imprint of a hiking boot. It has the most unpredictable weather in its skies, the most birdlife in its trees and

unquestionably the most mud on its tracks.

The island covers 1680 square km, measuring 65 km from north to south and 40 km from east to west. But its real beauty lies in its 755 km coast, which includes long beaches, impressive sand dunes and crystal clear bays ringed by lush rainforest. The interior is mostly bush and is generally broken by steep gullies and ridges, several emerging above the bushline. The highest point on Stewart Island, Mt Anglem, is only 976 metres, but the walking here can be almost as rugged as in mountainous areas in the North or South Islands.

Time slows down and almost stops for this isolated corner of the country. Visitors find life simpler, the pace unhurried and the atmosphere in the village of Halfmoon Bay relaxed. Trampers find it a delight in comparison with the busy and heavily used tracks of the South Island. The remoteness of Stewart Island, where the tracks are uncrowded after the Christmas to early January season and undeveloped beyond Port William, is a welcome change to many hikers.

The island has more than 220 km of tracks, maintained by DOC district officers at Halfmoon Bay (formerly Oban). These include the new Link Track, a three-day route cut in 1986, which connects huts at Port William and North Arm and provides the only short loop on the island. All the others require seven to 10 days. Today it is, understandably, the most popular trip for the estimated 5500 trampers who visit Stewart Island every year.

What's surprising about the trampers who arrive at Halfmoon Bay is that 60% of them are overseas travellers. They are obviously more intrigued by the island's remote southern position on the map than Kiwis are. The majority of them either hike the Link Track or head up to Christmas Village Bay where they then turn around and backtrack. It is estimated that less than 15% of all trampers who arrive at Stewart Island ever make it beyond Christmas Village.

Most tramping on Stewart Island is not easy. To hike beyond the fully planked and benched Link Track, parties should be experienced and well-equipped. You encounter mud just a few km from the Port William Hut and have to deal with it for much of the way, rain or shine. It's impossible to avoid on the Northern Circuit and most trampers just slosh right through it, ending each evening with a communal washing of boots, socks and feet. It varies from ankle-deep to knee-deep and even deeper at some ill-famed spots such as Ruggedy Flat and the track to Mt Anglem.

Gaiters are a good piece of equipment to have but if you are planning an extensive trip around Stewart Island you just have to accept the fact that your socks will be wet, your pants mud-splattered and your boots will never be the same colour again.

HISTORY

The Maoris have a legend about the creation of Stewart Island. They contend that a young man named Maui left the Polynesian Islands to go fishing. He paddled far into the sea and, out of sight of his homeland, dropped anchor. In time, his canoe became the South Island, a great fish he caught the North Island, and his anchor Stewart Island, holding everything in place.

Excavations in the area provided evidence that, as early as the 13th century, tribes of Polynesian origin migrated to the island to hunt moas. Maori settlements were thin and scattered however, because the people were unable to grow kumara (sweet potato), the main food of settlements to the north. They did make annual migrations to the outer islands seeking muttonbird, a favourite food, and to the main island searching for eel, shellfish and certain birds. At the time of the first European contact the main settlement was at Ruapuke Island,

with smaller groups at Port William, the Neck and Port Adventure.

The first European to sight the area was Captain Cook in 1770, but he left confused as to whether it was part of the South Island. He finally decided it was part of the mainland, naming it Cape South. By the early 1800s sealers were staying for months at a time to collect skins for the mother ship. There is evidence that American sealer O F Smith discovered Foveaux Strait in 1804, for it was known briefly as Smith's Strait. During the sealing boom a few years later it was given its present name, after a governor of New South Wales. The island itself derived its name from William Stewart, the first officer of the English sealer *Pegasus*. Stewart charted large sections of the coast during a sealing trip in 1809 and drafted the first detailed map of the island. He later had it published, imprinting his name on the region forever.

In 1825, a group of sealers and their Maori wives set up a permanent settlement on Codfish Island. Sealing was finished by the late 1820s and whaling replaced it temporarily. Stewart Island had been a port of call for whalers since the early 1800s as a place to recuperate after a season at the whaling bases. Small whaling bases were established on the island itself but they were never really profitable and didn't contribute significantly to the island's progress.

Neither did timber. Though the island was almost completely covered in bush, most of it was not millable and little was profitably accessible. Still the first mill on a commercial basis opened up at Kaipipi Bay in 1861, while in 1874 another was established at Halfmoon Bay in an area now named Mill Creek. Both stimulated the economy of the island to a small degree but in 1931 the timber industry lapsed, when the last remaining mill on Maori Beach closed down.

In 1886, gold was discovered at Port William in the wake of the great Otago and West Coast gold rushes. A small-scale rush resulted and further strikes were made at a few beaches on the north and west coast. The greatest output was between 1889 and 1894, when, ironically, the tin operations in the Tin Range above Port Pegasus turned out little tin but a fair amount of gold. The influx of miners was large enough then to warrant building a hotel and post office, the 'southernmost post office in New Zealand' until it closed on 3 August 1893.

The only enterprise that has endured is fishing. Initially fishermen were few in number and handicapped by the lack of regular transport to the mainland. But when a steamer service from Bluff began in 1885, the industry expanded, resulting in the construction of cleaning sheds on Ruapuke Island and a refrigerating plant in the North Arm of Port Pegasus in 1897.

Today fishing and, to a much lesser extent, tourism are the major occupations of most of the 400 residents in Halfmoon Bay. The main catch is crayfish for the export trade from June to January, while paua and blue cod are caught for the New Zealand market. A new development to the old industry started on Stewart Island in 1982 when the first of three sea-cage salmon farms were built in Big Glory Bay. The sheltered cold waters of Paterson Bay made it a desirable marine farming area and within 24 months salmon, raised from fingerlings to fish that weighed 2½ kg, were processed for sale.

The only other industry to survive the past is muttonbirding. As a direct result of the Deed of Cession signed in 1864, no Maoris except descendants of the original Maori owners of Rakiura are allowed to search and take muttonbirds from the island, and the only Europeans allowed this privilege are husbands or wives of legitimate birders.

The Sooty Shearwater, known affectionately as the muttonbird, nests in burrows on remote islets in the Stewart Island region, laying a single egg in November and hatching it towards the end of December. The parents stay with their chicks for three months and then depart on their annual migration in March. It's at this stage that the Maoris search out and capture chicks so laden with fat they can neither fly nor run very far. By May the remaining chicks have become proficient flyers and can follow their parents.

Although considered by many pakehas as greasy, muttonbirds are viewed as a great delicacy by the Maoris. It is the annual hunt, however, that has great significance with this segment of New Zealand's population. Muttonbirding is an important Maori custom that has successfully withstood the assault of European culture and exploitation.

CLIMATE

The weather also plays havoc with trampers. The overall climate of the island is surprisingly mild, considering its latitude. Temperatures are pleasant most of the year, cool in the summer, rarely cold in winter, and the only place snow falls is occasionally on the summit of Mt Anglem.

Annual rainfall at Halfmoon Bay is only 1600 mm but it occurs over 250 days of the year. Or as one ranger put it 'you get a little rain on a lot of days'. In the higher altitudes and along the south and west coasts, it averages 5000 mm of rain a year, providing trampers with a lot of rain on a lot of days. It's important to keep in mind that the daily weather, or better yet the hourly weather, changes frequently. It's not uncommon to experience two or three showers and clear blue skies by the time you have reached the next hut.

NATURAL HISTORY

For putting up with mud, hilly terrain and indecisive weather, the tramper is amply rewarded. The bush and birdlife on the island is unique. Beech, the tree that dominates the rest of New Zealand, is absent from Stewart Island. The predominant lowland bush is podocarp forest with exceptionally tall rimu, miro, totara and kamahi forming the canopy. Due to mild winters, frequent rainfalls and porous soil, most of the island is a lush forest held together by vines and carpeted in ferns and moss. It is so lush, thick and green, that the bush often appears to be choking the track.

The birdlife on the island is also unique. The ecological disasters (rats and cats) that have greatly affected the mainland have not had as much impact here, and Stewart Island is generally regarded as having one of the largest and most diverse bird populations in the country. Those intent on spotting a kiwi in the wild have a good opportunity while tramping here. There are more kiwis on Stewart Island than there are people and they are less nocturnal than their cousins to the north. The best areas to spot them are from Christmas Village Bay west, and particularly around Mason Bay.

Bush birds such as bellbirds, tuis, wood pigeons and fantails are often seen along the tracks, while parakeets and kakas (forest parrots), rare on the mainland, are occasionally spotted on Stewart Island. The island is also the home of several species of flightless penguin and colonies are often spotted near Long Harry Bay. The most famous bird, which trampers almost never see, is the kakapo, the world's only flightless nocturnal parrot. Thought to have been long extinct, the bird was re-discovered in the southern half of the island in 1977. An intense research program was undertaken as these birds represent the only breeding population left in New Zealand.

LINK TRACK

The Link Track was built to provide trampers with a short circular track of moderate difficulty as an alternative to the challenging 10-day route around the northern portion of the island. It immediately became the most popular tramp on Stewart Island and virtually replaced the five-day journey up to Christmas Bay as the standard trip for trampers with less than a week to spend

on the island. The walk requires three days and has been planked and benched to eliminate most of the mud this island is famous for. Nights are spent at the Port William Hut, and at the North Arm Hut, scheduled to be rebuilt and enlarged to a 20-bunk facility in 1989.

Access

Southern Air (tel (021) 89-129), located at the Invercargill Airport terminal, offers four flights on weekdays at 8 and 10 am and 1 and 5 pm, and three on weekends, at 10 am and 1 and 4 pm. The flight takes about 20 minutes and on a nice day affords a good view of Bluff Harbor, the Muttonbird Islands and the rugged interior of the island. On a poor day, you may simply not fly, but as a rule it's uncommon for flights to be cancelled for more than a day at a time. The one-way fare for adults is $55 but students and youth hostel members can go standby for $27.75. You land at the Stewart Island airstrip where a van greets all flights for the short ride into town.

The plane then returns to Invercargill with homeward-bound passengers and freight. In Halfmoon Bay, go to Stewart Island Travel (tel (021) 391-269) across from the DOC visitor centre to purchase a return ticket or to catch the van out to the airstrip.

You can also reach Halfmoon Bay by water. In 1985, the government-owned MV *Wairua*, which made the trip from Bluff to Stewart Island, was taken out of service and sold. A private firm, Stewart Island Charter Service (tel (021) 378-376), now makes the sailing on board the MV *Acheron*. The ship departs Bluff on Monday, Wednesday and Friday at 9 am and arrives at Halfmoon Bay at 11.15 am, leaving more than enough time to hike easily to the first hut at Port William. It departs the island at 2 pm and reaches Bluff at 4.15 pm. Trampers can reach Bluff on an H & H Travel Lines bus that departs its depot on Don and Kelvin Streets in Invercargill at 8 am. An H & H bus also greets the ferry when it returns from the island.

The cost is virtually the same if you travel by water or air. The ferry ticket is $33 one way but, again, YHA members and students can go standby for $19.20. Add the $6.20 bus fare to Bluff and the standby total is $25.40. The difference is the ferry goes rain, shine, hurricane or monsoon but the trip lasts almost 2½ hours. If the weather is calm the boat ride will be an extremely pleasant cruise. If conditions are poor, you may have trouble hanging onto your seat, not to mention your breakfast. Often called the roughest crossing in the world (by those who get sick on the boat no doubt), the strait has been known to toss the ship from side to side, break waves over the gunwale and leave the locals nodding and visitors horrified.

Places to Stay & Eat

Once ashore, most visitors find Halfmoon Bay to be a delightful little village. At the foot of the ferry dock there is *Anchor Merchants* the only store in town, which carries a surprisingly good selection of both fresh and dried food at very reasonable prices, especially when you consider its out-of-the-way location. Across from it is the *South Sea Hotel*, a lively little pub.

As Halfmoon Bay is a scenic town with a variety of short walks around it, plan to spend at least one night here, if not pressed for time. There is a variety of accommodation available, including a *DOC campground*. Follow Main St until it ends at a 4WD track signposted by a 'Northern Circuit' sign. It's another km up the track to the signposted spur indicating the campground. The area is a grassy clearing on a ridge with a picnic table, fire ring and rubbish bins. A pleasant spot to pitch a tent.

Closer to town is *Ferndale Caravan Park* (tel 52M) which offers tent sites for $6 per person, showers for $3 and a bunk in a large walled tent for $10 per person. The

park is 150 metres up Horseshoe Bay Rd from the wharf.

Hostel-type accommodation is available at *Ann Pullen* (tel (021) 391-065) further along the road from the caravan park, then the first left after you cross the bridge over Mill Creek. Pullen has a rustic cabin next to her home with five to six bunks, a small kitchen and a stove inside. The cost is $7 a night, which includes a shower.

Even further out is *Horseshoe Haven* (tel (021) 391-466), which has tent sites for $7 and a bunkroom lodge for $13 per person.

Information & Maps

Trampers heading to Stewart Island pass through Invercargill first where they can pick up information and maps at the DOC district office (tel (021) 44-589) in the State Insurance Building on Don St. Travel arrangements to cross the Foveaux Strait are also made here and the most popular way seems to be by air.

Just down Main St in Halfmoon Bay, the main town of the island, is the DOC visitor centre which is open daily from 8 am to 4.30 pm, though sometimes they close early – 'when people stop coming'. Inside there are some interesting displays and exhibits on the island's natural and human history along with brochures, books, maps and the latest weather reports. Leave your intentions here or in the registration box outside when the office is closed. There are also lockers inside where you can store extra gear It is $2.50 for small lockers, $5 for larger units that can easily hold a dufflebag.

You can expect to pay a hut and camping fee on Stewart Island after 1988. The fee most often mentioned is $5 for the use of either facility. In December and January there is a hut warden at Port William who will collect the fee. For the other huts and DOC campground pay them at the visitor centre.

The Link Track is covered on quads E48 and D48 of Infomap 260 series or by the Holidaymaker Map of Stewart Island, NZMS 336/10.

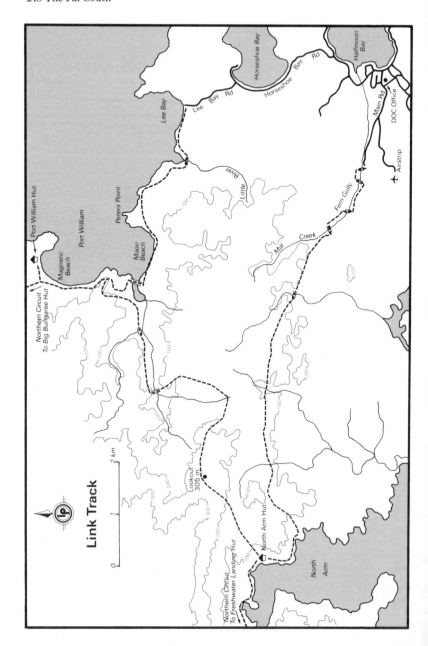

Link Track

The Track

The following trip, rated medium, is described from Port William to North Arm, the easiest direction to walk the route. For those tramping from North Arm to Port William, you should add two hours to the walking time for the uphill trek.

Stage 1: Halfmoon Bay to Port William

Walking Time: four to five hours

Accommodation: Port William Hut (30 bunks)

Beginning at the general store, the first five km is along Horseshoe Bay Rd to Lee Bay where the track begins. It then cuts through bush and in a km crosses a swingbridge over Little River Bridge where it skirts the tidal area on the edge of the forest before heading inland. Within two km the track descends onto Maori Beach and follows the smooth sand to reach a swingbridge at the far end, an hour's walk from Little River. A sawmill began operations here in 1913 and at one time a large wharf and a network of tramways were constructed to extract the rimu. By 1920 there were enough families living here to warrant opening a school. The onset of the Depression led to the closure of Stewart Island's last mill in 1931 and now regenerating forest surrounds the old steam haulers and tramways in the area.

From the bridge the track heads inland to skirt a headland and within a km passes the signposted junction of the Link Track to North Arm Hut. The track to Port William quickly descends the headland and swings close to Magnetic Beach where the jetty can be seen in the distance. It's possible at low tide to hike along the coast for the last leg to the jetty instead of following the track.

At 30 bunks, Port William is the largest hut on the island. In 1876 the government had grand plans for a settlement here and encouraged 50 families with free land to develop the timber resources and offshore fisheries. The settlement was a dismal failure, however, as the utopia the government had hoped for was plagued by isolation and loneliness. All that remains of the settlement today are the large gum trees next to the hut.

Occasionally a fisherman will dock at the jetty and clean his catch of blue cod. Often you can barter a few fillets from him which makes for an unexpected and delicious dinner.

Stage 2: Port William to North Arm

Walking Time: four to six hours

Accommodation: North Arm Hut (15 bunks)

Backtrack along Magnetic Beach to its south end where the track heads inland to cross the headland, almost two km from the Port William Hut. At a signposted junction, the Link Track heads west (right) and climbs over a hill before descending to a swingbridge over a branch of an unnamed stream that empties into Maori Beach. The track skirts the valley above the stream's true left (north) side for more than a km where it descends to a second bridge on the true right (south) side.

The walk becomes tedious as the track climbs over a number of hills as it heads south and fords another branch of the stream and then swings west. At this point it makes a 1½-km climb to the high point of 305 metres. The viewing point is signposted simply as 'lookout' and a tree stump allows you to see Paterson Inlet to the south. From here, the track descends sharply, levels out briefly and then descends a second time before ending at the North Arm Hut, reached in one to 1½ hours from the Lookout.

With the construction of the Link Track, plans have been made to replace the 15-bunk hut at North Arm with a new 20-bunk unit as early as 1989.

Stage 3: North Arm to Halfmoon Bay

Walking Time: four hours

The track departs from the hut and follows the coast of the sheltered bay before turning inland and climbing steeply 150 metres to the top of the first of many rolling plateaus traversed on the way to Fern Gully. The track follows the route of old bush tramways that at one time carried logs from here into the mills at Kaipipi Bay in 1861 and later to another at Mill Creek near Halfmoon Bay. The track climbs onto the plateaus and three times descends into small ravines and gullies between them to cross a stream, resuming the climb on the other side.

There is a footbridge over the third stream and from here the track ascends one last ridge before dropping to a clearing near Mill Creek where there is a 'Fern Gully' sign. There was a small mill here in 1889. From here the track skirts two small clearings and then enters an impressive tunnel of ferns. The number and variety of ferns are truly astounding. The track hugs Mill Creek, crossing several footbridges before emerging in 30 minutes at a DOC track sign on a 4WD track.

To the southwest the rough dirt road continues to Kaipipi Bay, which takes one hour to walk. To the east it continues for about a km, passing the DOC campground and finally merging into Main Rd, which can be followed to either the pub or the general store, depending on what you crave most after a tramp.

NORTHERN CIRCUIT

This is the classic trip around the northern half of Stewart Island. Also referred to as the Round-the-Island Track, the trip includes Mason Bay, a 14-km beach where prevailing westerly winds have formed a spectacular set of sand dunes. The beach itself can be an impressive sight, with the surf breaking hundreds of metres out and roaring onto the hard sand. Standing here, you truly feel you're on the edge of the world.

The entire loop is a difficult trip, for experienced parties only, requiring 10 to 12 days. Some parties cut it down to seven days by heading from Benson Peak to Freshwater Landing and skipping Mason Bay altogether. It seems like a shame to come so close to this magnificent bay only to bypass it in order to save time.

A much better solution is to incorporate a chartered flight to or from Mason Bay. Southern Air, which flies trampers over from Invercargill, also handles the short flight out to the bay on the west side of the island. The company uses a small four-seater plane and the trip lasts only 10 minutes, but it allows you to spend seven to eight days hiking to the bay along the best portions of the track and then skip some muddy sections along Scott Burn and Freshwater River. The cost is $115 per flight and the plane can hold three trampers and their packs. Arrangements for the flight can be made at the Southern Air desk at the Invercargill Airport or at Stewart Island Travel (tel (021) 391-269) in Halfmoon Bay.

There are also a number of charter boat operators in Halfmoon Bay where arrangements can be made to be dropped off up the coast, usually no further than Christmas Village Bay. The DOC visitor centre keeps a list of the current operators.

One highlight of the trip is the offshore fishing. At a number of coastal huts there are rocky points nearby where you can fish for blue cod. The best bait is limpet, the small shellfish that can be gathered easily off the rocks. Cut away the shell and toss your baited hook just off the rocks. Sometimes it's possible actually to see the cod rise to the bait.

Maps

The recreation map of Stewart Island, NZMS 336/10, covers the entire route but at 1:150,000 does not contain enough detail for most tramping parties. If that is the case, purchase quad D48 of the Infomap 260 series. This covers the entire route except for the well-benched tracks to Port William and North Arm from Halfmoon Bay.

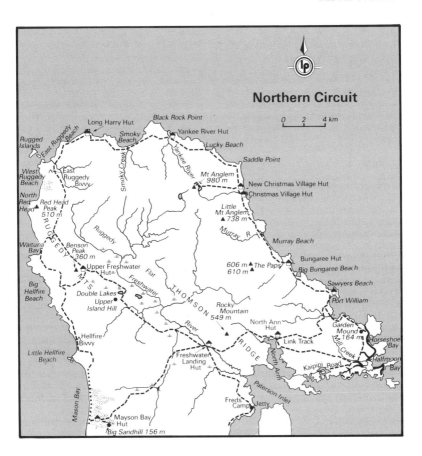

Northern Circuit

The Track

The following trip is rated difficult. The description begins at Port William and ends at North Arm. See the Link Track section for the track descriptions of the segments from Halfmoon Bay to Port William Hut and from North Arm Hut to Halfmoon Bay.

Stage 1: Port William to Christmas Village Hut

Walking Time: seven hours
Accommodation: Big Bungaree Hut (12 bunks); Old Christmas Village Hut (six bunks); New Christmas Village Hut (12 bunks)

From the Port William Hut, return along the side track over the small hump to the main track and head north. You climb a small saddle and cross a footbridge to Sawyers Beach and then head inland where the famous mud bashing of Stewart Island starts. Within 20 minutes the slipping and sliding up one hill and down the next begins, but in an hour you are rewarded with a view of the Muttonbird

Islands to the east. It's a good three km trek through the bush before the track begins a steady drop to Little Bungaree Beach.

From the beach, it crosses a small headland and then descends to Big Bungaree Beach and follows the golden curve of sand to the hut at the far end. The 12-bunk hut is only a three-hour walk from Port William but it is a scenic place to spend the rest of a short day.

The track resumes climbing from the hut and crosses a series of hills and gullies as it works its way inland from Gull Rock Point. In three km (about an hour's worth of slipping and sliding) the track descends sharply onto Murray Beach, catching many trampers unprepared for this two-km stretch of golden sand. Here is a good spot for a swim, shell collecting or paua and mussel hunting, but if you attempt to stretch out in the sun the sandflies will quickly drive you back into your clothes and onto the track.

Follow the beach and cross the swingbridge over Murray River at the north end to reach a side track that leads 100 metres upstream to a well-preserved steam engine half covered by bush. The engine is left over from mill operations of 1912 to 1913. A number of tramways were also built and the main track departs along one of them for a km and then resumes it's up and down hills and across numerous streams. In 3½ km, the track passes a spur track to the old Christmas Village Hut. The right-hand fork leads down to the old hut and then re-enters the bush to ascend to the main track.

The track climbs a hill and then descends to a swingbridge over a stream. On the north side, near the pebbled beach just north of Christmas Village Bay, is the new hut of the same name. The new Christmas Village Hut was built in 1986 and is a vast improvement over the original one, which was a rather dismal place to spend an evening.

Stage 2: Christmas Village to Yankee River
Walking Time: five to six hours
Accommodation: Yankee Hut (12 bunks)
Some spend an extra day at this hut to climb Mt Anglem, the highest point on Stewart Island. The junction to the summit track is just beyond the hut and the round trip is a six-hour walk. On a clear day the views from the top are excellent and include most of the island as well as the South Island in the distance. The mud on this side track, however, has been known to be exceptionally bad.

From the new hut, it's a steep climb to the junction with Mt Anglem Track, the trail that heads west (left). The main track heads north as it works its way through a rimu forest and remains dry for five km until it descends to a swingbridge and onto Lucky Beach. But there is little sand to entice anyone to linger here.

The track begins again at the west end of Lucky Beach and climbs through dense ferns and bush. For four km (two hours) the track covers the undulating terrain before making a long descent to the sluggish Yankee River. Just in time, and usually greeted with a sigh of relief, a signpost pointing to the hut five minutes downstream comes into view.

Stage 3: Yankee River to Long Harry Bay
Walking Time: five to six hours
Accommodation: Long Harry Hut (six bunks)
Backtrack to the main track. This crosses the Yankee River by a swingbridge and then rises steadily for 200 metres over the ridge of Black Rock Point before descending to Smoky Beach, two hours from the hut. The climb is a knee bender and the track is often muddy but the sandy beach, set off by rolls of huge sand dunes, is very scenic. If you reach it at low tide, it's often possible to collect paua from the exposed rocks.

The track continues along the beach for two km to its west end and then heads inland to cross Smoky Creek by way of a swingbridge. It climbs high above the beach and then begins a tough stretch where it climbs in and out of numerous bushclad gullies while crossing a half-dozen streams. Within three km of Smoky Creek Bridge (a good two-hour trek) the track makes a steady descent to Long Harry Hut, well above the ocean.

The old six-bunk hut is less than inspiring but the beach along Long Harry Bay is scenic. This is perhaps the best spot on the trip to view a penguin colony. The offshore fishing is also excellent here if you scramble onto a nearby rocky point to get away from the kelp beds.

Stage 4: Long Harry Bay to East Ruggedy Bivvy

Walking Time: three to four hours
Accommodation: East Ruggedy Bivvy (two bunks)

The track continues along a terrace behind the hut for a short distance before climbing along Cave Point Ridge. There are good views along the ridge before the track descends to the broken coast. The track follows the rugged coast briefly then enters the low scrub at a signpost. After a steep climb of 200 metres over a ridge, where there are more fine views, and a three-hour walk from Long Harry Bay, the track descends to a river with scenic East Ruggedy Beach beyond it.

The track moves inland from the beach and, marked by colourful fishing buoys, traverses sand dunes and scrub for a km until it reaches East Ruggedy Bivvy on a small stream. You can stay at the roomy two-bunk hut or head down the sidetrack to West Ruggedy Beach where there is a rock bivvy with room for four at the north end. The rock shelter is a 40-minute walk from East Ruggedy Bivvy.

Stage 5: East Ruggedy Bivvy to Benson Peak

Walking Time: five to six hours
Accommodations: Upper Freshwater Hut (six bunks)

From the end of the sandhills at the junction, the track works its way to the east side of the Ruggedy Range. As the track nears the head of Ruggedy Flat it encounters some extremely deep bogs and related mud holes although boardwalks now span the worst spots. Upon reaching the range the track turns south with good views of Red Head Peak to the west and in six km from East Ruggedy Bivvy it reaches the junction to Waituna Bay.

The southwest track (right-hand fork) heads to Waituna Bay and then continues south where it joins the track from Benson Peak near Big Hellfire Beach. There are no huts along this stretch but it is possible for a fit party to travel from East Ruggedy Bivvy to Little Hellfire Bivvy in a single day, which would take 10 to 11 hours). Otherwise take the southeast (left) track as it gradually sidles off the range to a six-bunk hut located on the east side of Benson Peak (360 metres). Upper Freshwater Hut is also known as Benson Peak Hut and features an open fireplace and six bunks. It's about five km (a two to three-hour hike) from the junction to Waituna Bay.

Stage 6: Benson Peak to Little Hellfire Beach

Walking Time: five hours
Accommodation: Hellfire Bivvy (two bunks)

After leaving the hut you walk through thick bush and over two gullies for 15 to 20 minutes before emerging onto an open tussock flat, a side arm of Ruggedy Flat. You follow the poles for three km through the tussock clearing until the track enters bush again and begins a short and steep climb to the top of a pass from where you can view Ruggedy Flat to the east or Big Hellfire Beach to the west. You can also reach the beach by following the sand dune for 200 metres down towards the ocean.

The track follows the main ridge of the coastal range, providing more views of the western shoreline of Stewart Island, before it descends sharply towards Richard Point. The track swings more to the south, works through a number of gullies and two km from the pass skirts a small beach. From here you are less than an hour from Little Hellfire Beach and just after crossing the next footbridge you come to the Hellfire Bivvy. The little hut is an unusual shelter draped in driftwood, buoys and other objects that have washed ashore. It's set among the sand dunes off the beach and has two bunks but can easily accommodate four people.

Stage 7: Little Hellfire Beach to Mason Bay

Walking Time: four hours
Accommodation: Mason Bay Hut (16 bunks)

Follow the beach for a km to the south end to pick up the signposted track. It quickly moves inland to climb a bush and scrub saddle around Mason Head before descending to the north end of Mason Bay. From here you follow the hard sandy beach, for one of the most scenic walks on the island and certainly the most rewarding to beachcombers and shell collectors. Mussels are abundant and are excellent when steamed with a clove or two of garlic. Paua is also available though many visitors, after cooking it for the first time, would just as soon chew on a rubber inner tube. (Pound the paua first and then slice very thin!)

After a 4½-km stroll, you near the mouth of Duck Creek where a sign points to Mason Hut. Follow the buoys and stream through the sand dunes to pick up the tractor track that leads to the hut. This is a pleasant facility with three rooms, 16 bunks and a range. The hut and the scenic wonders of Mason Bay make it hard not to spend a spare day here. During the day the sand dunes can be explored or the beach hiked another 10 km to the south. During the night you can watch for kiwis or just listen to them.

Stage 8: Mason Bay to North Arm

Walking Time: six to seven hours
Accommodation: Freshwater Landing (12 bunks); North Arm Hut (15 bunks)

The track that leaves Mason Bay is a tractor track and it quickly passes the Old Island Homestead, one of two on the west coast. It continues as a tractor path around Island Hill and down Scott Burn, and is surprisingly dry with boardwalks for the wettest parts. It's about a three-hour walk through manuka and scrub until the track reaches Freshwater River and a track junction. A track heads off northwest (left) onto Ruggedy Flat and eventually to the Upper Freshwater Hut (five hours). A track also heads down the river along its true right (south) side to Fred's Camp, a hut on the entrance of the South West Arm (four hours).

The main track crosses the swingbridge over Freshwater River to arrive at Freshwater Landing Hut. In the river there is a pair of jetties that make a good place for lunch. Avoid the side track to Rocky Mt and continue along the main track which begins with a gradual climb from the hut up Thomson Ridge. After 2½ km the climb becomes considerably steeper and the track here is often wet and slippery. Once above the scrub line, four km from the hut, much of the ridge is boardwalk to avoid boggy areas.

The descent off the ridge is also steep, but in an hour the track is sidling above the end of the North Arm and in 2½ km it reaches North Arm Hut. Plan on four hours to reach the hut from Freshwater Landing if conditions are good, five hours or even longer if it has been raining all day. It's a four-hour trek from North Arm to Halfmoon Bay so if you are planning to catch the 2 pm ferry back to Bluff it's best to be out of the hut by 9 am.

Index

Map references in **bold** type

Abel Tasman Coastal Park
    24, 120-126
    Coastal Track 32, 121-126,**124**
    Inland Track 126
Ada Flat 143
Ada Pass 155, 158
Ada River 158
Ahipara 49
Ahukawakawa Track 103
Aickens 179, 180
Anapai Bay Track 126
Anchorage Beach 124
Andrews River 184
Angelus Basin 152
Aniseed Valley 140, 141
Anne Saddle 155
Anti Crow River 175
Aorere River 131
Apollo Creek 139
Arch Point 125
Architect Creek 194
Arthur Creek 137, 211
Arthur River 229
Arthur's Pass National
    Park 24, 167-184
Atiwhakatu Stream 111, 113
Atlas Creek 139
Atuatumore Stream 63
Awaroa Bay 123, 126

Balloon Loop 238
Bark Bay 123, 125
Bealy River 172
Beehive Hills 100
Beer's Farm 235
Beer's Pool 238
Bell Falls 99
Bell Rock 229
Bellbird Ridge 132
Benson Peak 250, 253
Big Bay 233, 242
Big Bay-Lake Alabaster
    Loop 230, 242
Big Bungaree Beach 252
Big Creek 215
Big Hellfire Beach 253
Big River 131, 243
Billy Goat Track 62, 63
Bishop Burn 242
Bishops Cap 143
Black Rock Point 252
Blairs Landing 56
Blue Duck Creek 131
Blue Lake 87, 153
Blue Rock Stream 117

Bluff 49, 246
Boomerang Slip 99
Boulder Stream 117
Boyle Flat 159
Boyle River 156, 159, 184
Brady Creek 218
Brames Falls Track 100
Branches Flat 220
Bridal Veil Stream 205
Brides Veil Falls 215
Brod Bay 236
Brown River 131
Browning Pass 184
Browning Stream 143
Bryant Range 141
Bull Creek Track 155
Bullock Creek 166
Burnt Face 187
Bush's Beach 56

Cameron Stream 182
Cannibal Gorge 158
Canvastown 143
Cape Maria van Diemmen 50
Cape Reinga 52
Caples Track 33, 199, 207, 209-210
Capleston 167
Captain Creek 142
Carrington Ridge 112
Cascade Falls 125
Cascade Saddle 198, 199, 220
Cascade Saddle Route 34,
    214-216, **215**
Cascade Stream 92, 215
Cascade Track 149, 152
Casey Saddle-Binser Saddle
    Trek 184
Cass 184
Cass River 185
Cass Saddle 185
Cass-Lagoon Saddles Track 33,
    184-187, **186**
Cattle Flat 213
Cave Brook 131
Cave Point Ridge 253
Cedric Stream 151
Centre Pass 241
Chair Creek 232
Chime Creek 135
Chinamans Bluff 213
Chinamans Flat 211
Christmas Flats 197
Christmas Village Bay 243, 252
Christopher River 158
Claris 54
Clarke Slip 211
Clem Creek 116

Cleopatra's Pool 125
Cleughearn Peak 243
Clifton 127
Clinton Forks 225, 228
Clough Cableway 177
Coal Creek 236
Cobb Reservoir 137, 139
Cobb Valley 136, 137
Coffin's Creek 57
Collingwood 129
Cone Saddle Track 116
Conical Hill 205
Copland Pass 188
Copland Pass Trek 33, 190-194, **192**
Coroglen 62
Coromandel State Forest Park 28,
    59-63, **61**
Craigieburn State Forest
    Park 184-187
Crow River 138, 175
Crows Nest 229
Curtis Falls Track 101
Curzon Glacier 213

D'Urville Valley Track 32,
    152-155, **154**
Daleys Flat 213
Dancing Camp Dam 63
Darkies Ridge 52
Darran Mountains 229
Dart Glacier 199, 213, 216
Dart River 133, 199, 217
Dart Valley 211, 214, 215
Dashwood Stream 239
Dawson Falls 97, 101
Deadman's Track 205
Deadwood Creek 241
Deception River 172
Deception Valley 174
Deep Gorge 151
Demon Trail 230, 233
Dieffenbach Cliffs 99
Dilemma Creek 164, 166, 167
Dock Bay 235
Donelly Flat 112, 114
Dore Pass 228
Dredge Flat 213
Duck Creek 254
Dudley Knob 172
Duncan Bay 143
Dusky Sound 238
Dusky Track 34, 220,
    238-242, **240**

Earland Falls 206
East Matukituki Valley 219
East Ruggedy Beach 253

Eel Creek 232
Eglinton Valley 228
Egmont Village 97
Elfin Bay 206
Emerald Lakes 87
Emerald Pool 142
Emily Pass 203

Faerie Queen 158
Falls River 125
Fanthams Peak 100
Featherstone 109
Federation Corner 159
Fiordland National
    Park 24, 220-243
Fishtail Stream 142
Flagtop 152
Flanagan's Corner 131
Flora Track 137, 139
Foliage Hill 196
Forest Burn 238
Fossil Creek 166
Fox Glacier 217
Fox River 163, 167
Fraser Creek 210
Freshwater Landing 250, 254

Gairloch 241
Gentle Annie Hill 229
Gentle Annie Track 111, 115
George Sound Track 242-243
Giant Gate Falls 229
Gibbs Hill 127
Gillespie Pass 217, 219
Gilmore's Clearing 136
Glade Wharf 225
Glenorchy 199, 201, 202, 206, 210
Gloriana Peak 158
Goat Bay 126
Goat Pass 33, 170-174, **173**
Golden Bay 127, 129
Gorge Creek 174
Gorge Stream 117
Gouland Downs 131
Gowan Bridge 152
Graham Valley 137, 139
Great Barrier Island Trek 28,
    54-58, **55**
Grebe Valley 243
Green Lake 243
Greenlaw Creek 175
Greenstone Track 33, ,199,
    206-209, 210, **208**
Gull Rock Point 252
Gunner Creek 132
Gunner Downs 132
Gunns Camp 230

Haast River 198
Hacket Creek 140, 143
Halfmoon Bay 243, 246, 247

Hamilton Creek 185, 187
Hanamahihi 72
Hanamahihi Flats 73
Harman Pass 174, 184
Harper Creek 175
Harper Pass 33, 178-184, **180-181**
Harper River 187
Harris Saddle 201, 203, 205
Hasties Hill Track 101
Hauroko Burn 242
Havelock 143
Headlands Track 126
Heaphy Beach 132
Heaphy Track 32, 129-132, **130**
Helicopter Flat 135
Henry Burn 242
Henry Peake 103
Henry River 159
Henry Saddle 242
Herangi Hill 50
Hesse Glacier 217
Hidden Falls Creek 232
Hidden Lake 228
Hilda Burn 242
Hinapouri Tarn 151
Hinemaiaia Track 93
Hirakimata (Mt Hobson) 56,
    57, 58, 59
Hokuri Creek 233
Holdsworth Creek 114
Holdsworth Lookout 111
Holly Flats 99
Hollyford Face 205
Hollyford Track 34, 229-233, **231**
Hollyford Track 220
Hollyford Valley 205
Homer Creek 232
Hook Hill 99
Hooker Glacier 192
Hooker River 192
Hope 140
Hope Bridge 180
Hope River 183
Hopeless Creek 149
Hopurahine Landing 66
Hopurahine River 70
Hopuruahine Landing 75
Howard Track 152, 153
Huatere 49
Huiarau Stream 70
Hukatere 49
Humboldt Mountains 198, 203
Humphries Castle 101
Humphries Clearing 108
Hurunui River 182
Hydro Camp 62, 63

Ihaia Track 100
Inangahua Junction 167
Inland Pack Track 33, 163-167, **165**
Invercargill 239, 230, 246
Iris Burn 237

Iris Burn Valley 235
Island Hill 254

Jackson Creek 159
Jamestown 233
Jap Creek (Ruatea Stream) 92
Jerusalem Creek 233
Julia Track 177
Julius Summit 152
Jupiter Creek 139

Kahui Track 100
Kaiarara Plateau 56
Kaiarara Stream 56, 104
Kaiauai Track 104
Kaikau Stream 126
Kaimanawa State Forest
    Park 88-92
Kaipipi Bay 250
Kaipo River 91, 93
Kaipo Saddle 92, 93
Kaitaia 49
Kaitoke 114
Kaitoke Creek 58
Kaitoke Hot Springs 58
Kaiwhakauka Valley 109
Kakaiti Stream 79
Kakanui Stream 77
Kapowairua (Spirits Bay) 49, 52
Karamea 129, 133, 137
Karamea Bend 137
Karamea River 135, 139
Karangarua River 194, 197
Karangarua Valley Track 197
Katipo Creek 132
Kauaeranga River 62
Kauaeranga Valley 61
Kauri Dam 56
Kea Point Walk 192, 196
Keikie Stream 74
Kelly Range 179
Kelly Saddle 174, 175
Kendall Creek 139
Kenneth Burn 241
Kepler Track 34, 229, 233-238, **234**
Kerikeri 49
Kerin Forks 217, 219
Kerr Bay 147, 149
Ketetahi Hot Springs 84, 88
Key Summit 206
Kia Stream 159
Kilby Stream 125
Kinloch 203
Kintail Stream 241
Kirwans Track 167
Kiwi Saddle 183
Kiwiriki Bay 56
Kohaihai River 129
Kohi Saddle 106, 105
Kokatahi 184
Kokowai Stream 99
Korokoro Falls 69

Lagoon Saddle ¹85, 187
Lake Ada 229
Lake Alabaster 232, 233, 242
Lake Angelus 152
Lake Dive 100
Lake Drive Track 100
Lake Hankinson 242
Lake Harris 205
Lake Hauroko 238
Lake Howden 203, 206, 207
Lake Kaurapataka 181
Lake Laffy 242
Lake Mackenzie 203, 205
Lake Manapouri 220, 235, 238
Lake Mavis 172
Lake McKellar 207, 207
Lake McKerrow 230, 232
Lake Mintaro 228
Lake Monowai Route 243
Lake Roe 241, 242
Lake Rotoiti 147, 149
Lake Rotoroa 152, 155
Lake Sumner 183
Lake Sylvan 211
Lake Te Anau 228, 233, 235, 242
Lake Track 28, 66-70, **67**
Lake Waikareiti Track 75
Lake Waikaremoana 66, 75
Lake Wakatipu 199, 217
Lake Wanaka 214
Lakehead Track 149
Lame Duck 197
Lee River 143
Leslie River 137
Leslie-Karamea Track 32,
    136-139, **138**
Lewis Park National
    Reserve 155-160
Lewis Pass 158
Lewis River 132
Link Track 34, 243, 246-250, **248**
Little Bungaree Beach 252
Little Homer Saddle 232
Little River Bridge 249
Little Wanganui River 136
Liverpool Bivvy Track 221
Loch Maree 241
Locke Stream 182
Long Creek 187
Long Harry Bay 252
Long Reef 233
Lost Valley Creek 139
Lucky Beach 252
Luna Stream 135

Macfarlane Stream 242
MacKay Creek 229
Mackay Downs 131
MacKay Falls 229
Mackinnon Pass 228
Magdalen Valley 159
Magnetic Beach 249

Mahakirua Stream 72
Mahanga Range 153
Makahu 106
Makaka Creek 116
Makarora 199, 217
Makarora River 217, 218
Manangaatiuhi Stream 72
Manapouri 238
Manawatu Gorge 109
Mangaehu Stream 73
Mangahoanga Stream 75
Mangahume Stream 100
Mangamingi Stream 92
Manganui Gorge 101
Mangaoraka Walk 104
Mangapurua Stream 109
Mangapurua Track 108
Mangatawhero Stream 72, 75
Mangatepopo Track 86
Mangati Bay 57
Mangorei 101
Mangorei Track 103
Manuoha Trig Track 75-76
Maori Beach 249
Marahau 121, 122, 124
Marauiti Bay 69
Maraunui Bay 69
Marchant Stream 117
Mars Creek 139
Martins Bay 220, 229, 230, 233, 242
Maruia River 158
Mary Creek 177
Mason Bay 250, 254
Masterton 111
Matariki 133
Matemateaonga Walkway 32,
    105-108, **107**
Mates Creek 143
Matukituki 214
Matukituki River 199, 215
Maude Peak 103
Maungapiko Lookout 57
Maungarau Track 108
McHarrie Creek 136
McKellar Saddle 207, 210
McKerrow Island 232
McMillan Stream 183
McNabb Track 132
McPhee Creek 194
Medlands Beach 56
Mercury Creek 139
Mica Burn 239
Middy Creek 142
Milford Track 34, 220, 225-229, **227**
Mill Creek 250
Minarapa Stream 99, 103
Minginui 76
Mingha River 172
Mitre Peak 109
Moawhara Stream 73
Mohaka River 91
Mole Saddle 155

Moonstone Lake 139
Moss Creek 62
Moss Pass 152, 153, 155
Motueka 123
Motumuka Stream 74
Mt Ollivier 196
Mt Anglem 243, 252
Mt Anglem Track 252
Mt Aspiring 198
Mt Aspiring National
    Park 24, 198-220
Mt Awful 219
Mt Balloon 229
Mt Bruce 187
Mt Cedric 151
Mt Cook & Westlands National
    Parks 24, 187-197
Mt Egmont National
    Park 24, 93-104
    Round-the-Mountain Track
    32, 96-101, **98**
Mt Federation 159
Mt Hart 229
Mt Heal 58
Mt Hobson (Hirakimata) 57, 58, 59
Mt Holdsworth Circuit 32,
    111-114, **112**
Mt Humphries 108
Mt Longfellow 183
Mt Luxmore 235, 236
Mt Memphis 241
Mt Ngauruhoe Track 83-88, **85**
Mt Richmond State Forest
    Park 140-144
    Alpine Route 143
Mt Rintoul 143
Mt Robert 152
Mt Rowe 61, 62
Mt Ruapehu 87
Mt Starveall 143
Mt Temple 172
Mt Tongariri 86, 88
Mt Travers 150
Mt Umukarikari 93
Mt Whangaparapara 57
Muddy Creek 211
Mueller Glacier 196
Mueller Hut Walk 33, 194-196, **195**
Murray Beach 252
Murray Creek 132
Murray River 252
Murupara 76
Mutton Cove 127

Nelson Lakes National
    Park 24, 144-155
New Plymouth 97, 103
Ngahiramai 72
Ngarara Bluff 101
Ngaruroro River 92
Ninety-Mile Beach-Cape Regina
    Walkway 28, 49-52, **51**

North Arm 251
North Egmont 97, 101
North-West Nelson State Forest
Park 127-140
Northern Circuit Track 34,
250-254, **251**
Nugget Knob 135
Nydia Bay 143

Oamaru River 91
Oaonui Stream 100
Oban 243
Observation Beach 122
Ohaerena Flats 73
Ohakune 88
Ohaua 72
Ohinepango Springs 87, 88
Ohu Forest Camp 76
Okiwi 54
Old Man 143
Omaru Stream 108
Onamalutu Valley 143
One Mile Creek 178
Onepoto 66
Onetahuti Beach 126
Open Creek 194
Orbit Creek 139
Otehake River 181, 182
Otira 172, 174
Otira River 180, 181
Otira Valley 174
Oturere Stream 87

Paihia 49
Palaver Creek 194
Pancake Rocks 164, 166
Pandora Beach 52
Panekiri Bluff 66, 68
Panekiri Ridge 68
Pannikin Creek 136
Paparoa National Park 24, 161-167
Paparoa Range 167
Paradise 213, 214
Pass Burn 209
Peach Tree Hot Springs 58
Peak 151
Peel Stream 137
Pelorus River Track 32,
140-143, **141**
Pelorus Tops 143
Perry Creek 131
Perry Saddle 130, 131
Pfeifer Creek 181
Phil's Knob 158
Pig Flat 112
Pinchgut Track 152
Pinnacles Peaks 62, 63
Pipipi 108
Pipirike 105
Pleasant Ridge 238, 241
Pompolona Creek 228

Pororari River 166
Port Fitzroy 54, 56
Port William 243, 249, 251
Pouakai Range 103
Pouakai Track 32, 101-104, **102**
Poulter River 184
Pound Creek 126
Pukahunui Ridge Track 80
Pukepuke Route 75
Punakaiki 163, 164
Punakaiki River 164, 166
Punehu Canyon 100
Puniho Track 99
Punjabi Beach 166
Puteore Track 108
Pyke River 229, 232, 242
Pyramid Gorge 99
Pyramid Stream 99

Queens Reach 238
Queenstown 202
Quinns Flat 213

Rabbit Pass 219
Rai Valley 140
Rainbow Creek 232
Rainbow Reach 235, 238
Razorback Track 99, 101, 103
Red Head Peak 253
Rees River 199, 211
Rees Saddle 211, 212, 214, 217
Rees-Dart Track 34, 199,
211-214, **212**
Rere Lake 209
Rerehape Stream 73
Richard Point 253
Richmond Range 143
Roaring Burn Stream 229
Roaring Creek 206
Rob Roy Glacier 215
Rocks Creek 142
Rocky Burn 211
Rocky Lookout 112, 115
Rocky Mt 254
Roding River 143
Roebuck Creek 142
Roger Inlet 243
Rolleston Pack Track 158
Rolleston River 184
Rolling Junction 133
Rororoa 152
Rotoroa Track 153
Rough Creek 194
Route Burn 205, 211
Routeburn Track 33, 199, 201-206,
211, **204**
Ruatahuna 70, 75
Ruatea Stream (Jap Creek) 92
Ruatoki 70
Ruggedy Flat 244, 253, 254
Ruggedy Range 253

Sabine River 151, 153
Sabine Valley 147, 153
Sandfly Point 225, 226, 229
Sandy Bay 75
Sandy Bluff 213
Saturn Creek 138
Sawmill Creek 218
Sawyers Beach 251
Saxon Falls 139
Saxon River 131
Scott Burn 250, 254
Scott Creek 142, 194
Scott's Camp 132
Scott's Point 50
Scotty's Cable 178
Seaforth River 241
Seaforth Valley 241, 242
Sealy Tarns Track 196
Separation Point 121, 127
Seven Mile Creek 175, 178
Shakespeare Flat Track 131
Shallow Bay 238
Sheep Creek 131
Shiels Creek 194
Shiner Brook 131
Shotover River 220
Shotover River Walk 221
Shotover Saddle 220
Siberia Stream 219
Skinner Hill 99
Skinner Point 126
Slaty Peak 143
Slip Creek 233
Slip Flat 209
Slippery Creek 138
Smith Creek 117
Smoky Beach 252
Smoky Creek 252
Snowy Creek 212, 217
Soda Springs 86
Southern Crossing Track 118
Speargrass Track 152, 153
Spey River 238, 239
Spirits Bay (Kapowairua) 49, 50, 52
Splugeons Rock 137
St Arnaud 144, 147
St James Station 156
St James Walkway 33, 144,
156-160, **157**
St Quintin Falls 228
Stag Flats 136
Stanfields Whare 93
Starvaton Point 136
Steele Creek 208
Steele Creek Saddle 208
Steele Saddle 210
Stewart Island 243-254
Stone Creek Junction 135
Stony Hill Track 125
Stratford 105
Stratford Plateau 97
Strathmore 105

Sugar Loaf Stream 205
Summit Creek 150
Supper Cove 220, 238, 242
Sutherland Falls 229
Swamp Creek 232
Swan Burn 132

Tabernacle Lookout 135
Table Mountain 61, 62
Tableland Walk 139-140
Tadmor 133
Taipo River 135, 139, 175, 178
Taipoiti River 177
Takaka 122, 129, 137
Takurua 74
Tama Lakes 88
Tama Saddle 88
Tanawapiti Stream 106
Tangent Creek 136
Tapawera 133, 137
Tapotupotu Bay 50, 52
Tapuaenui Bay 70
Tapuiomaruahine Peak 92
Tarakena Rapids 73
Taramakau River 179, 181, 182
Taranaki Falls 86, 88
Taraua State Forest Park 109-118
Tarawamaomao Point 52
Tarn Creek 187
Tarn Nature Walk 158
Tasman Bay 127
Tauherenikau River 116, 117
Taumapou Flats 72, 75
Taumutu Stream 79
Taungatara Track 100
Taupeupe Saddle 75
Taupo 89
Tauranga-Taupo River 92, 93
Tauranikau Peak 63
Te Anau 201, 226, 235, 239
Te Iringa Circuit 28, 89-93, **91**
Te Kopua Bay 69
Te Kotoreotaunoa Point 69
Te Kumete 74
Te Mania Flats 72
Te Onepu Stream 75
Te Paki Coastal Park 48-52
Te Paki Stream 49, 50
Te Pukatea Bay 124
Te Puna 69
Te Waewae Bay 243
Te Wai-O-Tupuritia Stream 92
Te Werahi Beach 50, 51, 52
Te Whaiti-nui-a-toi Canyon 77
Te Wharau 75
Te Wharau Stream 69
Tekano Stream 194
Thames 60
Thomson Ridge 254
Thor Creek 139
Three Mile Stream 183

Three Pass Trip 184
Tieke Reach 105
Tikitiki Stream 90, 93
Tinline Bay 124
Tiraumea Track 152, 155
Tonga Quarry 125
Tonga Saddle 126
Tongario National Park 24, 80-88
Tongariro Traverse 88
Top Flat 210
Torrent Bay 123, 125
Torrent River 125
Totara Creek 115
Totara Flats Track 32, 114-117, **116**
Totara Saddle 141, 143
Totaranui 121, 122
Track Burn 243
Travers Falls 150
Travers River 149
Travers Saddle 150
Travers Valley 146
Travers-Sabine Circuit 32,
    146-152, **148**
Tregidga Creek 125
Tryphena 54
Tuatapere 239, 243
Tumbledown Creek 178
Turangi 93
Turkey Flat 175
Tutaki 152
Twilight Beach 50

Upper Deception River 174
Upper Hutt 114
Upper Mangamate Stream 77
Upper Tama Lake 86
Urewera National Park 24, 64-76

Venus Creek 139
Vern's Camp 77
Veronica Walk 104
Victoria Forest Park 167

Waiatupuritia Saddle 92
Waiau River 233, 238, 235
Waiau Valley 156, 159
Waiaua Gorge 100
Waiharakeke Bay 126
Waihohonu Stream 88, 87
Waihua-Mangamaiko Stream
    Route 75
Waikare River 70, 73
Waikare-whenua 74
Waimakariri River 174, 175, 184
Waimakariri-Harman Pass
    Route 33, 174-178, **176**
Wainui Bay 121
Waiohine River 115, 116
Waiopaoa 69
Waipakihi Route 93

Waipapakauri 49
Wairahi Stream 57
Wairaurahiri River 243
Wairere Stream 86, 88
Waitahora Lagoon 52
Waitapu Stream 50
Waitawhero Stream 92
Waitehetehe 69
Waitiki Landing 49, 50, 52
Waitotara Forest 108
Waituna Bay 253
Waitutu River 243
Waitutu Tramway Track 243
Waiweranui Track 100
Waiwhakaiho River 104
Waiwhakaiho Stream 99
Wakamarina Track 143
Walsh Creek 130, 164
Wanaka 199, 214 220
Wanganui River 109
Wangapeka River 133
Wangapeka Saddle 135
Wangapeka Track 32, 132-136,
    137, 139, **134**
Warren Burn 241
Warwick Castle 101
Waterfall Creek 182, 239
Waterfall Face 219
Watering Cove 124
Waters Creek 135
Webb Creek 62, 63
Weka Creek 131
Wekakura Creek 132
Welcome Flats 190, 194, 197
Werahi Beach 50
West Bay 147
West Matukituki Valley 220
West Ruggedy Beach 253
Westport 156
Whakapapa Village 84
Whakataka Trig Track 75
Whakatane River Track 29,
    70-75, **71**
Whakhoro 109
Whanganui Arm 70
Whanganui National
    Park 24, 104-108
Whangaparapara 54, 56, 57
Whangapoua Beach 56
Whariwharangi Bay 127
Whirinaki State Forest Park 76-80
Whirinaki Track 28, 76-80, **78**
Whitbourn Bridge 213
Whitbourn Glacier 213
White Horse Hill 192, 196
White River 175
White River Gorge 177
Whitehorn Pass 184
Wilberforce River 184
Wilkies Pool Track 101
Wilkin River 219
Wilkin Valley 199, 217

Wilkin-East Matukituki Route 219
Wilkin-Young Valleys Circuit 34,
   217-219, **218**
Windfall Flat 158

Windy Point 180

Yankee River 252
Yellow Point 124

Yerex Reach 238
Young Basin 219
Young River 217, 218

MAPS

Abel Tasman Coastal Track   124
Arthur's Pass Village   171
Cascade Saddle Route   215
Cass-Lagoon Saddle Track   186
Copland Pass   192
Coromandel State Forest Park   61
D'Urville Valley Track   154
Dusky Track   240
Goat Pass Track   173
Great Barrier Island Trek   55
Greenstone & Caples Tracks   208
Harper Pass   180-181
Heaphy Track   130
Hollyford Track   231
Inland Pack Track   165
Kepler Track   234
Lake Track   67
Lesley-Karamea Track   138
Link Track   248
Matemateaonga Walkway   107
Milford Track   227
Mt Egmont Round-the-Mountain
   Track   98

Mt Holdsworth Circuit   112
Mueller Hut   195
National Parks   23
Ninety-Mile Beach-Cape Regina
   Walkway   51
Northern Circuit   251
Pelorus River Track   141
Pouaki Track   102
Rees-Dart Track   212
Round Mt Ngauruhoe Track   85
Routeburn Track   204
St James Walkway   157
State Forest Parks   25
Te Iringa-Oamaru Circuit   91
Totara Flats Track   116
Travers-Sabine Circuit   148
Waimakariri-Harman Pass
   Route   176
Wangapeka Track   134
Whakatane River Track   71
Whirinaki Track   78
Wilkin-Young Valleys Circuit   218

Temperature

To convert °C to °F multipy by 1.8 and add 32

To convert °F to °C subtract 32 and multipy by ·55

Length, Distance & Area

	multipy by
inches to centimetres	2.54
centimetres to inches	0.39
feet to metres	0.30
metres to feet	3.28
yards to metres	0.91
metres to yards	1.09
miles to kilometres	1.61
kilometres to miles	0.62
acres to hectares	0.40
hectares to acres	2.47

Weight

	multipy by
ounces to grams	28.35
grams to ounces	0.035
pounds to kilograms	0.45
kilograms to pounds	2.21
British tons to kilograms	1016
US tons to kilograms	907

A British ton is 2240 lbs, a US ton is 2000 lbs

Volume

	multipy by
Imperial gallons to litres	4.55
litres to imperial gallons	0.22
US gallons to litres	3.79
litres to US gallons	0.26

5 imperial gallons equals 6 US gallons
a litre is slightly more than a US quart, slightly less
than a British one

Lonely Planet

Lonely Planet published its first book in 1973. Tony and Maureen Wheeler had made a lengthy overland trip from England to Australia and, in response to numerous 'how do you do it?' questions, Tony wrote and they published *Across Asia on the Cheap*. It became an instant local best-seller and inspired thoughts of a second travel guide. A year and a half in South-East Asia resulted in their second book, *South-East Asia on a Shoestring*, which they put together in a backstreet Chinese hotel in Singapore in 1975. The 'yellow book', as it quickly became known, soon became *the* guide to the region and has gone through five editions, always with its familiar yellow cover.

Soon other writers started to come to them with ideas for similar books – books that went off the beaten track and took an adventurous approach to travel, books that 'assumed you knew how to get your luggage off the carousel,' as one reviewer described them. Lonely Planet grew from a kitchen table operation to a spare room and then to its own office. It also started to develop an international reputation as the Lonely Planet logo began to appear in more and more countries. In 1982 *India – a travel survival kit* won the Thomas Cook award for the best guidebook of the year.

These days there are over 60 Lonely Planet titles. Nearly 30 people work at our office in Melbourne, Australia and another half dozen at our US office in Oakland, California.

At first Lonely Planet specialised exclusively in the Asia region but these days we are also developing major ranges of guidebooks to the Pacific region, to South America and to Africa. The list of walking guides is growing and Lonely Planet is producing a unique series of phrasebooks to 'unusual' languages. The emphasis continues to be on travel for travellers and Tony and Maureen still manage to fit in a number of trips each year and play a very active part in the writing and updating of Lonely Planet's guides.

Keeping guidebooks up to date is a constant battle which requires an ear to the ground and lots of walking, but technology also plays its part. All Lonely Planet guidebooks are now stored and updated on computer, and some authors even take lap-top computers into the field. Lonely Planet is also using computers to draw maps and eventually many of the maps will be stored on disk.

The people at Lonely Planet strongly feel that travellers can make a positive contribution to the countries they visit both by better appreciation of cultures and by the money they spend. In addition the company tries to make a direct contribution to the countries and regions it covers. Since 1986 a percentage of the income from each book has gone to aid groups and associations. This has included donations to famine relief in Africa, to aid projects in India, to agricultural projects in Nicaragua and other Central American countries and to Greenpeace's efforts to halt French nuclear testing in the Pacific. In 1988 over $40,000 was donated by Lonely Planet to these projects.

Lonely Planet Distributors

Australia & Papua New Guinea Lonely Planet Publications, PO Box 617, Hawthorn, Victoria 3122.
Canada Raincoast Books, 112 East 3rd Avenue, Vancouver, British Columbia V5T 1C8.
Denmark, Finland & Norway Scanvik Books aps, Store Kongensgade 59 A, DK-1264 Copenhagen K.
Hong Kong The Book Society, GPO Box 7804.
India & Nepal UBS Distributors, 5 Ansari Rd, New Delhi – 110002
Israel Geographical Tours Ltd, 8 Tverya St, Tel Aviv 63144.
Japan Intercontinental Marketing Corp, IPO Box 5056, Tokyo 100-31.
Netherlands Nilsson & Lamm bv, Postbus 195, Pampuslaan 212, 1380 AD Weesp.
New Zealand Transworld Publishers, PO Box 83-094, Edmonton PO, Auckland.
Singapore & Malaysia MPH Distributors, 601 Sims Drive, #03-21, Singapore 1438.
Spain Altair, Balmes 69, 08007 Barcelona.
Sweden Esselte Kartcentrum AB, Vasagatan 16, S-111 20 Stockholm.
Thailand Chalermnit, 108 Sukhumvit 53, Bangkok 10110.
UK Roger Lascelles, 47 York Rd, Brentford, Middlesex, TW8 0QP
USA Lonely Planet Publications, PO Box 2001A, Berkeley, CA 94702.
West Germany Buchvertrieb Gerda Schettler, Postfach 64, D3415 Hattorf a H.
All Other Countries refer to Australia address.

Keep in touch!

We love hearing from you and think you'd like to hear from us.

The Lonely Planet Newsletter covers the when, where, how and what of travel. (AND it's free!)

When...*is the right time to see reindeer in Finland?*
Where...*can you hear the best palm-wine music in Ghana?*
How...*do you get from Asunción to Areguá by steam train?*
What...*should you leave behind to avoid hassles with customs in Iran?*

To join our mailing list just contact us at any of our offices. (details below)

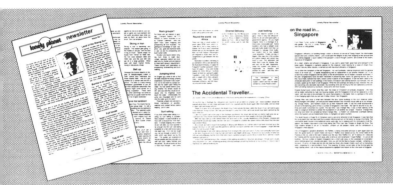

Every issue includes:

- a letter from Lonely Planet founders Tony and Maureen Wheeler
- travel diary from a Lonely Planet author - find out what it's really like out on the road
- feature article on an important and topical travel issue
- a selection of recent letters from our readers
- the latest travel news from all over the world
- details on Lonely Planet's new and forthcoming releases

Also available Lonely Planet T-shirts. 100% heavy weight cotton (S, M, L, XL)

LONELY PLANET PUBLICATIONS
Australia: PO Box 617, Hawthorn, 3122, Victoria (tel: 03-819 1877)
USA: Embarcadero West, 155 Filbert Street, Suite 251, Oakland, CA 94607 (tel: 510-893 8555)
UK: Devonshire House, 12 Barley Mow Passage, Chiswick, London W4 4PH (tel: 081-742 3161)

Guides to the Pacific

Australia – a travel survival kit
The complete low-down on Down Under – home of Ayers Rock, the Great Barrier Reef, extraordinary animals, cosmopolitan cities, rainforests, beaches ... and Lonely Planet!

Bushwalking in Australia
Two experienced and respected walkers give details of the best walks in every state, covering many different terrains and climates.

Islands of Australia's Great Barrier Reef – a travel survival kit
The Great Barrier Reef is one of the wonders of the world – and one of the great travel destinations! Whether you're looking for a tropical island resort or a secluded island hideaway, this guide has all the facts you'll need.

Sydney city guide
A wealth of information on Australia's most exciting city; all in a handy pocket-sized format.

Hawaii – a travel survival kit
Share in the delights of this island paradise – and avoid some of its high prices – with this practical guide. Covers all of Hawaii's well-known attractions, plus plenty of uncrowded sights and activities.

Melbourne city guide
From historic houses to fascinating churches and famous nudes to tapas bars, cafés and bistros – Melbourne is a dream for gourmands and a paradise for party goers.

New Zealand – a travel survival kit
This practical guide will help you discover the very best New Zealand has to offer – Maori dances and feasts; some of the most spectacular scenery in the world; and every outdoor activity imaginable.

Fiji – a travel survival kit
Whether you prefer to stay in camping grounds, international hotels, or something in-between, this comprehensive guide will help you to enjoy the beautiful Fijian archipelago.

New Caledonia – a travel survival kit
This guide shows how to discover all that he idyllic islands of New Caledonia have to offer – from French colonial culture to traditional Melanesian life.

Solomon Islands – a travel survival kit
The Solomon Islands are the best-kept secret of the Pacific. Discover remote tropical islands, jungle covered volcanoes and traditional Melanesian villages with this detailed guide.

Rarotonga & the Cook Islands – a travel survival kit

Rarotonga and the Cook Islands have history, beauty and magic to rival the better-known islands of Hawaii and Tahiti, but the world has virtually passed them by.

Micronesia – a travel survival kit

The glorious beaches, lagoons and reefs of these 2100 islands would dazzle even the most jaded traveller. This guide has all the details on island-hopping across the north Pacific.

Papua New Guinea – a travel survival kit

With its coastal cities, villages perched beside mighty rivers, palm-fringed beaches and rushing mountain streams, Papua New Guinea promises memorable travel.

Tahiti & French Polynesia – a travel survival kit

Tahiti's idyllic beauty has seduced sailors, artists and traveller for generations. The latest edition provides full details on the main island of Tahiti, the Tuamotos, Marquesas and other island groups. Invaluable information for independent travellers and package tourists alike.

Tonga – a travel survival kit

The only South Pacific country never to be colonised by Europeans, Tonga has also been ignored by tourists. The people of this far-flung island group offer some of the most sincere and unconditional hospitality in the world.

Samoa – a travel survival kit

Two remarkably different countries, Western Samoa and American Samoa offer some wonderful island escapes, and Polynesian culture at its best..

Also available:

Papua New Guinea phrasebook.

Lonely Planet Guidebooks

Lonely Planet guidebooks cover every accessible part of Asia as well as Australia, the Pacific, South America, Africa, the Middle East, Europe and parts of North America. There are five series: *travel survival kits*, covering a country for a range of budgets; *shoestring guides* with compact information for low-budget travel in a major region; *walking guides*; *city guides* and *phrasebooks*.

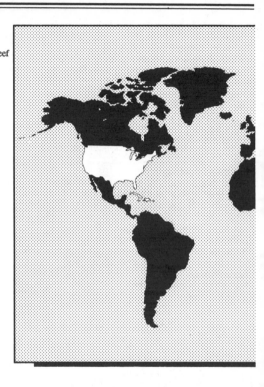

Australia & the Pacific
Australia
Bushwalking in Australia
Islands of Australia's Great Barrier Reef
Fiji
Melbourne city guide
Micronesia
New Caledonia
New Zealand
Tramping in New Zealand
Papua New Guinea
Papua New Guinea phrasebook
Rarotonga & the Cook Islands
Samoa
Solomon Islands
Sydney city guide
Tahiti & French Polynesia
Tonga
Vanuatu

South-East Asia
Bali & Lombok
Bangkok city guide
Myanmar (Burma)
Burmese phrasebook
Cambodia
Indonesia
Indonesia phrasebook
Malaysia, Singapore & Brunei
Philippines
Pilipino phrasebook
Singapore city guide
South-East Asia on a shoestring
Thailand
Thai phrasebook
Vietnam, Laos & Cambodia
Vietnamese phrasebook

North-East Asia
China
Mandarin Chinese phrasebook
Hong Kong, Macau & Canton
Japan
Japanese phrasebook
Korea
Korean phrasebook
Mongolia
North-East Asia on a shoestring
Taiwan
Tibet
Tibet phrasebook
Tokyo city guide

West Asia
Trekking in Turkey
Turkey
Turkish phrasebook
West Asia on a shoestring

Middle East
Arab Gulf States
Egypt & the Sudan
Egyptian Arabic phrasebook
Iran
Israel
Jordan & Syria
Yemen

Indian Ocean
Madagascar & Comoros
Maldives & Islands of the East Indian Ocean
Mauritius, Réunion & Seychelles

Mail Order

Lonely Planet guidebooks are distributed worldwide. They are also available by mail order from Lonely Planet, so if you have difficulty finding a title please write to us. US and Canadian residents should write to Embarcadero West, 155 Filbert St, Suite 251, Oakland CA 94607, USA; European residents should write to Devonshire House, 12 Barley Mow Passage, Chiswick, London W4 4PH; and residents of other countries to PO Box 617, Hawthorn, Victoria 3122, Australia.

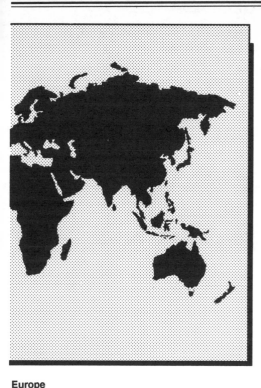

Indian Subcontinent
Bangladesh
India
Hindi/Urdu phrasebook
Trekking in the Indian Himalaya
Karakoram Highway
Kashmir, Ladakh & Zanskar
Nepal
Trekking in the Nepal Himalaya
Nepal phrasebook
Pakistan
Sri Lanka
Sri Lanka phrasebook

Africa
Africa on a shoestring
Central Africa
East Africa
Kenya
Swahili phrasebook
Morocco, Algeria & Tunisia
Moroccan Arabic phrasebook
South Africa, Lesotho & Swaziland
Zimbabwe, Botswana & Namibia
West Africa
Mexico
Baja California
Mexico

Central America
Central America on a shoestring
Costa Rica
La Ruta Maya

North America
Alaska
Canada
Hawaii

Europe
Eastern Europe on a shoestring
Eastern Europe phrasebook
Finland
Iceland, Greenland & the Faroe Islands
Mediterranean Europe on a shoestring
Mediterranean Europe phrasebook
Poland
Scandinavian & Baltic Europe on a shoestring
Scandinavian Europe phrasebook
Trekking in Spain
Trekking in Greece
USSR
Russian phrasebook
Western Europe on a shoestring
Western Europe phrasebook

South America
Argentina, Uruguay & Paraguay
Bolivia
Brazil
Brazilian phrasebook
Chile & Easter Island
Colombia
Ecuador & the Galápagos Islands
Latin American Spanish phrasebook
Peru
Quechua phrasebook
South America on a shoestring
Trekking in the Patagonian Andes

The Lonely Planet Story

Lonely Planet published its first book in 1973 in response to the numerous 'How did you do it?' questions Maureen and Tony Wheeler were asked after driving, bussing, hitching, sailing and railing their way from England to Australia.

Written at a kitchen table and hand collated, trimmed and stapled, *Across Asia on the Cheap* became an instant local bestseller, inspiring thoughts of another book.

Eighteen months in South-East Asia resulted in their second guide, *South-East Asia on a shoestring*, which they put together in a backstreet Chinese hotel in Singapore in 1975. The 'yellow bible' as it quickly became known to backpackers around the world, soon became *the* guide to the region. It has sold well over half a million copies and is now in its 7th edition, still retaining its familiar yellow cover.

Today there are over 100 Lonely Planet titles – books that have that same adventurous approach to travel as those early guides; books that 'assume you know how to get your luggage off the carousel' as one reviewer put it.

Although Lonely Planet initially specialised in guides to Asia, they now cover most regions of the world, including the Pacific, South America, Africa, the Middle East and Europe. The list of *walking guides* and *phrasebooks* (for 'unusual' languages such as Quechua, Swahili, Nepalese and Egyptian Arabic) is also growing rapidly.

The emphasis continues to be on travel for independent travellers. Tony and Maureen still travel for several months of each year and play an active part in the writing, updating and quality control of Lonely Planet's guides.

They have been joined by over 50 authors, 48 staff – mainly editors, cartographers, & designers – at our office in Melbourne, Australia and another 10 at our US office in Oakland, California. In 1991 Lonely Planet opened a London office to handle sales for Britain, Europe and Africa. Travellers themselves also make a valuable contribution to the guides through the feedback we receive in thousands of letters each year.

The people at Lonely Planet strongly believe that travellers can make a positive contribution to the countries they visit, both through their appreciation of the countries' culture, wildlife and natural features, and through the money they spend. In addition, the company makes a direct contribution to the countries and regions it covers. Since 1986 a percentage of the income from each book has been donated to ventures such as famine relief in Africa; aid projects in India; agricultural projects in Central America; Greenpeace's efforts to halt French nuclear testing in the Pacific and Amnesty International. In 1992 $45,000 was donated to these causes.

Lonely Planet's basic travel philosophy is summed up in Tony Wheeler's comment, 'Don't worry about whether your trip will work out. Just go!'